Cultivating Fields of Progress

Cultivating Fields of Progress

Agriculture and the International Labour Organization, 1920s–1950s

AMALIA RIBI FORCLAZ

OXFORD
UNIVERSITY PRESS

Great Clarendon Street, Oxford, OX2 6DP,
United Kingdom

Oxford University Press is a department of the University of Oxford.
It furthers the University's objective of excellence in research, scholarship,
and education by publishing worldwide. Oxford is a registered trade mark of
Oxford University Press in the UK and in certain other countries

© Amalia Ribi Forclaz 2025

The moral rights of the author have been asserted

All rights reserved. No part of this publication may be reproduced, stored in a retrieval system, transmitted, used for text and data mining, or used for training artificial intelligence, in any form or by any means, without the prior permission in writing of Oxford University Press, or as expressly permitted by law, by licence or under terms agreed with the appropriate reprographics rights organization. Enquiries concerning reproduction outside the scope of the above should be sent to the Rights Department, Oxford University Press, at the address above.

You must not circulate this work in any other form
and you must impose this same condition on any acquirer

Published in the United States of America by Oxford University Press
198 Madison Avenue, New York, NY 10016, United States of America

British Library Cataloguing in Publication Data
Data available

Library of Congress Control Number: 2024945349

ISBN 9780192849892

DOI: 10.1093/9780191945014.001.0001

Printed and bound by
CPI Group (UK) Ltd, Croydon, CR0 4YY

Links to third party websites are provided by Oxford in good faith and
for information only. Oxford disclaims any responsibility for the materials
contained in any third party website referenced in this work.

The manufacturer's authorised representative in the EU for product safety is
Oxford University Press España S.A. of El Parque Empresarial San Fernando
de Henares, Avenida de Castilla, 2 – 28830 Madrid (www.oup.es/en or product.safety@oup.com).
OUP España S.A. also acts as importer into Spain of products made by the manufacturer.

Acknowledgements

This book would not exist without the help of generous institutions, supportive colleagues, and caring friends and family members. I would like to start by thanking the Swiss National Science Foundation whose generous Ambizione fellowship made it possible for me to carry out the research for this project. In its early stages I spent time as a postdoctoral fellow at the Excellence Cluster in Heidelberg and at the Modern European History Centre of the University of Oxford. The project then accompanied me from research fellow to tenured associate professor at the Graduate Institute for International and Development Studies in Geneva. I have been lucky to spend the last twelve years in this supportive environment—an interdisciplinary cocoon on the shores of Lake Geneva.

The encouragement, constructive criticism, and friendship I have received from many of my colleagues inside and outside the Institute and across disciplines have made this journey a very enjoyable one. I have particularly benefited from scholarly exchanges, as well as from invigorating coffee breaks and inspiring chats with Annabelle Littoz-Monnet, Susanna Hecht, Marc Flandreau, Mahmoud Mohamedou, Davide Rodogno, Gopalan Balachandran, Nicole Bourbonnais, and Isabelle Schulte-Tenckhoff. Carolyn Biltoft's creative spirit and brilliant mind encouraged me to look behind the mountain of grey literature. Mischa Suter, Niccolò Mignemi, and Corinna Unger all read parts of the manuscript and helped me think more clearly. Isabelle Schulte-Tenckhoff was particularly generous with her time and offered to read the entire book providing detailed and constructive feedback. A special thank you goes to Daniela Almansi whose eagle eyes and devoted work helped to bring the final manuscript into shape. I am grateful to the anonymous reviewers for reading with a benevolent eye and pointing out potential improvements. I thank Cathryn Steele, Rachel Atkins, and the whole team at OUP for accompanying the manuscript from draft to book and for their dedication to it.

The book has also benefited from exchanges at international conferences and workshops with a lively international community of historians and social scientists interested in international organizations, in agriculture, and in rural development. Patricia Clavin, Madeleine Herren, Francesca Piana, Michele Sollai, Hannah Tyler, Corinna Unger, Liesbeth van de Grift, Sandrine Kott, Véronique Plata Stenger, Martin Bemmann, Olga Hidalgo Weber, Corinne Pernet, Sacha Zala, Cornelia Knab, Anne-Isabelle Richard, Miguel Bandeira Jerónimo, Tomoko Akami, Dorothea Hoehtker, Peter Moser, Jessica Richter, Juri Auderset, Marianna Fenzi, Kiran Patel, Heinrich Hartmann, Harald Fischer-Tiné, Julia

Tischler, and Larissa Da Silva Araujo all deserve a special mention. A big and belated thank you also goes to the fellow members of the Oslo International Research network who at the very early stages graciously commented on my papers. I also received valuable inputs from colleagues and graduate students in the Global Governance and International Environment Studies Centre at the Graduate Institute.

The book could not have seen the light of day without the help of a number of devoted archivists and librarians. I owe special thanks to Remo Becci and Jacques Rodriguez for their support and patience as I returned again and again to the archives of the International Labour Organization in Geneva, even after vowing to have 'finished' research. Fabio Ciccarelli at the Food and Agriculture Organization, archivists and librarians at the Social History Archives in Amsterdam and the staff at the headquarters of the Associated Country Women of the World, and the Columbia Rare Book and Manuscript Library have provided valuable assistance. I thank Charlotte Matthaei for sharing her memories of her aunt Louise and for giving me insights into her unpublished writings. I also thank the editors of the *Agricultural History Review* and of *Capitalism: A Journal of History and Economics* for letting me draw on small parts of previously published materials.

Family members—both current and ancestral—have played a major role in this book. It is the childhood stories told by my paternal grandparents about their agricultural undertakings in the mid- to late 1930s, and their tales of physical exhaustion, economic insecurity, and environmental uncertainty that have sparked my interest in agrarian lives and livelihoods. I then gained first-hand insights into the challenges in agriculture during the many summers I spent on the alpine farm of the lively and passionate Tognetti family. Angela, Mario and their extended family taught me everything there is to know about soil, goats, cheese-making, and the unpredictability of mountain farming. I thank them for sharing their lives and their knowledge.

Deepfelt thanks go to my husband, Alain, for his loving presence and unfailing support through life's many twists and turns. My daughters have shown patience, kindness, and the occasional exasperation, when I retired to write 'le livre' for hours on end. Their good humour and energy have sustained me. I wish that my father, born in 1937 on a makeshift farm without a roof, could have seen this book. His love of history and his keen sense of social justice were my upbringing. He passed away in February 2023 after a long and difficult illness and I deeply miss our conversations. His interest was in the lives of ordinary people, not in international organizations. But my hope is that he would have found something in here about that too. It is to him that this book is dedicated.

Contents

Introduction	1
Scholarship and Archives	7
Sources and Voices	11
Structure	13
1. Putting Agriculture on the Agenda	15
The Big Opening: Agriculture at the ILO	21
'The Most Despised and Least Protected'	26
Agricultural Workers Unite!	31
2. 'Nature Yields to No Law'	37
The Problem of Worktime	40
The Question of Housing	45
The Work of Women and Children	48
'A Less Obvious Need for Safeguarding'	52
3. Cultivating Knowledge	56
The Battle for Authority	62
Professionalizing Farming	67
Scientific Management of Agricultural Labour	72
Agrarian Reform and Other Controversies	76
4. Navigating the Crisis and Its Repercussions	80
Divided Perspectives	83
A Time for Action	88
Reopening the Debate on Hours of Work	92
From Sunrise to Sunset	98
5. New Voices of the Countryside	104
Uniting Agrarian Masses	106
Polarization	111
Peasants for Peace	114
A New Expert Committee	119
6. War, Disruption, and Transformation	125
Shifting Priorities	128
New Institutional Births and Slow Demises	130
Extending Social Policy to 'Dependent Territories'	137
Change and Continuity	141

7. The Tropics in Sight   145
   Expanding Unionist Horizons   152
   Framing Plantation Labour Globally   154
   Postcolonial Dynamics and Disputed Realities   159
   'The Gleam of Human Amelioration'?   165

   Conclusion: From Post-War Efforts to Present Challenges   169

Archival Sources and Bibliography   181
Index   201

Introduction

In the years following the First World War, the labour, lives, and productivity of farmers and agricultural workers worldwide emerged as a policy area for social and economic reform. During this period, and in line with internationalization processes in other fields, local rural associations, national and international interest groups, transnational expert networks, and international organizations increasingly shone a light on the agricultural sector. Agrarian worlds, their complex economic and social conditions as well as their often-unregulated labour practices represented a challenging and fertile ground for national and international policy-making.[1] Social reformers increasingly advocated the elaboration of international frameworks and a common language to deal with agricultural labour issues. The emergence of this new agrarian internationalism was defined by the transnational realities of globalized trade and attention to food security, and a growing concern that cut across ideologies about the poverty divide between urban and rural populations. Reflections on social improvements and agricultural modernizations were thus heavily entangled with projections of economic and social progress.

This book focuses on the shape that the social aspects of labour problems in agriculture took in the discussion chambers of international organizations. It does so by addressing a specific social and professional group that became the object of particular attention among international social reformers during the interwar years: the so-called agricultural workers (sometimes referred to in the sources as landworkers), a marginalized but large part of the global labour force.[2]

---

[1] Heinrich Hartmann and Julia Tischler, 'Introduction', in Hartmann and Tischler, eds, *Planting Seeds of Knowledge: Agriculture and Education in Rural Societies in the Twentieth Century* (New York, Oxford: Berghahn Books, 2023), 9–23; Joseph Morgan Hodge, *Triumph of the Expert: Agrarian Doctrines of Development and the Legacies of British Colonialism* (Athens, OH: Ohio University Press, 2007). For Europe, see for example Liesbeth van de Grift, Dietmar Müller, and Corinna Unger, 'Introduction', in van de Grift, Müller, and Unger, eds, *Living with the Land: Rural and Agricultural Actors in Twentieth-Century Europe: A Handbook* (Berlin: De Gruyter, 2022), 1–13; Liesbeth van De Grift and Amalia Ribi Forclaz, eds, *Governing the Rural in Interwar Europe* (London: Routledge, 2018); Corinna R. Unger, 'Agrarwissenschaftliche Expertise und ländliche Modernisierungsstrategien in der internationalen Entwicklungspolitik, 1920er bis 1980er Jahre', *Geschichte und Gesellschaft* 41 (2015), 552–79.

[2] For a discussion of the ILO's typology, see Chapter 1. On debates about fundamental questions of international terminology, see Chapter 5.

These male and female workers were narrowly defined as long-term, seasonal or occasional farm employees who did not own land or housing, did not manage their own farms, and whose livelihoods depended on waged agricultural work.[3] They were regarded by social reformers as vulnerable to exploitation, and, in line with the ideas of Karl Marx about the proletarianization of rural social relations, also as an increasingly politicized rural proletariat with specific social welfare needs and for whom it was necessary to create equal conditions with those of industrial workers.

At the centre of the account stands the Geneva-based International Labour Organization (hereafter ILO). Set up in 1919 as part of the Paris Peace accords, this specialized agency was mainly concerned with the social rights of industrial workers but quickly expanded its remit to the agricultural sector. Compared to other aspects of the ILO's work, which have been the subject of a rich body of scholarship, the Organization's agricultural focus has hitherto received little attention.[4] This is partly due to the fact that the ILO, by its own admission, did not succeed in achieving the same set of international instruments for agriculture as it did for industry, leading to a common perception that it did not do much for agriculture.[5] But the lack of legislation does not signify that there were no efforts to carry out rich and wide-reaching surveys on agricultural living conditions, study specific problems such as education and rural exodus, and generate international reports that framed rural economic and social issues in pioneering ways. Mapping these efforts and the accompanying debates and controversies is at the heart of this book. It is penned with the conviction that agriculture must be written back into international history and to a certain extent also into the historiography of international organizations and global labour. This research thus uses the records of the ILO and of related institutions and movements not as an end in themselves, but as an opportunity to listen in on a global range of voices on the question of agricultural labour conditions.

---

[3] On the diversity within this category, see Elise van Nederveen Meerkerk and Rolf Bauer, 'Introduction' in van Nederveen Meerkerk and Bauer, eds, *Global Agricultural Workers from the 17th to the 21st Century* (Leiden, Boston: Brill, 2023), 5.

[4] For some recent contributions, see Véronique Plata-Stenger, *Social Reform, Modernization and Technical Diplomacy: The ILO Contribution to Development 1930–46* (Oldenbourg: De Gruyter, 2020); Daniel Maul, *The International Labour Organization: 100 Years of Global Social Policy* (Berlin: De Gruyter; Geneva: International Labour Office, 2019); Sandrine Kott and Joelle Droux, eds, *Globalizing Social Rights: The International Labour Organization and Beyond* (Basingstoke: Palgrave, 2013); Ayla Aglan, Olivier Feiertag, and Dzovinar Kévonian eds, *Humaniser le travail. Régimes économiques, régimes politiques et organisation internationale du travail (1929–1969)* (Brussels: Peter Lang, 2011); Isabelle Lespinet-Moret and Vincent Viet, eds, *L'organisation internationale du travail. Origine, développement, avenir* (Rennes, Presses universitaires de Rennes, 2011); Magaly Rodriguez Garcia, Jasmien Van Daele, and Marcel Van der Linden, eds, *ILO Histories. Essays on the International Labour Organization and its Impact on the World during the Twentieth Century* (Bern: Peter Lang, 2010); Guy Fiti Sinclair, *To Reform the World: International Organizations and the Making of Modern States* (Oxford: Oxford University Press, 2017).

[5] A. Johnston, *The International Labour Organization: Its Work for Social and Economic Justice* (London: Europa Publications, 1970), 254.

With its focus on labour and social rights, the ILO offers a particularly interesting vantage point to observe the process of internationalization of agrarian questions. Its description of social problems in agriculture stands out for the unique transnational knowledge accumulated. One thing that the Organization did from the very beginning was to launch international enquiries on specific aspects of agricultural labour and living conditions in a bid to formulate international standards that would be supported by member governments.[6] While these efforts were often not successful, they nevertheless reveal the often contentious and sometimes polarized visions that existed among international actors. The paper trail left by experts, thinkers, reformers, trade unionist, agrarian interest groups, and farmers in and around the ILO allows us to explore the tensions between progressive social policies and the productivist agenda that characterized international debates on agricultural labour from the 1920s onwards. What is more, the ILO's research and legislative work on agriculture did not just cover labour arrangements on farms: it arguably started a much larger debate on the social stratification in the countryside, the power relationships between those who owned land and those who did not, and the nexus between local and global conditions, and rural and urban lifestyles. Because agricultural work and life often happened in the same place, labour issues were intrinsically linked to general living conditions. This raised intricate and controversial questions about how to change socio-cultural 'traditions', such as the practice in many Western European countries of housing farm labourers in the stables, where they slept with the cattle; or about how to agree on the limitation of worktime for farm employees in a setting in which work depended on natural factors such as climatic conditions and plant and animal health that could not always be humanly controlled or predicted.[7] In other words, agricultural labour problems also brought to the fore the spatial, atmospheric, and environmental constraints that made international standardization more complex and highly contested.

As the reader will discover, the figure of the agricultural worker (in French diplomatic language '*ouvrier agricole*') was seen as the poor, underrepresented, uneducated, and unprotected subject of the post-war world. The focus on the social and economic problems of this particular professional group provided the ILO with an entry point to reflect on rural problems more generally. While agriculture was by far the largest industry worldwide, the numerical importance of waged agricultural labour differed from country to country. In 1920, agriculture occupied around 70 per cent of the world's total labour force (compared to roughly 1 per cent of people working in mines and quarries and around 11 per cent

---

[6] On the ILO's scientific practice, see Marine Dhermy-Mairal, 'Du danger des enquêtes savantes. Faire oeuvre de science dans l'entre-deux-guerres au Bureau International du Travail', *Revue d'histoire moderne & contemporaine* 62, no. 4 (2015), 7–32.

[7] See Chapter 2.

in manufacturing).[8] In many European countries, even though their numbers had declined in relative terms since the late eighteenth century, still roughly 40 per cent of people made their living from agriculture as small farmers, big landowners, tenants, sharecroppers, or farmworkers.[9] Of these, the number of paid agricultural workers oscillated between 25 and 30 per cent in countries such as Bulgaria, Belgium, Denmark, Finland, France, and Hungary. Hired labourers constituted around 40 per cent of people working in agriculture in Italy and up to 60 per cent in Britain.[10] With the exception of Britain, waged workers formed a minority, but their importance for agricultural production and social stability was undisputed.

As will be shown, from 1920 onwards, the ILO took on the role of an international observatory for rural labour questions. Through the work of a specialist unit in the International Labour Office, the Agricultural Service, and through specialized expert commissions, the ILO identified a set of economic and social issues which it sought to document by launching international enquiries. The Organization participated in the construction of specialized knowledge on agrarian worlds: labour specialists and agricultural economists laid out what was perceived as the characteristic universal features of agricultural labour. By doing so, they cemented the binary opposition between industrial and agricultural modes of production and the idea of rural–urban inequality in development and living conditions that continue to shape international discussions today.[11] The ILO's enquiries, however, also highlighted that Europe, with its great regional diversity, large rural populations and significant variations in social and economic conditions, was far from embodying the pinnacle of human progress and capitalist modernity.[12]

The link between knowledge production, international governance, and agricultural development was inherent in the ILO's work and reflected similar processes that were taking place both nationally and internationally in government offices, private foundations, and research institutions in the interwar years.[13] The ILO, much like other international organizations was a producer of social knowledge and also of standards and practices, while also reflecting the

---

[8] Paul Bairoch and J. M. Limbor, 'Changes in Industrial Distribution of the World's Labour Force by Region, 1850–1960', *International Labour Review* 98, no. 4 (October 1968), 311–36.

[9] David Grigg, 'The World's Agricultural Labour Force 1800–1970', *Geography* 60, no. 3 (July 1975), 194–202.

[10] See Louise Ernestine Howard, *Labour in Agriculture: An International Survey* (Oxford: Oxford University Press, 1935), 27–52.

[11] See for example Eurofound, *Bridging the Rural–Urban Divide: Addressing Inequalities and Empowering Communities* (Luxembourg: Publications Office of the European Union, 2023).

[12] A similar point has been made by leading rural historians who have argued that focusing on rural actors in European history can contribute to 'provincializing' Europe's position in the world in line with Dipesh Chakrabarty's famous call. Van de Grift, Müller, and Unger, 'Living with the Land: Introduction', 2.

[13] For some examples, see the chapters in Hartmann and Tischler.

ideological concerns, cultural norms, and political and economic conditions of its time.[14] Due to the specific tripartite character of the Organization, its archive also offers a different perspective from the one that has usually been associated with the emergence of rural and agricultural populations as a focus of development thinking. The organization's tripartite structure and its connection to trade unions and employer organizations encouraged the production of specialized knowledge on the lives, working conditions, and social challenges faced by agricultural workers. The ILO's participation in the 'scientization of the social', its efforts to apply scientific methods and systematic approaches to studying social issues, also resulted in a more formalized understanding of the agrarian world and a reduction of complex realities.[15] The focus of the ILO differed from other reformist and developmentalist institutions and associations in meaningful ways. At the centre of its knowledge production was not the farmer but the often-forgotten class of agricultural workers which remained the central preoccupation of the ILO's internationalist reformist action throughout the period studied in this book.[16] The attention to labour conditions of agricultural workers rather than agricultural production systems, technological improvements, or the use of natural resources, thus also forces us to rethink the usual dichotomy in the literature between 'traditional' subsistence farming and 'modern' industrial farming. Rather than a history of the decline, survival, and rebirth of the peasantry as an object of international development after the Second World War, this story focuses on the agricultural worker as a constant in the global history of the twentieth century.[17]

The discussion shows that the ILO's campaign was not without its contradictions. It was motivated by a diffuse worry about potential rural unrest and 'revolution'—a danger which it sought to control by addressing what it deemed to be salient agricultural social questions. As the title of the book suggests, through its efforts to cultivate and advance international debate on conditions in agriculture, the ILO's aim was to work towards the social and economic progress of a population group and a whole sector which it viewed as important for national and international stability. In the eyes of the ILO, positive change was not (yet) expected to occur through technological fixes and developmentalist programmes, but

---

[14] On the link between knowledge production and social norms, see Sheila Jasanoff, ed., *States of Knowledge: The Co-Production of Science and Social Order* (London: Routledge, 2004).

[15] Raphael Lutz, 'Die Verwissenschaftlichung des sozialen als methodische und konzeptionelle Herausforderung für eine Sozialgeschichte des 20. Jahrhunderts', *Geschichte und Gesellschaft* 22 (1996), 165–93.

[16] On the neglect of this specific economic and social group, see also Susan Zimmermann, 'The Agrarian Working Class Put Somewhat Centre Stage: An Often Neglected Group of Workers in the Historiography of Labour in State-Socialist Hungary', *European Review of History* 25, no. 1 (2018), 79–100.

[17] On the term peasant, see Chapter 5. On re-peasantization, see Jan Douwe van der Ploeg, *The New Peasantries: Struggles for Autonomy and Sustainability in an Era of Empire and Globalization* (London: Earthscan, 2008). Eric Vanhaute, *Peasants in World History* (New York: Routledge, 2021).

through social reform and the reduction of inequalities between agricultural and industrial populations. The focus was on regulating working hours, improving education, and stabilizing wages. This does not mean, however, that the ILO was not conditioned by a logic of productivity. In fact, it also toyed with ideas of efficiency and improvement based on the industrial model—a concern that often sat uneasily with demands for social reform and greater welfare in farmwork.

Paradoxically, while arguing for equal standards for workers in agriculture and the industry, the picture that emerged was one of rural difference. The ILO's research, enquiries, and surveys cemented a picture of agriculture as still a mostly pre-industrial activity that was ruled by the natural constraints imposed by weather, climate, and seasons, which set the countryside apart from urban areas and hindered the amelioration of working conditions.

What also emerges from the narrative is that the ILO's agricultural social reforms were centred—at least in the first decades—on agricultural workers in Europe, with a focus on Western and Eastern European regions and the occasional inclusion of the United States of America and the self-governing British Dominions (Australia, Canada, and South Africa). There was little interest in extending the gaze to countries in Latin America and Asia, and colonial territories were completely absent from this discussion. This blind spot was due to various factors, including firstly a perceived urgency after the First World War to placate potential unrest amongst agricultural labourers across various European countries.[18] Secondly, colonial powers that sat in the ILO's Governing Body (the Organization's executive, which decided the agenda of the general assembly of members states called the International Labour Conference) were unwilling to seriously consider the labour situation in the colonies, and there existed a widespread perception, even among social reformers, that colonial territories were not yet ready for labour legislation.[19] Thirdly, international agricultural trade unions mobilized European farmworker only, leaving great parts of the rural population without representation. Finally, the ILO's conceptualization of agriculture in Europe as waged labour performed by free persons (albeit in very poor conditions) set it apart from those forms of agricultural labour in the colonies which involved elements of coercion.

Agricultural social reform was thus artificially separated from what came to be known and addressed as 'the native labour' issue from the mid-1920s onwards.[20]

---

[18] See Chapter 1.
[19] This was true for all aspects of the ILO's work, not just for agriculture. Maul, *The International Labour Organization*, 80.
[20] On the ILO's native labour code, see Luis Rodríguez-Piñero, *Indigenous Peoples, Postcolonialism, and International Law: The ILO Regime (1919–1989)* (Oxford University Press, 2005), 17–52. Susan Zimmermann, '"Special Circumstances in Geneva": The ILO and the World of Non-Metropolitan Labour in the Interwar Period', in Rodriguez Garcia, Van Daele, Van der Linden, eds, *ILO Histories*, 221–50; James P. Daughton, 'ILO Expertise and Colonial Violence in the Interwar Years', in Kott and Droux, eds, *Globalizing Social Rights*, 85–97.

This does not mean that disenfranchised groups and anti-colonial reformers did not engage with the debates or that the meeting rooms of the ILO were merely chambers of Western discourse. But as the book shows, despite recurring voices that challenged the ILO's vision and approaches, the Organization struggled to overcome its narrow geographical framework. Even though colonial labour problems were often agrarian in nature, and in spite of some common topics which included housing, worktime, recruitment, contracts, and wages, the ILO created a divide between agricultural and colonial labour problems that lasted throughout the interwar years.[21] This compartmentalization resulted in dichotomies between agricultural and industrial, European and colonial, and free and forced labour, which meant that until the 1940s there was no discussion on labour standards in the plantations, despite highly problematic labour conditions. The structure of the account reflects this shift but also shows its persisting ambiguities and contradictions within international debates.

Scholarship and Archives

The evolving discourse on social and economic reforms of agricultural labour in international institutions between the 1920s and 1950s is a largely untold history that has hitherto remained locked in archival repositories.[22] This contrasts with the flourishing interest in the role of international organizations as reformist agents more generally. In the last twenty years or so, these organizations have been used as 'transnational sites of study' in which ideas of social reform, economic development, and global security were negotiated and circulated.[23] The book thus joins a large body of research on the history of interwar and post-war institutions such as the League of Nations, the International Institute of Agriculture, the Food and Agriculture Organization, and other UN organizations.[24] It also draws

---

[21] See Chapter 4.
[22] Aspects of this history have so far been treated in the following studies as well as in my own work (for the latter see bibliography). Marie-Renée, Mouton, 'Les huit heures en agriculture? Un conflit entre la France et l'OIT', *Relations internationales* 4 (1975), 53–79: Marianne, Dahlén, *The Negotiable Child: The ILO Child Labour Campaign, 1919–1973*, Doctor of Laws thesis (Uppsala University 2007).
[23] Glenda Sluga, 'Editorial: The Transnational History of International Institutions', *Journal of Global History* 6 (2011), 219–22; Sandrine Kott, 'Les organisations internationales, terrains d'étude de la globalisation. Jalons pour une approche socio-historique', *Critique internationale* 52 (2011), 11–16; Carolyn S. Biltoft, 'Sundry World within the World: Decentred Histories and Institutional Archives', *Journal of World History* 31, no. 4 (December 2020), 729–60.
[24] Madeleine Herren, *Internationale Organisationen seit 1865: Eine Globalgeschichte der Internationalen Ordnung* (Darmstadt: Buchgesellschaft, 2009); Bob Reinalda, *Routledge History of International Organizations: from 1815 to the Present Day* (Abingdon: Routledge, 2009); Mark Mazower, *No Enchanted Palace: The End of Empire and the Ideological Origins of the United Nations* (Princeton, NJ: Princeton University Press, 2009); Sunil Amrith, *Decolonizing International Health: India and Southeast Asia, 1930–1965* (Cambridge: Palgrave Macmillan, 2006); Amy Staples, *The Birth of Development. How the World Bank, Food and Agriculture Organization, and World Health*

on the encompassing studies of the various internationalisms that emerged in the late nineteenth and early twentieth centuries, particularly the ones carried out by women, peace activists, social reformers, trade unionists, and anti-colonial activists.[25]

The rise of these movements and organizations has been well documented and their critical role in building transnational networks and transforming international diplomacy and global governance in the first half of the twentieth century no longer needs to be elucidated. The emergence of 'the rural' as a key site of local, national, and international governance has also been demonstrated both for Europe and the wider world.[26] Economic and technical aspects of agricultural cooperation during this period have received recent attention.[27] Yet, scholars tend to have a very incomplete picture of the men and women, officials, experts, diplomats, and activists who engaged in agrarian cooperation, defended social justice for agrarian workers, and saw the improvement of working and living conditions in agriculture as one of the greatest challenges of the interwar and post-war years. These actors include international administrators such as Louise Matthaei (later Lady Howard), who headed the ILO's Agricultural Service, a unit entirely focused on collecting and collating information on agricultural work; trade unionists such as Piet Hiemstra and the Scottish farmworkers' representative Joseph Duncan; and landowners and agronomists such as the Czech Ferdinand Klindera and the French Marquis Louis de Vogüé, who acted as experts in agricultural

---

Organization Changed the World, 1945–1965 (Kent, OH: Kent State University Press, 2006); Patricia Clavin, *Securing the World Economy. The Reinvention of the League of Nations, 1920–1946* (Oxford: Oxford University Press, 2013); Susan Pedersen, *The Guardians. The League of Nations and the Crisis of Empire* (Oxford: Oxford University Press, 2015); Guy Fiti Sinclair, *To Reform the World: International Organizations and the Making of Modern States* (Oxford: Oxford University Press, 2017); Sandrine Kott, *A World More Equal: An Internationalist Perspective on the Cold War* (New York: Columbia University Press, 2024) . For scholarship on the ILO, see footnote 2 in this chapter.

[25] Patricia Clavin and Glenda Sluga, eds, *Internationalisms: A Twentieth-Century History* (Cambridge: Cambridge University Press, 2017); Glenda Sluga, *Internationalism in the Age of Nationalism* (Philadelphia: University of Pennsylvania Press, 2013); Daniel Laqua, ed., *Internationalism Reconfigured: Transnational Ideas and Movements between the World Wars* (London: Tauris Academic Studies, 2011); Martin H. Geyer and Johannes Paulmann, eds, *The Mechanics of Internationalism: Culture, Society, and Politics from the 1840s to the First World War* (Oxford: Oxford University Press, 2001).

[26] See for example Amrith, *Decolonizing International Health*; Iris Borowy, *Coming to Terms with World Health: The League of Nations Health Organization 1921–1946* (Frankfurt am Main: Peter Lang, 2009).

[27] For histories of interwar economic cooperation in the agricultural sector, see Fritz Georg von Graevenitz, *Argument Europa: Internationalismus in der globalen Agrarkrise der Zwischenkriegszeit (1927–1937)* (Frankfurt am Main: Campus Verlag, 2017); Federico D'Onofrio and Niccolò Mignemi, 'The International Institute of Agriculture and the Information Infrastructure of World Trade (1905–1946)', *Histoire & Mesure* 48 (2023), 13–38; Martin Bemmann, 'Cartels, Grossraumwirtschaft and Statistical Knowledge: International Organizations and Their Efforts to Govern Europe's Forest Resources in the 1930s and 1940s', in van de Grift and Ribi Forclaz, eds, *Governing the Rural in Interwar Europe*, 233–58; Juan Pan-Montojo and Niccolò Mignemi, 'International Organizations and Agriculture, 1905 to 1945: Introduction', *Agricultural History Review* 62, no. 2 (2017), 237–53. See also Clavin, *Securing the World Economy*.

labour commissions. These experts do not usually figure in international and global histories of the twentieth century, even though their influence in international policy-making should not be underestimated. They all had diverging visions of the future of agrarian communities, but shared one common belief: since more than half of the world's population were engaged in agricultural work, the welfare and 'improvement' of the latter's socio-economic conditions was a pressing priority in international affairs.

The story told in this book is therefore a story of international cooperation and developmentalist thinking, as well as of labour and agriculture. It shines a light on the crucial social, economic, and political role attributed to the agricultural economy and the rural populations in the first half of the twentieth century. Rather than presenting an institutional study of the ILO's complex internal and external mechanisms, the book wants to make visible what we can understand from the archives of these organizations about agricultural transformation and more specifically about agricultural labour.[28] There is a fundamental contradiction in the new history of international institutions: despite being ubiquitous in national, regional, and imperial histories and despite arguably constituting the most prevalent and heterogeneous form of occupation across centuries, agricultural workers have so far only marginally figured in narratives of internationalism and international organizations.[29] To remedy this, the book combines different historiographies which are seldom brought together, connecting the scholarship on international organizations and the history of global governance with the history of agriculture and the history of labour. The latter two fields have in recent years experienced a remarkable process of rejuvenation and expansion. The new global labour history that has emerged in recent decades has reinvigorated the classic and declining field of European labour history, which used to focus on trade unionism and European movements. New studies have highlighted transnational connections between world regions and have demonstrated that wage labour was not the norm. They have also emphasized the blurry boundaries between free and unfree labour.[30] In agricultural history, the relationship between food production, farming, natural and human resources, and the environment has moved centre stage. Historians have explored transnational similarities and differences in the history of agricultural modernization and the evolution of the

---

[28] Carolyn Biltoft, *A Violent Peace: Media, Truth and Power at the League of Nations* (Chicago: University of Chicago Press, 2021).

[29] A recent exception is the collective volume by Elise van Nederveen Meerkerk and Rolf Bauer, eds, *Global Agricultural Workers from the 17th to the 21st Century* (Leiden, Boston: Brill, 2023).

[30] Marcel Van der Linden, 'Labour History: The Old, The New and the Global', *African Studies* 66 (2007), 169–80; Frederick Cooper, Thomas C. Holt, and Rebecca J. Scott, *Beyond Slavery: Explorations of Race, Labour, and Citizenship in Post-Emancipation Societies* (Chapel Hill: University of North Carolina Press, 2000); Alessandro Stanziani, *Labor on the Fringes of Empire: Voice, Exit, and the Law* (New York: Palgrave Macmillan, 2018); Alessandro Stanziani, 'Beyond Colonialism: Servants, Wage Earners and Indentured Migrants in Rural France and on Reunion Island (ca 1750–1900)', *Labour History* 54, no. 1 (2013), 64–87.

rural economy.³¹ Thanks to the work of global and imperial historians, agriculture has also become an important focus in the history of science, technology, and development.³² These new studies have revised the somewhat dated image of agricultural history as a backwater of modern history, concerned with non-industrialized, supposedly primitive forms of living, working, and producing, and with the traditions and folklore of a dwindling countryside.³³ Rather, as has become abundantly clear, during the interwar and immediate post-war years, agriculture and rural societies remained an essential social, economic, and political component of life in Europe and elsewhere.³⁴

Drawing on these recent advancements, the story highlights the economic, social, and political importance attributed to agricultural labour between 1920 and 1950. It shines a light on what was conceptualized as a pre-industrial form of labour in underdeveloped rural areas where a considerable number of poor workers lived with minimal incomes and lack of opportunities, and did not enjoy the rights of their urban counterparts.³⁵ By doing so, the book challenges the existing dichotomies and the traditional divisions that have characterized the study of supposedly industrialized European nations and the non-industrialized world in the twentieth century. Given the enduring labour exploitation in the agricultural sector, the long-term story of how the ILO has, since the First World War, tried to create analogous conditions in both industrial and agricultural contexts also resonates with current concerns about ongoing rural poverty, the social costs of the globalized food system, and the continued reliance on cheap, underpaid, and often exploited labour.³⁶ From the vantage point of labour reform, the history that emerges is one in which agriculture is central to the international history of the

---

[31] Pedro Lains and Vicente Pinilla, eds, *Agriculture and Economic Development in Europe since 1870* (London, New York: Routledge, 2009); Peter Moser and Tony Varley, eds, *Integration through Subordination: The Politics of Agricultural Modernization in Industrial Europe* (Brepols: Turnhout, 2013); Carin Martiin, Juan Pan-Montojo, and Paul Brassley, eds, *Agriculture in Capitalist Europe, 1945–1970: From Food Shortages to Food Surpluses* (Abingdon: Routledge, 2016); van de Grift and Ribi Forclaz, *Governing the Rural in Interwar Europe*. For an early effort at an international comparative study, see also Michael Tracy, *Government and Agriculture in Western Europe, 1880–1988* (New York: New York University Press, 1988).

[32] Hodge, *Triumph of the Expert*; Monica M. van Beusekom, *Negotiating Development: African Farmers and Colonial Experts at the Office du Niger, 1920–1960* (Oxford: James Currey, 2002); Harro Maat, 'Agriculture and Food Production', in Corinna R. Unger, Iris Borowy, and Corinne A. Pernet, eds, *The Routledge Handbook on the History of Development* (Abington, New York, 2022), 190–203; van de Grift, Müller, and Unger, 'Living with the Land: Introduction', 1–13.

[33] Tiago Saraiva, *Fascist Pigs: Technoscientific Organisms and the History of Fascism* (Cambridge, MA: MIT Press, 2016).

[34] Nicola Verdon, *Working the Land: A History of the Farmworker in England from 1850 to the Present Day* (London: Palgrave Macmillan, 2017).

[35] Carlo M. Cipolla, *Before the Industrial Revolution: European Society and Economy, 1000–1700* (New York: Norton, 1976).

[36] For the current situation, see International Labour Organization, *Policy Guidelines for the Promotion of Decent Work in the Agri-food Sector* (Geneva: May 2023). Jörg Gertel and Sarah Ruth Sippel, eds, *Seasonal Workers in Mediterranean Agriculture: The Social Costs of Eating Fresh* (London and New York: Routledge, 2014).

interwar and immediate post-war years. Through the ILO we can see how agriculture received institutional legitimacy, how the organization as well as a new group of international experts gained authority, and how knowledge was produced. By discussing a series of specific themes pertaining to the social protection of workers, to decent housing, and limited hours of work, the story also points to the tensions between the need for social improvements and the demand for greater productivity.

Sources and Voices

The archival records of international institutions and social reform movements used for this study are those of the ILO in Geneva, the International Institute of Agriculture in Rome, the International Landworkers' Federation in Amsterdam, the Associated Country Women of the World in London, as well as the publications and private papers of reformers, experts, and officials. Parts of these archives are more fragmented than others and, as will be revealed in the discussion, quite a large amount of material on agriculture has been destroyed either by forces of nature or by institutions.

The documents nevertheless offer an encompassing perspective on the various strands of intellectual and ideological forces that shaped international debates about agricultural labour in the interwar and post-war years. Inevitably, however, they tend to mirror the ideas. Many of the exchanges and interactions described in this book are those of urban 'technocrats' and reformers—such as socialist trade unionists, government ministers, and social scientists—and to a lesser extent of big landowners and small farmers with first-hand experience of agrarian work and living. Often the debates and social efforts took place not in the farms and fields of the countryside but in the offices of urban buildings in European cities. Due to the very nature of its mandate, the ILO's research created a narrative about the universality of rural problems, the socio-economic challenges faced by agrarian societies, and the main problems affecting agricultural workers.[37] The studies that aimed to present international comparative aspects were rarely based on direct engagement with agrarian societies and were mostly the result of a collection and collation of national reports, facts, and figures. However, as the book shows, there were also movements that challenged and sought to decentralize the dominance of international technocrats, calling for greater representation of those directly affected by the policies.

---

[37] Daniel T. Rodgers, 'Bearing Tales: Networks and Narratives in Social Policy transfer', *Journal of Global History* 9 (2014), 310–11.

Undeniably this is a story 'from above'. Those who work the land rather than writing reports remain in the background and only fragments of their experiences can be glimpsed. As historians of agriculture have posited, tracing the voice of farmers and farm labourers in official government sources and journalistic commentaries is tricky. Governmental officials, international experts, and their questionnaires put forward a series of questions that reflected their own interests and prioritized certain issues that were not necessarily those of the farming population.[38] Reports were often carefully edited and information considered political or otherwise delicate was omitted. Agricultural trade unionists were closer to the lives, concerns, and interests of farmworkers and their writings and comments provide a counterpoint to the seemingly technical and apolitical reports of international bureaucracies. But trade unions were also organized hierarchically, with codified rules, and a good dose of ideological baggage. The contributions of farmers such as Augusta Gillabert-Randin, published in agricultural journals and farm magazines, provide an alternative voice and opinion to those of international officials, but their readership and reception remains difficult to evaluate.[39] More direct insights into the lives of workers can also be gained from the few existing memoirs and autobiographical accounts, but those too need to be handled critically, as they raise questions about their representativeness and the relationship between individual life stories versus the broader collective experience of a social group.[40]

Despite their flaws, this book relies where possible on these sources, which offer details, personal opinions, and local insights that are absent from official documents. The testimonies of men and women with first-hand knowledge of agriculture and labour on the farms not only highlight the aspects that were invisibilized within the ILO such as the work of women on farms or features of waged agricultural work that might have been misunderstood or even misconstrued in international reports, or the apparent lack of attachment of farmworkers to the land. They also show that, contrary to the views prevalent in internationalist circles, farmworkers and farmers, far from being apolitical and isolated, were often aware of the international economic and social order and of the interconnectedness between local and global realities.

---

[38] Verdon, *Working the Land*, 18.

[39] Peter Moser and Marthe Gosteli, eds, *Une paysanne entre ferme, marché et associations: Textes d'Augusta Gillabert-Randin, 1918–1940* (Baden: hier+jetzt, 2005), 257; Nicola Verdon, 'The Modern Countrywoman: Farm Women, Domesticity and Social Change in Interwar Britain', *History Workshop Journal* 70, no. 1 (Autumn 2010), 86–107; Nicholas Goddard, 'The Development and Influence of Agricultural Periodicals and Newspapers, 1780–1880', *The Agricultural History Review* 31, no. 2, British Agricultural History Society (1983), 116–31. Janet Galligani Casey, 'Farm Women, Letters to the Editor, and the Limits of Autobiography Theory', *Journal of Modern Literature* 28, no. 1 (2004), 89–106.

[40] Verdon, *Working the Land*, 16; Gilbert Garrier, 'L'apport des récits de vie et des romans paysans', in Ronald Hubscher and Jean-Claude Farcy, eds, *La Moisson des autres: Les salariés agricoles aux XIXe et XX siècles* (Paris: Créaphis, 1996).

Structure

The material in the book is organized chronologically as well as thematically. The story begins by examining how, in the wake of the destruction brought on by the First World War, the countryside emerged as a site of social reform. Trade unionist lobbying drew attention to the plight of workers in the agricultural sector, which suffered from a lack of social legislation and employed some of the poorest people in Europe. The newly created ILO resolved to promote reforms related to housing, working hours, and the labour of women and children in its 1921 International Labour Conference, which raised controversy among specific governments and brought to the fore the diverging views of agricultural interest groups. Tensions emerged between those who were hoping for a common international understanding to address pressing social issues, and those who viewed agriculture as a domain that was too heterogenous and disorganized for international standardization.

From the mid-1920s onwards, the International Labour Office in Geneva emerged as a rural observatory. It carried out collaborative work with the older International Institute of Agriculture with which it created a joint expert commission, the Mixed Advisory Agricultural Committee. The aim of this committee was to compare national experiences and models, and to find common themes on which to conduct research that would help formulate a set of standards that were meant to close the gap between urban and rural workers. The geographical scope of these international discussions, which covered topics from vocational education to labour management and land reform, was exclusively centred on Europe even though disenfranchised groups had sought to engage with international debates as early as in 1919. There was a deep-seated reluctance to include agricultural labour in the colonies into these studies.

Using the Great Depression as a turning point, the story then examines how the Depression brought renewed attention to agricultural and rural economies and generated a renewed ambition to understand the specific economic and social characteristics of rural labour. The contentious question of limiting working hours on farms, which had been dropped in the early 1920s, came back to the fore, combining discussions on normative regulation with those about discipline, rationality, and scientific management. An enquiry on hours of work in agriculture exposed the limits of the ILO's often overly ambitious scientific work, as well as the inadequacy of its Eurocentric bias.

By the late 1930s, against the backdrop of a profound economic, political, and imperial crisis, the geography of agrarian debates was changing. The rise of agrarianist ideologies and the impending war affected internationalist networks, leading to a polarization between socialist and fascist agrarian reformers, with both sides using international organizations as platforms to promote their ideological and political interests. At the same time, non-European experts increasingly challenged the ILO's skewed and narrow focus on European waged farm labour, pointing to the large number of poor subsistence farmers that did not fall under the Organization's remit. Ongoing problems about the way in which agricultural labour was being recruited in the colonies and about forms of indentured labour that resembled servitude also came to the fore.

The Second World War disrupted the ILO's work and displaced its international secretariat. It also acted as a catalyst for the emergence of technical approaches to agricultural modernization, reconstruction, and development outside the organization. The creation of the United Nations and the Food and Agriculture Organization (and the death of the International Institute of Agriculture) posed new challenges to the ILO. Emerging Cold-War-related preoccupations with food security gave new meaning to agriculture in international diplomacy and also shifted the discourse to combating hunger and securing rural welfare on a global scale. Battling with the new world order and attempting to draw on its interwar work, the ILO struggled to reassert its position as a standard-setting agency and as a defender of social rights for people in agriculture.

In the late 1940s, changes in European agriculture, decolonization and the rise of non-European membership affected international debates on farmwork in Geneva. The ILO's agricultural work took a new turn with the creation of a Plantation Committee in 1948. By 1950, and in stark contrast with the 1920s, agriculture had become a problem associated with under-development in what today would be called the Global South.[41] The new focus on social conditions in large-scale agricultural undertakings highlighted another contradiction in the ILO's work: while the attention shifted to the welfare of agricultural labourers in non-industrialized countries in Southeast Asia, the focus on plantations as the sole object of study firmly maintained a colonial perspective—without, however, addressing Europe's violent past of colonial exploitation and unfree labour.

Cultivating Fields of Progress: Agriculture and the International Labour Organization, 1920s–1950s. Amalia Ribi Forclaz, Oxford University Press. © Amalia Ribi Forclaz 2025. DOI: 10.1093/9780191945014.003.0001

---

[41] On the limits and benefits of using this term, see Su Lin Lewis, 'Decolonising the History of Internationalism: Transnational Activism across the South', *Transactions of the Royal Historical Society* (2023), 1–25, 2.

1
Putting Agriculture on the Agenda

'It is very unfortunate that the Peace Treaty has not made special mention of agricultural workers. They are always a little forgotten, the poor men who are in the fields, busy digging, and enduring the burning sun. They are always forgotten. The workers in the cities, who are called industrial workers, know how to make themselves heard; they are feared, they are given justice, or at least a beginning of justice. But the agricultural workers, unfortunately for them, are more forgotten, because they do not have the means to defend themselves in the congresses.' Colombian delegate Antonio José Restrepo speaking at the third session of the International Labour Conference in 1921 (International Labour Office, *Record of Proceedings*, third session of the International Labour Conference, Geneva, 1921, 28)

In March 1919, a few weeks into the Versailles Peace Conference, Joseph Duncan, an agricultural labour leader and secretary of the Scottish Farm Servants' Union, wrote an inflammatory editorial pointing to existing discontent among the rural working class.[1] In the Union's journal, he described the dramatic social and economic consequences of the First World War and warned of increasing labour unrest, predicting that '[t]hose people who fondly believed that with the coming of the Armistice the nation would go back to "business as usual" are finding themselves woefully mistaken'. Duncan, who would later become a prominent leader of international agricultural trade union work, painted a desolate picture of conditions in post-war Europe, where 'the bones of millions of young men [were] lying rotting in the plains of Flanders', thousands of widows and fatherless children were suffering from hunger, hundreds of thousands of men and women were unemployed, and the 'wounded and maimed and blinded' were being 'thrown out on the scrap-heap', while political affairs were 'run by an unscrupulous gang of profiteers'.[2] It was no wonder, Duncan claimed, that self-respecting workers were reacting with growing political agitation and strike action. Soldiers who had risked their life for the nation now demanded 'useful work' 'under healthy and sane conditions', and were ready to engage in a political and social

---

[1] Biographical Note on Joseph Duncan, ILO Archives Geneva, I 1055/8/1.
[2] Newspaper cutting, *The Scottish Farm Servant,* March 1919, ILO Archives Geneva, AG 1/0/25.

revolution if needed.³ Nowhere was this new revolutionary spirit more apparent than among rural workers in the countryside.

The situation depicted by Duncan reflected the massive social and economic problems faced across all regions of Europe in the wake of the First World War, and the rise of social discontent not just among industrial workers but also within rural society.⁴ The war had mobilized millions of men and women and caused material damage to the countryside, decimating the rural workforce, destroying villages and fields, and bringing psychological trauma to farming families.⁵ International warfare had also led to trade disruption and affected food provisioning. Faced with rising food insecurity, governments more or less forcefully encouraged the population, especially women, to make up for the loss of labour by enlisting as farmworkers and participating in private food production.⁶

In the aftermath of the conflict, states were dealing with its social and economic consequences and taking measures to reconstruct their national and rural economies.⁷ Following the armistice in November 1918 and for most of 1919, Europe was still plagued by hunger. Food rationing continued leading to subsistence riots, disorder, and violence among rural populations—especially in Russia and Italy. From the summer of 1917, many war-torn countries had been facing practical and logistical challenges such as the return to the farms of wounded and mutilated discharged soldiers, but also more generally the need for social reforms and agricultural legislation.⁸ The October Revolution paved the way for transnational socialism and the 'globalization' of a Soviet model of economic and political organization.⁹ It gave rise to a new international workers' movement, with communist parties emerging across Eastern, Central, and Southern Europe.

---

³ Newspaper cutting, *The Scottish Farm Servant*, March 1919, ILO Archives Geneva, AG 1/0/25.
⁴ The impact of the First World War on agriculture has been well documented for many national contexts. For a good overview of the literature, see Matteo Ermacora, 'Rural Society', in Ute Daniel, Peter Gatrell, Oliver Janz, Heather Jones, Jennifer Keene, Alan Kramer, and Bill Nasson, eds, *1914–1918-online. International Encyclopedia of the First World War* (Berlin: Freie Universität Berlin, 2015), https://encyclopedia.1914-1918-online.net/article/rural_society. See also Benjamin Ziemann, 'Agrarian Society', in Jay Winter, ed., *The Cambridge History of the First World War*, vol. 3 (Cambridge: Cambridge University Press, 2014), 382–407.
⁵ Hugh Clout, *After the Ruins: Restoring the Countryside of Northern France after the Great War* (Exeter: University of Exeter Press, 1996); Eric Alary, *La Grande Guerre des civils* (Paris: Perrin, 2013), 306–12.
⁶ Keith Grieves, 'War Comes to the Fields. Sacrifice, Localism and Ploughing Up the English Countryside', in Ian Beckett, ed., *1917. Beyond the Western Front* (Leiden, Boston: Brill, 2009), 159, 168; Richard Perren, 'Farmers and Consumers under Strain: Allied Meat Supplies in the First World War', *Agricultural History Review* 53, no. 2 (2005); Anna Bravo, 'Italian Peasant Women and the First World War', in Arthur Marwick, Wendy Simpson, and Clive Emsley, eds, *Total War and Historical Change. Europe, 1914–1955* (Maidenhead: Open University Press, 1989), 45–73.
⁷ Nicola Verdon, *Working the Land: A History of the Farmworker in England from 1850 to the Present Day* (London: Palgrave Macmillan, 2017), 12.
⁸ Éric Alary, *L'Histoire des paysans français* (Paris: Perrin, 2016).
⁹ Steffi Marung, 'A "Leninian Moment"? Soviet Africanists and the Interpretation of the October Revolution, 1950s–1970s', *Journal für Entwicklungspolitik* 33, no 3 (2017), 21–48.

New and old states faced economic and political transformations such as the implementation of wide-reaching land reforms to avert the dangers of communist uprisings. Mounting conflict between land-owners and small tenants and landless labourers fuelled social instability in the countryside. Agricultural strikes in 1918 and 1919 among farmworkers in Italy, Spain, but also Poland, Sweden, and France, brought home the need for strong social signals.[10]

This chapter explores how, following the devastation caused by the First World War, the European countryside became a focal point of attention for trade unionists and social reformers, exposing both a new vitality of agrarian internationalism as well as the different perspectives of agricultural interest groups. As will be shown, Duncan's warning words indirectly raised a central question: to what extent would the economic, political, and social crisis, the suffering of civilians and the demands of rural people inform not only national politics but also the negotiations and debates among diplomats and internationalist reformers who, in the wake of the armistice, were turning to planning peace? And how would the social plights of agricultural populations be addressed in the new international and institutional order?

The Peace Conference had opened in Versailles a few weeks earlier, in January 1919, in the absence of Germany and with no clear agenda, setting off weeks of chaotic negotiation.[11] Among the many concerns, one that dominated the diplomatic debates about the post-war order was the question of what attitude should be adopted towards Germany in terms of reparations and disarmament. There were also major issues resulting from the collapse of former empires, the redrawing of state boundaries in Eastern and Central Europe, as well as the approach to former German colonies in Africa.[12] Evenings were dedicated to discussing the aims, scope, and design of various versions of an organization to promote international cooperation and security. Ideas for the creation of the League of Nations, a new diplomatic mechanism that would secure peace and arbitrate international disputes, had been circulating in British and American circles since the beginning of the war. Between January and May 1919, a commission of government delegates was tasked with hammering out the terms of the League's covenant and to accommodate the various expectations of the negotiating powers about the

---

[10] Franco Cazzola, 'Les salariés agricoles de la plaine du Pô. Naissance et déclin d'une classe "dangereuse"', in Ronald Hubscher and Jean-Claude Farcy, eds, *La Moisson des Autres: Les salariés agricoles aux XIXe et XXe siècles* (Paris: Créaphis, 1996), 161–2; Romain Bonnet, *La Terre et le Plomb. Violence politique, question agraire et crise du parlementarisme libéral dans l'Italie du premier après-guerre (1918–1922) et dans l'Espagne républicaine (1931–1935)*, PhD thesis (European University Institute, 2016).

[11] Sally Marks, 'Mistakes and Myths: The Allies, Germany, and the Versailles Treaty, 1918–1921', *The Journal of Modern History* 85, no. 3 (2013), 632–59, 637.

[12] For a history of the Paris Peace Conference, see Margaret MacMillan, *Paris 1919: Six Months that Changed the World* (New York: Random House, 2002); Allan Sharp, *The Versailles Settlement: Peacemaking in Paris, 1919* (Basingstoke, New York: Palgrave Macmillan, 2008).

Organization's promotion of social and political rights and the transformation it would bring to international diplomatic habits.[13]

But governments were by far not the only protagonists in Paris: the prospect of an intergovernmental organization that would make diplomacy accountable to 'public opinion' had drawn social reformers, anti-colonial activists, women's organizations, and trade unionists to the French capital.[14] Labour was one of the foci of this lobbying. From 1916, the international trade union movement had shown ambitions to be included in the shaping of the post-war world order.[15] Female trade union activists, for example, gathered in Paris to campaign for women's rights.[16] Drawing on the experiences of late-nineteenth-century and early-twentieth-century labour networks and expert meetings, especially European and American trade unionists had regrouped during the war. They demanded international recognition of labour rights, social insurance, the protection against sickness and accidents, the limitation of working hours, the regulation of rest, and health and safety measures.[17] At international trade union conferences, the inclusion of an international social-policy programme and a future labour office in the prospective peace arrangement were being discussed.[18]

In light of the continuing reverberations of the Bolshevik revolution and the threatening spread of social upheaval, governments too could not ignore the importance of the labour question and, by the end of 1918, diplomatic proposals for the establishment of a periodical International Labour Conference and an International Labour Office circulated in Paris.[19] In January 1919, a Commission on International Labour Legislation, composed of representatives of the Allied powers and a number of expert advisers, was established and tasked with drafting

---

[13] Peter J. Yearwood, *Guarantee of Peace: The League of Nations in British Policy 1914–1925* (Oxford: Oxford University Press, 2009); Glenda Sluga, *Internationalism in the Age of Nationalism* (Philadelphia: University of Pennsylvania Press, 2013), 47–9.

[14] Erez Manela, *The Wilsonian Moment: Self-Determination and the International Origins of Anti-Colonial Nationalism* (Oxford, New York: Oxford University Press, 2007), 2; Daniel Gorman, *The Emergence of International Society in the 1920s* (New York: Cambridge University Press, 2012).

[15] For a detailed history of the founding of the ILO, see James T. Shotwell, ed., *Origins of the International Labor Organization*, 2 vols (New York: Columbia University Press, 1934); Antony Alcock, *History of the International Labour Organisation* (Basingstoke: Macmillan, 1971), 3–17; Jasmien Van Daele, 'Engineering Social Peace. Networks, Ideas, and the Founding of the International Labour Organization', *International Review of Social History* 50, no. 3 (2005), 435–66.

[16] Dorothy Sue Cobble, 'The Other ILO Founders: 1919 and Its Legacies', in Eileen Boris, Dorothea Hoethker, and Susan Zimmermann, eds, *Women's ILO: Transnational Networks, Global Labour Standards, and Gender Equity, 1919 to Present* (Leiden, Boston: Brill, 2018), 38; Susan Zimmermann, 'A Struggle over Gender, Class and the Vote: Unequal International Interactions and the Formation of the "Female International" of Socialist Women', in O. Janz and D. Schönpflug, eds, *Gender History in a Transnational Perspective* (New York: Berghahn, 2014), 101–26.

[17] Carol Riegelman, 'War-Time Trade-Union and Socialist Proposals', in Shotwell, *Origins of the International Labor Organization*, 55.

[18] Reiner Tosstorff, 'The International Trade-Union Movement and the Founding of the International Labour Organization', *International Review of Social History* 50 (2005), 399–433.

[19] On the perceived dangers of communism and the emergence of communist parties, see Adam Tooze, *The Deluge: The Great War and the Remaking of the Global Order* (London, New York: Allen Lane, 2014), 418–19.

a convention for the creation of an international structure.[20] The result of this complex negotiation was the adoption of a draft constitution for an 'international parliament of labour' in the form of a permanent International Labour Conference that would regulate labour internationally.[21]

Between February and March 1919, the Commission on International Labour Legislation in Paris held extensive meetings to discuss the form and function of this new organization, which came to be known as the International Labour Organization.[22] The scope of its mandate was at the heart of the debate and, as it turned out, agriculture was not forgotten. The Italian delegation, which was concerned with the widespread radicalization among agricultural labourers in Italy that in the eyes of some conservative observers 'seemed on the verge of a Communist revolution', proposed that the principles of labour legislation be also extended to agriculture.[23] As a result, many of the deliberations of the Commission centred on agricultural labour representation and regulation.[24] At the centre of the discussion was the creation of 'equitable' labour legislation for workers in agriculture as in the industry, especially regarding the limitation of working hours, the labour of children, and a system of labour inspection in agriculture. In contrast, the Treaty of Versailles, which was signed a few months later in June 1919, and especially the part of its preamble which promised to improve the conditions of labour of a large number of people suffering from 'injustice, hardship, and privation', did not explicitly refer to agricultural workers but invoked an un-defined category of 'industrial labour'.[25] After discussion, delegates agreed that 'the English word 'industrial' included agriculture as well as industry' and therefore chose not to mention agricultural workers because they felt that their inclusion was already implied and that a specific mention would exclude other types of workers such as fishermen, construction workers employed on railways, tunnels, and canals, as well as domestic servants.[26] Industrial was thus meant to include all forms of labour subject to contracts and labour laws. The omission, however,

---

[20] H. B. Butler, 'The Washington Conference, 1919', in E. J. Solano, ed., *Labour as an International Problem* (London: Macmillan, 1920), 197–246.
[21] Alcock, *History of the International Labour Organization*, 24–6.
[22] Edward Phelan, 'The Labour Proposals before the Peace Conference', in Shotwell, *Origins of the International Labour Organization*, vol. 1, 199–220.
[23] International Labour Office, Minutes of the second session of the Governing Body, Paris, January 1920. Olivia Rossetti Agresti, *Anecdotage of an Interpreter: The Reminiscences of Olivia Rossetti Agresti* (1958), in the Oral History Collection of Columbia University, ch. 13, 2.
[24] See Paris Peace Conference, Commission on International Labour Legislation. Minutes of Proceedings published in ILO, *Official Bulletin* 1 (April 1919–August 1920), 207–11, 268.
[25] Cited in International Labour Office, *Record of Proceedings*, First session of the International Labour Conference, Washington, 29 October to 29 November 1919, 54.
[26] See Paris Peace Conference, Commission on International Labour Legislation. Minutes of Proceedings published in ILO, *Official Bulletin* 1 (April 1919–August 1920), 34. On the basis that the English term 'industrial' bore a different meaning from the French word '*industriel*', the wording was changed in the French text and substituted with 'professional'.

would cause considerable debate in coming years, when some government officials and experts interpreted it as a deliberate exclusion of agriculture.[27]

The Versailles Peace Agreement also missed the opportunity to integrate pre-war agricultural organizations in the new post-war framework and to clarify relations between them. One such organization was the International Institute of Agriculture, created in 1905 in Rome and whose American founder David Lubin had died of the Spanish flu in a Roman hotel only a few days before the start of the Peace Conference.[28] Another was the Commission Internationale d'Agriculture in Paris, a 'semi-official' forum for international cooperation between Europe's agrarian elites that existed since the 1880s and that was presided by the French agricultural minister Jules Méline.[29] Both organizations aimed at promoting inter-governmental cooperation to coordinate the trade and the pricing of agricultural products. And both had built extensive pre-war networks that would, however, not be formally integrated into the post-war institutional order. The International Institute of Agriculture, especially after the mid-1920s when it was increasingly invested with the interests and agenda of the Fascist government in Italy, tried to enter into closer relation with the League and aspired to have the status of a specialized agency like the ILO.[30] Even though it succeeded in achieving a joint agreement according to which the League's Financial and Economic Section and the Institute would draw on each other's expertise and bring their work 'into line' with each other, the Institute was never fully accepted by the League of Nations as an equal cooperation partner in agricultural affairs.[31]

In fact, very little in the Versailles Peace Treaty and the League of Nations Covenant regulated international cooperation on agriculture, an oversight which would come back to haunt the new international institutions in the coming years and raise ongoing issues of legitimacy and governance with regard to agricultural topics. Collaboration between the ILO and the League of Nations on agricultural questions was unsystematic throughout the interwar years. In the 1920s, the League, international security, disarmament, and the settling of

---

[27] On this, see Chapter 2.

[28] Rossetti Agresti, *Anecdotage of an Interpreter*, p. 25. On the International Institute of Agriculture, see also Chapter 3.

[29] Gilbert Noël, 'La solidarité agricole européenne: des congrès d'agriculture à la politique agricole commune', in Jordi Canal, Gilles Pécout, and Maurizio Ridolfi, eds, *Sociétés rurales du XXe siècle. France, Italie et Espagne* (Rome: École française de Rome, 2004), 311–25; Fritz Georg von Graevenitz, *Argument Europa: Internationalismus in der globalen Agrarkrise der Zwischenkriegszeit (1927–1937)* (Frankfurt am Main: Campus Verlag, 2017), 107–13; Federico D'Onofrio and Niccolò Mignemi, 'The International Institute of Agriculture and the Information Infrastructure of World Trade (1905–1946)', *Histoire & Mesure* 48 (2023), 13–38.

[30] Luciano Tosi, *Alle origini della FAO: Le relazioni tra l'Istituto Internazionale di Agricoltura e la Società delle Nazioni* (Milan: Franco Angeli, 1989), 60–85.

[31] On the relationship between the International Institute of Agriculture and the League, see League of Nations Archives, Geneva, R2800-10D-3727-2016 and R2800-10D-3369-2016.

international disputes, expanded its mandate to include international cooperation on a host of social welfare questions ranging from refugees to child protection and the abolition of slavery.[32] Relying on the expertise of other bodies, such as the International Institute of Agriculture and the ILO, it showed little active interest in agricultural questions. This would change in the wake of the Great Depression, when the League set up new expert commissions to discuss economic and trade issues in relation to specific agricultural commodities such as wheat and sugar.[33] League attention to rural issues would further increase in the 1930s, through its work on nutrition and rural hygiene and its exploration of the potential of agricultural credit and the role of cooperatives.[34] In contrast, the ILO would stay close to the promises of those fighting for the recognition of agricultural labour rights in Versailles. The institution remained focused on improving the working and living conditions of agricultural workers through labour legislation.

The Big Opening: Agriculture at the ILO

In July 1920, the permanent secretariat of the ILO, the so-called International Labour Office, took up its first headquarters in Geneva.[35] In the following months, the International Labour Office's bureaucratic machinery 'struggled into existence', hampered by a small budget and inadequate buildings. Some observers complained that offices were neither sufficiently heated nor ventilated, bathrooms were dirty, and afternoon tea was allegedly served in fire-buckets.[36] But the staff was highly motivated in spite of the aberrantly high living costs in Geneva and the difficulties in finding accommodation.[37] In its first two years, the ILO attracted as many as 20,000 job applications and resorted to competitive examinations to

---

[32] Liat Kozma, Magaly Rodriguez Garcia, and Davide Rodogno, eds, *The League of Nations' Work on Social Issues: Visions, Endeavours and Experiments* (Geneva: United Nations, 2016); Gorman, *The Emergence of International Society in the 1920s*; Susan Pedersen, 'Back to the League of Nations', *The American Historical Review* 112, no. 4 (2007), 1091–1117.

[33] On trade and economic cooperation, von Graevenitz, *Argument Europa*.

[34] On rural hygiene, Iris Borowy, *Coming to Terms with World Health: The League of Nations Health Organization, 1921–1946* (Frankfurt am Main: Peter Lang, 2009).

[35] A small preliminary group of ILO staff had moved from Paris to London before settling in Geneva, where a first ILO building (La Châtelaine in Pregny) was set up. The building now houses the headquarters of the International Committee of the Red Cross. Report of the Director to the third session of the International Labour Conference, Geneva, 1921, 13–21. In 1926, the ILO moved into a building (now the headquarters of the WTO) specifically constructed for the organization, where it remained until 1974.

[36] Alice Maud Allen, *Sophy Sanger: A Pioneer in Internationalism* (Glasgow: Robert Maclehose and Co., 1958), 182.

[37] Report of the Director to the third session of the International Labour Conference (Geneva: International Labour Office, 1921), 26. On housing see also Allen, *Sophy Sanger*, 174–84.

select the best candidates. Women and men were treated equally (at least in principle) and employed 'indifferently according to their capacity'.[38]

A first International Labour Conference had been held in Washington in October 1919, in which member states had proceeded to draw up six legal instruments, so-called conventions, setting out the basic principles of workers' rights, all of which formulated for factory workers.[39] These principles included limiting working hours in the industry to forty-eight hours per week, preventing unemployment, protecting women before and after childbirth, prohibiting night work, regulating the employment of women and children under fourteen, as well as protecting workers from hazardous substances such as anthrax and lead poisoning.[40]

The question of whether to include agriculture in this legal framework gave food to enduring debates. Some delegates in Washington thought that agriculture was best left alone and could not be included in international social legislation, due to its heterogeneity and the lack of existing information; others were adamant that social legislation should be extended to the farms at least across European countries. Especially when discussing the eight-hour day, various delegations (notably again the Italian one) criticized the proposed legislation for its exclusion of agricultural labourers. Czechoslovakian delegates too insisted that the protection of agricultural workers was 'exceedingly important for the economic and moral development of nations', and that the living and working conditions of this particular social group should be addressed in one of the next meetings.[41]

Many predicted that applying social standards to industrial workers alone would increase the divide between town and country and draw even more people from the land to the city, creating problems of labour resources and production. There was a perceived danger that whilst labour legislation was 'little by little guaranteeing the situation of the industrial workers, the attraction of the city' would grow 'stronger for the countryman'.[42] The latter, it was often stated, suffered from small earnings, lack of leisure, arduous work, inferior housing, and the general monotony of life. The Spanish labour representative, Francisco Largo Caballero, thus presented a motion that a special conference should be dedicated to social legislation in agriculture.

---

[38] Report of the Director to the third session of the International Labour Conference, (Geneva: International Labour Office, 1921), 25.

[39] International Labour Office, *Record of Proceedings*, First session of the International Labour Conference, Washington, 29 October to 29 November 1919, 41.

[40] For a first-hand description of the ILO's 1919 conference, see Allen, *Sophy Sanger*, 144; and Rossetti Agresti, *Anecdotage of an Interpreter*, ch. 12.

[41] International Labour Office, *Record of Proceedings*, First session of the International Labour Conference, Washington, 29 October to 29 November 1919, 54.

[42] International Labour Conference, Agricultural Questions, second item of the Agenda, Questionnaire (Geneva: International Labour Office, 1920), 10. International Labour Office, Minutes of the third session of the Governing Body, London, 22–25 March 1920. Appendix 7: Agenda of the third session of the International Labour Conference, 58.

Albert Thomas, the ILO's French socialist director, was adamant that the International Labour Office should make it clear from the outset that its object was to protect and raise the standard of life of all workers, both urban and rural. Trained in history and geography, Thomas was close to the French historian and founder of the Annales school Lucien Febvre, with whom he had studied at the prestigious École Normale Supérieure in Paris and who shared his interest in rural and agricultural history.[43] Thomas's expertise and reputation were based on his pre-war legislative work on providing pensions to urban and rural workers and on his wartime experience as a minister of armament during the First World War.[44] He was convinced that social peace could only be attained by extending legislation beyond urban surroundings to rural and agricultural workers. He was also aware of the economic and social importance of the countryside and of the stark differences in agricultural development across different regions in the North, East, South, and West of Europe—an awareness that he would further cultivate throughout the 1920s through multiple travels.[45] Thomas's affinities with rural issues was also reflected in his personal life. After acquiring a farmhouse and a herd of cows in the French countryside in 1924, he liked to boast to his correspondents that he had become a farmer, inviting them to visit his new property.[46] He also strategically used references to his rural ties and his cows to gain the trust of rural interlocutors and representatives of farmer organizations and agricultural trade unions during his travels abroad, especially in Eastern and Central Europe.[47] Thomas's understanding of farm life was arguably romanticized as can be gauged by his admiration for clean, tidy, and traditional middle-sized farmhouses managed by long-standing farming families.[48] He idealized the 'authentic' farmer, attached to his land, industrious, and engaged in the production of hearty food. Yet, he was also generally critical of right-wing populist peasant parties and large landholders and he was inclined to support the workers' organizations and to side with their demands.

The reasons why Thomas and other social reformers were in favour of an ILO mandate over agriculture had to do not only with the ILO's constitutionally enshrined and often advertised objective of 'social justice', but also with securing social stability, ensuring agricultural production, and averting the menace of a

---

[43] Lucien Febvre, 'Albert Thomas historien', *Annales d'histoire économique et sociale* 4 (July 1932), 381; Christophe Prochasson, 'Entre science et action sociale: le réseau Albert Thomas et le socialisme normallien 1900–1914', in Christian Topalov, ed., *Laboratoires du nouveau siècle. La nébuleuse réformatrice et ses réseaux en France 1880–1914* (Paris, 1999), 141–58.
[44] Ayla Aglan, 'Albert Thomas, historien du temps présent', *Les cahiers Irice* 2, no. 2 (2008), 23–38.
[45] Dorothea Hoethker and Sandrine Kott, eds, *À la rencontre de l'Europe au travail: récits de voyages d'Albert Thomas (1920–1932)* (Sorbonne/Bureau International du Travail, 2015).
[46] Letter, Thomas to de Vogüé, 14 October 1924, ILO Archives Geneva, AG 0/10/22.
[47] Thomas's notes on a trip to Hungary, in Hoethker and Kott, *À la rencontre de l'Europe au travail*, 170.
[48] Thomas's notes on a trip to Hungary, in Hoethker and Kott, *À la rencontre de l'Europe au travail*, 173.

communist uprising. In Thomas's words, agriculture was of 'immense value' both economically and socially, and its role for 'social stability' was essential.[49] Underpaid and overworked, with no or little access to land, the rural workforce was considered as particularly volatile. The necessity for the political and economic integration of rural populations everywhere in Europe and particularly in the new states of Eastern and Central Europe, as well as the dangers of ideological and populist instrumentalization from the right and left, was reason enough to put agriculture centre stage.[50] Other concerns had to do with the perceived instability of rural–urban migration in national context. To the ILO's Governing Body, the allegedly 'alarming tendency' of country people to migrate from the country to cities was a source of concern and a motivation for social reform.[51] In the ILO's early conference meetings, the threat of rural exodus was used as an argument in favour of ensuring more equal rights and living and working conditions between rural and urban workers. Bad housing and long working hours were thought to encourage the rural workforce to leave the land.[52] There was no doubt, in the Governing Body's mind, that social legislation to improve farmworkers' work conditions would be an effective way of decreasing rural exodus, if not bringing it to an end.[53] Surprisingly, however, at least until the Second World War, the ILO was much less concerned with the international migration of rural workers and it did not discuss this aspect in more depth.

Historians of the ILO have stressed that it was the organization's aim to offer a peaceful alternative to class conflict by enabling a dialogue on social reform without questioning capitalist industrialization and economic productivity.[54] This also applied to the agricultural sector. Reformers were concerned with the lure of bolshevism, which supposedly posed a potential threat not only to the industrial masses but also to workers on farm. The Soviet reorganization of agriculture and the regime's decision to forcefully move Russian peasants into collective farms with the ambition to create larger industrialized and mechanized kolkhozes

[49] See Thomas's travel notes during a trip to Czechoslovakia in 1927. Hoethker and Kott, À la rencontre de l'Europe au travail, 125. Thomas made similar reflections when travelling to Poland.

[50] Charles S. Maier, *Recasting Bourgeois Europe: Stabilization in France, Germany, and Italy in the Decade after World War I* (Princeton: Princeton University Press, 1988); Derek Howard Aldcroft, *Europe's Third World: The European Periphery in the Interwar Years* (Aldershot, UK: Ashgate, 2006); Helga Schultz and Angela Harre, eds, *Bauerngesellschaften auf dem Weg in die Moderne: Agrarismus in Ostmitteleuropa 1880 bis 1960* (Wiesbaden: Harrassowitz Verlag, 2010).

[51] For a discussion of the agenda, see International Labour Office, Minutes of the third session of the Governing Body, London, 22–25 March 1920. Appendix 7: Agenda of the third session of the International Labour Conference, 58.

[52] Amalia Ribi Forclaz, 'A Bed, a Cover, and Possibly a Pillow: Improving the Living Conditions of Agricultural Workers in the Interwar Years', *Capitalism. A Journal of History and Economics* 3, no. 1 (2022), 136–59.

[53] International Labour Office, Minutes of the third session of the Governing Body, London, 22–25 March 1920, 58.

[54] Shotwell, *Origins of the International Labour Organization*, 18; Van Daele, 'Engineering Social Peace'.

appeared on the ILO's radar as early as 1919.⁵⁵ In fact, one of the ILO Governing Body's first commissions was set up to study bolshevism and (among other topics) Soviet agrarian reform.⁵⁶ An enquiry into labour conditions in Soviet Russia carried out on Russian soil was to provide 'accurate and impartial information' to prevent 'dangerous illusions' about the superiority of Soviet labour and industry from spreading among the working class.⁵⁷ The commission was ultimately unsuccessful and never made it to the Soviet Union. However, this did not stop the International Labour Office from establishing a Russian Section that continued to collect information on the Soviet economy and industrial organization.⁵⁸

In March 1920, a majority of the ILO's Governing Body voted in favour of putting agriculture on the agenda.⁵⁹ By seriously considering the extension of labour rights to agriculture, Thomas was expanding the ILO's mandate far beyond what more conservative forces had initially imagined. The integration of agriculture into the ILO's framework meant that the Organization inadvertently touched on a delicate subject that had the potential to upset those who thought of the countryside as a 'rural idyll', a wholesome counterpart to urban decay and industrial modernity.⁶⁰ Critiquing the social and economic conditions of agriculture proposed a different vision than the one embodied by those farming lobbies and parties that idealized the farming population as a bedrock of the nation, composed of hard-working patriots rooted in the land of their ancestors and acting as a bulwark against the claims of communist workers.⁶¹

In contrast, left-wing social reformers and trade unionists tended to point to the social inequalities between rural and urban living, the persistence of patriarchal relationships and exploitative labour conditions in the countryside, and the need for social, economic, and technical improvements. As will become clear, the ILO was trying to mediate between the two and bridge the distance between

---

⁵⁵ Lynne Viola, V. P. Danilov, N. A. Ivitskii, and Denis Kozlov, eds, *The War against the Peasantry, 1927-1930: The Tragedy of the Soviet Countryside* (New Haven: Yale University Press, 2005).

⁵⁶ On the 'bolshevik enquiry', see International Labour Office, Minutes of the third session of the Governing Body, London, 22-25 March 1920, 49-57 (on bolshevik agricultural policies, 55-7). See also Marine Dhermy-Mairal and Laure Piguet, 'Enquiring into Others: The International Labour Office's Attempts to Grasp the Early Soviet Labour System (1920)', *Cadernos Sociedade e Trabalho* (Lisbon: MTSSS/GEP, 2021), 149-62.

⁵⁷ On the origins of and diplomatic difficulties accompanying this inquiry, see Report of the Director to the third session of the International Labour Conference, Geneva, 1921, 218.

⁵⁸ Report of the Director to the fourth session of the International Labour Conference, Geneva, 1922, 851-2. The information on Russia was published in the form of a supplement of the *Industrial and Labour Information*.

⁵⁹ International Labour Office, Minutes of the third session of the Governing Body, London, 22-25 March 1920, 32-4.

⁶⁰ Jeremy Burchardt, 'The Rural Idyll: A Critique', in Verity Elson and Rosemary Shirley, eds, *Creating the Countryside: The Rural Idyll Past and Present* (London: Paul Holberton, 2017), 64-73.

⁶¹ See for example the works of Ernst Laur as cited in Jérémie Forney, 'Idéologie agrarienne et identité professionelle des agriculteurs: la complexité des images du paysan Suisse', *Yearbook of Socioeconomics in Agriculture* 4, no. 1 (June 2011), 13-33.

landowners, independent farmers, and workers. But the ILO's ambition to conceptualize agricultural labour as a domain of social reform that necessitated the (tripartite) cooperation of states, employers, and workers' organizations, and to filter half a century of industrial social reform programmes into the agricultural sector, was not only unprecedented: it also meant addressing a set of contested issues on which there was but scarce data, let alone international cooperation. As the Governing Body of the International Labour Office anticipated, topics such as the length of the working day on European farms, social insurance for unemployment and accidents in agriculture, the protection of women and children from night work on farms, as well as issues of education and housing, were bound to cause 'serious political or other difficulties'.[62] A labour conference dealing with these issues would have to 'exercise great discretion'.[63]

'The Most Despised and Least Protected'

Of the many segments of the rural economy, a source of particular concern for international social reformers was the class of labourers called 'agricultural workers' or '*ouvriers agricoles*', narrowly defined as farm employees who did not own land or housing, did not manage their own farm, and whose livelihoods completely depended on waged agricultural work. As early as in 1919, the ILO's Governing Body had decided that should agriculture be included, it would be 'necessary to define carefully the agricultural problem' and to prioritize a focus on hired farm labour.[64] Described as hard-working and hard-headed, proud and strong, but also poor, landless, illiterate, and generally despised and stigmatized, this social group included a wide spectrum of workers, from day labourers to permanent farm servants, often also women and migrants.[65] In the late nineteenth century, this particular class of workers had entered the collective imagination thanks to Max Weber, who in his early sociological surveys had identified the '*Landarbeiter*' (landworker) as an impoverished worker, especially vulnerable but also highly mobile during agricultural crises, thus posing a particular challenge to national social policy, political economy, and territoriality.[66]

---

[62] International Labour Office, Minutes of the third session of the Governing Body, London, 22–25 March 1920. Appendix 7: Agenda of the third session of the International Labour Conference, 56–7.
[63] International Labour Office, Minutes of the third session of the Governing Body, London, 22–25 March 1920. Appendix 7: Agenda of the third session of the International Labour Conference, 56–7.
[64] International Labour Office, *Record of Proceedings*, First session of the International Labour Conference, Washington, 29 October to 29 November 1919, 41.
[65] For the diversity of this group see Elise van Nederveen Meerkerk and Rolf Bauer, 'Introduction' in van Nederveen Meerkerk and Bauer, eds, *Global Agricultural Workers from the 17th to the 21st Century* (Leiden, Boston: Brill, 2023), 1–29.
[66] Max Weber, *Die Verhältnisse der Landarbeiter im ostelbischen Deutschland (Preussische Provinzen Ost- und Westpreussen, Pommern, Posen, Schlesien, Brandenburg, Grossherzogtümer Mecklenburg, Kreis Herzogtum Lauenburg)* (Leipzig: Duncker & Humblot, 1892).

By 1920, European agricultural workers were regarded by many social reformers as an underclass of workers that was subjected to the worst of both the industrial and agrarian worlds. In the eyes of newly emerging international agricultural trade unions, those faceless figures appeared collectively as 'the most despised and least protected' workers in the post-war economy.[67] A description corroborated by historians who, for instance with regard to Britain, have characterized the relationship between farm owners and labourers as 'exploitative' and the farm as 'the scene of constant potential conflict'.[68] Badly housed, inadequately fed, and with little prospects of social improvement, these working poor lived at the bottom of the social ladder. Not unlike other social segments such as migrant workers, sailors, and vagrants, they were the object of urban anxieties and prejudice.[69] Social enquiries and first-person accounts, such as those of the French social scientist Jacques Valdour, helped to cement this view.[70] Valdour (whose real name was Louis Martin) wrote about the material conditions of agricultural workers, their habits, language, and morality. He painted the picture of a population group that worked long hours for little pay, suffered from hard physical labour and fatigue, was housed in dismal conditions, lacked basic education and hygiene, and was prone to vagrancy.[71]

Of course, even within Western Europe, the rural workforce was not as undifferentiated as the term 'agricultural worker' might suggest: as historians have shown in a variety of national contexts, the agricultural workforce was hierarchically structured and differentiated into various degrees of skilled occupations, from unskilled farmhands to the specialized horse- and ploughmen, mountain herdsmen, dairymaids, engine men, and forest workers. These figures did not all have the same experience nor did they receive the same pay or housing.[72] But they shared some common working conditions across many countries: the French '*ouvrier agricole*', the Italian '*bracciante*', the British 'landworker', and the German '*Landarbeiter*' were subjected to informal contracts, irregular and seasonally fluctuating wages (often including remuneration in kind such as food, housing, and clothes), child labour, and insalubrious housing conditions on

---

[67] Opening words of Jan Oudegeest, representative of the International Federation of Trade Unions at the First International Congress of Landworkers. International Labour Office, *First International Congress of Landworkers' Unions affiliated to the International Federation of Trade Unions Amsterdam, 17–19 August 1920*, Studies and Reports, Series K, no. 1 (Geneva: International Labour Office, 1920), 5.

[68] Alun Howkins, *Poor Labouring Men: Rural Radicalism in Norfolk 1870–1923* (Boston: Routledge and Kegan Paul, 1985), 15.

[69] Gopalan Balachandran, 'Subaltern Cosmopolitanism in the Imperial Metropole: Notes towards a Prehistory of Racism and Multiculturalism', *Working Papers in International History* 8 (September 2011).

[70] Jacques Valdour, *L'ouvrier agricole: Observations vécues* (Paris: Arthur Rousseau, 1919).

[71] See Chapter 2.

[72] Verdon, *Working the Land*, 14. For a contemporary account of specializations in French agriculture, see Michel Augé-Laribé, 'Labour Conditions in French Agriculture', *International Labour Review* 25, no. 1 (1932), 30–1; Hubscher and Farcy, *La Moisson des autres*, 66.

the farm.[73] Sometimes described as 'docile' due to their illiteracy and lack of education, these rural workers were viewed by social reformers as largely unorganized, repressed, and submissive.[74]

In fact, these stereotypes contrasted with the reality of frequent local strikes, rebellions, and upheavals that often remained unaccounted for in official statistics. Contemporary experts on agricultural labour observed that the widespread assumption that strikes 'had no place in agriculture' was wrong and that this belief was due to the fact that farm strikes remained largely unrecorded.[75] Instead, episodes of labour unrest could surge very quickly when economic circumstances changed: altercations could occur as a result of unsatisfactory working and living conditions (especially long hours, bad food and lodging, low wages, and frequent accidents) or when a rise in prices would prompt workers to demand a greater share in the profits.[76] The early twentieth century had provided many examples of this: women working as weeders in Italian rice fields repeatedly mobilized for a shorter working day and their action culminated in a general strike in 1906.[77] Between 1906 and 1912, various labour conflicts around long working hours, low wages, and bad food and lodging occurred among the vineyard-workers in the North and South of France.[78] Overseas, discontent with work, pay, and sanitary conditions led to sometimes violent unrest among farmworkers, such as in the so-called wheatland strike of migrant hop pickers in California in 1913.[79] A similar picture of frequent agricultural labour strikes was painted by the African-American social reformer and author Booker T. Washington in his *Man Farthest Down*, which recounted his tour of Europe in 1910. Booker even dedicated a chapter to the 'labour insurrection' of landless farm labourers in Italy and Hungary, which he described as 'the most bloody and the most far-reaching in influence' of any labour strikes in Europe.[80] The potential for violent social conflict thus contradicted the prevailing stereotype of rural populations as apolitical, isolated, and unorganized.

---

[73] For France, see Hubscher and Farcy, *La Moisson des autres*; for Italy, see Asher Hobson, 'The Landless Agricultural Laborer in Italy', *The Journal of Land & Public Utility Economics* 1, no. 4 (1925), 425–34; Elda Gentili Zappi, *If Eight Hours Seem Too Few: Mobilization of Women Workers in the Italian Rice Fields* (New York: State University of New York Press, 1991); for Britain, see Howkins, *Poor Labouring Men*; Verdon, *Working the Land*.

[74] Hubscher and Farcy, *La Moisson des autres*, 25.

[75] For an incomplete list of the local strikes that had taken place in European countries since the late nineteenth century: see Louise E. Howard, *Labour in Agriculture: An International Survey* (Oxford: Oxford University Press, 1935), 323–5.

[76] Howard, *Labour in Agriculture*, 323–5.

[77] Gentili Zappi, *If Eight Hours Seem Too Few*.

[78] J. Harvey Smith, 'Agricultural Workers and the French Wine-Growers' Revolt of 1907', *Past & Present* 79, no. 1 (May 1978), 101–25; Yves Rinaudo, 'Ouvriers agricoles provençaux en grève, 1890–1939', in Hubscher and Farcy, *La Moisson des autres*, 281–301.

[79] David Vaught, *Cultivating California. Growers, Specialty Crops, and Labor, 1875–1920* (Baltimore: John Hopkins University Press, 2002), 130–1.

[80] Booker T. Washington with the collaboration of Robert E. Park, *The Man Farthest Down: A Record of Observation and Study in Europe* (Garden City: Double Day, 2012).

Strikes and unrest were not the only problem associated with this social group: since the late nineteenth century, one of the most salient issues regarding the relationship between rural and urban economies was that of rural–urban migration, referred to as 'rural exodus'. The drift from the country to cities against a backdrop of industrialization, urbanization, and agricultural crisis was a well-rehearsed trope harnessed by the political right and left alike. According to contemporary observers, the lowest rural classes, least attached to the land and suffering from the worst housing and living conditions, were especially keen to leave farmwork and emigrate to the cities, where they became involved in socialist movements.[81] More generally, it was feared that agricultural work was disliked by the younger generation, who increasingly viewed farming as 'too painful' an occupation that left insufficient time for leisure and recreation.[82]

One of the major problems identified by social reformers was the lack of social legislation, seen as a source of inequality between industrial and agricultural workers. Until the First World War, in Western Europe, the social legislation to protect agricultural workers was scarce.[83] The war acted as a catalyst for change, and in its aftermath, social legislation was being considered and implemented, albeit inconsistently, in various Western European countries: in Germany, France, Italy, and Britain, for example, reforms consisted of establishing minimum wages for agricultural labourers and tenant farmers, promoting technical education, and, in the case of Italy, providing compulsory insurance against accidents.[84] As an international institution, the ILO understood its role as a mediator between different interest groups and a standardizer of social and economic improvements in the agricultural sector. This also included reforms intended to counteract pre-war processes of rural exodus and to encourage agricultural production, for instance through new legislation that facilitated access to agricultural credit, and the generalization of insurance schemes against hail or livestock loss.

From the start, the ILO's focus was limited to waged and white agricultural workers in industrialized countries. Especially in the early years of the Organization, the locus of industrialization and economic productivity was seen as essentially Western European. The ILO distinguished between economically advanced countries referred to as of 'chief industrial importance'—a measurement that depended on the size of the country's industrial population, the length of its railway track, and the importance of its mercantile marine. This controversially excluded the rural economy and artisanal production and thus left out large

---

[81] Émile Vandervelde, *L'exode rural et le retour aux champs* (Paris: Felix Alcan, 1903).

[82] Augusta Gillabert-Randin, 'L'emploi des loisirs à la campagne III', *L'industrie laitière Suisse* (19 June 1925), in Peter Moser and Marthe Gosteli, eds, *Une paysanne entre ferme, marché et associations: Textes d'Augusta Gillabert-Randin, 1918–1940* (Baden: hier+jetzt, 2005), 144.

[83] Alun Howkins, 'Labor History and the Rural Poor, 1850–1980', *Rural History* 1, no. 1 (1990), 113–22.

[84] See report on the Corn Production Act, 1917, in *International Review of Agricultural Economics* (October 1917), 67. Also, Verdon, *Working the Land*, ch. 6.

agrarian economies with relatively little industrial output. The above criteria were used to determine who would be granted membership of the Governing Body: in the early 1920s (with the notable exception of India, which had taken issue with the ILO's narrow approach), it comprised industrialized countries such as Belgium, Canada, France, Germany, Great Britain, Italy, and Japan.[85] This meant that while the ILO boasted various Latin American, East Asian, and Middle Eastern countries among its members, the Organization's day-to-day affairs were in the hands of mostly Western European civil servants.[86]

The initial absence of Russia and the United States of America from the Organization (both joined in 1934) further hampered the ILO's universal ambitions.[87] Their absence deprived the ILO of important agricultural knowledge and expertise: in the case of the United States, it meant that the ILO could not access a leading network of governmental and academic research institutions.[88] In the case of Russia, the ILO had to resort to second-hand information and never quite gained a full picture of the evolution of Soviet agrarian transformation and the effects of new agricultural economic and social policies in the country.[89] The non-participation of these two powers that disapproved of European imperialism also meant that colonial power did not experience much international scrutiny.[90] Colonial labour was regarded as a prerogative of imperial metropoles and even though the International Labour Office occupied a seat on the League's Permanent Mandates Commission and from 1922 onwards an ILO expert on 'native labour' questions participated in the League's Slavery Commission, the discussions on agricultural working conditions were never intended to apply to workers in dependent territories.[91] For much of the interwar years, agricultural workers

---

[85] Report of the Director to the fourth session of the International Labour Conference, Geneva, 1922, 653. For the story of how India succeeded in obtaining a seat on the Governing Body, see Thomas Gidney, 'The Development Dichotomy: Colonial India's Accession to the ILO's Governing Body (1919–1922)', *Journal of Global History* 18, no. 2 (2023), 259–80.

[86] Véronique Plata-Stenger, *Social Reform, Modernization and Technical Diplomacy. The ILO Contribution to Development 1930–46* (Oldenbourg: De Gruyter, 2020), 62–3; Olga Hidalgo-Weber, *La Grande-Bretagne et l'Organisation internationale du travail (1919–1946): Une nouvelle forme d'internationalisme* (Louvain-la-Neuve: Academia—L'Harmattan, 2017). Magaly Rodriguez Garcia, Jasmien Van Daele, and Marcel Van der Linden, eds, *ILO Histories: Essays on the International Labour Organization and its Impact on the World during the Twentieth Century* (Bern: Peter Lang, 2010); Sandrine Kott and Joelle Droux, eds, *Globalizing Social Rights: The International Labour Organization and Beyond* (Basingstoke: Palgrave, 2013).

[87] Report of the Director to the fourth session of the International Labour Conference, Geneva, 1922, 683.

[88] Hannah Tyler, 'In Numbers We Trust? A History of the US Department of Agriculture and Its Agricultural Surveys during the 1920s', *Histoire & Mesure* 48 (2023), 39–46.

[89] Bruisch, Katja, *Als das Dorf noch Zukunft war: Agrarismus und Expertise zwischen Zarenreich und Sowjetunion* (Cologne et al: Böhlau, 2014); James W. Heinzen, *Inventing a Soviet Countryside: State Power and the Transformation of Rural Russia, 1917–1929* (Pittsburgh, PA: University of Pittsburgh Press, 2004).

[90] Daniel Maul, *The International Labour Organization: 100 Years of Global Social Policy* (Berlin: De Gruyter; Geneva: International Labour Office, 2019), 80.

[91] On these blindspots, see Chapters 4 and 7. On the ILO's involvement in the League's colonial affairs, Luis Rodríguez-Piñero, *Indigenous Peoples, Postcolonialism, and International Law: The ILO*

outside Europe remained largely invisible in ILO debate. This was especially true for so-called 'tropical' agriculture—an adjective which denoted not just a geographical space outside the temperate zones of the world but also an ambivalent colonial imaginary which combined notions of rich and exotic vegetation and difficult climates, with racialized assumptions about lazy workers.[92] Throughout the interwar years, information on their living conditions circulated only very sporadically, despite the well-known pre-war scandals over labour exploitation and forced cultivation schemes on rubber plantations in the Congo and in South America.[93] It is only in the 1950s that the ILO would address waged agricultural labour in Asian, Latin American, and African countries through its Plantation Committee.[94]

Agricultural Workers Unite!

In taking on agricultural work conditions as one of its reformist fields, the ILO was also facing organizational and structural challenges. Its tripartite system required equal representation of employers and employees in addition to government delegates. In the agricultural sector, this requirement raised difficult issues of definition and categorization and was further complexified by a perceived lack of unionization and organization among rural workers. For women farmworkers, for example, their readiness to strike and engage in spontaneous rebellion did not automatically imply a willingness to form trade unions and other associations, go to meetings, and follow organizational rules.[95] Whereas industrial workers had benefited from unionization and organization on a national and international scale since the late nineteenth century, national agricultural trade unions (with a few exceptions, such as Italy and Britain) were a recent phenomenon, even where local ones had existed for decades.[96] And while the identification with the aims of

---

Regime (1919–1989) (Oxford University Press, 2005), 27–9. Also, Susan Zimmermann, '"Special Circumstances in Geneva": The ILO and the World of Non-Metropolitan Labour in the Interwar Period', in Rodriguez Garcia, Van Daele, and Van der Linden, *ILO Histories*, 221–50.

[92] David Arnold, '"Illusory Riches": Representations of the Tropical World, 1840–1950', *Singapore Journal of Tropical Geography* 21, no. 1 (2000), 6–18; Daniel Clayton and Gavin Bowd, 'Geography, Tropicality and Postcolonialism: Anglophone and Francophone Readings of the Work of Pierre Gourou', *L'Espace Géographique* 3 (2006), 208–21.

[93] Kevin Grant, *A Civilized Savagery: Britain and the New Slaveries in Africa, 1884–1926* (New York, 2005); Amalia Ribi Forclaz, *Humanitarian Imperialism: The Politics of Anti-Slavery Activism, 1880–1940* (Oxford: Oxford University Press, 2015); Anne Booth, 'Varieties of Exploitation in Colonial Settings: Dutch and Belgian Policies in Indonesia and the Congo and Their Legacies', in Ewout Frankema and Frans Buelens, eds, *Colonial Exploitation and Economic Development: The Belgian Congo and the Netherlands Indies Compared* (London: Routledge, 2016).

[94] On this, see Chapter 7.

[95] Gentili Zappi, *If Eight Hours Seem Too Few*, 13.

[96] In 1920 the British Union changed its name from British National Agricultural Labourers and Rural Workers Union to the National Union of Agricultural Workers. Reg Groves, *Sharpen the Sickle! The History of the farmworkers' Union* (London: Merlin Press Limited, 2011), 139. The French

the working class as a whole and with its more organized claims for social justice arguably grew after the First World War, large-scale and institutionalized mobilization of farmworkers remained scarce as an international study of the ILO carried out in the mid-1920s revealed.[97]

In the wake of the First World War, two international (but mostly European) farm unions emerged alongside national ones.[98] The most important one was the International Landworkers' Federation, a socialist (but anti-communist) organization of exclusively European agricultural workers' unions created in 1920. It was led by Piet Hiemstra, who was the secretary of the Dutch Federation of Agricultural, Horticultural, and Dairy Workers (Nederlandsche Bond van Arbeiders in het Landbouw- Tuinbouw- en Zuivelbedrijf).[99] The son of farmers, Hiemstra spent his early years as a farmworker before becoming a full-time unionist and the first general secretary of the International Landworkers' Federation. Much of the history of this organization has been lost but the fragments of its records speak to its internationalist ambitions.[100] The International Landworkers' Federation was affiliated to the main international trade union movement, the International Federation of Trade Unions, and it brought together agricultural trade unionists from twenty European countries. Italy counted 845,635 members, Germany 780,000 members; Great Britain was represented with three unions and a total of 360,000 members; Austrian participation amounted to 51,000 members; Denmark 30,000; Sweden 20,000; Holland 15,500; and Belgium 1700.[101] Initially based in Utrecht, the International Landworkers' Federation moved to Berlin in 1924. In spite of financial (and later political) difficulties, it remained the main advocate of European agricultural workers throughout the interwar years, and the ILO's most important interlocutor on agricultural issues. A second international agricultural union, the International Federation of

National Federation of Agricultural Workers was created in 1919 when local unions decided to merge. Adolphe Hodée (secretary of the French National Federation of Agricultural Workers), 'Landworker in France', *The Landworker* (October 1920), 6. See also Ronald Hubscher, 'Révolution aux champs. La Fédération nationale des travailleurs de l'agriculture (1920–1981)', in Hubscher and Farcy, *La Moisson des autres*, 343–59.

[97] International Labour Office, *The Representation and Organisation of Agricultural Workers*, Studies and Reports, Series K (Agriculture), no. 8 (Geneva: International Labour Office, 1928).

[98] International Labour Office, *Labour Problems in Agriculture: General Report for the Thirty-Third Session of the International Labour Conference* (Geneva: International Labour Office, 1950), 36–7.

[99] On the first congress in Amsterdam, see International Labour Office, *First International Congress of Landworkers' Unions affiliated to the International Federation of Trade Unions (Amsterdam, 17–19 August 1920)*, Studies and Reports, Series K, no. 1 (Geneva, International Labour Office: 1920).

[100] The archives of the International Landworkers' Federation were bombed by the Germans. At the ILO office, the relevant files are missing without explanation. The only existing study is an unpublished history of the International Landworkers' Federation which was prepared by the United States Department of Labor in 1957. Leon A. Dale, 'The International Landworkers' Federation' (United States Department of Labour, 1957).

[101] At the end of the 1920s a Palestinian association became the first extra-European adherent to the International Landworkers' Federation. See also International Labour Office, 'Representation and Organisation of Agricultural Workers', 72–4.

Christian Landworkers' Unions, was created in 1920 but did not have the same weight in international debates.[102] It was much smaller than the International Landworkers' Federation, with a total membership of about 230,000 members in France, Belgium, Germany, and Holland.[103]

In August 1920, the International Landworkers' Federation held its foundational meeting and first congress at an international conference of agricultural trade unions in Amsterdam. The congress brought together twenty-two delegates from Great Britain, Germany, Austria, Sweden, Denmark, Belgium, Italy, and Holland, representing a total of over two million agricultural workers in Europe.[104] Beside general secretary Hiemstra, the Federation's executive committee comprised representatives of some of the largest existing national unions. One of them was the Italian feminist and socialist Argentina Altobelli, leader of the Italian Federation of Agricultural Workers (Federterra or Federazione Nazionale dei Lavoratori della Terra), founded in 1901. Altobelli, who was the only woman in the Federation's leadership, was well known and could boast two decades of experience as an organizer of rural cooperatives and a campaigner for land nationalization.[105] Other executive members included the gardener and Socialist politician Georg Schmidt, leader of the German Landworkers' Union (Deutscher Landarbeiterverband). Schmidt wrote various studies on Germany's landworkers, wages, and employment relations, as well as general agricultural policy. Together with Hiemstra, he would become one of the leading correspondents for the ILO.[106] Also present were Oscar Levinson, the secretary of the Danish Landworkers' Union (Landarbejederforbundet i Danmark), W. R. Smith of the National Union of Agricultural Workers in Britain, and Duncan of the Scottish Farm Servants' Union.[107] The Polish and Czechoslovakian unions sent supportive messages, apologizing for their absence due to the inability to secure passports.

By linking for the first time several national agricultural trade unions, the first congress of the International Landworkers' Federation opened a new era of agrarian workers' internationalism and a welcome platform for the representation of their demands. Agricultural trade unionists in Britain praised Hiemstra's leadership, vision, and insistence on the need for international cooperation, solidarity,

---

[102] In French 'Fédération internationale des syndicats chrétiens de travailleurs de la terre', in German 'Internationaler Bund Christlicher Landarbeiterverbände'. International Labour Office, 'First International Congress of Landworkers' Unions'.

[103] Internationaler Bund Christlicher Landarbeiterverbände, ILO Archives Geneva, AG 800/0/3AG 800/0/4.

[104] International Labour Office, 'First International Congress of Landworkers' Unions'.

[105] Silvia Bianciardi, *Argentina Altobelli e la 'buona battaglia'* (Milan: Franco Angeli, 2013).

[106] Georg Schmidt, *Lohnformen and Arbeitsverhältnisse in der Landwirtschaft: ein Beitrag zur Beurteilung der Lage der deutschen Landarbeiterschaft* (Berlin: Deutscher Landarbeiterverband, 1913).

[107] International Labour Office, 'First International Congress of Landworkers' Unions', 3. On the fascist assault on the Federterra in early 1920 and the 'disparity of peasant interests' in Italy, see Maier, *Recasting Bourgeois Europe*, 305–50, 309; Jonathan Dunnage, *Twentieth-Century Italy. A Social History* (London: Routledge, 2002).

and better organization among workers against war and capitalist domination. In the eyes of British farmworkers, the congress showed a 'clear grasp of agricultural problems from the workers' standpoint'.[108] The creation of a permanent office in Utrecht also opened up new possibilities for transnational networking and coordination, the circulation of information on wages and employment conditions, and the standardization of legislation across countries.[109] There was also an expectation that the new organization could offer financial support in case of strike action and that it would take steps to prevent farmers and other agricultural employers from substituting the strikers with cheap migrant labour. In other words, one of the primary concerns of the affiliated unions (at least in the beginning) was also the protection of domestic agricultural workers and national interests.[110] This also meant that non-European countries such as China, Japan, Argentina, and Brazil, where social legislation was 'less advanced', were seen as a potential danger and workers from these countries were not considered as possible members.[111]

From the beginning it was clear that the Federation's most important and defining relationships would be with the International Labour Office. In its first meeting (where the International Labour Office was also represented), trade unionists agreed on a set of themes and joint demands that strongly endorsed the ILO's ambition to adapt industrial labour standards to agriculture. The International Landworkers' Federation also insisted that agricultural workers should no longer be considered 'like Cinderellas', in other words ignored and marginalized, and that they deserved the same attention as their industrial counterparts.[112] Thus, the Federation demanded a reduction of working hours (to nine in summer and seven in winter), the banning of child labour for children under the age of fourteen, and a free Saturday afternoon for women working in agriculture. Good technical education, better housing and generally an improvement of the living conditions were also part of the demands.[113]

The common front put forward by agricultural trade unionists, however, was more brittle than its official communications seemed to show. At the time of its creation, debates within the International Landworkers' Federation about whether to include sharecroppers and small farmers, whose relationship with farmers and larger landowners was more complex than a simple work contract, caused tensions in national organizations. The disparity of interests between various groups of agricultural workers meant that the integration of other, more hybrid categories of labourers that were doing paid work as well as farming their own plot was rejected. Soon, some of the adhering national

---

[108] 'Long Live the Landworkers' International', *The Landworker* (October 1920), 3.
[109] 'Long Live the Landworkers' International', 3.
[110] International Labour Office, 'First International Congress of Landworkers' Unions', 4–5.
[111] See intervention by Oudegeest, 'First International Congress of Landworkers' Unions', 12.
[112] 'First International Congress of Landworkers' Unions', 8.
[113] 'First International Congress of Landworkers' Unions', 4–5.

unions would also face political difficulties. The numerically strongest member, the Italian organization Federterra, was dissolved by Mussolini in 1922, thus eroding the Federation's financial backing.[114]

In contrast to trade unionists, agricultural employers were slower to organize, but the threat of an International Labour Conference that would address agricultural labour conditions acted as a catalyst. The ILO's decision, controversial from the start, engendered considerable hostility among those countries who saw themselves as 'old-established states where an independent peasant population existed'.[115] Protest came especially from the French and Swiss governments who were fiercely against an ILO mandate on agriculture and its aim to discuss the reduction of working hours.[116] Farmers' representatives too, especially those supporting protectionist government policies, did not view the ILO's agricultural discussion favourably. Thus, the Swiss Farmers' Union (Schweizerischer Bauernverband), under the famous (conservative) leadership of Ernst Laur, an internationally renowned agronomist and Professor at the ETH in Zurich, went as far as distributing a manifesto urging governments to resist the international regulation of agriculture.[117]

Laur's attempt at mobilizing employers did not escape the attention of agricultural trade unions. In February 1921 the cover page of *The Landworker* warned its readers to be 'On Guard!' and featured an article in which Hiemstra dramatically reported how farmers associations were preparing a vigorous campaign against the application of the Washington conventions on protective measures for industrial workers to agriculture.[118] Hiemstra strongly condemned the Swiss Farmers Union for issuing a manifesto to employers' organizations worldwide, pressing for combined action against international laws about agriculture. He was particularly upset that Laur had the audacity to advise governments to exercise their influence and sabotage international debates by appointing delegates opposed to international labour legislation.[119] Although Hiemstra did not think that

---

[114] On the history of Italian agricultural labour unions, see Manuela Martini, 'Conflits sociaux et organisations paysannes dans les campagnes italiennes, du *Risorgimento* à l'arrivée du fascisme au pouvoir', *Ruralia* 16/17 (2005), http://journals.openedition.org/ruralia/1072 (last access 27 January 2024).

[115] International Labour Office, Minutes of the sixth session of the Governing Body, Geneva, January 1921.

[116] On the domestic context of French opposition, see also Marie-Renée Mouton, 'Les huit heures en agriculture? Un conflit entre la France et l'OIT', *Relations internationales* 4 (1975), 53–79.

[117] Circular letter dated 8 October 1920, sent by the Union Suisse des Paysans in Brougg to various agricultural organizations, ILO Archives Geneva, AG, D 603/103 in subject catalogue. On Laur, see Werner Baumann: 'Laur, Ernst', in Historisches Lexikon der Schweiz (HLS), Online: https://hls-dhs-dss.ch/de/articles/029856/2006-12-15/ (last accessed 19 April 2024).

[118] Piet Hiemstra, 'On Guard!', *The Landworker* (February 1921).

[119] Hiemstra claimed that as a response to the International Landworkers' Federation, a number of farmers' organizations representing the employer side had been created in France, Switzerland, Belgium, Spain, Italy, Ireland, Luxembourg, Poland, Portugal, Czechoslovakia, and Yugoslavia. However, as later records in the archive testify, a federation of these organizations never actually came into being. Hiemstra, 'On Guard!'.

'governments would dare to lend themselves to [such] a policy', he warned that those representing labour interests in Geneva needed 'to be prepared for anything that may happen' and to show that 'land workers were firmly resolved to resist to the utmost any likely attempt to shelve their requests'.[120]

In many ways, the mobilization of landowners and farm managers remained a phantom menace. Neither the French government nor Laur—despite their existing far-reaching agrarianist networks—were successful in mobilizing agricultural employers and in rallying wider support for their opposition to the ILO. This was partly to do with the vague target of Laur's rallying cry: after all, employers in European agriculture—unlike factory owners and business entrepreneurs—were mostly farmers who worked the land alongside their employees. Like their hired workers, they were far less organized than employers in the industrial sector. Until the mid-1920s, there would be no concerted attempt at establishing an organization that represented the collective interests of farmers.[121] And even then, the movement did not take off. The lack of mobilization on the part of employers' might also explain why the ILO was able to proceed with its third conference, dedicated to agriculture, in autumn 1921.

Cultivating Fields of Progress: Agriculture and the International Labour Organization, 1920s–1950s. Amalia Ribi Forclaz, Oxford University Press. © Amalia Ribi Forclaz 2025. DOI: 10.1093/9780191945014.003.0002

---

[120] Hiemstra, 'On Guard!'.
[121] On attempts to organize an international movement of agricultural organizations in Bern in the mid-1920s, see Asher Hobson, 'An International Organization of National Farm Associations', *Journal of Farm Economics* 10, no. 7 (April 1928), 215.

2
'Nature Yields to No Law'

> *'Agriculture is a seasonal industry and it is necessary to make hay while the sun shines. As well might we try to regulate the sun, the moon, the stars, the wind, the rain, the snow, and the habits of the animals.'*
> S. R. Parsons speaking at the third session of the International Labour Conference in 1921 (International Labour Office, Third Session of the International Labour Conference, Geneva 1921)

In late October 1921, the International Labour Office opened for its third session—the first dedicated to agriculture—in Geneva. The conference boasted an ambitious agenda whose items fell into two categories: Firstly, there were the adaptation of the so-called Washington conventions to agriculture, including the regulation of hours of work, measures against unemployment and the protection of women and children.[1] Secondly, the agenda featured a set of issues specifically formulated for the needs of agricultural workers, such as the introduction and standardization of vocational education (since in the eyes of social reformers many workers were unskilled) and the improvement of accommodation and housing (since the existing practices of housing workers in stables were seen as unhygienic and morally inacceptable). Other items for international discussion were the right to organize and strike; the adoption of social insurance to protect agricultural workers against accidents, sickness and invalidity; and the creation of pension schemes, all of which were still very limited in most countries.[2]

This chapter will examine how some of these questions, particularly education, housing, and the work of women and children, were discussed in the new international space offered by the ILO. The chapter argues that these so-called 'technical' agricultural questions were in fact moral, political, social, and economic issues that sparked controversy among member governments and highlighted the diverging views of agricultural interest groups. As the chapter will show, conflicts arose between those advocating for a unified international approach to what they

---

[1] For a discussion of the agenda, see International Labour Office, Minutes of the third session of the Governing Body, London, 22–5 March 1920. Appendix 7: Agenda of the third session of the International Labour Conference, 58. For the definite agenda, see International Labour Office, Minutes of the fourth session of the Governing Body, Genoa, 8–9 June 1920. Appendix 4: Agenda for the Conference of 1921, 40.

[2] International Labour Office, *Report on Special Measure for the Protection of Agricultural Workers* (Geneva: International Labour Office, 1921).

saw as pressing social issues in agriculture and those who believed that agriculture was too varied and disorganized for standardization at the international level.

In June 1921 over 400 delegates from thirty-seven countries from all regions of Europe and from Latin America, China, Oceania, and Southeast Asia came together in Geneva for three full weeks of intense conference meetings. They were split into different working groups to respect the ILO's tripartite consultation of employers, employees, and government delegates. Most of the representatives were accustomed to discussing industrial labour problems and had little knowledge about agriculture, a fact that was criticized by agricultural trade unionists.[3] Among the few exceptions were two women: the leader of Federterra, Argentina Altobelli, who had been invited to attend, and Swiss farmer Augusta Gillabert-Randin, who had stepped in at the last minute for another Swiss delegate.[4]

The British workers' delegate, trade unionist Edward L. Poulton, qualified the gathering as 'the nearest approach yet achieved to the Parliament of the whole world'.[5] Nevertheless, Russia and the United States—both important actors in the global agricultural economy—were conspicuously absent.[6] Although Russia was not present, however, the plight of its peasants, faced with a terrible famine in the Volga region, was vividly exposed to the delegates in a long address by the League's High Commissioner for Refugees, Fridtjof Nansen: the latter had been invited to join an unofficial meeting of the conference to urge governments to abandon any partisan politics and to mitigate the disaster through a coordinated humanitarian intervention.[7]

Before launching into discussions, the ILO's Governing Body had to address the complaints of the French government, which reiterated its doubts about the ILO's legitimacy to tackle agricultural issues.[8] French government representatives cautioned that agriculture was too diverse to be addressed efficiently in an international forum. They also argued that the timing for what they thought of as risky and premature 'international experimentations' was particularly bad, given the

---

[3] International Labour Office, *Record of Proceedings*, third session of the International Labour Conference (Geneva: International Labour Office, 1921), 336.

[4] Her name was misspelled in the proceedings as 'Gillabert-Roudin'. International Labour Office, *Record of Proceedings*, third session of the International Labour Conference (Geneva: International Labour Office, 1921), 336. See also Chapter 1.

[5] International Labour Office, *Record of Proceedings*, third session of the International Labour Conference (Geneva: International Labour Office, 1921), 11.

[6] On the absence of Russia and the USA, see Report of the Director to the fourth session of the International Labour Conference (Geneva: International Labour Office, 1922), 633.

[7] Report of the Director to the fourth session of the International Labour Conference, Geneva, 1922, 634–5. On Fridtjof Nansen's mission to Russia, see Carl-Emil Vogt, 'Fridtjof Nansen et l'aide alimentaire européenne à la Russie et à l'Ukraine bolchévique en 1921–1923', *Matériaux pour l'histoire de notre temps* 95 (2009), 5–12.

[8] Report of the Director to the fourth session of the International Labour Conference Geneva: International Labour Office, 1922), 700.

recent war and the need for agricultural production growth.⁹ What the French did not explicitly say was that they rejected international intervention into what they considered to be strictly domestic agricultural policies. Their opposition went as far as to file an official query with the newly established International Court of Justice in La Haye asking it to advise on whether the ILO was 'competent to deal with questions of agricultural labour' and 'how far its powers' would extend in this matter.¹⁰ This attitude, however, was not shared by the French workers' delegate and leading international trade unionist Léon Jouhaux, who regretted having to oppose his own government.¹¹ Jouhaux, a close friend of Albert Thomas, eloquently defended the ILO's right to discuss agricultural work and would continue to do so for the next three decades.¹²

The French opposition was also met by a spontaneous wave of protests in favour of agricultural cooperation by representatives of countries such as Colombia and Chile and by workers' delegates from India and Japan. Colombian government delegate Antonio José Restrepo, for example, met with applause and laughter when he stated that many new countries in the world, including Colombia, were 'agrarian countries'. 'Deleting agriculture from our program', Restrepo warned the audience, 'is like saying to us, the representatives of these countries: Go away, you have nothing to do here.' For an International Labour Conference to exclude 'the relationship between the landed proprietor and the workman who digs, the man planting cotton, [...] the man who breeds cattle, the man who keeps the cows in the fields, the man who cuts corn' would be an 'unjustified' and 'remarkable' contradiction.¹³ To the Chilean delegate Manuel Rivas-Vicuna, the inclusion of agriculture in international social reform was equally a question of principle and he insisted that, 'on the general grounds of humanity', agricultural labourers should be given the same protection as any other workers.¹⁴ In the end, the French and Swiss government delegates who had opposed the discussions successfully obtained that some of the demands supported by agricultural trade unions such as the reduction of working hours be deleted from the agenda. However, they did not manage to jeopardize the

---

⁹ See International Labour Office, *The International Labour Organization and Agriculture* (Geneva: International Labour Office, 1924), 4.

¹⁰ For the procedure, see Advisory Opinion, Permanent Court of International Justice, 12 August 1922, League of Nations Archives Geneva, Col. 206, Box 12, File 117. Also, Marie-Renée Mouton, 'Les huit heures en agriculture? Un conflit entre la France et l'OIT', *Relations internationales* 4 (1975), 53–79.

¹¹ International Labour Office, *Record of Proceedings*, third session of the International Labour Conference (Geneva: International Labour Office, 1921), 22–4.

¹² On Jouhaux, see his obituary in *International Labour Review* 70, no. 3 (1954), 241–57.

¹³ Restrepo speaking at the third session of the International Labour Conference. International Labour Office, *Record of Proceedings*, third session of the International Labour Conference (Geneva: International Labour Office, 1921), 28.

¹⁴ Rivas-Vicuna speaking at the third session of the International Labour Conference. International Labour Office, *Record of Proceedings*, third session of the International Labour Conference (Geneva: International Labour Office, 1921), 28.

conference as such. An agricultural trade unionist who observed the proceedings even noted that the Swiss and the French were 'completely defeated' when trying to oppose the debate on agriculture.[15]

The Problem of Worktime

One point that was particularly contentious was the question of regulating work time in agriculture. In the case of industrial workers, this issue had been one of the primary concerns of the international movement for labour legislation as early as in the nineteenth century, when ideas about the impact of excessive working hours on health and productivity started gaining international traction.[16] The late nineteenth and early twentieth centuries also saw the rise of a science of work, including research into the optimization and physiological limits of the working body.[17] Social reforms and concerns with limiting physical exhaustion, mental fatigue, and waste of labour whilst maximizing energy and output drove considerations about reducing the working day.[18] Such ideas were also influenced by the economic and political notion that the industrial labour force was the 'capital of the nation' and should therefore not be wasted or mismanaged.[19] In the wake of the First World War, and in the light of heightened political unrest, the regulation of the working day for industrial workers spread across Western Europe, often becoming the object of militant strikes—for example in Switzerland in 1918, as well as in Britain.[20] France emerged as a model by adopting the eight-hour day in April 1919: this socialist proposal was intended not only to reduce unemployment, which was anticipated after demobilization, but also to diminish the psychological and physical costs of increasingly mechanized work, and to insure more time for family life and self-education.[21]

---

[15] R. B. Walker, 'The World of Farmworkers', *The Landworker* (April 1921), 2.

[16] Paul Boilley, 'La journée de huit heures et le travail intensif', *La revue socialiste* 11 (January–June 1890), 712-15; Judith F. Stone, *The Search for Social Peace: Reform Legislation in France, 1890–1914* (Albany: State University of New York, 1985); Max Weber, 'Zur Psychophysik der industriellen Arbeit', *Archiv für Sozialwissenschaft* 28 (1908), 227.

[17] On this and on changing understandings of productivity, see Peter-Paul Bänziger and Mischa Suter, eds, *Histories of Productivity: Genealogical Perspectives on the Body and Modern Economy* (London: Routledge, 2016).

[18] Anson Rabinbach, *The Human Motor: Energy, Fatigue and the Origins of Modernity* (New York: Basic Books, 1990); Florian Tennstedt, *Vom Proleten zum Industriearbeiter: Arbeiterbewegung und Sozialpolitik in Deutschland 1800 bis 1914* (Cologne: Bund-Verlag, 1983); Lars Bluma and Karsten Uhl, eds, *Kontrollierte Arbeit—disziplinierte Körper? Zur Sozial- und Kulturgeschichte der Industriearbeit im 19. und 20. Jahrhundert* (Bielefeld: Transcript Verlag, 2012).

[19] Anson Rabinbach, *The Eclipse of the Utopias of Labor* (New York: Fordham University Press, 2018), 56.

[20] Gary Cross, 'Les Trois Huits: Labor Movements, International Reform, and the Origins of the Eight-Hour Day, 1919–1924', *French Historical Studies* 14, no. 2 (Autumn 1985), 240-68, 244.

[21] Cross, 'Les Trois Huits', 243.

In 1919 the issue of working hours in industry had been put on the agenda of the very first International Labour Conference. This had led to the adoption of a convention that defined the eight-hour day and forty-eight-hour week for workers in extractive industries such as mines and quarries, manufacturing, construction, and transportation. It excluded seafarers and agricultural labourers.[22] Even though the convention was regarded as a major achievement at the time it did not have the desired effect on national legislation. States were unwilling to ratify the international instrument unless their economic competitors would do the same. The convention thus failed to secure sufficient ratifications that would legally bind the countries to its terms, and thus did not become the instrument of international labour policy it was designed to be.[23]

In the case of agriculture, the question of hours was even more contested and deemed too problematic to even consider. The matter raised complex issues about the relationship between time and nature in farming, the weight of rural customs and traditional labour arrangements, and the complexity of organizing, planning, and managing farmwork.[24] At the third session of the International Labour Conference in 1921, two years after endorsing the forty-eight-hour week for industrial workers, the International Labour Office set out to discuss the application of this measure to the agricultural sector.[25] The proposal encountered considerable opposition, not least from the French government and farmers' organizations that objected to any intervention in this matter.[26] The item was voted to be taken off the agenda by a small majority, and postponed to a future session.[27] The prevailing idea was that agriculture was a pre-industrial activity, governed by nature, climate, and unpredictable weather, all of which escaped international regulation. Not the clock but nature's rhythm ruled the farm, and the motto 'nature yields to no law' was often cited.[28] This was a view corroborated by contemporary social scientists. As renowned American rural sociologist Carl C. Taylor put it, the main difference between agriculture and industry was

---

[22] Steven Bauer, 'The Road to the Eight-Hour Day', translated by Alfred Maylander, *Monthly Labor Review* 9, no. 2 (August 1919), 41–65; International Labour Organization, Convention no. 1, Hours of Work (Industry), (1919).

[23] Antony Alcock, *History of the International Labour Organization* (Basingstoke: Macmillan, 1971), 56–8.

[24] E. P. Thompson, 'Time, Work-Discipline, and Industrial Capitalism', *Past and Present* 38 (December 1967), 56–97.

[25] See Chapter 1.

[26] International Labour Office, *Report on the Adaptation to the Agricultural Labour of the Washington Decisions Concerning the Regulation of Hours of Work* (Geneva: International Labour Office, 1921).

[27] International Labour Office, *Record of Proceedings*, third session of the International Labour Conference (Geneva: International Labour Office, 1921), vol. 1, 90–131. The necessary two-thirds majority for an item to be retained on the agenda was missed by only few votes. See Louise Ernestine Howard, *Labour in Agriculture* (London: Oxford University Press, 1935), 114.

[28] International Labour Office, *The Eight-Hour Day Act and Its Application to Agriculture in Czechoslovakia*, Studies and Reports, Series K, no. 5 (Geneva: International Labour Office, 1921), 87.

that the latter was not 'cast into jeopardy by the precariousness of forces which lie beyond human control'. In agriculture, work relied heavily on natural light, crops depended on the right amount of rain, harvests could be destroyed by hailstorms, wind could turn meadows into deserts. By contrast, in the industry 'the weather is shut out by factory walls and roofs. The climate and seasons are made or modified by artificial heat and electric fans. Even the sun's light is dispensed with as an essential element for working hours.'[29]

The perceived dichotomy between agricultural and industrial work conditions also served as a pretext not to address the paternalistic character of social arrangements in agricultural milieus. Even reformers doubted the possibility of regulation due to the highly specific nature of the agricultural 'workplace'. As was often argued, its open and often fragmented disposition with regard to land and labour (at least in the European context—the situation was different in plantations) posed definite challenges to managerial oversight and rationalizations.[30] There was also an understanding that agricultural work did not bear the same risk of mental and nervous fatigue as mechanized industrial work.[31] Moreover, the fact that it was task-oriented and that its tasks depended on allegedly uncontrollable factors made the application of clock time impossible. Thomas himself admitted in the early 1920s that the limitation of working hours in agriculture was not yet 'ripe for international discussion', and the initial promise to put the question on the agenda was delayed.[32] This indicates that many reformers did not want to question the status quo of the agricultural labour force in Europe where it was characterized by poverty and low wages, let alone in the colonies. It also illustrates that the ILO could only push for international standardization when there were existing models of national legislation.

One of the few available models was Czechoslovakia, which, together with Spain, had undertaken regulations to limit working hours in agriculture. In December 1920, in a bid to gain insights into the feasibility of a limited working day in agriculture, the International Labour Office participated in an enquiry run by the Czechoslovakian ministry of social welfare to assess the results of worktime reduction since 1919.[33] Guido Pardo, a member of the Italian delegation at

---

[29] Carl C. Taylor, *Rural Sociology: A Study of Rural Problems* (New York and London: Harper, 1926), 463.

[30] On workplace and managerial control of working bodies, see Ava Baron and Eileen Boris, 'The Body as a Useful Category for Working-Class History', *Labor* 4, no. 2 (2007), 23–43, 35–6.

[31] On the rise of so-called psychological and industrial fatigue due to mechanization process in the industry, see E. P. Cathcart, *The Human Factor in Industry* (London: Oxford University Press, 1928).

[32] Letter, Hiemstra (International Landworkers' Federation) to International Labour Office, Utrecht, 31 May 1923; reply by Albert Thomas, 11 June 1923, ILO Archives Geneva, D 606/001.

[33] International Labour Office, *The Eight-Hour Day Act*, Studies and Reports, Series K, no. 5 (Geneva: International Labour Office, 1921). On Czechoslovakia, see also Chapter 3. Katherine Lebow, Małgorzata Mazurek, and Joanna Wawrzyniak, 'Making Modern Social Science: The Global Imagination in East Central and Southeastern Europe after Versailles', *Contemporary European History* 28, no. 2 (May 2019), 137–42.

the Paris Peace Conference and Chief of the Russian Section, was sent to Prague on behalf of the International Labour Office to collect evidence from landowners, government representatives, and workers' organizations. Pardo's enquiry was particularly informative: it showed that the short-term social and economic impact of the eight-hour day in agriculture had remained largely theoretical, as the reform was almost instantly modified by collective agreements. Unsurprisingly, the findings also revealed the ideological fault lines of the debate: workers' representatives praised the reduction of working hours, arguing that it had led to an 'amelioration in [...] material and moral conditions', a heightened awareness among farmworkers of the value of their work, and the development of an 'esprit de corps'. In addition, workers who owned as small plot of land had more time to cultivate it and, overall, workers organizations observed a decrease in rural exodus.[34]

This positive feedback stood in strong contrast with that of employers' organizations, which blamed the reduction of worktime for an increase in unionization, disputes, and strikes, and generally deplored that workers were proving less accommodating since the worktime reduction act of 1919.[35] Some blamed the act for a general 'wave of idleness' and slackness, and even held it responsible for difficult harvests and loss of crop.[36] Generally, employers painted a gloomy picture of the impact of labour regulations and particularly of work time limitations on post-war production. They argued that these measures would force big landowners to drop intensive cultivation. Some also questioned the growth of spare time and complained that agricultural workers used it for politics and trade union work rather than for 'self-development'.[37] Employers criticized that workers did not use their free time for more acceptable activities such as evening classes or reading groups.[38]

All in all, the diverging positions of farm owners versus farmworkers that emerged from the Czechoslovakian enquiry mirrored the general divide that existed at the time of the conference. It highlighted not only the social stratification of the rural countryside but also the different degrees to which people in agriculture were connected to the land. When the question of hours of work in agriculture was dropped in 1921, trade unionists were disappointed and criticized the International Labour Organization for bowing to a minority and giving in to French and Swiss opposition.[39] Agricultural trade unions angrily commented that the ILO's 'inaction', dysfunctionality and excessive bureaucracy threatened to

[34] International Labour Office, 'The Eight-Hour Day Act', 72–3.
[35] International Labour Office, 'The Eight-Hour Day Act', 94.
[36] International Labour Office, 'The Eight-Hour Day Act', 58.
[37] International Labour Office, 'The Eight-Hour Day Act', 65 and 91. Employers expected workers to improve themselves and their 'intellectual level' through evening classes, readings, and generally by changing their 'habits'.
[38] International Labour Office, 'The Eight-Hour Day Act', 65 and 91.
[39] Mouton, 'Les huit heures en agriculture?', 53–79.

render it useless for agricultural workers' interests. They also predicted that its strategic avoidance of crucial labour issues would send the ILO 'to an early grave'.[40]

Others, however, did not share this disappointment and were convinced that the questions had been rightly abandoned. In particular, farmers and politicians with first-hand knowledge of rural conditions were quick to dismiss 'the doctrinaire debaters of Geneva' who had insisted on limiting working hours according to industrial models.[41] They pointed out that the consideration of such legislation was out of touch with the realities of farming communities and would endanger productivity and farming incomes. Writing in the column of a dairy journal a few months after the conference, and in the wake of a summer tempest which destroyed much of her harvest, Swiss farmer Augusta Gillabert-Randin, for example, ironically quipped: 'Nature [...] has given us the eight hours of work that were so fervently discussed last autumn in Geneva. But where is the contentment that must come from this? Between moderate work and relative poverty or intensive work and abundance, agriculture knows no middle ground. [...] So blessed be the experience we have had this disastrous summer, let us wish for hard work rather than holidays and let us no longer complain about the length of our summer days.'[42] Gillabert-Randin, a widowed mother of five who after the First World War had found herself in charge of a 20-hectare farm, was an agrarian reformer and an active campaigner for women's rights. Through her writings, her membership in farmers' associations, and the organization of rural women's cooperatives, she sought to overturn what she saw as a patriarchal rural system that deprived women of political and economic agency.[43] Her positive interpretation of longer working days as a sign of bountiful harvests which would translate into economic welfare shows the divergent positions that existed even among the more progressive and forward-thinking segments of the farming population with regard to this issue. The very characteristic of farming, many agreed, was not to measure hours but follow the rhythm imposed by nature. In short, the ILO found itself attacked from all fronts: employers criticized it for raising the issue, trade unions condemned it for not raising it enough, and farmers, for being out of touch.

---

[40] [No author], 'Drawing the Farming World Together', *The Landworker* (September 1923), 11, ILO Archives Geneva, D 606/001.

[41] Howard, *Labour in Agriculture*, 115.

[42] Augusta Gillabert-Randin, 'Albert Thomas and the ILO', *L'industrie laitière Suisse* (8 September 1922), in Peter Moser and Marthe Gosteli, eds, *Une paysanne entre ferme, marché et associations: Textes d'Augusta Gillabert-Randin 1918–1940* (Baden: hier+jetzt, 2005), 136.

[43] For an introduction to Randin's life and work in Switzerland, see Moser and Gosteli, eds, *Une Paysanne entre Ferme, Marché et Associations*, 13–29.

The Question of Housing

Another question prominently discussed at the third session of the International Labour Conference in 1921 was the question of housing. The issue was specifically formulated to address the conditions of agricultural work that touched not only on labour contracts but also on agrarian ways of life. It shows that from the very start, the ILO did not limit itself to the discussion of technical and legislative aspects of 'working conditions' only, but that its reformist vision also extended to the morally loaded issues of 'living conditions'.[44] In the eyes of social reformers, the housing problem, and the widespread accommodation of farmworkers in stables without proper beds, running water, or other minimal sanitary equipment, epitomized the gaps between rural and urban living and between more industrialized versus less industrialized areas.

Agricultural trade unionists insisted on the improvement of housing, asking for 'dwellings fit for human habitation' for both seasonal workers and permanent farm servants.[45] They also condemned the inequalities in urban and rural housing, arguing that whereas factory work entailed a clear demarcation between work and home, the so-called 'living-in' conditions of farmworkers placed the latter in an inferior position. Their workplace was often identical with their living space, which blurred the boundaries between work and free time. In other words, the main difference between the urban worker and the farmworker was that the latter was housed under variable but generally bad conditions on the farm. This practice, which dated back at least to the eighteenth century, was dictated by the nature of the work, the need for proximity and availability, and by the frequent impossibility to commute due to the isolation of the farms. As the ILO remarked, however, rare were the farmers that invested in suitable accommodation, and many agricultural workers were left to rest in the most primitive conditions. This divide in living conditions threatened to encourage the rural worker to abandon the land in search of the promise of progress offered by the glitter of 'city life'. One official who was particularly well acquainted with the problem in Britain and France did not mince her words when stating that 'there is a good deal of definitely very bad rural housing in all countries and of this very bad housing the wage-paid agricultural workers get quite the worst; the conditions under which some of these workers live are intolerable'.[46]

---

[44] For a detailed discussion of the problem of agricultural housing in the interwar years, see Amalia Ribi Forclaz, 'A Bed, a Cover, and Possibly a Pillow: Improving the Living Conditions of Agricultural Workers in the Interwar Years', *Capitalism. A Journal of History and Economics* 3, no. 1 (2022), 136–59.

[45] International Labour Office, *First International Congress of Landworkers' Unions affiliated to the International Federation of Trade Unions, Amsterdam, 17–19 August 1920*, Studies and Reports, Series K, no. 1 (Geneva: International Labour Office, 1920), 9.

[46] Howard, *Labour in Agriculture*, 134–5.

The International Labour office was not the first to address problems of housing. In 1913, poet and novelist May Kendall had co-written with philanthropist Seebohm Rowntree a survey on agricultural workers' lives in which she criticized the housing conditions of agricultural labourers in Britain. Kendall described how these workers lived in 'extremely dark and extremely damp' cottages with rats as tenants, 'coffin'-sized bedrooms, and water that needed to be boiled before drinking.[47] The subject of housing was also at the heart of other social enquiries, such as the one penned by Jacques Valdour on agricultural working life in France.[48] Valdour's research method was to disguise himself as a worker in various settings—he also wrote about other social groups including seamen, miners, and chauffeurs—and then report about his personal experience. Shortly before the war, he posed as an agricultural worker in an undercover investigation on a farm of a rich landowner half an hour from Paris.[49] Commenting on his living arrangement, he noted: 'Our accommodation is miserable: in the oxen stables, we sleep in a sort of wooden cage hung on the wall and furnished with a straw mattress, a pair of sheets and a blanket. The stables receive air and light only through the door. Through their heavy, odour-laden atmosphere we reach our sleeping cages [...]. Nothing is provided for the most basic toilette. There is a bucket for washing the horses, there is none for the men to wash themselves.'[50]

Such descriptions were soon corroborated by international investigations. In what would become a standard practice, before the start of the 1921 conference, the International Labour Office sought to assemble as many 'facts' on these housing problems as possible.[51] Summarizing the knowledge gained, the International Labour Office noted a lack of suitable accommodation and—as one international official pointed out—the 'sordid' and 'drab' conditions in which farmworkers all over Europe were sleeping.[52] In many cases, 'housing' was nothing more than a sack of hay in a stable. Reminiscent of the sleeping practices of peasants in medieval Europe, the workers often rested in their day clothes on straw mattresses or

---

[47] Benjamin Seebohm Rowntree and May Kendall, *How the Labourer Lives: A Study of the Rural Labour Problem* (London: Thomas Nelson, 1913).

[48] Jacques Valdour, *L'ouvrier agricole: Observations vécues* (Paris: Arthur Rousseau, 1919).

[49] Bernard Valade, 'Un marginal de la science sociale: Jacques Valdour', *Revue européenne des sciences sociales* 5, no. 1 (2013), online version http://journals.openedition.org/ress/2344; DOI: 10.4000/ress.2344 (last accessed 30 Avril 2019); Keizo Isobe, 'Aux marges de la description géographique et de l'enquête sociale: Notes sur Jacques Valdour', in P. Claval, ed., *Autour de Vidal de la Blache* (Paris: CNRS Éditions, 1993), 65–9.

[50] 'Notre logement est misérable: nous disposons dans les écuries à bœufs, de sortes de cages en bois accrochées au mur et garnies d'une paillasse, d'une paire de draps et d'une couverture. Les écuries ne reçoivent d'air et de lumière que par la porte. À travers leurs atmosphères lourdes et chargées d'odeur nous gagnons nos cages à dormir. Rien n'est mis à notre disposition pour la toilette la plus sommaire. Il y a un seau pour laver les chevaux, il n'y en a pas pour que les hommes se lavent.' Valdour, *L'ouvrier agricole*, 24–5.

[51] For a discussion on ILO research and surveys, see Chapter 3.

[52] International Labour Organization, *Technical Survey of Agricultural Questions* (Geneva: International Labour Office, 1921), 461–504.

makeshift beds on the floor, close to the animals.[53] In other cases the 'bed' was 'hung from the roof over the stalls or [...] raised on four posts and reached by a ladder'.[54] In the countries where the problem was acknowledged, regulations prescribed at least some distance between workers and animals as well as separate doors into sleeping quarters. This was the case in Sweden, where agricultural workers were locally organized and a 1919 public health act had laid down rules for rural dwelling.[55] In Denmark, Germany, and Italy, the accommodation of agricultural workers was the subject of some protective legislation. In France, this was not the case and regulations on housing and hygiene remained insufficient. The infamous practice of sleeping in the stables on straw, called '*couchage dans la paille*', was repeatedly discussed in the French parliament until the late 1920s.

In short, the dismal picture that emerged from the ILO's collection of national reports was that farmers often paid more attention to the animals' sleeping quarters than to those of farmworkers. Wholly dependent on the farmer, the agricultural workers' access to a bed and to water for personal hygiene was often compromised. Reports pointed to the availability of clean water supplies for the horses but not for workers. 'The stable for the beasts themselves in one district may be far better than the houses provided for the men and women who look after them in another!', one writer observed.[56] Despite the structural differences across regions and countries, the International Labour Office identified a set of common problems that would later be defined by social scientists as 'basic physiological human needs', such as access to a sheltered, warm, and clean sleeping space, fresh air, and water for hygiene.[57] Beyond the description of these basic standards, the summary report descended into intricate details, such as the question of availability of bedsheets and how often they were changed, ranging from fortnightly in 'better kept farms' to twice a year in some countries where the custom was 'to clean sheets in May and at on All Saints' Day in November.[58]

But unhygienic sleeping conditions were only part of the problem. The ILO report reflected widespread concern across Europe about how agricultural labour, although legally free, retained some vestiges of feudal labour arrangements even in so-called advanced countries. In many Western European countries, for instance, accommodation (often together with meals) was included in the contract of employment and thus counted as part of the wage. This kind of contract, agricultural workers unions observed, rendered the farmworker dependent on the farm owner and lessened the former's bargaining power.

---

[53] International Labour Organization, *Technical Survey of Agricultural Questions*. On medieval European sleeping fashions, see Brian Fagan and Nadia Durrani, *What We Did in Bed: A Horizontal History* (New Haven, CT: Yale University Press, 2019), 25–6.
[54] International Labour Organization, *Technical Survey of Agricultural Questions*, 5.
[55] International Labour Organization, *Report on Special Measures*, 59.
[56] Howard, *Labour in Agriculture*, 134–5.
[57] Abraham Maslow, 'A Theory of Human Motivation', *Psychological Review* 50, no. 4 (1943), 370.
[58] International Labour Organization, *Technical Survey of Agricultural Questions*.

The living-in issue also touched on a more general problem of isolation and marginalization. As detailed in ILO records, agricultural workers were considered part of the household and there were no labour inspections on the farm. This created 'an intimate' and often paternalistic relationship, in which much of the day-to-day business was placed under the authority of the farmers, working hours were rarely respected, and workers were partly paid in kind rather than in wages.[59] According to one ILO official, the worldwide practice of assigning accommodation under the employer's own roof also meant that losing a job (a frequent occurrence due to the seasonality of the labour demand, the specificity of the agricultural calendar, and the volatility of the market) entailed losing one's 'home'. Whereas farmworkers could be dismissed rather easily, the contracts did not spare those who left before the agreed term: in some European countries, agricultural workers needed permission to move, marry or change occupation, and new employers could be fined for harbouring walkaways.[60]

What emerged from the ILO's report was a contradictory picture: even in industrialized and economically advanced countries of so-called 'chief industrial importance' the 'living-in' conditions of agricultural workers needed to be improved and threatened to taint the standards of 'civilization' usually associated with Western Europe.[61] Strikingly, the agricultural conditions that were discussed in Geneva were shining a light on the grievances of Europe's rural populations and the continent's very own 'heart of darkness'. Drawing on the knowledge it had assembled, the International Labour Office argued that workers should at least be provided with a bed, a woollen cover, and possibly a pillow. A light, ventilation, a 'minimum cubic air space', access to clean water as well as a locked cupboard to store personal possessions were discussed as desirable extras.[62]

The Work of Women and Children

Agricultural labour was often presented as different from the industrial norm. Government delegates and employers liked to point out that in contrast to industrial undertakings, agriculture was subject to informal contracts, customary and traditional arrangements, and family decisions that many governments were reluctant to address. Nowhere was this more evident than in the discussion on the work of women and children in agriculture. One of the first conventions that the ILO had adopted at its first meeting in Washington in October 1919 was about

---

[59] Howard Newby, Colin Bell, David Rose, and Peter Saunders, *Property, Paternalism and Power* (Madison: University of Wisconsin Press, 1987).

[60] Howard, *Labour in Agriculture*, 59.

[61] Gerrit W. Gong, *The Standard of 'Civilization' in International Society* (Oxford: Clarendon Press, 1984).

[62] International Labour Organization, *Report on Special Measures*, 42–70.

the protection of women before and after childbirth, the prohibition of night work as well as the prohibition of employing children under the age of fourteen in the industry.[63] Agricultural trade unionist and women's organizations wanted these measures to apply to women and children in agriculture too. The International Landworkers' Federation strongly condemned the use of child labour in farming and stated that children should be protected 'even against their parents'.[64] The International Congress of Working Women, meanwhile, asserted that protective measures should be extended to women.

In order to prepare the ground for an international convention regulating the labour of women on farms, in the spring of 1920 the International Labour Office had dispatched a questionnaire specifically dealing with women and asking governments whether they considered it possible that women employed in agriculture should benefit from the measures passed at Washington for the protection of women. The questions included: to what categories of female agricultural workers should these measures be extended and whether there should be a distinction between agricultural businesses 'employing only a few women separately' and 'those which employ female labour in groups of several women'.[65] There were also more technical issues, such as the question of how the term 'night' should be defined in agriculture for regulatory purposes. For the industry, the Washington conventions stipulated a period of eleven consecutive hours of rest for women.[66]

The reaction of the governments mirrored the discrepancies between reality and perception, and the apprehensions found in national debates on women's work in agriculture.[67] Whilst women had gained greater visibility during the First World War, often taking over from men in managing the farm and working the land, this did not necessarily mean that their contribution was widely acknowledged nor that there was a will to protect their social rights. In their reports, member states suggested that women played a marginal role in the agricultural workforce—a picture that contrasted strongly with empirical facts and observations. Part of the reason for this distortion was that the ILO was asking about 'female agricultural worker', which it defined as a full-time farm employee and

---

[63] Nora Natchkova and Céline Schoeni, 'The ILO, Feminists and Expert Networks: The Challenges of a Protective Policy (1919-1934)', in Sandrine Kott and Joëlle Droux, eds, *Globalizing Social Rights: The International Labour Organization and Beyond* (Basingstoke: Palgrave, 2013), 49–64. On the details of these conventions and how they extended previous regulations, see Report of the Director to the fourth session of the International Labour Conference (Geneva: International Labour Office, 1922), 792–3.

[64] International Labour Office, 'First International Congress of Landworkers' Unions', 5.

[65] International Labour Conference, Agricultural Questions, second item of the Agenda, Questionnaire, Geneva, 1920, 55. On this, see also Marianne Dahlén, *The Negotiable Child: The ILO Child Labour Campaign, 1919-1973*, Doctor of Laws thesis (Uppsala University, 2007), 149–70.

[66] International Labour Conference, Agricultural Questions, second item of the Agenda, Questionnaire (Geneva: International Labour Office, 1920).

[67] Nicola Verdon, 'Agricultural Labour and the Contested Nature of Women's Work in Interwar England and Wales', *The Historical Journal* 52, no. 1 (2009), 109–30.

those were relatively rare compared to the large number of women seasonally or casually participating in agricultural labour or working without wages on family farms.

Thus, the Canadian government reported that the number of women in agriculture was 'very small'; Denmark and Finland claimed that women were only employed on an exceptional basis, whereas in fact women formed an essential part of seasonal, casual, and (unpaid) family labour.[68] What is more, there was an implicit focus on white European workers only. The conditions of colonial workers in extra-European territories were deliberately excluded: the Government of South Africa thus professed with clear racial undertones that there were no 'white women [...] employed in agriculture' in the country and that therefore 'no reply to the questionnaire [was] necessary'.[69] The lack of interest, study, and information on the living and working conditions of Asian, African, and Latin American agricultural workers would remain a constant throughout most of the interwar years.

There was also more generally an unwillingness among the conference participants to consider seriously the type of work that women were carrying out. For example, the extent to which work in agriculture was comparable in hardship and fatigue to work in the industry was strongly debated. At the 1921 conference, many delegates insisted that agricultural labour was different and not detrimental to women's health and not hazardous in any way.[70] Concerning the issue of night rest, governments put forward, for example, that in contrast to the industry, night work in agriculture was rare. Every kind of agricultural work (apart from milking in the early hours and unpredictable activities such as tending to lambing and calving, or getting harvests in during night storms), they posited, was 'practically dependent on daylight'.[71] Paradoxically, however, they also insisted that the Washington provisions about a night rest of eleven consecutive hours was unrealistic for farmers and should be shortened to seven hours (from 9 pm to 4 am) to allow for early morning work.[72] Especially in conservative agrarian circles, the view prevailed that farm work offered personal satisfaction, greater health benefits and less exposure to toxic environments compared to industrial work. This argument was also put forward when it came to protecting women during and after the birth of their children. Evoking the famous trope of the rural idyll of life

[68] Verdon, 'Agricultural Labour'.

[69] International Labour Office, *Report on the Adaptation to Agricultural Labour of the Washington Decisions Concerning the Protection of Women and Children*, Report III (B) (Geneva: International Labour Office, 1921), 17.

[70] Resolution of the International Congress of Working Women. International Labour Office, *Record of Proceedings*, third session of the International Labour Conference (Geneva: International Labour Office, 1921), 803.

[71] International Labour Office, *Report on the Adaptation to Agricultural Labour of the Washington Decisions Concerning the Protection of Women and Children*, 32.

[72] See reply of Finland in International Labour Office, *Report on the Adaptation to the Agricultural Labour of the Washington Decisions Concerning the Protection of Women and Children*, 38–9.

on the land in harmony with nature, the Polish government delegate theorized that life and work were 'more healthy in agriculture' and that therefore 'a cessation of work' before or after giving birth was 'not necessary' for women.[73]

Similar views existed on the labour of children, at least in the eyes of industrialists and employers. Agricultural trade unionists condemned the use of child labour, which was a common feature across farms all over the world, and which they saw as a danger to the availability and fairness of adult male work. But this attitude was not widespread and many did not see the need to limit the work of children in agriculture.[74] Launching its preparatory work for the conference, the International Labour Office pointed to the lack of direct legislation, arguing that in contrast with the industrial sector, the 'child farmworker' had received comparatively little attention. In many national cases, labour laws explicitly excluded agriculture from their provisions. Before the war, some European states had made efforts to put in place some safeguards for rural children by using education laws to control their admission to employment.[75] Thus, in the early twentieth century and in the wake of the First World War, a handful of countries across Europe had passed laws that made children's work conditional on school attendance, limiting it during the school term while allowing for longer work time during term breaks. In some countries, limitations also were put in place for specific activities such as weeding or working in the rice fields in Italy, and for the use of machinery, which was prohibited in Denmark for children under the age of twelve. In Austria and Czechoslovakia, where children were banned from working in factories before the age of twelve, they were allowed to carry out 'light work' on the farm from the age of ten.[76] Overall, it was acceptable for children to work on the family farm and everywhere educational laws adapted to the realities of farm work, not the other way round, thus allowing for all sorts of exemptions for necessary or urgent fieldwork.

As the International Labour Office became aware when surveying the state of legislation on this matter, there existed a general view across European countries that life and work in the open air were conducive to the child's physical and mental development. The International Labour Office deplored that governments downplayed the risks of such work and did not realize that children were set tasks beyond their strength and that they were exposed to 'special dangers' including exposure to strenuous manual labour, the carrying of heavy loads and accidents with tools and machines.[77] When member states were asked by the International

---

[73] International Labour Office, *Report on the Adaptation to the Agricultural Labour of the Washington Decisions Concerning the Protection of Women and Children*, Report III (B) (Geneva: International Labour Office, 1921), 16–17.
[74] On this see also Dahlén, *The Negotiable Child*, 149–70.
[75] [No author], 'Control of Employment of Children in Agriculture in Europe', *International Labour Review* 4, no. 2 (November 1921), 191.
[76] [No author], 'Control of Employment of Children in Agriculture in Europe', 192.
[77] [No author], 'Control of Employment of Children in Agriculture', 190.

Labour Office whether they thought child labour should be allowed (and if so with what restrictions), or whether it should be completely banned, the great majority of the sixteen governments consulted before the conference were not in favour of international regulation.[78] The French argued that child labour in agriculture could be regarded as 'a healthy sport graduated according to the strength of the child'. The Swiss government similarly romanticized agriculture—at least in small holdings—'as the most suitable of all occupations for the employment of children' due to the nature of work, its variety, and the fact that is was performed in the open air. Others thought that as long as that type of work did not encroach on education or sleeping hours, the legislation on education was sufficient to regulate abuse.[79] Generally, responses from the governments also pointed to their confusion about whether the object of the enquiry were children working periodically on family holdings, supervised by their parents, or children working for wages elsewhere, which in the minds of government officials warranted greater restrictions.

'A Less Obvious Need for Safeguarding'

Despite the buoyancy with which a majority of delegates had initially voted to retain the agricultural questions on the agenda of the conference in 1921, the mood was more subdued when it came to discussing concrete instruments of international legislation. It soon became clear that there was quite a large opinion gap between those defending the side of employers, who feared that any social legislation would hinder a production growth at a particularly delicate time for the post-war economy, and the workers' delegates, who emphatically championed more stringent social measures. The former were generally hostile to what they considered international interference and did not hesitate to ridicule the ILO's attempt.

One of their recurring arguments against legislation was that agriculture was subject to nature and to ever-changing atmospheric conditions. The perils of interfering with natural laws were an often-cited reason for excluding workers in the fields and on the farms from legislative consideration. For instance, the Canadian employer's delegate S. R. Parsons noted that international legislation was not 'practical', as it could not account for seasonal, regional and national variations as well as the climatic and weather conditions that determined how and

---

[78] International Labour Conference, Agricultural Questions, second item of the Agenda, Questionnaire, Geneva, 1920, 55. The questions concerned whether child labour should be completely banned during school term, allowed before or after school hours, or limited only to children helping their own parents on the family farm. On this, see also Dahlén, *The Negotiable Child*, 149–70.

[79] International Labour Conference, Agricultural Questions, second item of the Agenda, Questionnaire, Geneva, 1920, 56.

when work was carried out. 'Agriculture', he emphatically argued, 'is a seasonal industry and it is necessary to make hay while the sun shines. As well might we try to regulate the sun, the moon, the stars, the wind, the rain, the snow, and the habits of the animals.'[80]

Not surprisingly, the resolutions subsequently passed for agricultural workers by the 1921 conference were much weaker and more inconsistent than those adopted in Washington in 1919 for industrial workers. The conference resulted in the drafting of three conventions: one on the right of agricultural workers to unionize; another regulating the employment of children in agriculture; and a third protecting agricultural wage-earners against work accidents.[81] Unlike the convention about child labour in the industry, which had banned the employment of children under the age of fourteen, the one on agriculture allowed their employment provided that the total annual school attendance would not be reduced to less than eight months.[82] Further crucial issues that had been regulated by conventions for the industry, such as the question of maternity protection, women's work and night work, were addressed through less stringent, non-binding recommendations.[83]

Women delegates who had been invited to take part in the commissions were especially disappointed by this outcome and criticized the fact that in the process of adapting existing industrial labour rights to agriculture, international legislation had been considerably watered down.[84] Altobelli, who was in the news for her open support of striking farmworkers in Northern Italy, told conference participants that women's protection in agriculture was a question of 'humanity' and 'civilization'. Settling on a non-binding recommendation rather than a convention, she insisted, would send the wrong signal and would be useless.[85] The technical adviser to the Cuban government Laura de Zayas Bazan, a women's right's

[80] International Labour Office, *Record of Proceedings*, third session of the International Labour Conference, Geneva, 1921, 102–3.
[81] International Labour Organization, Convention no. 11, Right of Association in Agriculture (1921); Convention no. 10, Minimum Age in Agriculture (1921); Convention no. 12, Workmen's Compensation in Agriculture (1921). For the draft conventions and recommendations adopted by the conference, see International Labour Office, *Record of Proceedings*, third session of the International Labour Conference, Geneva, 1921, 832–52. International Labour Office, *Report on the Adaptation to Agricultural Labour of the Washington Decisions Concerning Women and Children*.
[82] International Labour Organization, Convention no. 11, Right of Association in Agriculture (1921); Convention no. 10, Minimum Age in Agriculture (1921).
[83] International Labour Organization, Recommendation no. 11, Unemployment in Agriculture (1921); Recommendation no. 12, Maternity Protection in Agriculture (1921); Recommendation no. 13, Night Work of Women in Agriculture (1921); Recommendation no. 14, Night Work of Children and Young Persons in Agriculture (1921); Recommendation no. 15, Vocational Education in Agriculture (1921); Recommendation no. 16, Living-in Conditions in Agriculture (1921); Recommendation no. 17, Social Insurance in Agriculture (1921).
[84] International Labour Office, *Record of Proceedings*, third session of the International Labour Conference, Geneva, 1921, 122.
[85] On Altobelli's presence at the 1921 conference, see Olivia Rossetti Agresti, *Anecdotage of an Interpreter. The Reminiscences of Olivia Rossetti Agresti* (1958), in the Oral History Collection of Columbia University, ch. 13, 6–7.

activist, teacher, and writer from Havana, mused in an extraordinary public statement that so much time and money were spent to improve the cultivation of plants and the breeding of animals, whereas so little was dedicated to improving the situation of farm women.[86] Norwegian delegate Betzy Kjelsberg pointed out, not without irony, that as a mother of six she knew that 'childbirth is just as strenuous and serious and affair for women in the rural world as it is for women in the industrial world' and that what was needed was therefore a convention, not a recommendation.[87] The Belgian workers' delegate Corneille Mertens also criticized the vague formulations of the proposed recommendations on women's night work in agriculture, arguing that the inclusion of conditional phrases when saying that minimum rest would be granted to farm women 'if possible' was tantamount to saying that nothing would be done.[88] The degree to which women insisted on the need for proper international legislation is indicative of their fundamental role in the rural economy, a fact which was not acknowledged by the vast majority of delegates at the ILO conference.

The situation was similar for international legislation on the 'living-in conditions' in agriculture. Although many national reports had pointed to the dismal housing conditions of agricultural workers, including the proximity with animals and the lack of ventilation and bedding, governments were generally unwilling to accept that international legislation should provide a normative framework. Some, such as the Swiss government, pointed out that it was precisely the regional and national diversity of climates, seasons, and land tenure, so characteristic of agriculture, which made the drafting of a convention impossible. Thus, the great majority of governments claimed that divergences in conditions did not allow for international legislation. They objected to drafting a convention on housing of agricultural workers, preferring to work towards a less stringent recommendation that did not carry any legal obligation. The result was a concise text which invited signatories to 'take steps to ensure' that workers would be provided 'with rooms that can be heated', 'separate beds for each worker and provisions for cleanliness', and the end of using 'stables, cowhouses and open sheds [...] for sleeping quarters'.[89] What this showed was that even when faced with evidence of important lacunae in social legislation, economic, social, and political considerations outweighed reformist ones.

---

[86] International Labour Office, *Record of Proceedings*, third session of the International Labour Conference, Geneva, 1921, 274.

[87] Intervention of Betzy Kjelsberg, International Labour Office, *Record of Proceedings*, third session of the International Labour Conference, Geneva, 1921, 274.

[88] See speech of Corneille Mertens, president of the Belgian workers' delegation, in International Labour Office, *Record of Proceedings*, third session of the International Labour Conference, Geneva, 1921, 267. International Labour Organization, Recommendation no. 13, Night Work of Women in Agriculture (1921).

[89] International Labour Organization, *Recommendation No. 16, Living-in Conditions (Agriculture)*, 1921, Article 3.

Nevertheless, many ILO officials, trade unionists, and other commentators praised the work of the conference as ground-breaking. Lord Burnham, who had presided over the conference, hailed the achievements of the 1921 meetings as 'the triumphant completion of epoch-making work'.[90] Agricultural trade unionist R. B. Walker, a representative of British farmworkers in Geneva, praised the conference in the union's flagship journal as 'something approaching a worldwide consideration of that most neglected section of the workers: those who are on the land'.[91] Walker concluded that while the international legislation issued by the International Labour Office had limited power and did not put agricultural workers on the same footing as industrial ones, its symbolic and representative character was important. It represented the first ever effort to address challenges faced by an often overlooked part of the global population.[92]

The very few attendees of the conference who actually worked on farms thought so too. Gillabert-Randin, one of a dozen female delegates and one of the rare people with first-hand knowledge of agriculture, mused that despite its sometimes unrealistic demands, the symbolic implications of the conference were not to be dismissed. In a Swiss dairy magazine, she evoked the logistical and financial costs of holding months of discussions, meetings, and conference talks in Geneva to arrive 'at a small, tiny improvement perhaps on one or other of the points under consideration'. 'Is it worth the effort?', she rhetorically asked her readers.[93] Her answer was that of a true internationalist, namely that the moral efforts of mutual comprehension between people of different nationalities were more important for world peace than the enormous sums engulfed by military budgets.[94] In fact, although observers could not know it at the time, the ILO's 1921 conference would remain the most important event for agricultural discussions until the outbreak of the next war.

Cultivating Fields of Progress: Agriculture and the International Labour Organization, 1920s–1950s. Amalia Ribi Forclaz, Oxford University Press. © Amalia Ribi Forclaz 2025. DOI: 10.1093/9780191945014.003.0003

---

[90] International Labour Office, *Record of Proceedings*, third session of the International Labour Conference, Geneva, 1921, 583.
[91] Walker, 'The World of Farmworkers', 11.
[92] Walker, 'The World of Farmworkers', 11.
[93] Augusta Gillabert-Randin, 'Les assises du travail (suite et fin)', *L'industrie laitière Suisse* (18 November 1921), in Peter Moser and Marthe Gosteli, eds, *Une paysanne entre ferme, marché et associations: Textes d'Augusta Gillabert-Randin 1918–1940* (Baden: hier+jetzt, 2005), 237.
[94] Gillabert-Randin, 'Les assises du travail (suite et fin)', 238.

3
Cultivating Knowledge

'The need at the present time is [...] to take up patiently and systematically various phases of the rural problem, find out the facts in regard to them and interpret them in their relation to the larger social movements going on in the modern western world.' Paul Vogt, Introduction to Rural Sociology, 1917, 5

When taking on agriculture as part of its mission, the International Labour Office followed the same dual strategy it applied to industrial work: firstly, to formulate international labour standards as legal instruments to improve labour and social conditions for workers; and secondly, to function as 'a great organization for scientific investigation on social questions'.[1] With regard to agriculture, the ILO's adoption of a set of conventions and recommendations for agricultural workers had caused quite a stir in its early years. But the work stalled after the conference of 1921, highlighting that adoption and ratification of international instruments were two different things.[2] In August 1922 the competence of the ILO to regulate agricultural labour was officially confirmed by the Court of International Justice, which ruled that nothing in the treaty of Versailles indicated that agriculture should be excluded from labour improvements as long as this concerned waged labourers.[3] Yet governments made little efforts to acknowledge the existence of the new set of legal instruments formulated in 1921.[4] Ratifications of conventions on agricultural work, which would have created some legal obligations in the form of domestic legislative approval for the ratifying member states, were very slow and the International Labour Office received only sporadic reports on their implementation.[5] By the mid-1920s, Albert Thomas could hardly disguise his frustration with the lack of effort of member countries to align themselves with

---

[1] Report of the Director to the third session of the International Labour Conference, Geneva, 1921, 249.

[2] See Chapter 1.

[3] For the advisory opinion of the court, Advisory Opinion, Permanent Court of International Justice, 12 August 1922, League of Nations Archives Geneva, Col. 206, Box 12, File 117.

[4] For details, see International Labour Office, *The International Labour Organization and Agriculture* (Geneva: International Labour Office, 1924), 4.

[5] By the mid-1920s, the convention on minimum age had been ratified by seven member states including Sweden, Poland, Japan, Italy, Ireland, Estonia, and Austria and the convention on the right to unionize was ratified by a slightly bigger group of countries including Austria, Bulgaria, Belgium, Chile, Estonia, Finland, Germany, India, Ireland, Italy, Latvia, Poland, the Netherlands, Sweden, the United Kingdom, and Burma.

the ILO recommendations on agriculture. As the ILO's director accurately analysed, some agrarian and economic circles were 'consciously opposed to granting any sort of protection to agricultural workers' because they were afraid that this would 'introduce an unnecessary element of disturbance' into the present agricultural order.[6]

There was not much the International Labour Office could do about the lack of implementation. However, from the mid-1920s onwards, it did progress in the collation of international studies on agriculture. This chapter will explore the work carried out by a small group of specialists in the ILO in collaboration with the older International Institute of Agriculture in Rome to collect data and collate international surveys and reports that contained mostly qualitative and to a much lesser extent quantitative information, often also with some analytical statements. As the chapter argues, the resulting 'social knowledge' sought to describe in unprecedented ways the social and economic behaviours, organization, and outlook of agricultural workers as a collective group. Like other such types of knowledge, one aim of the collected data was to formulate empirically founded claims about the past, present, and future of agricultural work.[7]

At the heart of this work was the so-called Agricultural Section (later Agricultural Service), one of the earliest administrative units in charge of preparing documentation for conferences and meetings.[8] The Service was primarily concerned with collecting information on national agricultural legislation and policy in terms not only of labour but also of land use, housing, education, and other related issues.[9] Initially described as 'absurdly small' in view of the momentous task it was supposed to undertake, it was placed under the direction of Walter Alexander Riddell, a clergyman and former deputy minister of the Department of Labour in Ontario.[10] Little is known about his work in the Service, as his personal file could not be found. A larger imprint was left by his successor, British academic Louise Matthaei, who headed the Service from 1924 until 1933, considerably expanding

---

[6] International Labour Office, *Record of Proceedings*, eighth session of the International Labour Conference (Geneva: International Labour Office, 1926), 424–5.

[7] For a definition of 'social knowledge' and its role, see Charles Camic, Neil Gross, and Michele Lamont, 'The Study of Social Knowledge Making', in Camic, Gross, and Lamont, eds, *Social Knowledge in the Making* (Chicago: University of Chicago Press, 2011), 3–4. The ILO also engaged in the production of economic knowledge: Marine Dhermy-Mairal, 'Du danger des enquêtes savantes. Faire oeuvre de science dans l'entre-deux-guerres au Bureau International du Travail', *Revue d'histoire moderne & contemporaine* 62, no. 4 (2015), 7–32.

[8] For early discussions on setting up a separate section on agriculture (in view of the 1921 conference), see International Labour Office, Minutes of the second session of the Governing Body (Paris: International Labour Office, 1920), 30, 41. For a detailed overview of the administrative structure of the ILO headquarters and its many sections, see Report of the Director to the third session of the International Labour Conference (Geneva: International Labour Office, 1921), 14 ff. On the technical services, 19–20.

[9] Memo Harold Butler, 8 April 1921, ILO Archives Geneva, P 6/6/1.

[10] There is unfortunately no file on Riddell at the ILO's historical archives. He is mentioned in Report of the Director to the third session of the International Labour Conference (Geneva: International Labour Office, 1921), 20.

its field of interest. Born in 1880, Matthaei had studied at Newnham College, Cambridge, where she went on to teach as a classics fellow before the war, and had become a well-published author on Greek tragedy. Before and during the First World War, Matthaei was in close contact with leading internationalist thinkers, notably the writer and editor Leonard Woolf, husband of Virginia Woolf, for whom she worked as an assistant.[11] The combination of her interest in the classics and her engagement in interwar international affairs was not unusual at the time, and Matthaei wrote about international politics and participated in anti-war demonstrations.[12] After falling out with Cambridge due to her German heritage and anti-war stance, Matthaei, who was fluent in German, French, Italian, and English, arrived in Geneva in 1921 to work for the ILO's Publication Section before moving up the echelons of the Labour Office.

Matthaei was assisted in her task by two other permanent officials who would both shape the work of the Agricultural Service until the Second World War. The first was Italian agronomist and socialist exile Olindo Gorni, a specialist on Italian and more generally Mediterranean agriculture.[13] Matthaei described him as somebody with 'extensive' and 'valuable' knowledge, 'intimately acquainted with Italian agriculture and Italian labour'.[14] Gorni carried out research on a variety of topics, including agrarian reform and collective agreements in agriculture.[15] The second permanent member of staff was the Danish economist Fritz Wilhelm von Bülow, a recent graduate in social and political economy from the University of Copenhagen.[16] While Gorni was lauded by his superiors for his '*esprit scientifique*', von Bülow's work was perceived as more action-oriented.[17] He was praised as 'one of those who best understands that our scientific studies must not be carried out *in abstracto*, but always with a view to possible action'.[18] Throughout the 1920s and until the Great Depression, this trio of experts would try to fulfil their duty

---

[11] For a succinct biographical account of Matthaei's life, see Sybil Oldfield, 'Howard, Louise Ernestine, Lady Howard (1880–1969)', *Oxford Dictionary of National Biography* (Oxford: Oxford University Press, 2004), http://www.oxforddnb.com/view/article/37576 (last accessed 28 January 2024)]. For glimpses of her interwar activities, see Amalia Ribi Forclaz, 'A New Target for International Social Reform', *Contemporary European History* 20, no. 3 (2011), 307–29. On her later support for organic farming, see Philip Conford, *The Origins of the Organic Movement* (Edinburgh: Floris, 2001); Gregory Barton, *The Global History of Organic Farming* (Oxford: Oxford University Press, 2018).

[12] Glenda Sluga, 'From F. Melian Stawell to E. Greene Balch: International and Internationalist Thinking at the Gender Margins, 1919–1947', in Owens Patricia, Rietzler Katharina, Hutchings, Kimberly, Dunstan, Sara C., eds, *Women's International Thought: A New History* (Cambridge: Cambridge University Press, 2021), 223–243.

[13] Mauro Cerrutti, 'Olindo Gorni', *Dictionnaire historique de la suisse*, https://hls-dhs dss.ch/fr/articles/027942/2004-10-27 (last accessed 5 February 2024).

[14] Note by Matthaei, 3 March 1927, ILO Archives Geneva, file Gorni, P 1615.

[15] ILO Archives Geneva, file Gorni, P 1615. The file contains reports from the early 1920s to the late 1930s which provide insights into the work, research, and scientific missions of the Agricultural Service. See 'Copy of report by Chief of Service, 14. 1. 1925'.

[16] Biographical note in von Bülow's personal file, ILO Archives Geneva, P 1733 (von Bülow). On Gorni, see also Chapter 5.

[17] Note Maurette 3.11.1931, ILO Archives Geneva, file Gorni, P 1615.

[18] Note Matthaei, 16 December 1930, ILO Archives Geneva, P 1733.

with relentless passion and in spite of various obstacles. Although largely in favour of including agriculture in the discussion, the means which Thomas put at the disposal of research on this topic were limited. This would create continuous tensions, especially with Matthaei, who repeatedly tried to get funding for research and publications, including foreign language assistants with expertise on Eastern Europe. But funding for additional staff, new studies, and publications remained scarce, and Matthaei constantly deplored that she had to 'neglect' Eastern European, Latin American, and African agriculture.[19]

When the ILO's Agricultural Service began its systematic research on agriculture, the practice was already well established among government institutions, academic bodies, private philanthropic foundations, and individual scientists in domestic and international contexts.[20] The eighteenth and nineteenth centuries had seen the emergence of scientific institutions, labs, and experimental stations specializing in botany, geography, entomology, agronomy, and the study of soils.[21] From the late nineteenth century onwards, the collection of so-called social and economic knowledge on production, labour, and social conditions began to emerge in the form of statistics, legal documents, and empirical surveys. British and other colonial scientists played a crucial rule in extending this knowledge to imperial settings, embracing agriculture as a significant area of scientific enquiry.[22] Around the First World War, attention to rural ways of life increased further as a school of American rural sociologists developed a new focus on rural communities, family, and village organization. Their work was mainly concerned with social change, exodus, and rural–urban relations, and generally outlined the existence of a 'rural problem'.[23] By the early 1920s a global web of institutions, movements, and interest groups combined

---

[19] Notes L. E. Matthaei, 8 September 1929 and 2 January 1931, ILO Archives Geneva, P 6/6/1.

[20] Frank Uekötter, *Die Wahrheit ist auf dem Feld. Eine Wissensgeschichte der deutschen Landwirtschaft* (Göttingen: Vandenhoeck & Ruprecht, 2010); Elizabeth B. Jones, 'Seeing Is Believing: Sites/Sights of Agricultural Improvement in Germany (1840–1914)', *Rural History* 30, no. 1 (2019), 37–51; Federico d'Onofrio, *Knowing to Transform: Three Ways for Agricultural Economists to Observe Italy, 1900–1940*, PhD thesis (University of Utrecht, 2013); Tore C. Olsson, *Agrarian Crossings: Reformers and the Remaking of the US and Mexican Countryside* (Princeton: Princeton University Press, 2017); Jonathan Harwood, *Technology's Dilemma. Agricultural Colleges Between Science and Practice in Germany, 1860–1934* (Frankfurt: P. Lang, 2005).

[21] William K. Storey, 'Plants, Power and Development: Founding the Imperial Department of Agriculture for the West Indies, 1880–1940', in Sheila Jasanoff, ed., *States of Knowledge: The Co-Production of Science and Social Order* (London: Routledge, 2004), 109–30.

[22] Helen Tilley, *Africa as a Living Laboratory: Empire, Development, and the Problem of Scientific Knowledge, 1870–1950* (Chicago: University of Chicago Press, 2011); Joseph Morgan Hodge, *Triumph of the Expert: Agrarian Doctrines of Development and the Legacies of British Colonialism* (Athens, OH: Ohio University Press, 2007); Michele Sollai, 'How to Feed an Empire? Agrarian Science, Indigenous Farming and Wheat Autarky in Italian-Occupied Ethiopia, 1937–1941', *Agricultural History* 96, no. 2 (2002), 379–416.

[23] See for example Paul Vogt, *Introduction to Rural Sociology* (New York: Appleton & Co., 1917); J. C. Galpin, *Rural Life* (New York: The Century Co., 1918); J. C. Galpin, *Rural Social Problems* (New York: The Century Co., 1924); E. R. Grovers, *The Rural Mind and Social Welfare* (Chicago: University of Chicago Press, 1922); J. M. Gillette, *Rural Sociology* (New York: Macmillan, 1922).

scientific study and social reform, knowledge production, and welfare projects. The ILO was rapidly becoming one of them.[24]

Matthaei had no direct influence on the choice of items placed on the agenda of the ILO's legislative body, and due to the restricted human and financial resources placed at her disposal, the possibilities of thematic expansion and regional specialization were limited. She decided that the priority of the Agricultural Service should be collecting data and existing legislation on waged agricultural labour globally. This was a considerable challenge, as reliable information on work conditions in agriculture was scarce and difficult to come by. In the 1920s many countries lacked agricultural legislation, which made comparative surveys impossible. Even when material was available, the notoriously understaffed service struggled to access it because of language difficulties.[25] Matthaei did her best to reach out to the scarce agricultural trade unions that existed at the time. She also corresponded with other international institutions, such as the International Institute of Agriculture, the League of Nations Health Section and the global agricultural census project of the Rockefeller Foundation, always with a view to promote collaborative work and exchange on specific aspects that had an impact on working and living conditions in agriculture such as cost of labour and housing for hired agricultural workers.[26]

The Agricultural Service did not just narrowly cover labour arrangements on the farms. The research was also concerned with larger debates on social stratification in the rural countryside, on the power relationships, and on the relationship between local and global conditions, on gender questions, and rural and urban lifestyles. As such, the Service contributed to the emerging field of rural sociology which in the early 1920s was geared towards understanding the socio-economic and cultural impact of industrialization and urbanization on the rural countryside.[27] The application of new social sciences to projects of rural planning and reform was becoming a global phenomenon at the time.[28] The ILO's specific advantage as an international organization was that it could—at least theoretically—integrate a plurality of voices, simultaneously asking its member governments as well as other interest groups such as agricultural labour unions and employer

---

[24] Heinrich Hartmann and Julia Tischler, 'Introduction' in Hartmann and Tischler, eds, *Planting Seeds of Knowledge: Agriculture and Education in Rural Societies in the Twentieth Century* (New York, Oxford: Berghahn Books, 2023).

[25] See note L. E. Howard, 17 March 1933, ILO Archives Geneva, P 6/6/1.

[26] On this see Amalia Ribi Forclaz, 'Agriculture, American Expertise, and the Quest for Global Data: Leon Estabrook and the First World Agricultural Census of 1930', *Journal of Global History* 11, no. 1 (2016), 57–58.

[27] Bertrand Hervieu and Francois Purseigle, 'The Sociology of Agricultural Worlds: From a Sociology of Change to a Sociology of Coexistence', *Review of Agricultural and Environmental Studies* 96, no. 1 (2015), 59–90.

[28] Raluca Muşat, 'Prototypes for Modern Living: Planning, Sociology and the Model Village in Interwar Romania', *Social History* 39 (2014), 157–184. Also, Muşat, 'Making the Countryside Global: The Bucharest School of Sociology and International Networks of Knowledge', *Contemporary European History* 28 (2019), 205–19.

organizations to submit their answers. These voices, however, remained arguably limited for reasons outside its control and which had mostly to do with the lack of international agricultural trade unions.

The basis of the ILO's research work had been laid out from the Organization's very beginning. With the 1921 conference, the International Labour Office had made a remarkable entry into the field of agriculture—an achievement supported by extensive preliminary research. Despite its limited resources, narrow time frame, and general lack of specific information, the Agricultural Service had made efforts to compile everything it could find on the agricultural working day, women and children's labour, rural schools, rural housing, and workers' associations and unions.[29] The library of the International Labour Office, which by 1920–21 was expanding at an 'extraordinarily rapid rate', contributed by assembling bibliographies and by requesting works on agriculture from all corners of the globe.[30] These preliminary efforts resulted in the compilation of an unparalleled transnational study, published as a 600-page 'technical survey' of agricultural issues that had been hitherto firmly under the control of local and regional authorities and that were now presented to an international audience.[31]

In those early years, the ILO established a specific method of research that consisted in launching international enquiries in order to provide the participants with documentation. This preparatory work was carried out in two steps: first, the relevant technical services of the office, which Thomas conceived as 'research laboratories' and 'liaison centres', independently sourced material and data from specialized national offices and interested parties. The latter included ministries of agriculture, agricultural experts and academics, farmers' organizations, and trade unions, which were asked to provide information about existing national legislation, statistical inquiries, and previous research.[32] On the basis of this first step, questionnaires were then formulated by ILO experts and circulated to survey the current state of affairs and gauge the attitude of member governments towards international regulation.[33]

---

[29] For a discussion of the agenda, see International Labour Office, Minutes of the third session of the Governing Body, London, 22–25 March 1920. Appendix 7: Agenda of the third session of the International Labour Conference, 58. For the definitive agenda, see International Labour Office, Minutes of the fourth session of the Governing Body, Genoa, 8–9 June 1920. Appendix 4: Agenda for the Conference of 1921, 40.

[30] Report of the Director to the third session of the International Labour Conference, Geneva, 1921, 209–10.

[31] International Labour Organization, *Technical Survey of Agricultural Questions* (Geneva: International Labour Office, 1921).

[32] For a description of how the various divisions collected material for an enquiry, see Report of the Director to the fourth session of the International Labour Conference (Geneva: International Labour Office, 1922), 837.

[33] International Labour Organization, *Report on Special Measures for the Protection of Agricultural Workers* (Geneva: International Labour Office, 1921), 42–70. On the method of the questionnaire, see International Labour Conference, Agricultural Questions, second item of the Agenda, Questionnaire (Geneva : International Labour Office, 1920), 3–4.

There were both advantages and drawbacks to this method: the combination of independent research and international enquiries enabled the ILO to gather rich and wide-ranging information about topics on which there was little data.[34] It also allowed the ILO to compare and contrast different national realities and to compile summaries and overviews of international conditions on specific issues. This not only filled a glaring gap in the meagre body of knowledge on labour conditions in agriculture, which had traditionally focused on the industry: in its aim to find out about patterns and structures of labour arrangements, the ILO also went far beyond the boundaries of its work and tackled broader socio-economic issues. What emerged was simultaneously a vision of the broader common characteristics of the European postwar countryside that awaited international solutions as well as the realization that local situations were vastly different.[35] However, the collection and collation of information was not without problems. Generally, it was difficult for the International Labour Office to check the veracity of the evidence submitted by governments.[36] A good example is the questionnaire on the conditions of women in agriculture, prepared and dispatched in the spring of 1920, which, as previously shown, in fact resulted in statistical misrepresentation and invisibilization of women workers.[37]

The Battle for Authority

The creation of the Agricultural Service demonstrated the International Labour Office's ambition to establish itself as an international rural observatory. This also produced some tensions and competition with other institutions, especially the International Institute of Agriculture which had survived the war in Rome and was waiting to reactivate and expand its pre-war work.[38] The Institute could

---

[34] International Labour Organization, *Technical Survey of Agricultural Questions,* VIII. On the mechanisms of this knowledge production before the conference and the consultation of governments and ministries, see Edward Joseph Phelan, 'The Contribution of the ILO. to Peace', *International Labour Review* 59, no. 6 (1949), 617–18.
[35] Muşat, Raluca 'Making the Countryside Global', 208.
[36] International Labour Organization, *Technical Survey of Agricultural Questions,* VIII.
[37] On this, see Chapter 2.
[38] For the role of the International Institute of Agriculture in producing and circulating agricultural knowledge, see Niccolò Mignemi, 'Rome, capitale mondiale de la documentation agricole: de la bibliothèque de l'Institut international d'Agriculture à la David Lubin Memorial Library de la FAO', *Mélanges de l'École française de Rome. Italie et Méditerranée modernes et contemporaines,* no. 132-1 (2020), 215–35; Niccolò Mignemi, 'Agriculteurs du monde entier, associez-vous! Robert de Rocquigny: du Musée social à l'Institut International d'Agriculture', *Histoire et Sociétés Rurales* 1, no. 45 (2016), 43–67. On early internationalist efforts, see Amy Staples, *The Birth of Development: How the World Bank, Food and Agriculture Organization, and World Health Organization Changed the World, 1945–1965* (Kent, OH.: Kent State University Press, 2006), 64–71. See also Sergio Marchisio, Antonietta di Blase, *The Food and Agriculture Organization (FAO)* (Dordrecht: M. Nijhoff, 1991); Luciano Tosi, *Alle origini della FAO. Le relazioni tra l'Istituto Internazionale di Agricoltura e la Società delle Nazioni* (Milan: Franco Angeli, 1989).

count on the continued support of experts and delegates but it was kept at bay by the League of Nations, in which it had sought and failed to be officially integrated.[39] At the 1921 International Labour Conference, Norwegian delegate and agricultural expert Anders Fjelstad, who had participated in the meetings of the Institute before the war, had emphatically drawn attention to the fact that there already was an international institution solely dedicated to agriculture, and that there was a risk of overlap.[40]

In fact, the goals, structure, and functioning of the two organizations were fundamentally different. The ILO was almost exclusively concerned with the working and living conditions of hired agricultural labourers, whom it described as poor, landless, and in need of social protection. This focus was reiterated in one of its major studies, carried out in the mid-1920s about the definition of these workers, their organization in trade unions, and their representation within the International Labour Office.[41] The International Institute of Agriculture catered to a different crowd. The Roman organization implicitly conceptualized 'farmers' as producers, businessmen, and employers who depended on trade and economic cooperation. They should be granted access to 'world data' that would help them plan production according to the needs of the market.[42] The work of the International Institute of Agriculture concentrated on collecting and circulating information on agricultural production and trade in crops, as well as on the dissemination of research on scientific advances, plant diseases, and meteorological conditions.

Before the war, the Institute had successfully encouraged an increasing number of states to collect and share agricultural figures, and it continued to do so in the early 1920s.[43] One of the most ambitious projects in this regard, which would occupy the International Institute of Agriculture between 1924 and 1929, was a worldwide agricultural census carried out with the financial support of the Rockefeller Foundation with the aim to gain an overview of world production.[44] As the director of the Institute, Italian statistician Umberto Ricci put it, with a little disguised side-blow to the International Labour Office, 'a simple one-page survey [of agricultural statistics]' that provided the forecast of wheat harvests was 'more valuable than a five-hundred-page volume dealing with the progress made

---

[39] Tosi, *Alle origini della FAO*.
[40] International Labour Office, *Record of Proceedings*, third session of the International Labour Conference (Geneva: International Labour Office, 1921), 98. See also Anders Fjelstad, 'Memorandum on International Cooperation in Agriculture', published as an annex to the above, 816.
[41] International Labour Office, *The Representation and Organisation of Agricultural Workers*, Studies and Reports, Series K (Agriculture), no. 8 (Geneva: International Labour Office, 1928). See also Chapter 1.
[42] Louis Dop, *Le Présent et l'avenir de l'institut international d'agriculture* (Rome: Imprimerie de L'institut international d'agriculture 1912), 50.
[43] Federico D'Onofrio and Niccolò Mignemi, 'The International Institute of Agriculture and the Information Infrastructure of World Trade (1905–1946)', *Histoire & Mesure* 48 (2023), 13–38.
[44] Ribi Forclaz, 'Agriculture, American Expertise, and the Quest for Global Data', 44–65.

[...] by agricultural legislation'.⁴⁵ The Institute's primary attention was to numbers. Social reform and legislation were very marginally on the Institute's agenda, and anything that could have an impact on national policy or amount to an international treaty was 'carefully removed from the programme' so as not to put off member governments.⁴⁶ Not surprisingly, agricultural labour unions did not have much regard for the Roman organization. One of the leaders of the International Landworkers' Federation, Georg Schmidt, quite openly stated that he did not expect any improvement of social policies from the Institute.⁴⁷

From the start, the relationship between the two institutions in Rome and Geneva, which both claimed to safeguard the interest of agriculture, was marked by rivalry and mistrust. In the spring of 1923, they entered a marriage of convenience that would last throughout the interwar years: an interinstitutional expert group, the Mixed Advisory Agricultural Committee, was created to coordinate their work on agriculture.⁴⁸ This was the first—and, for a decade, the sole—expert commission on agriculture on the side of the ILO. It was invested with great expectations, as one of its mandates was to help set an international agenda for the discussion of agricultural problems and to support the Organization by launching research on specific issues. Opening the first meeting, the chairman tried to set an optimistic tone, voicing his hopes that cooperation between the 'two world-famous' institutions would yield happy results 'for the whole of humanity'.⁴⁹

In reality, much of the initial debates within the Committee were spent on making sure that neither the ILO nor the International Institute of Agriculture would overstep their mandates.⁵⁰ From the start, the expert members of the Committee tried to devise joint projects and enquiries on which both institutions could compromise. They had to work hard to overcome the competitive mindset and the battles over legitimacy that marked the meetings. Representatives of the International Institute of Agriculture prided themselves on their pre-war experience, their complete dedication to agrarian questions, and the large documentation which the ILO did not yet have.⁵¹ The latter's director, in response,

---

⁴⁵ Umberto Ricci, 'Le Service de la statistique générale, ce qu'il est et ce qu'il pourrait devenir'. International Institute of Agriculture, Minutes of Permanent Committee, 1920, FAO Archives Rome, 1 IIA 73, 586.

⁴⁶ Dop, *Le Présent et l'avenir*, 52.

⁴⁷ Letter, Georg Schmidt to Matthaei, 29 September 1927, ILO Archives Geneva, AG 1000/01/1.

⁴⁸ For the discussions around the constitution of such a committee, see International Labour Office, Minutes of the twelfth session of the Governing Body, Rome, April 1922, 128–30.

⁴⁹ Polish diplomat and delegate to the ILO's Governing Body Franciszek Sokal substituting for Arthur Fontaine. Mixed Advisory Agricultural Committee, First session, 26 June 1922, ILO Archives Geneva, AG 800/3/4.

⁵⁰ The Mixed Advisory Agricultural Committee (also called the Joint Advisory Committee on Agriculture) was described by Thomas as a 'Committee of a very special character set up in agreement with a kindred institution [...] to avoid needless duplication and conflict by loyal collaboration'. Report of the Director to the fourth session of the International Labour Conference (International Labour Office: Geneva, 1922), 858, 871–3.

⁵¹ Mixed Advisory Agricultural Committee, First session, 26 June 1922, ILO Archives Geneva, AG 800/3/4.

insisted that his institution could boast greater legitimacy because it comprised not only voices from experts, governments, and employers, but also from agricultural workers. Supporters of the Roman organization derided these claims of representing the underdog as 'completely unrealistic' because of the globality of the subject, the differences between countries, and the heterogeneity of the farming classes.[52]

It was therefore apparent from the start that many of the ILO's choice subjects, such as labour, hours of work, remuneration, and social protection, would not figure in the work of the Committee. The latter treated more loosely defined common interests, and dealt with agricultural and rural issues in a wider sense. Rather disappointingly, at least in the eyes of agricultural trade unionists who were closely watching the ILO, the Mixed Advisory Agricultural Committee was only to meet every three years and would comprise three representatives for each institution, most of whom only had scarce knowledge of social and labour questions in agriculture.[53] This situation was to be improved through the mobilization of a host of additional ad hoc experts 'with international titles and recognition' who would be punctually invited to participate in the Committee's discussions.[54]

Most of these experts emanated from pre-war European networks. One of the leading figures was the French landowner and agronomist Marquis Louis de Vogüé.[55] Born in 1868, De Vogüé presided over various French agricultural societies and was regarded by Thomas as a leading figure in international agricultural policy and a supporter of the ILO's mission. De Vogüé was an active member of the nineteenth-century Commission Internationale d'Agriculture and would become its president in 1924. Other experts included Carlo Dragoni, Professor of Agriculture at the University of Rome and general secretary of the International Institute of Agriculture; and Jules Gautier, Vice-President of the Commission Internationale d'Agriculture. They were joined by José Zulueta y Gomis, a Spanish politician and member of various Catalan agricultural employers' organizations. There was a will to balance the interests of different groups and to have a fair representation of workers' point of view. Georg Schmidt was appointed as a representative of farmworkers. So was Joseph Duncan, a 'recognized authority' on agricultural labour.[56] In an effort to include female

---

[52] Mixed Advisory Agricultural Committee, First session, 26 June 1922, ILO Archives Geneva, AG 800/3/4.

[53] The ILO representatives were the French president of the ILO's Governing Body Arthur Fontaine; the Danish chairman of the employers group Hans Oersted; and the German worker's delegate Theodor Leipart. The International Institute of Agriculture was represented by British civil servant Sir Thomas Elliott, Italian politician Count Edardo Soderini, and Anders Fjelstad.

[54] Thomas Elliott in Mixed Advisory Agricultural Committee, first session, 26 June 1922, ILO Archives Geneva, AG 800/3/4, 28.

[55] See foreword by Louis de Vogüé in Marcel Paisant, *La Commission Internationale d'Agriculture et son rôle dans l'économie europenne* (Paris, 1936).

[56] Letter, Fleuri to Cabrini, 3 April 1923, Mixed Advisory Agricultural Committee, Correspondence concerning experts for the first meeting, ILO Archives Geneva, AG 801/2.

trade unionists, Altobelli was briefly considered as a potential candidate but was dropped on the grounds that adherence to her trade union Federterra was decreasing by the day, due to political changes in Italy.

Both the International Institute of Agriculture and the ILO agreed that in order to be effective, the expertise should go 'beyond England, Italy and France' and include experts from Eastern European countries of leading agrarian importance.[57] This led to the appointment of the Czech politician, landowner, and agricultural expert Ferdinand Klindera.[58] A minority of participants also wanted the Committee to engage with extra-European countries, which later resulted in the recruitment of experts such as the Japanese agronomist Yasushi Sawamura and an expert from Latin America.[59] However, in contrast with this opening onto the world, the Committee's themes and debates were to remain largely centred on Europe.

Many of the agricultural issues discussed by the Mixed Advisory Agricultural Committee during the interwar years were situated at the crossroads of general rural studies, agricultural economics, and rural sociology. The topics identified from the mid-1920s onwards as areas of joint interest had one thing in common: they were all concerned with anticipating the important structural changes that were happening in the rural countryside after the First World War. Topics such as agricultural education or the organization of rural workers aimed at identifying ways to transform the lower segments of agrarian societies by promoting greater organization and planning and infusing them with new values and by controlling the level of skills needed. They were also at least partly fuelled by fears of rural depopulation, mass migration, vagrancy, urban slumming, and unemployment. In numerical terms the mass flight remained a myth, but to contemporary farmers and experts, the political, economic, and social threats that such migration potentially posed to agricultural production and the rural 'way of life' were real.[60]

In his 1917 work on rural sociology, Paul Vogt identified the exodus as one of the major 'rural problems' of Western nations and as an obstacle to the development of a stable and productive rural countryside. German agronomists painted a similar picture.[61] Jacques Valdour regarded the exodus in the French context as the source of various ailments: land remained uncultivated because of a lack of labour, and the immigration of 'foreign hands' especially from Belgium, Poland,

---

[57] Sokal to Thomas, 12 June 1923, Mixed Advisory Agricultural Committee, Correspondence concerning experts for first meeting, ILO Archives Geneva, AG 801/2.

[58] Mixed Advisory Agricultural Committee, Correspondence concerning experts for the first meeting, ILO Archives Geneva, AG 801/2.

[59] Mixed Advisory Agricultural Committee, First session, Plenary Meeting, 24 August 1923, ILO Archives, AG 801/9.

[60] Edouard Lynch, 'Interwar France and the Rural Exodus: The National Myth in Peril', *Rural History* 21, no. 2 (2010), 165–76; Ernst Langthaler, 'Landflucht, Agrarsystem und Moderne: Deutschland 1933–1939', in Jochen Oltmer, ed., *Nationalsozialistisches Migrationsregime und 'Volksgemeinschaft'* (Paderborn: Schöningh, 2012), 111–36.

[61] Friedrich Aeroboe, *Die ländliche Arbeiterfrage nach dem Kriege* (Berlin: Parey, 1922).

Italy, and Spain resulted in the 'denationalization' of the land.[62] Even though he did not directly cite immigration as a problem, Thomas viewed the rural exodus as a catalyst for social instability, and one of the most alarming issues with regard to agriculture. The rural labour force, so Thomas claimed, was being drawn towards cities by other occupations, resulting in a decrease of cultivated land, disappearance of small farms, and proletarianization of the 'agricultural middle class'. The exodus was seen as 'a real disease' with 'complex causes', urgently calling for 'remedies'.[63] Even Carl C. Taylor, who questioned this catastrophist rhetoric, admitted that the prospect of better schools, regular wages, short hours, entertainment, bright lights, street cars, and clean clothes was an irresistible lure for the rural poor living in supposedly backward villages.[64]

It was therefore primordial to strengthen the workers' bond to the land by improving their work but also their conditions. Many issues, however, were marred by the competition between the two institutions or by conflicting views between employers and workers organizations. The topic of agricultural cooperatives and the role they could play in improving workers' economic conditions, for example, was considered, after discussion, too complex to tackle in a joint enquiry, and the study was left to the International Institute of Agriculture, which had already carried out work on this.[65] Workers' representatives would have liked to see an enquiry on the question of labour inspection on farms, but employers objected that agriculture worked along different laws and it would be wrong and 'completely undesirable' to apply industrial principles to it, so no further enquiry was undertaken.[66] One of the rare issues, however, on which everyone seemed to agree and the Committee successfully collaborated was that of vocational agricultural education.[67]

Professionalizing Farming

Among the most prominent areas of research and reform on the ILO agenda was the improvement and standardization of agricultural education, which was

---

[62] Jacques Valdour, *L'ouvrier agricole: Observations vécues* (Paris: Arthur Rousseau, 1919), 294.
[63] Report of the Director to the Twelfth International Labour Conference (Geneva: International Labour Office, 1929), 223.
[64] Carl C. Taylor, *Rural Sociology: A Study of Rural Problems* (New York and London: Harper, 1926), 13.
[65] Mixed Advisory Agricultural Committee, first session, plenary meeting, August 1923, ILO Archives Geneva, AG 801/10.
[66] Mixed Advisory Agricultural Committee, first session, plenary meeting, August 1923, ILO Archives Geneva, AG 801/10.
[67] Report of the Mixed Advisory Agricultural Committee, second session, 5–7 November 1925, ILO Archives Geneva, AG 802/5. For a list of enquiries and research work, see Programme of the Agricultural Service, 1925–26, in Mixed Advisory Agricultural Committee, ILO Archives Geneva, AG 802/4.

inherently linked to other preoccupations such as improving efficiency and scientific management of workers on farms.[68] Vocational education, together with the promotion of agricultural cooperatives and better housing, was seen as less controversial than the question of hours of work, which the Agricultural Service had repeatedly suggested as a topic of investigation but which—at least for the time being—was deemed as too problematic.[69] Rural and agricultural education had long been at the heart of social reform and modernization ideas and it was viewed as the most important stepping stone in the professionalization of farming. Historically, the formal and informal diffusion of agricultural knowledge through governmental activities, agricultural societies, and scientific networks had seen varying degrees of implementation since the eighteenth century.[70] The redefinition of agricultural work as a combination of manual labour and scientific knowledge that necessitated technical training, rather than a traditional occupation handed down from one generation to the next, was a slow process. The practice of generational learning had survived through the Enlightenment and was difficult to eradicate.[71] And although more formal forms of education were established from the late eighteenth century onwards, the emergence of vocational education for agriculture was comparatively slow. Since the beginning of the twentieth century, the problem of how to train dispersed and farm-bound agriculturists had been debated in Western Europe and the United States, with a focus on itinerant lectures and extension training.[72] Colonial governments too were concerned with agricultural education as a means to develop what they viewed as unskilled and backward rural populations with a poor work ethic into productive, efficient, and rational farmers.[73]

---

[68] For a more detailed discussion, see Amalia Ribi Forclaz, 'Shaping the Future of Farming: The International Labour Organization and Agricultural Education in the Interwar Years', *The Agricultural History Review*, 65, no. 2 (2017), 320–339.

[69] For a discussion of hours of work in the early 1920s, see Chapter 2 and for the revisiting of the topic in the mid-1930s, see Chapter 4.

[70] Yves Segers and Leen Van Molle (eds), *Agricultural Knowledge Networks in Rural Europe, 1700–2000*, (Woodbridge: The Boydell Press, 2022).

[71] On this see Peter Jones, *Agricultural Enlightenment: Knowledge, Technology, and Nature, 1750–1840* (Oxford: Oxford University Press, 2016).

[72] For France, see Stéphane Lembré, 'The Experience of Itinerant Agricultural Education in the Nord Region (1900–1939)', *Histoire et Sociétés rurales* 34, no. 2 (2010), 149–80; Michel Boulet, ed., *Les enjeux de la formation des acteurs de l'agriculture, 1760–1945* (Dijon: Educagri, 2000). For Italy, see d'Onofrio, *Knowing to Transform*; for Britain, see Paul Brassley, 'Agricultural Education, Training and Advice in the UK, 1850–2000', in Nadine Vivier, ed., *The State and Rural Societies: Policy and Education in Europe, 1750–2000* (Brepols: Turnhout, 2008); Caitlin Adams, 'Rural Education and Reform between the Wars', in Paul Brassley, Jeremy Burchardt, and Lynne Thompson, eds, *The English Countryside between the Wars: Regeneration or Decline?* (Woodbridge: Boydell & Brewer, 2006), 36–52.

[73] Hartmann and Tischler, *Planting Seeds of Knowledge*; Harry Gamble, 'Peasants of the Empire. Rural Schools and the Colonial Imaginary in 1930s French West Africa', *Cahiers d'études africaines* 195 (2009), 775–804; Julia Tischler, 'Education and the Agrarian Question in South Africa, c. 1900–40', *The Journal of African History* 57, no. 2 (2016), 251–70.

Leaning on such precedents, Thomas argued in 1922 that improving agricultural education was central to social progress and to stabilizing the rural workforce.[74] According to the ILO's Governing Body, all classes of agricultural labourers, and particularly poorer workers, were in need of accessible vocational instruction to learn about the best systems of cultivation.[75] Examples such as Denmark, where folk schools had ensured progressive education in rural areas and thus contributed to agricultural modernization, were seen as models. There was a firm belief that vocational education—by which experts meant the education of workers in such crafts as pruning, grafting of plans, the use of machinery, animal husbandry, knowledge on wine, and cheese-making—could create a skilled agricultural labour force.

By redefining the future of agricultural work as technical and vocational, the ILO wanted to align it with other skill-based professions.[76] Turning agricultural labour into a skilled job, experts thought, would retain people in agriculture, help standardize methods and encourage a move towards 'a more rational exercise of agriculture' which included the adoption of new technologies.[77] The main goal was to change the general perception that agricultural work was unskilled work and to maximize the output of human labour. In the words of Taylor, '[T]he old assumption that anyone could make an efficient farm labourer is false in the extreme. […] Farming demands a longer apprenticeship than any manual occupation in existence. It demands this apprenticeship in addition to the best scientific agricultural education which can be had.'[78]

We have seen in previous chapters that in 1920 the International Labour Office had run a number of enquiries on child labour and the condition of women in preparation for the third session of the International Labour Conference. Another such enquiry dealt with the state of rural education in its member countries, leading to a recommendation that governments should promote the improvement of vocational training and make it specifically available to agricultural wage-earners who had less access to schools and scientific literature and were not coveted by government advisers and technical experts.[79] The research carried out at the time also brought to light a lack of data on the state of rural schools and institutions in different countries across the globe, which made further international regulation

---

[74] Report of the Director to the fourth session of the International Labour Conference (Geneva: International Labour Office, 1922), 873.
[75] International Labour Office, Minutes of the third session of the Governing Body, London, 22–25 March 1920. Appendix 7: Agenda of the third session of the International Labour Conference, 58.
[76] For an important reflection on the connections between knowledge, skills, and training, see Raphael Lutz, 'Knowledge, Skills, Craft? The Skilled Worker in West German Industry and the Resilience of Vocational Training, 1970–2000', *German History* 37, no. 3 (2019), 359–73.
[77] Paul Devinat, *Scientific Management in Europe*, Studies and Reports, Series B (Economic Conditions), no. 17 (Geneva: International Labour Office, 1927).
[78] Taylor, *Rural Sociology*, 72–3.
[79] Recommendation concerning the development of technical agricultural education, third session of the International Labour Conference (1921).

difficult.[80] In response to this problem, in 1923 the Mixed Advisory Agricultural Committee launched a more elaborate survey.[81] Much of the preparatory work was done by the ILO's Agricultural Service, and von Bülow was put in charge of the enquiry.[82] Not surprisingly, as the Committee set out to discuss the aim of the study, its members expressed diverging views about the aims and forms of agricultural education: according to Zulueta y Gomis, its primary object was 'to teach [children and young men] to think correctly about agricultural matters, to facilitate an exact notion of agricultural phenomena, [and] to teach them to recognize natural laws which govern agriculture', including arithmetic, physics, chemistry, and biology.[83] The Italian senator and delegate representing the International Institute of Agriculture, Count Edoardo Soderini, held a much more pragmatic view, and cautioned that education needed to be 'practical' as well as accessible to ensure that farmers were sending their children to school.[84] As Soderini pointed out, the well-known resistance to change of farming societies was a major stumbling block: 'There would be a lot to do on this, but it is very difficult. It would be necessary to find means to make the child [of the peasant] go to school, but the first not to send him there is his father!!!'[85] To Soderini, the problem was that rural societies continued to rely on empirical teachings, transferring knowledge and know-how from generation to generation—a cause of economic and social stagnation. The challenge was to impart enough education to benefit production, 'encourage agriculture', and help maintain a balanced rural society.[86] In the eyes of some reformers, too much education was to be avoided as this was potentially risky and would encourage the children of agricultural workers to leave the occupation of their parents.

After much discussion, the aims of the study were defined as to compile a survey of existing agricultural instruction throughout the world, and to compare various methods of instruction to highlight gaps and possible improvements.[87] To gather this data, in the spring of 1924 the Mixed Advisory Agricultural Committee dispatched a questionnaire to ILO member countries (and, through the International Institute of Agriculture, also to the United States and Russia), asking

---

[80] On social knowledge as a prerequisite for labour regulation, see Anson Rabinbach, *The Eclipse of the Utopias of Labor* (New York: Fordham University Press, 2018), 53.

[81] Mixed Advisory Agricultural Committee, first session, appendix: Report submitted by the experts, ILO Archives Geneva, AG 801/7.

[82] Memo Harold Butler, 8 April 1921, ILO Archives Geneva, P 6/6/1.

[83] Mixed Agricultural Commission, first session, 22 August 1923, ILO Archives Geneva, AG 801/10, 21-2.

[84] Report of the Mixed Advisory Agricultural Committee, second session, 5-7 November 1925, ILO Archives Geneva, AG 802/5.

[85] Soderini, 26 June 1922, ILO Archives Geneva, AG 800/3/4.

[86] International Labour Office, *Vocational Education in Agriculture,* Studies and Reports, Series 9 (Geneva: International Labour Office, 1929), 67.

[87] Report of the experts on vocational agricultural instruction submitted to the Mixed Advisory Agricultural Committee, November 1925, ILO Archives Geneva, AG 802/5.

for information on national legislation, institutions, and the various categories of agricultural education ranging from lower-grade schools to evening classes, higher education, and extension programmes. Methods of teaching were also part of the enquiry.[88] Many of the questions concerned elementary education and whether the ruralization of the curriculum included agricultural subjects and 'encouraged children to remain on the land'.[89] This in itself was a controversial issue among both rural sociologists and the staff of the Agricultural Service, who underlined that 'rural people' rejected 'the idea of using the rural school as a means of keeping the children on the farm'.[90]

Thirty-one countries in and outside Europe responded to the questionnaire, and their answers were collated and analysed in an elaborate final report six years after the start of the enquiry.[91] Neither the United States nor the USSR replied, despite having been invited to do so.[92] Some countries revealed detailed information on institutions, numbers of pupils, and courses offered. Other answers were much shorter and less informative. All, however, highlighted that only a 'mere fraction' of the agricultural population received formal agricultural training, which in the eyes of the ILO meant that they had no 'real knowledge' of their occupation.[93] Seen through the lens of labour reformers, the absence of education resulted in rural communities that were not only poor, but also 'shy', 'suspicious', 'diffident' in nature, and 'deficient in general culture'.[94] This state of affairs, together with other problems such as the absence of adequate housing, infrastructure, and health provisions, was producing a socially, politically, and economically inferior agricultural class that was vulnerable to change and economic crisis.[95] But there were also economic considerations: lack of education led to inefficient work, high labour costs for the farmers—which was the object of another study carried out around the same time—and generally sub-standard productivity on farms.[96]

The ILO study on agricultural education did not provide direct policy recommendations, but the conclusions of the enquiry were clear: the aim of agricultural

---

[88] Report of the experts on vocational agricultural instruction submitted to the Mixed Advisory Agricultural Committee, November 1925, ILO Archives Geneva, AG 802.
[89] Mixed Advisory Agricultural Committee, first session. Appendix: Report submitted by the experts including questionnaire, section B. ILO Archives Geneva, AG 801/7.
[90] Taylor, *Rural Sociology*, 285. For an American survey on this question, see A. S. Jensen, 'Rural Opinion of Educational Philosophy', *Journal of Rural Education* (November 1925).
[91] International Labour Office, 'Vocational Education'.
[92] ILO, 'Vocational Education'. The study contains an overview of vocational agricultural education in twenty-nine countries across the globe, covering North, East, South and West European countries, as well as Canada, South Africa, Australia, Argentina, Chile, Cuba, Haiti, British India, China, and Japan.
[93] ILO, 'Vocational Education', 38.
[94] ILO, 'Vocational Education', 30. On the general acceptance of such prejudice, see also Jim Handy, '"Almost Idiotic Wretchedness": A Long History of Blaming Peasants', *Journal of Peasant Studies* 36, no. 2 (2009), 325–44.
[95] ILO, 'Vocational Education', 45.
[96] International Labour Office, *The Relation of Labour Cost to Total Costs of Production in Agriculture* (Geneva: International Labour Office, 1926).

education should be to professionalize farming and to make the most of the land. This would also benefit industrial populations, as the latter depended on 'having cultivation done by educated people who, by increasing the yield of the land, decrease the price of its product'. In the absence of formal educational facilities and services, one way to achieve a minimal dissemination of technical knowledge, in the eyes of the experts of the Mixed Advisory Agricultural Committee, was the use of rural cinema for propaganda. Following a proposition by the Italian members of the Committee, the international institute for cinematographic education was tasked with writing a memorandum on the possibilities of using film to teach agricultural workers about improved cultivation and production, the prevention of accidents, and the appropriate use of leisure time.[97]

This approach to educating rural people revealed the power dynamics between well-meaning but patronizing experts and government representatives who ruled the discussion in the Committee on the one hand and, on the other, the much weaker voice of the workers. Creating an efficient agricultural sector whilst preserving a clear distinction between rural and urban life was at the heart of the ILO's considerations. As a secondary benefit, the ILO claimed, the popularization of vocational education among agricultural workers would improve their professional skills and represent the best means 'to raise their social level', thereby uplifting farmworkers as a group through a new appreciation of their role.[98] The combined aims of economic productivity and social uplifting were a leitmotif of the ILO's rhetoric and would continue to characterize much of its research and legislative efforts.

Scientific Management of Agricultural Labour

The central role of productivity in the ILO's conceptualization of social improvement also became apparent in its later enquiries, which sought to apply new theories and practices of scientific management to agriculture along Taylorist lines. From the mid-1920s onwards, both the International Labour Office and the International Institute of Agriculture manifested an interest in the possibilities of a 'scientific organization' of farm work and the improvement of work efficiency as well as work ethic.[99] The 'uneconomic use' and general 'waste' of labour in

---

[97] Report of the Mixed Advisory Agricultural Committee, fourth session, Rome, November 1929, ILO Archives Geneva, AG 804/1, 7.

[98] Report of the International Labour Office on agricultural vocational training, undated and unsigned, 1927, ILO Archives Geneva, AG 803/1/2.

[99] The following paragraphs draw on Amalia Ribi Forclaz and Carolyn Taratko, 'Experimenting with Scientific Management: New Approaches to Agricultural Labour in the Twentieth Century', in Liesbeth van de Grift, Dietmar Müller, and Corinna Unger, eds, *Living with the Land: Rural and Agricultural Actors in Twentieth-Century Europe: A Handbook* (Berlin: De Gruyter, 2022), 205–25; Deborah Fitzgerald, *Every Farm a Factory: The Industrial Ideal in American Agriculture* (New Haven,

agriculture was increasingly appearing as an obstacle to progress. This was a time when scientific management-related congresses and conferences flourished, and a new field concerned with the 'rationalization of farm labour' emerged, seeking to combine economic and social agendas.[100] Agricultural experts and particularly agricultural economists in the United States and Europe increasingly refused to accept at face value the natural limits to agricultural work imposed by climate and fatigue and preferred to view it as a missed opportunity to improve work processes by implementing low-cost fixes, borrowed from Taylorist management practices in the industry.[101] The belief was that instead of blindly following traditional habits and inherited customs, a better planning of the working day and organization of the farm and its labourer would shorten work time and increase output.

Like its more familiar applications to industrial contexts, the application of scientific management to agricultural labour was seen by the ILO as a way not only to stimulate productivity, but also to close a widening gap between industrial and agricultural development and to turn the countryside into a more uniform entity that would be manageable, predictable, socially stable and productive, in spite of local and climatic variations and recurring economic crises.[102] Thanks to the research work of its Agricultural Service, the ILO was aware of scientific management studies carried out in Europe after the mid-1920s.[103] One of the first and best known ones were the experimental farms in Pommritz, where German agricultural experts experimented with logistical arrangements on the farm, cultivation practices, but also ways of remuneration that would incite workers to seek bigger outputs.[104] Similar research was carried out at the Polish Institute of Scientific Management in Warsaw. There Karol Adamiecki sought ways to improve the planning of agricultural labour and minimize the unpredictable impact of non-human factors such as seasonal change, weather conditions, and

---

CT and London: Yale University Press, 2003); Juri Auderset, 'Manufacturing Agricultural Working Knowledge: The Scientific Study of Agricultural Work in Industrial Europe, 1920s–60s', *Rural History* 32, no. 2 (October 2021), 233–48.

[100] This topic remains understudied even in today's booming new labour history. For an exception and an important study of the 'nascent industrial ideal' in the United States' agriculture in the 1920s, see Fitzgerald, *Every Farm a Factory*. See also Auderset, 'Manufacturing Agricultural Working Knowledge'; Ribi Forclaz and Taratko, 'Experimenting with Scientific Management'.

[101] Devinat, 'Scientific Management in Europe'; Wilhelm Seedorf, *Die Vervollkommnung der Landarbeit und die bessere Ausbildung der Landarbeiter unter besonderer Berücksichtigung des Taylor-Systems* (Berlin: Deutsche Landbuchhandlung, 1919). On the ILO's affinities with Taylorist ideas, see Thomas Cayet, 'Travailler à la marge: le Bureau International du Travail et l'organisation scientifique du travail (1923–1933)', *Le Mouvement social* 3, no. 228 (2009), 39–56.

[102] Charles Maier, 'Between Taylorism and Technocracy: European Ideologies and the Vision of Industrial Productivity in the 1920s', *Journal of Contemporary History* 5, no. 2 (1970), 27–61.

[103] For an overview, see Institut International d'Agriculture, *L'organisation scientifique du travail agricole en Europe* (Rome: Imprimerie de la Chambre des Députés Charles Colombo, 1931).

[104] International Labour Office, 'The Science of Farm Labour: Scientific Management and German Agriculture', *International Labour Review* 15, no. 3 (1927), 379–413; Georg Derlitzki, 'Die Landarbeitsforschung, dargestellt an den Arbeiten der Versuchsanstalt für Landarbeitslehre Pommritz', in Georg Derlitzki, ed., *Berichte über Landarbeit* (Stuttgart, 1927).

animal behaviour.¹⁰⁵ In Britain, research was carried out at the National Institute of Industrial Psychology under the leadership of Walter Dunlop, who ran a series of studies on ways to improve the output of fruit-pickers on an experimental farm in Kent.¹⁰⁶ More comprehensive experiments in farm labour management were also carried out in France by Adolphe Javal, a professor of medicine and biochemist turned farmer who undertook steps to align agricultural work on his farm 'as far as possible to industrial formulae and scientific methods' in a bid to lower labour costs and halt rural exodus.¹⁰⁷

In 1926, the ILO launched its own enquiry on Taylorism in agriculture, hoping to collect information from member governments on their own experiences of new applications of scientific management. Regrettably, the records regarding this enquiry were destroyed in the 1970s, but it appears that information was collected in Austria, Belgium, France, Great Britain, Hungary, Italy, Poland, Spain, and the United States. What this initiative shows, however, is that for a short while at least, scientific management was seen as a promising way to improve farmwork and stabilize the labour supply by diminishing fatigue and minimizing waste of labour through a more efficient use of tools and better planning of the day. Related measures about better housing and hygiene such as the installations of a toilet and showers, were adopted to avoid disease, sickness, and loss of human labour and livestock. All these improvements, it was thought, would not only boost agricultural productivity but also keep the workers committed to stay and unlikely to strike, a frequent occurrence during harvest times.¹⁰⁸

What all these efforts had in common was the claim that scientific management represented the magic solution to problems of productivity as well as social welfare. A principal concern of the ILO was to make up for an existing gap in social protection between agricultural and industrial workers, and to decrease fatigue by limiting the duration of the working day. Adapting conditions in agriculture to an industrial ideal was also motivated by a wish to rationalize and discipline agricultural labour and its natural rhythm, and to render it more efficient, and avoid unnecessary costs. In the eyes of the ILO, the two-fold goal of social improvement and profitable rationalization was not contradictory (although trade unions saw things differently). As a memorandum of the Mixed Advisory Agricultural Committee revealed, 'a better return on human labour' was at the heart of most of the Committee's work and agricultural investigations, whether

---

¹⁰⁵ Institut International d'Agriculture, *L'organisation scientifique du travail*, 34; Ribi Forclaz and Taratko, 'Experimenting with Scientific Management'.

¹⁰⁶ Walter Dunlop, *An Investigation of Certain Processes and Conditions on Farms* (London: National Institute of Industrial Psychology, 1927); Walter Dunlop, 'Labour Efficiency Investigations in English Farming', *International Labour Review* 21, no. 5 (1930), 700–10.

¹⁰⁷ Adolphe Javal, *La Confession d'un agriculteur* (Paris: Fayard, 1929). See also Louise Ernestine Howard, *Labour in Agriculture: An International Survey* (Oxford: Oxford University Press, 1935).

¹⁰⁸ On farm labour strikes, see Nicola Verdon, *Working the Land: A History of the Farmworker in England from 1850 to the Present* (London: Palgrave Macmillan, 2017).

they touched on agricultural education, the prevention of illness and accident, rural exodus or questions of working hours, rest periods, and leisure times.[109]

This last concern was very common among farmers and social reformers. As the Czechoslovakian enquiry in 1921 had demonstrated, the question of time and labour management on farms also entailed providing workers with useful and 'judicious' activities during their spare time.[110] For industrial workers, the creation of allotments was seen as means to render their lives 'more pleasurable and more independent of the vicissitudes of industrial life'.[111] For farm labourers, the propositions ranged from giving them access to a garden or plot of land for personal use, to the organization of music or drama societies or the expansion of radios and rural cinemas. A model for this was provided by the American Country Life Movement which promoted a 'constructive use of leisure time' through the organization of activities such as trips, camps, music groups, plays, and games.[112]

Ultimately, however, the ILO's interest in the scientific management of agriculture did not yield more concrete results. An attempt to turn it into an institutionalized field of enquiry in cooperation with the International Management Institute in Geneva was cut short by the economic downturn. The Great Depression and the rise of unemployment led ILO officials to wonder whether industrial rationalization was partly to blame for the economic disaster.[113] Although never directly mentioned, negative press about the coercive soviet policy of agrarian collectivization and the transformation of peasants into workers might also have played a role in the abandonment of rationalization and in the return to the initial question of reducing working hours.[114]

What also transpired from these enquiries was the idea that improvements could only be made if the status quo was transformed, the standard of living improved, the attachment of workers to the land and to their occupation secured, and productivity increased. Change was necessary but the amount and types of changes needed to be carefully monitored. As we have already seen, movements from below such as uprisings, strikes and revolutions were perceived as detrimental to social peace. Specific and targeted intervention such as the spread of vocational education were promising if handled well. But what about those large-scale reforms that were enacted at state level to transform land ownership, improve legislation, and intensify and rationalize cultivation? Could these be conducive to

---

[109] Fifth session of the Mixed Advisory Agricultural Committee, November 1930, ILO Archives Geneva, AG 805.
[110] Report of the Mixed Advisory Agricultural Committee, November 1925, ILO Archives Geneva, AG 802/5. See Chapter 2.
[111] Report of the Mixed Advisory Agricultural Committee, November 1925, ILO Archives Geneva, AG 802/5.
[112] American Country Life Association to the International Commission for the Improvement of Rural Life in Brussels, East Lansing, 21 June 1926, ILO Archives Geneva, AG 1000/14/1.
[113] On the impact of the Depression on the ILO's agricultural work see Chapter 4.
[114] On this, see Ribi Forclaz and Taratko, 'Experimenting with Scientific Management', 214–15.

social progress and stability?[115] This was one of the next questions debated by the Mixed Advisory Agricultural Committee.

Agrarian Reform and Other Controversies

The land redistributions that took place in Poland, Czechoslovakia, Romania, Estonia, Latvia, and Lithuania during and after the war were regarded by ILO officials as one of the major agrarian transformations of the post-war years.[116] Almost everywhere in Eastern and Central Europe, new post-war agrarian legislation had been put in place to divide up large estates, but also to modify the structure of existing peasant holdings by reconsolidating scattered plots.[117] These controversial reforms were driven by agrarian parties and by nationalist ambitions to strengthen the newly emerged nation states and integrate rural minorities, while also promoting new ways of organizing agricultural production, and avert the danger of communist uprisings.[118] Thomas himself showed a strong interest in land reforms when visiting the Baltic states in the 1920s, revealing his fascination with organizational and technological improvements.[119] But he also noted that the impact of these reforms on rural populations was not yet fully understood. The question was of wider relevance, as it ultimately also touched on the deeper issue of the relationship between land ownership and labour. The idea that the people working the land should also own it was becoming a rallying cry across partisan lines: in 1920, and in line with the views of Marxist philosopher Karl Kautsky on the socialization of agriculture, the executive committee of the International Landworkers' Federation had spoken in favour of land redistribution.[120] The democratization of land tenure and the need to improve social mobility and

---

[115] Report of the third session of the Mixed Advisory Agricultural Committee, January 1927, Annex: Questionnaire on agrarian reform, ILO Archives Geneva, AG 803/4.

[116] For a brief overview, see Klaus Richter, 'Post-War Agrarian Economic Policies (East Central Europe)', in Ute Daniel, Peter Gatrell, Oliver Janz, Heather Jones, Jennifer Keene, Alan Kramer, and Bill Nasson, eds, *1914–1918-online. International Encyclopedia of the First World War* (Berlin: Freie Universität Berlin, 2015), https://encyclopedia.1914-1918-online.net/article/post-war_agrarian_economic_policies_east_central_europe; Sarahelen Thompson, 'Agrarian Reform in Eastern Europe Following World War I: Motives and Outcomes', *American Journal of Agricultural Economics* 75, no. 3 (1993), 840–4.

[117] Adam Rose, 'Agricultural Workers and Agrarian Reform in Central Europe, *International Labour Review* 18, no. 3 (September 1928), 308.

[118] Dietmar Müller and Angela Harre, eds, *Transforming Rural Societies. Agrarian Property and Agrarianism in East Central Europe in the Nineteenth and Twentieth centuries* (Innsbruck: Studienverlag, 2011); Helga Schultz and Angela Harre, eds, *Bauerngesellschaften auf dem Weg in die Moderne. Agrarismus in Ostmitteleuropa, 1880 bis 1960* (Wiesbaden: Harrassowitz, 2010).

[119] See Thomas's travel notes about Estonia, Latvia and Lithuania in the late 1920s, in Dorothea Hoethker and Sandrine Kott, eds, *À la rencontre de l'Europe au travail: récits de voyages d'Albert Thomas (1920–1932)* (Sorbonne/Bureau International du Travail, 2015).

[120] Internationale Landarbeiter Föderation, 'Bericht der Internationalen Landarbeiterkonferenz abgehalten am 17–19 August 1920', IISH Archives Amsterdam, 34–7; Karl Kautsky, *Sozialisierung der Landwirtschaft* (Berlin: Otto Elsner, 1919).

the ascent of farmworkers to positions of farm tenants and owners were also discussed by liberal governments such as Britain and the United States.[121]

By 1925, the ILO's Agricultural Service considered that the time was ripe for an assessment of the social and economic effects of land reform policies on the agrarian working class, and the subject became one of the joint areas of research of the Mixed Advisory Agricultural Committee.[122] An enquiry was launched to collect information on agrarian reforms in Eastern and Central Europe. This mirrored a general interest in these geographical spaces, which held an ambiguous place in the minds of experts: some saw them as peripheral, impoverished cradles of potential social unrest; others, as centres of modernity and rural transformation that also fulfilled a strategic and territorial role between Russia and the West.[123] When it came to planning the enquiry, the International Institute of Agriculture did most of the preparatory work. In 1925, it presented the International Labour Office in 1925 with a lengthy draft questionnaire of twenty-nine pages that included numerous questions about the origins of and rationale for land redistribution, statistical information about people engaged in agriculture, the outcomes of the reforms with regard to the creation of new farm types, and the impact on former landowners and agricultural workers.[124]

But the enquiry was off to a bad start. It irritated French expert Jules Gautier, who pointed out that analysing agrarian reforms from a scientific and statistical perspective alone would do nothing but hide their wide-reaching, social, economic, but also psychological impact on rural people's lives.[125] The draft questionnaire was also criticized by officials within the ILO for creating the dangerous impression that the Organization was in favor of agrarian reforms rather than merely seeking information on the subject.[126] Discussions with the International institute of Agriculture also revealed its reluctance to incorporate more of the ILO's social concerns into the enquiry.[127] In fact, relations between the two organizations were continually problematic and there were considerable tensions. This was not

---

[121] On how hired labourers could rise to land ownership, see W. J. Spillman, 'The Agricultural Ladder', *The American Economic Review* 9, no. 1 (1919), 170–9. On plans for land reform in pre-war Britain, see Ian Packer, *Lloyd George, Liberalism and the Land: The Land Issue and Party Politics in England, 1906–1914* (New York: Boydell and Brewer, 2001).
[122] On the reasons why the ILO felt mandated to review the question of agrarian reform, see note Maurette to Thomas, ILO Archives Geneva, AG 802/4.
[123] Alan Dingsdale, *Mapping Modernities: Geographies of Central and Eastern Europe, 1920–2000* (London: Routledge, 2002); Katherine Lebow, Małgorzata Mazurek, and Joanna Wawrzyniak, 'Making Modern Social Science: The Global Imagination in East Central and Southeastern Europe after Versailles', *Contemporary European History* 28, no. 2 (May 2019), 137–42, 138, 139.
[124] Questionnaire on agrarian reform prepared by the International Institute of Agriculture, ILO Archives Geneva, AG 100/0/0.
[125] Jules Gautier, Note pour Monsieur Arthur Fontaine (undated, December 1925), ILO Archives Geneva, AG 100/0/0.
[126] Letter, Thomas to Fontaine, 12 January 1926, ILO Archives Geneva, AG 100/0/0.
[127] Letter, Arthur Fontaine to Albert Thomas, Paris, 11 December 1925, ILO Archives Geneva, AG 100/0/0.

helped by the fact that the International Institute of Agriculture, which was seeing a surge of interest from the fascist government since the mid-1920s, was increasingly putting forward the social and economic policies of the Italian government in the field of agriculture. Matthaei was also annoyed with the Institute's unreliable communication and she considered it a 'gross breach of faith' that the latter was encroaching on the ILO's mandate by discussing issues such as working hours and wages in agriculture, despite agreements that each organization would keep to its specific territory.[128] Communication was bad, and Albert Thomas sarcastically noted that the Institute's recently appointed director Giuseppe De Michelis had a tendency to 'pretend to be the sole scientific representative of agriculture, and the only one that needed to be consulted'.[129] De Michelis was a Swiss-educated Italian diplomat who represented the Italian government in the ILO between 1921 and 1935, and also held important functions within the League of Nations and as a director of the International Institute of Agriculture from 1925 onwards. He embodied the paradoxes of fascist internationalism: its enthusiasm for international bureaucracies and planning, and its close engagement with liberal internationalism, not least to promote and project the Italian regime's policies globally.[130]

As no common ground could be found about which questions should be included or left out, the ILO decided to undertake its own research on agrarian reform in a limited number of countries including Czechoslovakia, Estonia, Latvia, Romania, and Japan.[131] Russia was excluded because of its special character: those in charge of selecting the case studies reasoned that the transformations in land use were the result of a violent and chaotic communist revolution and not planned by the state.[132] The reality was also that the ILO lacked information on Russia and probably preferred to side-step this thorny issue. Unfortunately, like many other agriculture-related materials, the archival records of these studies were later destroyed. All we have left are the published accounts in the *International Labour Review*.[133]

---

[128] Note Matthaei 14 April 1927, ILO Archives Geneva, AG 800. See also the lengthy discussions about how to avoid encroachment in the Mixed Advisory Agricultural Committee.

[129] Note 'personelle tout à fait confidentielle', Albert Thomas to Maurette, undated, ILO Archives Geneva, AG 800.

[130] On De Michelis see Jens Steffek, 'Fascist Internationalism', *Millennium: Journal of International Studies*, 44, no. 1 (2015), 3–22. On the role fascist internationalism in agricultural cooperation, see also Chapter 5.

[131] Collection of Information on Agrarian Reform in Czechoslovakia, 1924. ILO Archives Geneva, AG 100/101/17 The following files were unfortunately destroyed in 1971: Agrarian Reform Hungary, ILO Archives Geneva, AG 100/101/31; Agrarian reform Japan 1925, ILO Archives Geneva, AG 100/101/35; Agrarian reform Poland 1925, ILO Archives Geneva, AG 100/101/50.

[132] On this, see Lars T. Lih, *Bread and Authority in Russia 1914–1921* (Berkeley: University of California Press, 1990). Also, Katja Bruisch, 'Knowledge and Power in the Making of the Soviet Village', in Ribi Forclaz and van de Grift, eds, *Governing the Rural in Interwar Europe* (London: Routledge, 2018).

[133] [No author], 'New Agrarian Legislation in Central Europe', *International Labour Review* 6, no. 3 (September 1922); [No author], 'Social Aspects of Land Reform in Czechoslovakia', *International Labour Review* 12, nos. 1 and 2 (July and August 1925); Martna Mihkel 'Social Aspects of Land Reform in Estonia', *International Labour Review* 13, no. 1 (January 1926); F. W. v. Bülow, 'Social Aspects of Agrarian Reform in Latvia', *International Labour Review* 13, no. 3 (September 1928).

The resulting accounts were not the tales of empowerment and upward mobility that one might expect: from the reports it seemed that agricultural workers formerly employed on large estates in Central Europe had, in contrast to small peasants, not benefitted from the reform and were at risk of becoming an unemployed and impoverished rural proletariat.[134] This conclusion strengthened the ILO's position that social change should happen through the standardization of labour legislation and through 'technical improvements' such as education, better housing, and cooperative and professional organization rather than through large-scale land reforms that endangered the social equilibrium.

As we have seen, the joint enquiries of the International Labour Office and the International Institute of Agriculture in the second half of the 1920s shared a general concern with charting and understanding rural transformations such as land reform and rural–urban migration, limiting and controlling the alleged disintegration of rural societies, as well as stabilizing relations between town and countryside. In the minds of agricultural experts and international officials, such knowledge was needed to identify possible areas of social reform that would help stabilize the perceived state of flux of agricultural societies. The collection and collation of information was thus regarded as a first step towards proposing solutions to the rural problem. More than an actual vision of rural 'modernization', what social reformers and ILO experts proposed were improvements such as the standardization of agricultural education or the dissemination of home economics knowledge, without upsetting the existing socio-economic structures. These joint studies also reinforced the perceived differences between rural and urban worlds, and the wish that they should remain separate. The paradox of this ambiguous approach came to the fore in the 1930s, when the question of worktime in agriculture was put back on the table.

Cultivating Fields of Progress: Agriculture and the International Labour Organization, 1920s–1950s. Amalia Ribi Forclaz, Oxford University Press. © Amalia Ribi Forclaz 2025. DOI: 10.1093/9780191945014.003.0004

---

[134] Rose, 'Agricultural Workers', 336.

4
Navigating the Crisis and Its Repercussions

> 'Those who are living in the hope that, when the intensity of the present depression is weakened, we shall quietly slip back again to the industrial and social alignments we knew before 1914, must be blind to the forces which the world upheaval has let loose [...]. The landworkers [...] have moved away from their old isolation and will not be content to remain outside the current of economic and social movements. They have made their contacts, national and international.'
>
> Joseph Duncan, 'A New Policy for Agricultural Labour', *International Labour Review* 25, no. 2 (February 1932).

In the early 1930s, international debates about agriculture became engulfed in a rhetoric of depression and crisis. Prices of agricultural commodities collapsed, farm incomes fell, and conditions in agriculture worsened both globally and locally.[1] By 1931 the Great Depression was affecting the living conditions of agrarian producers and labourers worldwide, leading to increasing debt, poverty, and political polarization among rural populations and paving the way for a new wave of social unrest and strikes.[2] Many governments reacted by intensifying interventionist economic policies, stepping up social and technological reforms, and by expanding protectionist measures.[3] Observers noted anxiously that the economic

---

[1] Gérard Béaur and Francesco Chiapparino, eds, *Agriculture and the Great Depression: The Rural Crisis of the 1930s in Europe and the Americas* (London: Routledge, 2023); Jakob B. Madsen, 'Agricultural Crises and the International Transmission of the Great Depression', *The Journal of Economic History* 61, no. 2, (2001), 327–65; Giovanni Federico, *Feeding the World: An Economic History of Agriculture, 1800–2000* (Princeton: Princeton University Press, 2005), 22–3.

[2] On specific countries, see also Niccolò Mignemi, *Nel regno della fame. Il mondo contadino italiano fra gli anni Trenta e gli anni Cinquanta* (Rome: Aracne, 2010); Robert O. Paxton, *French Peasant Fascism: Henry Dorgères's Greenshirts and the Crises of French Agriculture, 1929–1939* (New York, Oxford: Oxford University Press, 1997); Paul Brassley, 'British Farming Between the Wars', in Paul Brassley, Jeremy Burchardt, and Lynne Thompson, eds, *The English Countryside between the Wars: Regeneration Or Decline?* (Woodbridge: Boydell & Brewer, 2006).

[3] Adam Tooze, *The Deluge: The Great War and the Remaking of Global Order* (London, New York: Allen Lane, 2014); Lourenzo Fernandez-Prieto, Juan Pan-Montojo, and Miguel Cabo, eds, *Agriculture in the Age of Fascism: Authoritarian Technocracy and Rural Modernization, 1922–1945*, series *Rural History in Europe* 13 (Turnhout: Brepols, 2014).

crisis was showing no signs of abating and that it posed a considerable threat to political stability and social peace.[4]

The Great Depression also affected the research and policy agenda of international institutions. Proliferating nationalist economic policies and mounting tensions in international relations were endangering diplomatic relations and putting a damper on the governments' belief in the capacity of international organizations to secure peace and prosperity. As the League's institutions started to lose the confidence of both governments and activists, the imperial logic that had shaped, dictated, and limited much of the work of international institutions since 1920 was also losing momentum.[5] But contrary to these trends, as the history of the League of Nations demonstrates, economic and social cooperation, international statistical investigations, and exchange of expertise did not diminish but rather increased and brought renewed attention to rural problems that had been discussed in the early 1920s.[6] In the pages that follow, the chapter will look at how the economic crisis renewed the ILO's focus on agricultural and rural economies and brought back to the table the controversial question of working hours, which had been abandoned in the early 1920s. As the chapter argues, this was a time of heightened internationalist awareness of the interconnectedness of social and economic questions as well as of the interdependence of industrial (urban) and agricultural (rural) economies.

A case in point is the ILO's research work on rural exodus. Throughout the 1920s, both the International Institute of Agriculture and the ILO had touched on this subject in their common meetings, agreeing to carry out further enquiries under joint responsibility. The members of the Mixed Advisory Agricultural Committee thought that this question was important from a social and economic point of view, but that both the phenomenon and the factors feeding it were only poorly understood. In September 1930 the Agricultural Service was tasked with launching a multi-country study on the factors of rural exodus.[7] The aim was to

---

[4] Jules Alquier, *L'agriculture dans l'évolution de la crise Mondiale* (Paris: Alcan, 1933); Michel Augé-Laribé, 'La crise agricole et ses effets sur la classe paysanne en France', *Revue internationale d'agriculture* (1931), 174–80.

[5] Susan Pedersen, *The Guardians: The League of Nations and the Crisis of Empire* (Oxford: Oxford University Press, 2015); Mark Mazower, *No Enchanted Palace: The End of Empire and the Ideological Origins of the United Nations* (Princeton, NJ: Princeton University Press, 2009).

[6] Patricia Clavin, *Securing the World Economy: The Reinvention of the League of Nations, 1920–1946* (Oxford: Oxford University Press, 2013); Madeleine Lynch Dungy, 'The Global Agricultural Crisis and British Diplomacy in the League of Nations in 1931', *The Agricultural History Review* 65, no. 2 (2017), 297–319; Olivier Feiertag, 'Humaniser la crise économique (1929–1934): l'expertise du BIT dans la crise de mondialisation des années 1930', in Ayla Aglan, Olivier Feiertag, and Dzovinar Kévonian, eds, *Humaniser le travail. Régimes économiques, régimes politiques et organisation internationale du travail (1929–1969)* (Brussels: Peter Lang, 2011), 19–38. Quinn Slobodian, *Globalists: The End of Empire and the Birth of Neoliberalism* (Cambridge, MA: Harvard University Press, 2018), Chapter 2.

[7] Note Matthaei to Maurette, 5 September 1930, ILO Archives Geneva, AG 100/109/02.

carry out on-the-spot investigations in countries where rural exodus was either 'typical' or 'pathological', and to publish the results as a series of monographs that would offer a detailed analysis of each specific situation.[8] The original plan was to start with enquiries in France, Germany, and Czechoslovakia, where Gorni and von Bülow undertook preliminary visits.[9] French and German authorities appeared less than thrilled at the prospect of having an ILO expert inspect their countryside and declared that they would be 'unable to assist'. German authorities, in particular, replied with a 'courteous, but extremely firm' refusal. Although sympathetic to the aims of the study, they felt singled out and asked that the selection of the countries be discussed within the Governing Body.[10] As von Bülow put it, the thought of a 'monograph' and 'experts' had 'frightened' the government.[11]

The refusal brought to light the limits of the ILO's autonomy in collecting information, and its reliance on government approval. Finally, after much delay, a personal intervention by Thomas coaxed Germany into accepting the enquiry, and von Bülow was given the green light in May 1931, at a time of great political change. The visit's outlook was much wider than the original focus on rural exodus. In fact, it seemed that the exodus was a pretext to gain an appreciation of the more general economic and social conditions of agricultural labour in Germany. Together with an expert from the International Institute of Agriculture, von Bülow spent almost a month visiting the country, inspecting placement agencies and labour exchanges in Berlin, and meeting with local government representatives, administrators of the Central Labour Exchange, rural engineering services, as well as industrial and agricultural employers' associations and agricultural workers' unions.[12]

The two experts travelled widely across the countryside, inspecting old and new estates, settlements, and types of rural housing. Strikingly, the insights gained did not agree with the theoretical and general ideas on rural exodus mentioned earlier. Rather, von Bülow came away with the impression that more than a voluntary exodus of workers, the problem in Eastern Germany and the region bordering Poland was that people were driven out of agriculture ('*Landverdrängung*') because of the rationalization and reduction of labour on the big estates and of the general economic changes induced by the economic crisis. As von Bülow underlined, agricultural workers were not so much attracted to city life as 'to

---

[8] Report of the Mixed Advisory Agricultural Committee, fourth session, November 1929, Rome, ILO Archives Geneva, AG 804/1.
[9] Copy of Note to research division and Agricultural Service, signed HBB, 3 September 1930, ILO Archives Geneva, AG 100/109/02.
[10] Copy of Note to research division and Agricultural Service, signed HBB, 3 September 1930, ILO Archives Geneva, AG 100/109/02.
[11] Note on telephonic conversation between Mr von Bülow and Miss Matthaei, 29 July 1930, ILO Archives Geneva, AG 100/109/02.
[12] von Bülow, Report on study journey on rural exodus in Germany, 3–27 May 1931, ILO Archives Geneva, AG 100/109/02. von Bülow was accompanied on this trip by Dr Böker from the International Institute of Agriculture.

some extent forced to emigrate.'[13] In the state of Saxony, where von Bülow travelled next, the situation was different: industrial growth in the province had pulled people out of agricultural labour, but in times of economic crisis the unemployed tended to return to farm work. Agricultural employers, however, complained about the fluctuations and instabilities of labour availability, especially with regard to female workers who would quit as soon as their husbands found employment in the industry.[14]

The German study tour brought home more forcefully than the usual surveys how regional variations required different solutions, thereby indirectly putting a question mark on the ILO's normative work. It also showed the quick evolution of the problem and the learning effect it had on the ILO. Already by 1932, in the midst of the world depression, the ILO's understanding of the exodus was much more nuanced, and interpretations would further evolve in the mid-1930s. Whereas the published monograph on Germany spoke of the 'economic political and social disadvantages' of rural migration for the agricultural sector and of its 'detrimental' effects on the rural community, a second investigation carried out by von Bülow in Czechoslovakia and published two years later came to a different conclusion. There, the exodus was closely linked to post-war land reform and the building of a new nation state. The study on Czechoslovakia underlined that such exodus was both a result of economic progress and a condition for material development.[15] This conclusion foreshadowed a post-war vision of European agriculture in which the rural exodus would be seen as the natural and necessary outcome of mechanization and modernization.

Divided Perspectives

By the summer of 1931, rural issues were at the forefront of many international gatherings. In the spring, the League's Economic Committee circulated a draft report on the agricultural crisis, analysing the reasons for the crisis which it attributed to 'a disturbance of the balance between production and consumption'.[16] According to agricultural experts, the disturbance was due to a panoply of factors, including upheavals in world trade and monetary fluctuations after the

---

[13] von Bülow, Report on study journey on rural exodus in Germany, 3–27 May 1931, 4, ILO Archives Geneva, AG 100/109/02.
[14] von Bülow, Report on study journey on rural exodus in Germany, 3–27 May 1931, 5, ILO Archives Geneva, AG 100/109/02.
[15] International Labour Office and International Institute of Agriculture, *Studies on Movements of Agricultural Population: I, The Rural Exodus in Germany* (Geneva: International Labour Office, 1933); International Labour Office and International Institute of Agriculture, *Studies on Movements of Agricultural Population: II, The Rural Exodus in Czechoslovakia* (Geneva: International Labour Office, 1935).
[16] League of Nations Economic Committee, Agricultural Crisis, Geneva 1931. League of Nations Archives, R2805-10D-26670-2016.

First World War, followed by a period of overproduction and surpluses that was influenced by changes in consumption and technological improvements which in turn created problems of pricing and debt, and ultimately also fostered competition and inequalities between farming systems.[17] A few months later, the League of Nation's Health Organization organized the first of a series of rural hygiene conferences to which the Agricultural Service contributed a report on rural housing and on child labour in agriculture in European countries.[18] While the League focused on trade issues and on rural welfare more generally, the social and economic impact of the economic crisis on farmers and farmworkers and the issue of international agricultural cooperation were at the heart of many other international gatherings. Rural economists such as the French Michel Augé-Laribé, the American Asher Hobson, and the Australian Frank McDougall spoke at a proliferating number of agricultural conferences about the dangers of protectionist policies and insisted on the necessity of cooperation and regulation.[19] The International Institute of Agriculture, for example, supplemented its usual statistical output with a series of annual summaries on economic tendencies in agriculture, highlighting a 'considerable aggravation' of the Depression and its impact on the prices of agricultural products, which had continued to decline.[20] International agricultural trade unions too were demanding greater attention to some of the questions that had been deemed not ripe for discussion in the early 1920s, including the issues of wages and excessive worktime.

Moreover, new organizations emerged, mobilizing and generating new types of expertise and agendas, such as the Associated Country Women of the World and the International Conference of Agricultural Economists. The two organizations were both created in the late 1920s and went on to hold annual conferences that put agriculture centre stage. The Associated Country Women of the World viewed itself as the 'champion of a neglected and disregarded section of the world's population' and offered rural women a new international platform to highlight their roles and views.[21] The organization was led by middle- and upper-class women who were involved in the Women's Institute, a movement

---

[17] League of Nations Economic Committee, Agricultural Crisis, Geneva 1931. League of Nations Archives, R2805-10D-26670-2016.

[18] ILO Archives Geneva, AG 1000/44/1. Iris Borowy, *Coming to Terms With World Health: The League of Nations Health Organization, 1921–1946* (Frankfurt am Main: Peter Lang, 2009), 329–32.

[19] See file Augé-Laribé in the Archives of the Graduate Institute Geneva 130/1.

[20] International Institute of Agriculture, *The Agricultural Situation in 1929–30* (Rome, 1931); International Institute of Agriculture, *The Agricultural Situation in 1930–31* (Rome, 1932).

[21] See leaflet 'The Associated Country Women of the World: A Noble Endeavour – Achievement and Further Ambitions', undated, ACWW Archives, London. For a history of the ACWW and its leader, see Linda M. Ambrose, *A Great Rural Sisterhood: Madge Robertson Watt and the ACWW* (Toronto: University of Toronto Press, 2015). Amalia Ribi Forclaz, 'Guardians of the Countryside: The Associated Countrywomen of the World (ACWW) and International Rural Governance in the interwar years', in Ribi Forclaz and van de Grift, eds, *Governing the Rural in Interwar Europe* (London: Routledge, 2018).

created to revitalize rural communities and give women a more prominent place in village economy and society. A minority of ACWW members were active farmers and farmer's wives, or married to big landowners in the dominions and colonies.[22] Notably, unlike trade unions, the organization did not prioritize the specific and technical aspects of labour and social rights: rather, its conferences articulated broader socio-economic and cultural ideas of rurality, rural living, and its preservation, especially in view of increasing economic hardship.[23]

The International Conference of Agricultural Economists, on the other hand, showcased the growing interest, specialization and international scientific cooperation in the field of agricultural economics. Founded in England by British agronomist Leonard Elmhirst together with a group of British and American colleagues, the new association had as its aim the development of agricultural economics as a science and the promotion of the practical application of the results of economic investigations in order to improve the economic and social conditions of rural life.[24] From 1929 it met every two years to exchange on economic and social problems in agriculture. Its discussions ranged from land tenure and farm management and marketing to the economic situation in European agriculture and the causes of the international depression.[25]

The ILO's Louise Matthaei was in correspondence with both organizations, whose meetings she regularly attended, and took inspiration from their proceedings. Already in late 1930, Matthaei had begun to make plans for an international study of how the economic downturn might affect agricultural workers. In view of a meeting of the Mixed Advisory Agricultural Committee, hastily convoked in Geneva in December of that year, Thomas tasked her with preparing documentation on the impact of the 'world agricultural crisis' on rural workers.[26] For Matthaei, this was an opportunity to put the spotlight back on agricultural workers, a focus which had dwindled since the ILO's early work in 1921. Matthaei ambitioned to run an international enquiry and to collect as much primary evidence as possible on workers' social and economic conditions. She compiled a questionnaire for member governments on the impacts of the economic crisis on agricultural wages, living standards, children's education, the use of family labour,

---

[22] 'Biographies of Women Who Went to Stockholm', ACWW Archives, London.
[23] See conference of the Associated Country Women of the World in London, 27 May 1932, on 'Rural Women's Organization and the Agricultural Crisis'. See also Liaison Committee on Rural Women's and Homemakers' Organisations, *What the Country Women of the World Are Doing* (London: Chapman and Hall, 1932). League of Nations Archives, R5669-50-26016-568.
[24] John Ross Raeburn and Owen J. Jones, *The History of the International Association of Agricultural Economists: Towards Rural Welfare World Wide* (Aldershot and Brookfield: Dartmouth Publishing Company Ltd, 1990). I thank Hannah Tyler for pointing me to this history. Hannah Tyler, 'In Numbers We Trust? A History of the US Department of Agriculture and Its Agricultural Surveys during the 1920s', *Histoire & Mesure* 48 (2023), 39–46.
[25] Proceedings of the International Conference of Agricultural Economists, ILO Archives Geneva, 1000/47/1.
[26] Circular letter Thomas, 20 November 1930. ILO Archives Geneva, AG 805/0.

unemployment, and relief measures.[27] In an accompanying note, she stressed 'the extreme gravity' of the Depression and the 'menace it constitutes to agricultural life and in particular to the life of the workers'. She also presaged that 'the situation show[ed] no signs of improvement' and emphatically argued that in such circumstances it was 'the obvious function of the Office to ascertain the exact extent of the evil'.[28] But internally, there was no support for an international enquiry. The director of the ILO's research division, Fernand Maurette, dismissed (somewhat patronizingly) Matthaei's projected study as too formal, too extensive, and requiring too much input that governments would be unlikely to provide. Maurette sarcastically commented that it was unrealistic, in the current climate, to demand information 'on something other than numbers or laws, i.e. on views and ideas that require government officials to put their brains to work a bit'.[29] He also questioned the use of the term 'crisis', arguing that it was too soon to tell.[30] In some way this attitude was symptomatic of the treatment of agriculture at the ILO: the primary sector was deemed too important to be left aside, but not important enough to fully invest the Organization's resources. Also, there was a persistent concern amongst the higher echelons that agricultural issues might become overly political.

Following Maurette's intervention, Matthaei's draft was turned into a small memorandum and submitted for discussion to the experts of the Mixed Advisory Agricultural Committee.[31] In December 1930 the six Committee members met with eleven ad hoc experts to discuss the issue.[32] Many of the attendees, including Joseph Duncan, Jules Gautier, the Marquis de Vogüé, Georg Schmidt and Ferdinand Klindera, had been previously involved in these meetings. But there were also newcomers such as Frank McDougall, who, during the interwar years, would acquire some fame in the new nutrition debate of the League of Nations. Also present was the Swiss agronomist Ernst Laur, whom Thomas had flattered into accepting an invitation despite the fact that the former had spent a decade criticizing the ILO for its agricultural work.

---

[27] Draft questionnaire on 'The Effects of the Agricultural Crisis on Agricultural Labour', December 1930, ILO Archives Geneva, AG 805/0, 8. Annexed Memorandum on the effect of the agricultural crisis on agricultural labour.

[28] L. E. Matthaei, 'Note sur la crise agricole mondiale et ses remèdes', 8 December 1930, ILO Archives Geneva, AG 805/0.

[29] Note Maurette to Matthaei, 28 October 1930, ILO Archives Geneva, AG 805.

[30] 'Memorandum on the effect of the agricultural crisis on agricultural labour', 8 December 1930, ILO Archives Geneva, AG 805/0.

[31] It was later published as Louise Ernestine Matthaei, 'Some Effects of the Agricultural Depression on Agricultural Labour', *International Labour Review* 23, no. 4 (April 1931). It should be noted that while the *International Labour Review* paints a bleak picture, more recent studies come to a different conclusion and depict some rural areas in the 1930s as experiencing a mixture of decline and regeneration. See for instance John Martin, *The Development of Modern Agriculture: British Farming since 1931* (London: Macmillan, 2000).

[32] Mixed Advisory Agricultural Committee, fifth session, 9–10 December 1930, ILO Archives Geneva, AG 805/1.

Generally, experts attending the meeting agreed that agricultural workers faced precarious conditions and that significant disparities existed with regard to social protection and national legislation between these workers and their industrial counterparts. However, the Committee's discussions also revealed differing views on the meaning of the economic crisis for agriculture and the extent of economic decline in rural areas. Some experts, such as McDougall, advised against calling the economic downturn a 'crisis', noting that agricultural depression had been ongoing since the First World War. According to him, the post-war period—which was marked by global deflation—could be described as a succession of crises.[33] In his words, the global countryside had witnessed 'widespread ruin and distress between 1921 and 1924', followed by 'a very partial recovery', only to degenerate again into 'a period of terrible difficulties as early as 1928, difficulties which show[ed] no signs of abating'.[34]

Experts were also not unanimous about the effects of the Depression on the living and working conditions of landless agricultural workers. Conservative landowners such as the Marquis de Vogüé were quick to claim that the agricultural workers were better off than industrial workers during the crisis, as part of their wages was paid in kind and they were 'lodged and boarded' by their employee.[35] To which Thomas remarked that during a recent trip to France he had himself experienced that the food provided to agricultural workers was of poor quality and had become even worse because of the general drop in prices that had affected the farmer's income.[36] Even in progressive places such as Czechoslovakia, Klindera pointed out, the Depression had put a stop to the provision of services such as access to public baths for the workers and childcare for working mothers. Overall, however, the discussions also pointed to deeper underlying changes in the agricultural labour force caused by mechanization (mainly outside Europe, as illustrated by McDougall's example of Australia) and the use of agricultural chemicals, both of which required technical skills that would ultimately lead to a reduction of agricultural labour and to a long-term transformation of the sector.[37] These aspects, especially the impact of mechanization on farm labour, had been tentatively researched by the Agricultural Service for North America, where during the 1920s combines, threshers, harvesters, and tractors had spread much more widely than in Europe, but there was generally little information about this topic.[38]

---

[33] Tooze calls the depression of 1920 'the most underrated event in twentieth century world history'. Tooze, *The Deluge*, 354.
[34] See footnote in Matthaei, 'Some Effects', 471–2. This view has also been corroborated by Béaur and Chiapparino, *Agriculture and the Great Depression*.
[35] Matthaei, 'Some Effects', 465.
[36] Mixed Advisory Agricultural Committee, fifth session, 9–10 December 1930, ILO Archives Geneva, AG 805/1, 22–4.
[37] Mixed Advisory Agricultural Committee, fifth session, 9–10 December 1930, ILO Archives Geneva, AG 805/1, 22–4.
[38] W. A. Riddell, 'The Influence of Machinery on Agricultural Conditions in North America', *International Labour Review* 13 (March 1926), 309–26. E. L. Matthaei, 'More Mechanisation in Farming', *International Labour Review* 23, no. 3 (March 1931).

Representatives of farm labourers' unions tended to be more outspoken and combative about the downturn and possible countermeasures. They also challenged the notion that inequality could be explained away with the special nature of agricultural work. As Duncan who had become the president of the International Landworkers' Federation would later put it, agriculture as a sector required new international policies to address social issues affecting agricultural workers.[39] There was 'no excuse for not applying the same social standards to agriculture than to industry', and the attitude towards agricultural labourers as 'second-class citizens' needed to change.[40] Echoing his earlier statements issued after the First World War, he also warned against maintaining the status quo, arguing that the world was profoundly changing.[41] Duncan anticipated greater mobilization among the rural workforce: 'Those who are living in the hope that, when the intensity of the present depression is weakened, we shall quietly slip back again to the industrial and social alignments we knew before 1914, must be blind to the forces which the world upheaval has let loose [...]. The landworkers [...] have moved away from their old isolation and will not be content to remain outside the current of economic and social movements. They have made their contacts, national and international.'[42] Agrarian mobilization from below, Duncan suggested, had increased since the First World War, and it had become a significant force to contend with. One point on which trade unions were insisting was an international standardization of worktime in agriculture, making conditions more equal to those of industrial workers. This was a question that the ILO had side-stepped throughout the 1920s, claiming that it was too complex for international regulation and that the time was not yet ripe for an international debate.[43] As the following discussion shows, the economic crisis generated a renewed ambition to address this issue and understand the specific economic and social characteristics of rural labour organization.

A Time for Action

In the spring of 1932, the ILO was struck by a 'cruel stroke of destiny' when its director Thomas died suddenly on 8 May 1932.[44] For agrarian interest groups that had fought for the international recognition of their social claims, Thomas's

---

[39] Joseph Duncan, 'A New Policy for Agricultural Labour', *International Labour Review* 25, no. 2 (February 1932).
[40] Duncan, 'A New Policy', 185.
[41] See Chapter 1.
[42] Duncan, 'A New Policy', 187.
[43] See Chapter 2.
[44] Report of the Director to the Seventeenth International Labour Conference, Geneva, 8–30 June 1933, 5–6.

passing was a major blow. His commitment to include agricultural labour in the ILO's mandate against the will of more conservative forces had been a motor of international agrarian networking and mobilization throughout the 1920s. Thomas had shown a strong interest in agrarian life and work, which he believed to be essential to national and international stability, and had made continued efforts to liaise with representatives of agricultural labour interests.[45] As Léon Jouhaux put it in a public tribute, 'the workers of the world had the fullest possible confidence in him'.[46]

The new director Harold Butler, former British civil servant and deputy director of the ILO since 1920, took over the Organization's leadership at a particular difficult time.[47] Butler, who would remain in office until 1938, was dealing with internal and external challenges. Internally, there was widespread mistrust among the various services, and many officials were unhappy and frustrated.[48] This also showed within the ILO's Agricultural Service: Matthaei, one of strongest advocates for the ILO's agricultural work, left the Organization in 1933. Officially, the reason she gave was her marriage to the renowned botanist Albert Howard. Unofficially, she had become tired of the constant battles for funds and of the condescending attitudes of her superiors.[49] In a final note to her hierarchical superiors, in which she evoked her time in the Agricultural Service, Matthaei deplored 'that she had been greatly hampered in her work', especially by shortage of staff.[50] She also criticized the lack of visibility and attention given to agriculture in general, a cause to which she continued to dedicate her time and work. Under her married name Louise Howard, she would go on to publish a monograph that ambitioned to paint a universal picture of the labour problem in agriculture and that drew on the research collected during her time at the ILO.[51] Reviewers celebrated it as a window into the social and economic difficulties of the agricultural labour classes.[52]

Externally, the global depression was also highlighting the shortcomings of the ILO's perspective which primarily considered European agricultural contexts and did not adequately address the needs and challenges faced by workers

---

[45] See Chapter 1.
[46] International Labour Office, *Record of Proceedings*, Seventeenth International Labour Conference, Geneva, 8–30 June 1933, 5.
[47] For Butler's biography, see also Jaci Leigh Eisenberg, 'Butler, Harold Beresford', in Bob Reinalda, Kent J. Kille, and Jaci Leigh Eisenberg, eds, *IO Bio: Biographical Dictionary of Secretaries-General of International Organizations*, www.ru.nl/fm/iobio (last accessed 28 January 2024).
[48] Alice Maud Allen, *Sophy Sanger. A Pioneer in Internationalism* (Glasgow: Robert Maclehose and Co., 1958), 192.
[49] See Chapter 3.
[50] Note Howard to Maurette, 17 March 1933, ILO P 6/6/1.
[51] See Louise Ernestine Howard, *Labour in Agriculture: An International Survey* (Oxford: Oxford University Press, 1935).
[52] Josiah C. Folsom, 'Review of *Labour in Agriculture: An International Survey* by Louise E. Howard', *Journal of Farm Economics* 18, no. 2 (May 1936), 439–44.

outside of Europe. By 1932 the problem of mass unemployment had become global, hitting industrial workers from Europe to North America and highlighting the urgency of economic and social measures. To the ILO, the situation in the labour market not only threatened to generate mass poverty and social unrest, but also represented a waste of productive labour.[53] 'The world has now passed through its third winter of acute unemployment with all the untold misery, the waste of talent and energy, and the frustration of hope which it entails', Butler reported, emphasizing that the ILO was 'capable of playing an important part in the reconstruction of industrial life'.[54] Butler recognized that unemployment and its effects on housing, food, nutrition, and general health of workers and their families was a primary concern that the ILO needed to address in ways that would be relevant for the workers.[55] The ILO's Governing Body had created a Unemployment Committee that suggested possible steps to alleviate the problem, including the development—through cooperative governmental efforts—of systems of relief and but also the launching of international public works as a way to reemploy people and businesses.[56]

Like many economists in Geneva, Butler, who was a personal friend of John Maynard Keynes, endorsed active policy interventions and believed in international financial cooperation to stabilize the economy.[57] He was keen to collaborate with the League of Nations to discuss problems of international production and trade and the possibilities of international agreements that would support the economy. Thus, in late spring 1933, the International Labour Office forwarded a list of economic and financial 'remedies' to the League-sponsored World Monetary and Economic Conference, scheduled to take place in London with representatives of sixty-five nations.[58] Farmworkers' representatives were not impressed by this multilateral effort at addressing the Depression: they viewed the ILO's financial and economic policy proposals as a departure from the Organization's original dedication to social justice. Michael Duffy, who described himself as a 'rural worker', deplored that the resolutions had little to say about agriculture and

---

[53] Daniel Maul, *The International Labour Organization: 100 Years of Global Social Policy* (Berlin: De Gruyter; Geneva: International Labour Office, 2019), 85–6.

[54] Report of the Director to the Seventeenth International Labour Conference, Geneva, 8–30 June 1933, 17.

[55] Rod Mamudi, *A Survey of the Great Depression as recorded in the International Labour Review, 1931–1939* (Geneva: International Labour Office, 2009).

[56] Antony Alcock, *History of the International Labour Organization* (Basingstoke: Macmillan, 1971), 100–1.

[57] Isabelle Lespinet-Moret and Ingrid Liebeskind-Sauthier, 'Albert Thomas, le BIT et le chômage: expertise, catégorisation et action politique internationale', *Les cahiers Irice* 2, no. 2 (2008), 157–79.

[58] Resolution addressed to the World Monetary and Economic Conference, submitted by Sir Atul Chatterjee, Government representative of the Governing Body. International Labour Office, *Record of Proceedings*, Seventeenth International Labour Conference, Geneva, 8–30 June 1933. Appendix XIV, 686. Herbert Samuel, 'The World Economic Conference', *International Affairs (Royal Institute of International Affairs 1931–1939)* 12, no. 4 (July 1933); Patricia Clavin, 'Explaining the Failure of the World Economic Conference', in Harold James, ed., *The Interwar Depression in an International Context* (Munich: Oldenbourg Wissenschaftsverlag, 2002), 77–99.

even less about agricultural workers. Taking aim at what he considered to be the meaningless output of Geneva institutions, he quipped: 'I know that if you were to ask any rural worker what he thought of the mess into which those who control the existing system of production and distribution have allowed the world to get, he would use language which would be very much more emphatic than the language of this resolution.'[59] Speaking for the workers he represented, Duffy warned: 'We have had enough of long, drawn-out conferences where diplomats make fine speeches and experts prepare voluminous memoranda. What we want now is a conference that will recognize that the time for talk is past and the time for action is come.'[60]

At least in terms of broadening its geographical perspective and paying attention to agriculture globally, the ILO was moving in the right direction. In June 1933, the International Labour Conference presided by Italian government delegate de Michelis had for the first time featured an official delegation of 'observers' from the United States.[61] Speaking at the conference, various delegates from Southern and Eastern Europe and from Latin American countries had brought to the fore the economic and social interdependence of industrial and agricultural development. Some even went as far as to postulate that 'the centre of gravity of the economic world crisis, together with its solution' lay in the social and economic improvements in agriculture.[62] As a first step, the conference had included agriculture in the discussions of three of the questions on the agenda, namely invalidity, old age and widows' and orphans' insurance.[63] These discussions had resulted in the adoption of three new agricultural conventions which applied to manual and non-manual workers in agriculture, as well as agricultural apprentices and domestic servants in agricultural household. What workers demanded from the ILO, however, was to take effective measures against unemployment by shortening hours of work to keep a greater number of workers employed. This proposal echoed some of the measures that had been implemented by member governments and put forward by the ILO leadership as a remedy to alleviate the crisis.[64]

[59] International Labour Office, *Record of Proceedings*, Seventeenth International Labour Conference, Geneva, 8–30 June 1933, 37.
[60] International Labour Office, *Record of Proceedings*, Seventeenth International Labour Conference, Geneva, 8–30 June 1933, 37.
[61] On de Michelis, see chapter 3.
[62] See contributions of delegates from Italy, Uruguay, and Czechoslovakia, in International Labour Office, *Record of Proceedings*, Seventeenth International Labour Conference, Geneva, 8–30 June 1933.
[63] International Labour Office, *Record of Proceedings*, Seventeenth International Labour Conference, Geneva, 8–30 June 1933. International Labour Organization, Convention no. 36, Old Age Insurance (Agriculture), Convention no. 38 Invalidity Insurance (Agriculture), and Convention no. 40 Survivors Insurance (Agriculture), all adopted in 1933.
[64] On the management of working hours through national legislation, see Mamudi, *A Survey of the Great Depression*, 6–7.

Reopening the Debate on Hours of Work

It is significant that the controversial issue of limiting the working day on the farm (the so-called 'hours of work'), which had been briefly discussed in 1920 and 1921 but abandoned thereafter, came back on the table in the midst of the economic crisis. As discussed in Chapter 2, the proposal at the time had encountered steep opposition, not least from the French government and farmers' organizations that objected to any intervention in this matter.[65] For much of the 1920s, the question of hours had remained contested and deemed too problematic to even consider. Demands by agricultural trade unionists to place the question back on the agenda after it was taken off in 1921 had remained unsuccessful, and the legal reduction of hours of work for farm labourers had not received any direct regulatory attention. It was a well-known fact that farmworkers often worked as many as fourteen hours a day on understaffed farms, often in harsh conditions, exposed to noise, dust, and heat, and with no time to take care of physical health issues that came with the job.[66] Yet, Governments and ILO officials alike were sceptical that the issue could be discussed internationally, and employers were completely opposed to it, as limiting worktime in agriculture raised fears about lower productivity and increased labour cost. In farming especially, such limitations were regarded as a potential disruption of customary and traditional arrangements that had prevailed for centuries.[67]

For a brief moment, in the late 1920s, the issue of hours of work had also been fleetingly discussed in the context of a debate on the use of forced labour. Tasked with shining a light on so-called 'indigenous' labour in the colonies, which, contrary to its modern definition, at the time meant colonial labour, the ILO's Native Labour Section had prepared an enquiry to clarify the limits of the use of involuntary work in those regions.[68] One item in the questionnaire sent out in preparation for international legislation stipulated that forced labour should not be carried out for more than eight hours a day.[69] Workers' representatives in favour of abolishing this practice were adamant that if forced labour was allowed to continue, the limitations of hours should at least be taken into consideration. A South African workers' delegate argued that 'if men are forcibly taken from

---

[65] International Labour Office, *Report on the Adaptation to the Agricultural Labour of the Washington Decisions Concerning the Regulation of Hours of Work* (Geneva, 1921).

[66] For a description of the conditions of a hired farmworker in Britain, see Fred Kitchen, *Brother to the Ox: The Autobiography of a farm labourer* (London, 1939; 1981 edn), 53–7, 200–1.

[67] See Chapter 2.

[68] Daniel Maul, 'The International Labour Organization and the Struggle against Forced Labour from 1919 to the Present', *Labor History* 48, no. 4 (2007), 477–500. On the problem of terminology and the interwar meaning of 'indigenous', see Luis Rodríguez-Piñero, *Indigenous Peoples, Postcolonialism, and International Law: The ILO Regime (1919–1989)* (Oxford University Press, 2005), 18 and 41.

[69] Alcock, *History of the International Labour Organization*, 87.

their homes, from their simple daily routine of labour and relaxation and thorn into labour camps or railroad gangs and forced to undertake strange and unpleasant tasks for the benefits of their European rulers', they should at least benefit from a minimum of protection, namely 'a strict limitation of the working day [to] eight hours'.[70]

But employers and government delegates taking part in the discussion pointed out that as the question had not been resolved for 'free' workers in Europe, addressing it for colonial workers would likely lead to discontent amongst European workers who had not received similar attention. They also somewhat flippantly accused the workers' delegate of wanting to introduce capitalism (defined here specifically as an economic system based on waged labour) in the colonies, thus shifting 'traditional' or 'local' practices of labour recruitment and mobilization. Roland Venables Vernon, government advisor for the British Empire, mocked the allegedly unreasonable demands of the workers' delegates who—he quipped—would have insisted on establishing 'an eight-hour day in the Garden of Eden'. To the workers' dismay, Vernon went so far as to romanticize and idealize forced labour, arguing that the 'traditional' and 'customary' labour performed by a community for their chief was a 'living thing', in other words a vital part of cultural traditions 'that should not be killed'.[71] This minimization of the negative effects of forced labour echoed some of the earlier arguments about preserving 'traditions' and 'customary arrangements' cited in discussions about limiting working hours in agriculture in Europe.[72] When in 1930 the International Labour Conference set out to formulate a convention that abolished the use of forced labour for private purposes, the question of hours had disappeared from the agenda and forced labour was considered permissible in the context of agriculture. Thus, rather than being addressed in both colonial and non-colonial contexts, the issue of excessive hours in agriculture was intentionally and artificially divided, suggesting that the length of the working day did not matter in the colonial context. The practical differentiation between agricultural and industrial labour, colonial and non-colonial, free and forced labour made it more difficult to have a unified and coherent debate about labor rights and conditions in agricultural settings, as each category was treated separately, thus overlooking commonalities and shared concerns across different geographical contexts and regions of the world.

In the 1930s, the issue of hours in agriculture was revisited at least for industrialized countries. The problem of unemployment had given new relevance to this question, aligning it with the ILO's established interest in questions of

---

[70] International Labour Office, *Record of Proceedings*, Twelfth International Labour Conference, Geneva, 30 May to 29 June 1929, 581.
[71] International Labour Office, *Record of Proceedings*, Twelfth International Labour Conference, Geneva, 30 May to 29 June 1929, 520.
[72] See Chapter 2.

rationalization and efficiency. The tumult caused by the economic downturn led the ILO to consider once again its original ambition to create equal conditions for labourers in agriculture and industry. Although the atmosphere of global uncertainty that reigned in the early 1930s presented notable similarities to the 1920s, this time the issue of the working day was approached under a new light, namely as a way to respond to the international economic situation and as a measure to limit unemployment. Already under Thomas, instigated by the Unemployment Committee of the ILO's Governing Body, the International Labour Office had set out to examine whether the reduction of working hours might help increase the employment of a larger number of workers during the economic crisis.[73] This idea was discussed as a possible way to prevent dismissals and encourage the re-hiring of salaried employees.

Butler picked up the issue in the wake of Thomas's demise, arguing that the revision of hours of work was one of the main tasks of the ILO and a way to ensure equality, productivity, and avoid waste of agricultural labour.[74] However, the relationship between reduced hours and improved productivity was not uncontested: even advocates of the relatively new discipline of industrial psychology debated its application to the industrial sector. As German psychologist Otto Lipmann argued in the *International Labour Review*, 'the existing data on the relation between hours of work and output' remained unsatisfactory. 'From an exclusively economic point of view the problem is to determine not the maximum but the optimum hours of work, which are shown to vary with industry, occupation, race, and individual capacities.'[75] In his review of existing research, Lipmann showed that the quality and quantity of hourly output was dependent on a complex combination of physiological and psychological factors, including the number of hours, degree of fatigue, nutrition, wages, the will to work, the intensity of work, and finally, the organization of the work place.[76]

But from a point of view of balancing social improvements with economic productivity, the idea of limiting hours was attractive. It was also strongly endorsed by farmworkers' representatives, who were impatient for the International Labour Office to reopen the debate, provided that wages would not be reduced.[77] They viewed the limitation of worktime as a possible measure to restore economic stability while guaranteeing employment and maintaining purchasing power. Employers were much more critical, pointing out that a reduction of

---

[73] International Labour Office, 'Reduction of Hours of Work: Report of the Tripartite Conference', Seventeenth International Labour Conference, Geneva, 8–30 June 1933.

[74] Report of the Director to the Seventeenth International Labour Conference, Geneva, 8–30 June 1933, 63–7.

[75] Otto Lipmann, 'Hours of Work and Output', *International Labour Review* 9, no. 4 (April 1924), 481.

[76] Lipmann, 'Hours of Work and Output', 487.

[77] Report of Secretary and Proceedings of the Seventh Congress of the International Landworkers' Federation, London, 2–3 July 1935, IISH Archives Amsterdam, INT 2926-8, 48.

hours might increase production costs and therefore selling prices, and that such measures could work only if applied internationally, which was unrealistic. At the 1933 International Labour Conference, de Michelis representing the Italian government had made a proposal to examine 'the possibility of adopting a reduction of hours of work in order to combat unemployment'—a proposition that was also strongly supported by the Spanish government.[78] A workers' delegate likened this support to 'an oasis in a desert of despair', a source of hope in challenging times.[79]

The fact that the issue was discussed in detail reflected a renewed surge in interest in agricultural labour conditions. This was also apparent, in the creation of a new temporary Committee of Agricultural Work composed of members of the ILO's Governing Body (despite much resistance by those representing the interests of agricultural employers and businesses).[80] The Committee remained in place until 1936 and was to enable a more adequate study of agricultural problems within the International Labour Office. Its aim, in particular, was to ensure that the ILO would have greater autonomy when addressing agricultural issues, especially those which the Mixed Advisory Agricultural Committee had failed to look at systematically. In terms of expertise, however, there was not much innovation nor were there significantly new ideas or methods. The new Committee was composed of the same experts that also participated for the ILO in the Mixed Advisory Agricultural Committee. The main difference was that they could now meet every three months rather than every three years, and without having to consider the interests of the International Institute of Agriculture.[81]

One of the Committee's first tasks was to launch a technical study on hours of work in agriculture, for which the Agricultural Service set out to prepare a questionnaire to be sent out internationally. The ILO's new and unprecedented enquiry on hours of work in agriculture, which began in the winter of 1934, stands out as much for its technical and knowledge-producing aspirations as for its unrealistic ambitions. As with every issue addressed by the International Labour Office, the main goal of the research was to collect information from member countries to get an impression of local conditions. In December 1934, a draft plan for a technical study on working hours in farming was circulated internally.[82]

---

[78] International Labour Office, *Record of Proceedings*, Seventeenth International Labour Conference, Geneva, 8–30 June 1933, 16–18.
[79] International Labour Office, *Record of Proceedings*, Seventeenth International Labour Conference, Geneva, 8–30 June 1933, 62.
[80] International Labour Office, Minutes of the sixty-second session of the Governing Body, April 1933 (Geneva: International Labour Office 1933), 42–3.
[81] For the meetings of the Committee on Agricultural Work, see ILO Archives Geneva, AG 800/4/5/1.
[82] The draft was supervised by the new Committee on Agricultural Work of the Governing Body. International Labour Office, Committee of Agricultural Work of the Governing Body, Draft Plan of a Technical Study of Hours of Work in Agriculture, ILO Archives Geneva, AG 1 (Agriculture- Reduction of Hours of Work 1933–34), 48.

The study, drawn up by the Agricultural Service (now led by von Bülow, who had succeeded Matthaei after her departure in 1933), sought to gather information on annual work time, seasonal distribution, beginnings and endings of the working day, and daily breaks.[83] On the one hand, the ILO aimed to understand 'the length of the working day from the worker's point of view'; on the other hand, it sought to clarify the relationship between the efficiency and length of working hours.[84] The enquiry also asked for information on natural, geographic and economic conditions, landscape, climate, and soil to contextualize these data with regard to production, as well as information about the size and organization of farms, and the agricultural labour market.[85] The aim was not merely to assemble statistical information, as had been the case with the first world agricultural census project run by the International Institute of Agriculture in previous years.[86] The architects of the new study wanted to elucidate the question of 'whether shorter hours of work provide scope for the employment of more workers'.[87]

This collection of both social and economic knowledge was not unusual for the ILO, but the extent and specificity of the questions demonstrated its renewed determination to clarify the role of waged labour in the agricultural economy. The introductory note of the draft study painted the problem of working hours in agriculture as 'extremely complex and of a special character', and warned that it could not be addressed just by transposing the methods applied in the manufacturing industries.[88] 'Differences and divergences from locality to locality and between various types of farms', ' extreme dependence on natural factors', 'seasonal variations in the volume of work', and peculiarities in the social structure rendered labour in agriculture fundamentally distinct from labour in the industry.[89] The International Labour Office argued that 'the first object of an international technical study' must be 'to ascertain the actual hours worked throughout the world, to examine the various factors which can be regarded as decisive in determining the length of the working day, and to state to what extent [...] uniformity [...] and common features of the problem are to be found'.[90]

---

[83] Note von Bülow to Weaver, Di Palma, and Butler, 1 December 1933, Agriculture, ILO Archives Geneva, AG 1, 48.
[84] International Labour Office, Committee of Agricultural Work of the Governing Body, Draft Plan of a Technical Study of Hours of Work in Agriculture, 1934, ILO Archives Geneva, AG 1, 1–2.
[85] International Labour Office, Committee of Agricultural Work of the Governing Body, Draft Plan of a Technical Study of Hours of Work in Agriculture, 1934, ILO Archives Geneva, AG 1.
[86] See Chapter 3.
[87] International Labour office, Committee of Agricultural Work of the Governing Body, Draft Plan of a Technical Study on Hours of Work in Agriculture, 1934, ILO Archives Geneva, AG 1, 5.
[88] International Labour Office, Committee of Agricultural Work of the Governing Body, Plan of a Technical Study of Hours of Work in Agriculture, ILO Archives Geneva, AG 1, 3–4.
[89] International Labour Office, Committee of Agricultural Work of the Governing Body, Plan of a Technical Study of Hours of Work in Agriculture, ILO Archives Geneva, AG 1, 5.
[90] International Labour Office, Committee of Agricultural Work of the Governing Body, Plan of a Technical Study of Hours of Work in Agriculture, ILO Archives Geneva, AG 1, 4.

Another point of interest was to investigate the evolution of agricultural labour, especially whether the introduction of various machines had reduced the number of hours.[91] More covert items on the agenda included finding out whether there was a 'certain correlation between the length of the working day and agricultural prosperity or wage-level'.[92] In simpler terms, this suggested comparing different farming practices to see how work hours could relate to the success of agricultural operations and the income of workers. This reflected concerns with efficiency and labour-power and preoccupations with the 'human motor', as much as with labour conditions.[93] The control of human labour in the production process and the protection of the rights of labourers went hand in hand and, in the long run, the idea was to establish norms and rules that would smooth out existing differences between industrial and agricultural working classes, thereby enabling managerial control.[94]

The study also highlighted a general prejudice against farm labour and the perception that it was generally unorganized and inefficient. ILO experts thus maintained that excessive working hours could not be attributed solely to natural conditions and custom, but that lack of planning and a failure to modernize agricultural practices were also contributing to the problem. A preliminary outlook in the *International Labour Review* posited that 'not all factors affecting hours of work in agriculture arise out of purely natural conditions'.[95] Rather in line with new theories of scientific management in agriculture, there were other factors hampering productivity, such as the waste of time in cultivating distant areas, the inefficient layout of farm buildings, and poor planning of specific tasks. In conclusion, the general tendency to waste time and labour meant that agricultural activities could not 'secure its adherents more than a very modest living even at the cost of very long hours'.[96]

Identifying whether long hours in agriculture were justified and whether conditions could be improved, both economically and socially, seemed an ideal way to get at the heart of the question of agrarian progress.[97] But the plan was so ambitious that it seemed doomed from the start. As British professor of agricultural economics and founding member of the International Association of

---

[91] See Louise Ernestine Matthaei, 'More Mechanisation in Farming', *International Labour Review* 23, no. 3 (March 1931).
[92] International Labour Office, Committee of Agricultural Work of the Governing Body, Plan of a Technical Study of Hours of Work in Agriculture, ILO Archives Geneva, AG 1, 20.
[93] Anson Rabinbach, *The Human Motor: Energy, Fatigue and the Origins of Modernity* (New York: Basic Books, 1990).
[94] On discourse, norms, regulations and ways to enhance managerial control, see Ava Baron and Eileen Boris, 'The Body as a Useful Category for Working-Class History', *Labor* 4, no. 2 (2007), 25.
[95] International Labour Office, 'The Present Regulation of Working Hours in Agriculture', *International Labour Review* 25, no. 1 (1932), 79.
[96] International Labour Office, 'The Present Regulation of Working Hours in Agriculture', *International Labour Review* 25, no. 1 (1932), 79.
[97] On Kautsky and the agrarian question, see Chapter 3.

Agricultural Economists A. W. Ashby pointed out to Duncan when asked to comment on the draft enquiry, such an international investigation of time measurements in agriculture was unprecedented and 'would be a fairly stiff job to cover', even in countries in which agricultural labour statistics existed.[98] Ashby also cautioned that none of the professional agricultural economists had 'ever specifically worked on any of the social or general aspects of hours of labour'.[99]

Others were more concerned about how such a study would affect the interests of landowners and agricultural employers. The International Institute of Agriculture, which defended the interests of the latter, immediately reacted to the ILO's plans by mobilizing farmers and employers organizations, asking for their opinions on whether the eight-hour day could be applied to agriculture and, if so, how and with what exceptions.[100] Whereas unfortunately we do not know what they responded, those defending the interests of landowners and farmers undoubtedly considered the ILO's enquiry as a threat and were prepared to counter any regulatory attempts. Thus, once again, the ILO found itself attacked on all fronts.

From Sunrise to Sunset

In the spring of 1934, the International Labour Office circulated the draft plan of the study among a select group of experts; a few months later, reactions and comments flowed in to Geneva. The majority of responses came from European countries, with the notable exceptions of Argentina, Brazil, and Australia.[101] Although agricultural areas in the so-called tropics, meaning largely the warmer, non-temperate, geographical zones, were gaining recognition amongst agricultural economists as significant contributors in global agricultural production, no colonial territories featured in this enquiry. The exclusion of colonies and of so-called 'native labourers' suggests that even though there had been previous discussions, social reformers were still reluctant to extend reforms to the territories that continued to be under the control of colonial powers .

When submitting the draft study, the International Labour Office had sought out the opinions of 'experts' among existing contacts, some of whom directly identified with the interests of agricultural employers while others represented agricultural trade unions. Both groups were sceptical about the enquiry and its

---

[98] Letter, Ashby to Duncan, 17 July 1934, ILO Archives Geneva, AG 1/0/25.
[99] Letter, Ashby to Duncan, 17 July 1934, ILO Archives Geneva, AG 1/0/25.
[100] De Vogué for the Commission Permanente des Associations Agricoles CIPA at the International Institute of Agriculture, 25 April 1933, ILO Archives Geneva, AG 1 (Agriculture-Reduction of Hours of Work 1933–34).
[101] Replies to the questionnaire were sent by Argentina, Australia, Brazil, Denmark, France, United Kingdom, Hungary, the Netherlands, Norway, Poland, and Sweden.

potential political implications. Jules Gautier, Vice-President of the Commission Internationale d'Agriculture, cautioned Butler that the ILO would do well to stress that the study merely aimed at collecting information and not at formulating any type of international norms. 'Without this precaution you risk receiving protests against a project considered dangerous by many, rather than objective answers to your questions.'[102]

More surprisingly, perhaps, agricultural workers unions were sometimes equally reluctant to provide the necessary information. Many of these unions had been and were affected by the rise of fascism, with disastrous consequences for the international agricultural trade union movement. With the Nazi government's ascent to power in February 1933, Germany and later Austria witnessed the 'assimilation' (nazification) of free trade unions and the dismissal of previous leaders.[103] Similar issues emerged shortly after with agricultural trade unions in Spain and Hungary, leading to a loss of affiliates and disastrous financial consequences for the International Landworkers' Federation. Administratively, the Nazi rise to power led to the resignation of the Federation's secretary Georg Schmidt and its relocation to the Netherlands. In that process the archives and all the valuable connections were lost, leaving the Organization on a weak footing.

Thus, although international agricultural trade unionists had initially urged the International Labour Office to include the opinions of local unions, this was easier said than done. When approached, the British National Union of Agricultural Workers replied that it was 'unable to carry out this enquiry'. British trade unionists were reluctant to consult their members on the question of hours, arguing that in the economic and political climate of the time such a step might be greeted with suspicion and mistrust. 'We have to be careful how far we press them on this matter as it is not very easy for them to give the necessary information and great care has to be taken not to worry our membership unduly.'[104] In fact, many of these unions were facing considerable difficulties, from political repression to dissolution.[105] Their reluctance to answer the ILO enquiry also shows that they perceived its dual character and the fact that it could also be used as an instrument for rationalization.

---

[102] Jules Gautier, Président Fédération Nationale des Associations Agricoles, to Butler, Paris, 16 May 1934, ILO Archives Geneva, AG 1/0/22 (Hours of work 1934–39, France).
[103] International Landworkers' Federation, Report of Secretary and Proceedings of the Seventh Landworkers Congress in London, 2–3 July 1935, ILO Archives Geneva, AG 1000/7/10. See also Note von Bülow, 13 March 1934, IISH Archives Amsterdam, INT 2926-28, 70–1.
[104] W. Holmes, General Secretary of the National Union of Agricultural Workers, to Bristow [sic, should be von Bülow], ILO Agricultural Service, 22 October 1934, ILO Archives Geneva, AG 1/0/25.
[105] Note von Bülow, 13 March 1934, ILO Archives Geneva, AG 1; see also the meetings of the Executive Committee of the International Landworkers' Federation on 7 June 1933, ILO Archives Geneva, AG 1000/7/9. Report of Secretary and Proceedings of the Seventh Landworkers Congress in London, 2–3 July 1935, IISH Archives Amsterdam, INT 2926-28, 70–1.

Consequently, the International Labour Office had to rely on information that came almost exclusively from government departments.[106] Rather unsurprisingly, what generally emerged from the country reports was that agricultural work was commonly much longer than industrial work—twelve hours was the norm—and that it was still largely manual and dependent on environmental factors. All reports, without exception, opened with a remark on the naturally determined length of the working day. Invariably and in all the languages the reports defined the working day as lasting from 'sunrise to sunset' ('*vom Sonnenaufgang bis zum Sonnenuntergang*', '*du lever au coucher du soleil*', and so forth).[107] The straightforward explanation was that agricultural work depended on natural light and that seasonal tasks such as ploughing and harvesting were weather-dependent and needed to be carried out within a specific time window.

This emphasis on the process and timing of agricultural work being dictated by natural conditions corroborated earlier statements about nature ruling agricultural work and not yielding to any man-made laws or international rules.[108] With regard to the implications of such prolonged working days for the health and well-being of workers, assessments varied. Since natural light and general 'atmospheric conditions' were determining working hours, many reports detailed how the labourers would get up, wash up and have breakfast at least half an hour before sunrise, so as to be ready to start work as soon as possible. This also meant, as some were quick to point out, that on cloudy or rainy days the labourers would get up later and work less hours.

The reports also featured the old trope that the natural context made for a healthier workplace than the industry. Especially in Europe, the idea still prevailed that agricultural work, being 'done in the open air', did not expose the workers to the same risks and hygiene issues. Jules Gautier who reported on France, for example, commented that working in the fields was 'cut by frequent and prolonged rest periods which do not exist in industrial work' and that 'in the end, the total duration of the effective work of an agricultural worker [was] not much greater than that of a city worker'.[109] Argentine expert Emilio A. Coni, a Professor at the University of Buenos Aires and League of Nations economic expert, similarly insisted that—unlike industrial work—agricultural work was characterized by frequent breaks, usually determined by a concern for the health

---

[106] See preliminary reports from Argentina, Australia, Brazil, Denmark, France, United Kingdom, Hungary, the Netherlands, Norway, Poland, and Sweden. ILO Archives Geneva, AG 1/0/2, AG 1/0/4, AG 1/0/9, AG 1/0/18, AG 1/0/22, AG 1/0/25, AG 1/0/31, AG 1/0/42, AG 1/0/45, AG 1/0/50, and AG 1/0/58.

[107] See reports for Argentina ('from sunrise to sunset'), Hungary ('von Sonnenaufgang bis zu Sonnenuntergang'), Poland ('la durée du travail en agriculture et adaptée au lever et coucher du soleil'). ILO Archives Geneva, AG 1/0/2, AG 1/0/31, and AG 1/0/50.

[108] See Chapter 2.

[109] Response from H. Bonnet, Directeur Général Office Central de la Main-d'Œuvre Agricole, ILO Archives Geneva, AG 1/0/22 (Hours of work 1934–39, France), 27.

of animals. 'If animals are used for ploughing, they must be given about ten minutes' rest in the hour, and the ploughman can also rest during this time.' As a consequence, the 'hours in the afternoon are usually shorter than in the morning, for the sweating horses must not be caught by the evening chill, so that if it is cold, work ceases half an hour or three-quarters of an hour before sunset'.[110] Such responses indirectly highlighted an issue that had already appeared in the context of housing: the well-being and efficiency of farm animals were at least as important (if not more) to the farmer than those of workers—yet another point of distinction between the agrarian and industrial worlds.

Many insisted that the working day on a farm varied across different groups of workers and depended on differences in status and contract. Duncan, one of the experts reporting for Britain, emphasized that a distinction should be made between 'productive labour' and simple attendance, for instance in the case of shepherds and cattlemen who, in his view, did little physical work apart from watching the sheep on the hill.[111] Writing on the situation in Argentina, Coni, who viewed the limitation of hours as inapplicable and prejudicial to the cultivators/employers, also relativized the length of the working day. He emphasized that the number of hours was largely dependent on the type of farm and crop and that not all work was physically demanding. Sitting on a horse-drawn plough was not the same as harvesting—which was the most physically demanding labour and required longer hours, due to the stringent time constraints and dependency on natural conditions. Coni also put forward that a statutory limitation of work time would run counter to the interests of the piece-rate worker, who was paid for output and not for hours.[112]

Beside this rather romanticized view on working along natural rhythms, Geneva also received gloomier feedback that revealed deep historical legacies of exploitation and coercion in agriculture and a general lack of data. As an expert from the department of labour in Rio de Janeiro pointed out in his preliminary report on agricultural worktime in Brazil, in his country, where big land ownership was the norm, the conditions of the agricultural worker were 'extremely precarious' and subject 'to the arbitrariness of the employers'.[113] This, the expert observed, was the legacy of centuries of exploitation of African slaves for agricultural labour in Brazil: even after abolition, field labour retained its abusive and racialized character. Because there were no regulations and the work was 'from sun to sun', with all hours of the day being used, it was impossible for the Brazilian ministry of labour to present any documentation for the ILO's investigation.[114]

---

[110] ILO Archives Geneva, AG 1/0/2, 3.
[111] Duncan to Butler, 2 May 1934, ILO Archives Geneva, AG 1/0/25.
[112] ILO Archives Geneva, AG 1/0/2.
[113] Report of National Labour Department, Rio de Janeiro, ILO Archives Geneva, AG 1/0/9, 7.
[114] Report of National Labour Department, Rio de Janeiro, ILO Archives Geneva, AG 1/0/9, 7.

The inclusion of Brazil and Argentina in the enquiry testitifies to the ILO's initially timid ambitions to increasingly expand the debates to non-European countries. The response of these countries also foreshadowed an area of work on which the ILO had dragged its feet. Especially the report from Brazil put the spotlight on problems of labour racialization and exploitation in agriculture. The enquiry also highlighted other issues. Not only did the office lack information on large agrarian countries such as the Soviet Union and the United States. Even with regard to Europe, on which there was more information, it was difficult to agree on pursuing a study in view of formulating international legislation. Many respondents, although largely in favour of the enquiry and its 'excellent plan', pointed out the impossibility of implementing it. They stressed the 'enormous obstacles' to drafting a convention on working hours in agriculture.[115] The adjectives 'extremely complex' and 'impossible' were frequently used in the preliminary responses. Moreover, some correspondents strongly doubted that the reduction of hours would have any impact on unemployment: according to the French expert, the fact that the agricultural labour market in France had to rely on foreign labour was proof enough that there was no unemployment in French agriculture and that a convention would therefore be useless.[116]

Despite its promising beginning, the enquiry on working hours was ultimately abandoned because of its perceived infeasibility. For agricultural trade unionists this was highly disappointing, especially given that the ILO adopted a convention on the forty-hour work week for industrial workers in 1934, which was regarded as a major step in the improvement of working and living conditions.[117] The failed enquiry showcases one of the main paradoxes of the ILO's work on agriculture, insofar as its extensive preparations and research work did not lead to any international legislation. This also helped cement the erroneous perception, among later officials, that the Organization had woefully neglected agricultural labour. As for the working hours, the problem would be raised once more before the war, in 1938, during the meetings of a new agricultural expert commission, the newly appointed Permanent Agricultural Committee.[118] By then, new voices had emerged from the Global South and particularly from Latin American countries which would put the agricultural workers centre stage. It would take a Second World War, however, to implement the regulation of hours, both in Europe and overseas, including in 1948 in Austria, Bulgaria, France, Haiti, Norway, and Yugoslavia; in 1949 in the German Democratic Republic and Hungary; in 1950 in Romania;

---

[115] See reply Prof. Coni, Argentina, ILO Archives Geneva, AG 1/0/2, 1.
[116] Response Bonnet for France, ILO Archives Geneva, AG 1/0/22, 27.
[117] International Labour Organization, convention no. 47, 40-hour week industry, 1935. Maul, *The International Labour Organization*, 89.
[118] See International Labour Office, 'The Regulation of Hours of Work in Agriculture', *International Labour Review* 77, no. 6 (1958), 538–52.

in 1951 in the Indian plantations, Indonesia, and Israel; in 1952 in Belgium; in 1953 in Vietnam; and in 1956 in Tunisia.[119]

The enquiry carried out by the International Labour Office on working hours in the early 1930s ultimately shows that the ILO was slow to move away from its narrow focus on the waged agricultural working class in Europe. On the one hand, the collection of specific knowledge on the working day can be read as an effort to break with the conservative views of agriculture as a 'peculiar' institution, whose inherent social and economic organization required flexible and often exploitative work arrangements.[120] Yet the enquiry also appears as a profoundly unrealistic and limited undertaking. Like previous enquiries, it was characterized by a pervasive European bias which was increasingly contested at a time when colonial labour issues were becoming more visible internationally. In this sense, this was a missed opportunity for the ILO to widen its gaze and consider agricultural labour more globally. Something that it would be forced to do with the approaching war and an increasing global mobilization from below.

Cultivating Fields of Progress: Agriculture and the International Labour Organization, 1920s–1950s. Amalia Ribi Forclaz, Oxford University Press. © Amalia Ribi Forclaz 2025. DOI: 10.1093/9780191945014.003.0005

[119] International Labour Office, 'Regulation of Hours of Work in Agriculture', 549.
[120] Expression used in Plan of a technical study on hours of work in agriculture, ILO Archives Geneva, AG 1, 7.

5
New Voices of the Countryside

> *'The farmers and peasants wish to collaborate in the institutions at Geneva, but they do not wish to be received like poor relations. Could not peasants be given a larger place in the League and the organizations that have been created, could not this "expert's mentality" be avoided according to which only those who have for years been separated from the real life of the countryside are held to understand its problems?'*
> Peasant Peace Conference, 'A New Force for the League of Nations, the Peasant Peace Movement', February 1938. Archives of the International Institute for Social History in Amsterdam (hereafter IISH Archives Amsterdam), RUP 181–5

In the mid-1930s, the ILO's work on agriculture began to change in tone and outreach, mostly as a result of new international currents. Due to the mutual reinforcement of the economic crisis and growing political mobilization, new political movements stepped into the fray, from women's organizations to fascist and leftist ones, targeting rural populations, rural issues, and agricultural policies. They sought to revive international debates on agricultural living and working conditions and also to challenge what was seen as the insufficient efforts of international organizations in this domain. Viewed from the perspective of agricultural trade unionists, the track record of the ILO looked poor. The Mixed Advisory Agricultural Committee had met regularly to discuss rural issues and had launched various enquiries but the pace was considered too slow by those defending the interests of the workers.[1] The debate on hours of work had looked promising at first but yielded no concrete results. Other questions, such as allowing farmworkers to benefit from paid holidays, were seen as 'not ripe for discussion', and agricultural workers continued to be viewed as an inferior class.[2] The fact that the ILO had made no significant progress in agricultural legislation angered the leaders of agricultural trade unions, who felt that their demands had been sidelined.

This was a delicate time for the ILO. For one, there was a marked growth in mobilization and social unrest in the agricultural sector: from farms outside Paris

---

[1] See previous chapter.
[2] International Labour Office, Minutes of the sixty-fifth session of the Governing Body, Geneva, 22–24 January 1934, 51.

to Californian wheat fields and plantations in colonial territories, agricultural labourers joined strikes and movements of protest, against a backdrop of state repression, poverty, and declining living standards.³ From the mid-1930s onwards, agricultural and rural worlds were also increasingly invested with larger societal blueprints. The use of policies and programmes to control nature and people extended across fascist, socialist, and liberal states, often accompanied by a nationalist discourse.⁴ The fact that the ILO had so far failed to present a consistent social policy and agricultural labour standards that would be emulated by its member governments did not bode well for future international cooperation.

This chapter moves away from the internal bureaucracy of the ILO to look at the new organizations and movements around the ILO, which spoke on behalf of rural populations, seeking to engage with internationalist circles in Geneva but also to put forth diverging claims and in the name of distinct value systems. As the chapter shows, although the ILO remained the common reference point for these novel regional actors, this was a time when international agricultural policy discussions were increasingly decentred from Geneva and a new language appeared which highlighted the politicized nature of agricultural mobilization and challenged the ILO's central status as the main international hub for agricultural social policy. As the emergence of a new agricultural expert commission will show, the ILO was also undergoing some important transformations that shifted both its geographical and conceptual outlook and would ultimately also bring closer attention to agrarian issues. By early 1936 and following the adherence of the United States in 1934, the ILO had started taking action to strengthen its global outreach by holding an international conference of American states in Santiago de Chile—the first of the ILO's so-called Regional Conferences.⁵ As historians have argued, 1936 reflected the beginning of the Organization's 'global turn'.⁶ This new type of meetings shifted the geographical locus and outreach of

---

³ On the increase of agricultural strikes in Ireland between 1936 and 1939, see Jean-Claude Farcy, 'Les grèves agricoles de 1936–1937 dans le bassin parisien', in Ronald Hubscher and Jean-Claude Farcy, eds, *La Moisson des Autres: Les salariés agricoles aux XIXe et XXe siècles* (Paris: Créaphis,1996), 303; Jordi Domènech and Thomas Jeffrey Miley, 'Structural Change, Collective Action, and Social Unrest in 1930s Spain', *IFCS Working Papers in Economic History* (Universidad Carlos III de Madrid, Instituto Figuerola: 2013). On labour unrest in the colonies, see Chapter 6 and 7.

⁴ Kiran Klaus Patel, 'The Green Heart of Governance: Rural Europe during the Interwar Years', in Amalia Ribi Forclaz and Liesbeth van de Grift, eds, *Governing the Rural in Interwar Europe* (London: Routledge, 2018).

⁵ Jill Jensen, 'From Geneva to the Americas: The International Labor Organization and Inter-American Social Security Standards, 1936–1948', *International Labor and Working-Class History*, no. 80 (2011), 215–40.

⁶ Véronique Plata-Stenger, *Social Reform, Modernization and Technical Diplomacy: The ILO contribution to Development 1930–46* (Oldenbourg: De Gruyter, 2020), 62–3; Magaly Rodriguez Garcia, Jasmien Van Daele, and Marcel Van der Linden, eds, *ILO Histories. Essays on the International Labour Organization and Its Impact on the World during the Twentieth Century* (Bern: Peter Lang, 2010); Sandrine Kott and Joelle Droux, eds, *Globalizing Social Rights: The International Labour Organization and Beyond* (Basingstoke: Palgrave, 2013); Daniel Maul, *Human Rights, Development and Decolonization: The International Labour Organization, 1940–70* (New York: Palgrave Macmillan, 2012).

agricultural debates, and calls were made for the ILO to pay greater attention to agrarian problems in the countries of the Americas, and also to collect documentation on the conditions of landless rural populations outside Europe.[7]

Uniting Agrarian Masses

One of the movements, which emerged in September 1936 on the international scene in a period of increasing international tensions, was a group claiming to represent the poorer segments of agricultural populations. The movement was led by Guido Miglioli, an Italian pacifist who campaigned on behalf of landless day labourers and against their exploitation by large landowners. Miglioli was an Italian catholic with communist sympathies who did not adhere to the liberal tenets of Geneva. Since the early 1920s he had built strong links with the Krestintern, a soviet peasant organization formed by the Communist International in the early 1920s.[8] He was derided in the Italian press as a 'bolshevik of Jesus' and had exiled himself in 1927, travelling all over Europe to hold anti-fascist conferences.[9] Miglioli also spent time in the Soviet Union to study collectivization and the ensuing agrarian transformations before settling down in Paris.[10] From there, in reaction to the Italian invasion of Abyssinia which took place in the autumn of 1935 and to the escalation of the Spanish civil war in the following months, Miglioli liaised with French intellectuals to mobilize agrarian interest groups in the name of peace. The result was the organization of a Conférence Agraire Internationale, set under the umbrella of the sponsorship of the International Peace Campaign (in French 'Rassemblement Universel pour la Paix'), a Franco-British organization led by Lord Robert Cecil and launched in 1936 to coordinate the work of pacifist groups.[11]

In September 1936, Miglioli's new agrarian movement was one of the social groups represented at the International Peace Campaign's inaugural conference

---

[7] See for example Enrique Munguía, 'The Agrarian Problem in Mexico: I', *International Labour Review* 36, no. 1 (1937), 49–85.

[8] The local dimension of Miglioli's early political engagement and his place as a left-wing Catholic have been studied by John M. Foot, 'White Bolsheviks? The Catholic Left and the Socialists in Italy, 1919-1920, *The Historical Journal* 40, no. 2 (1997), 415–33; Giuseppe Sircana, 'Guido Miglioli', *Dizionario Biografico degli Italiani*, vol. 74 (Rome: Istituto dell'Enciclopedia Italiana, 2010).

[9] [Author unknown], 'I bolscevichi di Gesù', *Corriere della Sera* (21 March 1920). On Miglioli's life in exile in the late 1920s and 30s, see Franco Leonori, *No guerra, ma terra! Guido Miglioli, una vita per i contadini* (Milan, Rome: CEI, 1969), 75–92.

[10] Guido Miglioli, *Le village soviétique* (Paris: Librairie du Travail, 1927).

[11] Peter Farrugia, 'Mésentente Cordiale: Anglo-French Collaboration in the Rassemblement Universel pour la paix', *Synergies. Royaume-Uni et Irlande* 4 (2011), 105–16; Rachel Mazuy, 'Le Rassemblement Universel pour la Paix: une organisation de masse?', *Matériaux pour l'Histoire de Notre Temps* 20, no. 1 (1993), 40–4.

in Brussels.¹² The aim of Miglioli's initiative was to draw attention to agricultural populations, without making any distinction between groups or classes. He wanted to improve the representation of this rural population on an international level, and mobilize them as a pacifist force in support of the International Peace Campaign.¹³ Sustained by a transnational network of agrarian reformers, politicians, and agricultural experts, the central message of the conference was an appeal for 'the peasants and agricultural workers of all countries' to mobilize and support pacifist initiatives, warning them of the looming war. The organizers declared to be 'the representatives of the peasants' and evoked the 'unanimous desire' of 'agrarian masses' that peace be maintained, and that humanity be saved from the evils of war.¹⁴ This was in essence not just a call for mobilization, but also a declaration of support for international cooperation and friendship. The economic and political crisis, the organizers claimed, could only be resolved by overcoming ideological differences between European regimes and by allowing greater representation of international agrarian masses in Geneva.¹⁵

Such a call also echoed increasingly strong demands from Latin American countries within the ILO to put agricultural workers centre stage. In January 1936, the first Regional Conference of American member states in Santiago de Chile pointed to the economic and social importance of their large rural populations. The Chilean delegation had proposed to add 'the working and living conditions of agricultural workers' as a special item to the agenda (which initially comprised questions of minimum wages and rationalization in the textile industry, as well as revisions of the child labour convention).¹⁶ The delegations from Latin America stressed the 'decisive numerical importance' of people working in agriculture, their political and economic role, and the need to extend social insurance schemes to that particular section of the population.¹⁷ This echoed earlier statements by

---

¹² Rassemblement Universel pour la Paix, Conférence Agraire Internationale, Brussels, 3–6 September 1936, ILO Archives Geneva, AG 1000/78. (Dates of the conference vary; the actual event took place on 4–5 September.)

¹³ Conférence Agraire Internationale, 'Documents préparatoires'; 'Appeal to the Peasants and Agricultural Workers of all countries', IISH Archives Amsterdam, RUP 76.

¹⁴ Conférence Agraire Internationale, 'Les masses agraires pour la paix', *Bulletin de la Conférence Agraire Internationale* 1, Brussels, 1936, IISH Archives Amsterdam, RUP 77; Conférence Agraire Internationale, 'Die Bauern für den Frieden', Internationaler Informationsdienst, nos. 1–3, Brussels, August 1936, IISH Archives Amsterdam, RUP 77; Dr Guido Miglioli, 'Coordination et action des masses agraires pour le paix', three booklets, Brussels, 1936, IISH Archives Amsterdam, RUP 79; Conférence Agraire Internationale, 'Rapport sur la conférence, 1936– 1937', IISH Archives Amsterdam, RUP 80.

¹⁵ 'La Crise agricole ne peut être vaincue que par le retour d'une atmosphère de paix', newspaper cutting, undated, IISH Archives Amsterdam, RUP 80.

¹⁶ Record of Proceedings of the Labour Conference of the American States which are members of the International Labour Organization, Santiago (Chile), 2–14 January 1936 (Geneva: International Labour Office, 1936).

¹⁷ Record of Proceedings of the Labour Conference of the American States which are members of the International Labour Organization, Santiago (Chile), 2–14 January 1936 (Geneva: International Labour Office, 1936), 123.

Latin American representatives who had cautioned the ILO, in one of its first conferences, not to forget agricultural workers in Latin America.[18] As Mexican government representative Adolfo Cienfuegos put it at the 1936 meeting: 'Agricultural workers [in Latin America] are the most numerous and the most important, because of the large political power they represent and the important economic entity they constitute, as well as the large potential reserves. It is of great political and economic interest to study all phenomena concerning the agricultural population, but of those phenomena their labour is one of the most important.'[19]

For now the Latin Americans and the European agrarian movements did not combine. The organizing committee of the Conférence Agraire Internationale instead brought together mostly European interest groups with different visions and ideological backgrounds, of which a minority was familiar with the ILO's work and had participated in previous conferences.[20] The 350 supporters and participants in the meeting were an eclectic and colourful assemblage of French leftist intellectuals, socialist and communist sympathizers, trade unionists, agronomists, Marxist economists, and representatives of Eastern European peasant parties.[21] Among them was Piet Hiemstra who represented the International Landworkers' Federation, and C. J. Kuiper, secretary of the Fédération Internationale des Travailleurs Agricoles Chrétiens. Other participants included the French politicians and experts in agrarian reform and social policy such as Pascal Carrion, Guy Menant, and Henry Noilhan. Also present were the Marxist economist David Mitrany, and representatives of the Eastern European peasant parties of Romania, Czechoslovakia, and Yugoslavia, and, last but not least, the Bulgarian Vasil Kolarov—a member of the Moscow Krestintern. More surprisingly, perhaps, the conference also attracted liberal attendees: Daniel Hall, who was the former director of the Rothamsted Institute, the leading British agricultural experiment station, attended as a representative of the United Kingdom, together with a group of Oxford professors. There were also some notable absences: the Parti Agraire et Paysan Français, for example, declined the invitation on the grounds that the meeting promoted communist sentiments.[22] Catholic movements stayed away for similar reasons.

The scope of the Conférence Agraire Internationale was twofold: to propagate an anti-fascist and pacifist message about the threat posed to peace by forces that

---

[18] See Chapter 1.
[19] International Labour Office, *Record of Proceedings of the Labour Conference of the American States Which Are Members of the International Labour Organisation*, Santiago (Chile), 2–14 January 1936, 255 and 123.
[20] Circular letter by the Comité d'Initiative de la Conférence Agraire, 8 August 1936, IISH Archives Amsterdam, RUP 67.
[21] 'La conférence agraire internationale de Bruxelles, adhésions et projets', newspaper cutting, undated, ILO Archives Geneva, AG 1000/78.
[22] Conférence Agraire Internationale, *Le Monde Agraire et la Paix* (Paris: Editions Agraires Internationales, 1936), 285.

promoted international division, military expansion, and authoritarian control, and to highlight the suffering of farmers and farmworkers caused by the reverberations of the political and economic crisis. The conference wanted to represent and bring together different groups working the land, from hired workers to small farmers and bigger landowners. As the conference organizers argued, economic crisis and preparations for war were 'suffocating the population, and farmers and agricultural workers [were] the first to bear the crushing burden'. In its publicity materials, the conference highlighted the worries of the countryside and considered what possible remedies could bring solace.[23] At a superficial level, the rhetoric echoed Louise Matthaei's earlier words about the extent of the agricultural crisis, but the focus was different. What organizers were concerned with was not just the economic crisis but the increasingly tense international relations and what was described as 'an atmosphere of war'.[24]

In preparation for the conference, attendees had received a questionnaire about the negative impact of military rearmament on agriculture in various European countries, asking them for suggestions on how to propagate pacifism among the rural masses and how to strengthen the international governance of agriculture. The questions were rhetorical and aimed at raising attention to the fact that the war would endanger rural prosperity and technical progress, and put an end to cooperation and trade. There was also an element of critique of international institutions as the questionnaire highlighted the underrepresentation of so-called 'agricultural masses' at the League of Nations as well as the fact that the latter was not in contact 'with the life and aspirations' of people working in agriculture.[25]

The congress itself followed the classic format of scientific presentations, which were delivered by an illustrious list of academic experts and politicians. Their interventions dealt with war and the economy in general but also with improving rural living conditions through better education facilities and health services. A section dedicated to farm women addressed rural hygiene and the scientific management of labour. In contrast to previous international agricultural meetings within the ILO, colonial agricultural issues and the living conditions of colonial peasants and rural workers featured largely at the conference. In a section dedicated to colonial agricultural policy, well-known French socialist feminist and militant anti-imperialist Léo Wanner spoke of the situation of Arab peasants in North Africa and of the pauperization of rural masses, which she largely

---

[23] Rassemblement Universel pour la Paix, Conférence Agraire Internationale, Brussels, 3–6 September 1936, ILO Archives Geneva, AG 1000/78.
[24] Rassemblement Universel pour la Paix, Conférence Agraire Internationale, Brussels, 3–6 September 1936, ILO Archives Geneva, AG 1000/78.
[25] 'Questionnaire' (undated), Conférence Agraire Internationale, IISH Archives Amsterdam, RUP 67.

attributed to colonial exploitation.[26] British geographer, sociologist, and forestry expert Arthur Geddes focused on Indian peasants, reminding the attendants that the conditions of the latter were impacting on Europe's economy and that they would in turn be impacted by the outbreak of a new world war.[27] Finally, William Macmillan, a specialist on South Africa and member of various imperial reformist pressure groups, spoke about agriculture on the African continent, underlining the exploitative conditions of African agricultural workers on farms owned by white settlers.[28] A final paper on the fate of Chinese peasants since the Manchurian invasion completed this section.[29]

Such openly critical views on the social and economic conditions of agrarian populations in the colonies (including direct and indirect criticism of Italy's recent invasion of Ethiopia) were bound to cause considerable unease within the League of Nations and more specifically the ILO. Even more so because one of the main goals of the conference organizers was to encourage the League of Nations and particularly the ILO to offer explicit endorsement to the conference. Miglioli sent an invitation to Butler to this effect, asking for the ILO to adhere to the congress and send an official delegate.[30] The support of liberal institutions was seen as necessary for the success of new international groups.

The ILO immediately undertook some careful research on Miglioli and his affinities with Moscow.[31] The memos that circulated described the conference as a radical event 'of an extreme left-wing character', and noted that it constituted a potentially dangerous 'popular agrarian front' that had successfully convinced more moderate and well-established international associations to adhere.[32] The ILO did not wish to be dragged into what it saw as a 'politicized' event, and wanted to avoid the impression that it was officially supporting this new initiative. However, as Butler was also aware of the international significance of the meeting and of some of the adhering organizations, he hesitated about how to respond.

Miglioli, meanwhile, tried to mobilize his contacts within the ILO to build support for his movement. These included Olindo Gorni, one of the long-term members of the Agricultural Service.[33] Gorni, who had been forced to seek exile

[26] 'La politique agraire coloniale, politique de guerre, par Mme Leo Wanner', in Conférence Agraire Internationale, *Le Monde Agraire et la Paix*, 205–13.
[27] 'Paysan d'Orient et Paysan d'Occident, par le professeur Arthur Geddes', in Conférence Agraire Internationale, *Le Monde Agraire et la Paix*, 213–19.
[28] 'La répartition des colonies et le problème paysan, par le Professeur Macmillan', in Conférence Agraire Internationale, *Le Monde Agraire et la Paix*, 219–23.
[29] 'Le paysan chinois et la paix, par la section paysanne de l'UPLN', in Conférence Agraire Internationale, *Le Monde Agraire et la Paix*, 224–8.
[30] Letter, Miglioli to Butler, International Labour Office, 20 August 1936, ILO Archives Geneva, AG 1000/78.
[31] Letter, Phelan to Miglioli, 28 August 1936, ILO Archives Geneva, AG 1000/78. Memo Childs and Phelan, 19 August 1936, ILO Archives Geneva, AG 1000/78.
[32] Memo von Bülow to Childs and Phelan, 19 August 1936, ILO Archives Geneva, AG 1000/78.
[33] Letter, Miglioli to Gorni, 12 August 1936, ILO Archives Geneva, AG 1000/78; Mauro Cerutti, 'Olindo Gorni', *Dictionnarire historique de la Suisse*, https://hls-dhs-dss.ch/fr/articles/027942/2004-10-27 (last accessed 28 January 2024).

in Geneva in 1924 because of his political views, knew Miglioli from anti-fascist circles. As part of a clandestine anti-fascist organization which he helped create together with writer Ignazio Silone, Gorni had also been subject to harassment by fascist police. He had even been imprisoned in Italy for a few days during a trip home, even though he was travelling as an official of the International Labour Office.[34] Gorni, although sympathetic to Miglioli's cause, was not in a position to openly support the event. In the end, on the pretext that the Conférence Agraire Internationale was happening at the same time as the International Conference of Agricultural Economists in Scotland, the International Labour Office apologized for not being able to officially participate, but sent its Brussels correspondent, Max Gottschalk, as an unofficial observer.[35]

The Conférence Agraire Internationale received a fair amount of attention in the press. It also led to the publication of a volume on the 'the agrarian world and peace', which offered a detailed reproduction of all the interventions given on the topic. The meeting shifted the focus away from governments to the role and power of the people. For all that, it did not otherwise result in any practical steps to put the rhetoric of peasant mobilization into action.[36] For example, there is no evidence that the agrarian movement did actively participate in the popular campaigns that the International Peace Campaign launched after the first meeting in Brussels and which included the founding of a Peace Pavilion at the *Exposition internationale des arts et techniques dans la vie moderne* in Paris in 1937 as well as the popular boycott of Japanese goods to condemn its aggression of China.[37] Other activities and ambitions of the agrarian pacifist movement, such as the organization of an 'international peasant's day for peace' and the sending of a delegation to the League of Nations assembly, equally failed to materialize.[38] The Conférence Agraire Internationale of 1936 would not remain a singular event, but was followed two years later by a similar international meeting, the so-called Peasant Peace Conference in Geneva, which would reiterate similar claims with a new global outlook.

Polarization

By 1937, agrarian social policy discussions were becoming overtly politicized for ideological ends by the left and right, which now blatantly competed for dominance on agrarian issues which held a central place in their visions of society and progress. International platforms were also increasingly used for purely nationalist goals and organizations and events that were meant to promote

---

[34] Letter, Miglioli to Gorni, 12 August 1936, ILO Archives Geneva, AG 1000/78.
[35] Note von Bülow, 2 December 1936, ILO Archives Geneva, AG 1000/78.
[36] Conférence Agraire Internationale, *Le Monde Agraire et la Paix*.
[37] Farrugia, 'Mésentente Cordiale'.
[38] Journée paysanne internationale pour la Paix, ILO Archives Geneva, AG 1000/78.

international cooperation began to be utilized by countries to promote their own national interests. Italy is a case in point. From the mid-1920s onwards, international observers witnessed a striking growth of Italian agrarian organizations and international associations in line with the regime's interest in autarkic production and ruralization policies.[39] Mussolini's overt attempts at controlling the international field were also causing a battle within the International Institute of Agriculture. American agricultural experts particularly resented the numerical dominance of Italian experts and politicians, which increasingly used the Institute to showcase Italian policies.[40] By the early 1930s, Italy styled itself as the centre of agrarian internationalism.[41] In September 1932, an 'international agricultural month' ('*mois agricole international*') had been held in Rome, in an attempt to put Italian agriculture in the limelight. Italy had also organized an international congress on vocational agricultural education.

The following years saw the emergence of a cluster of Italian-led international agrarian organizations that claimed to cover every agricultural domain from the press to education, social problems, credit, chemical fertilizers, rural broadcasting, libraries, and specific crops.[42] These organizations all pivoted around the central figure of Franco Angelini, a farm owner who, since 1920, had held multiple positions in fascist agricultural trade unions, farmers unions, and agricultural expert commissions.[43] By the second half of the 1930s, Angelini's invitations to the ILO to adhere to Italian agrarian congresses and acknowledge new organizations were so frequent that the head of the ILO's Agricultural Service laconically remarked on 'yet another agricultural congress and another invitation [from] Mr Angelini who thus adds another international organization to his collection'.[44]

---

[39] On fascist agricultural policies, see Tiago Saraiva, 'Fascist Modernist Landscapes: Wheat, Dams, Forests, and the Making of the Portuguese New State', *Environmental History* 21, no. 1 (2016), 54–75; Marco Armiero, 'Introduction: Fascism and Nature', *Modern Italy* 19, no. 3 (2014), 241–5; Marc B. Tauger, 'Stalin, Soviet Agriculture, and Collectivization', in Frank Trentmann and Just Flemming, eds, *Food and Conflict in Europe in the Age of the Two World Wars* (Basingstoke: Palgrave Macmillan, 2006), 109–42.

[40] See Amalia Ribi Forclaz, 'Agriculture, American Expertise, and the Quest for Global Data: Leon Estabrook and the First World Agricultural Census of 1930', *Journal of Global History* 11, no. 1 (2016), 44–65.

[41] On fascist (and agrarian) internationalism, see Madeleine Herren, 'Fascist Internationalism', in Patricia Clavin and Glenda Sluga, eds, *Internationalisms: A Twentieth-Century History* (Cambridge: Cambridge University Press, 2017), 191–212. Also, Jens Steffek, 'Fascist Internationalism', *Millennium: Journal of International Studies* 44, no. 1 (2015), 3–22.

[42] Among these organizations were the International Federation of Agricultural Technicians Associations (*Fédération Internationale des Associations des Techniciens Agronomes*, FITA); The International Federation of Agricultural Press (*Fédération Internationale de la Presse Agricole*); the International Office for Agricultural Education (*Bureau International de l'Enseignement Agricole*); the International Conferences for Agricultural Credit and for Chemical Fertilizers (*Conférences Internationales du Crédit Agricole* and *Conférences Internationales des Engrais Chimiques*); the International Centre for Rural Radio Broadcasting (*Centre International de Radiophonie Rurale*); the International Tobacco Centre (*Centre International du Tabac*); and the International Agricultural Library Committee (*Comité International des Bibliothèques Agricoles*).

[43] On Angelini, see Perry Willson, *Peasant Women and Politics in Fascist Italy: The Massaie Rurali* (London: Routledge, 2002).

[44] Note von Bülow to Freymond, 1 September 1938, ILO Archives Geneva, AG 0/10/01/13/2.

To Miglioli, the constitution of these new international organizations for agriculture in Rome showed that fascism was trying to strengthen its position in Europe and in international organizations by giving itself a respectable international political programme, building on the results of previous work in the agricultural field.[45] And although Italy left the League of Nations and the ILO in December 1937, the move did not signal a withdrawal from agrarian internationalism.[46] In August 1938, Angelini created yet another organization to challenge the ILO: the International Office for Social Problems in Agriculture (Ufficio Internazionale per i Problemi Sociali in Agricoltura) which blatantly rivalled the ILO's focus on social affairs.[47]

What can generally be observed in the second half of the 1930s is a steep increase in attendance and adherences to international congresses and conferences dealing with agriculture, and generally a marked interest in social and economic questions. At its meeting held in La Haye in 1937, the Commission Internationale d'Agriculture, which in 1936 had changed its name to Confédération Internationale d'Agriculture, saw a record participation of about 1,000 attendees.[48] Participation in the meeting also included for the first time representatives from North and South American Countries such as Canada, the United States, Argentina, and Chile.[49] The conference was very broadly concerned with the political economy of agriculture, and covered both economic and social issues—from meat and wine production to agricultural education. Rather unusually for this type of technical meeting, the international situation also figured prominently on the programme. The conference even issued a peace manifesto, emphasizing its concern about the increasing insecurity and problematic relations between nations, and pointing to the 'terrifying consequences' that a new war would have not only for economic prosperity but also for all human activity and the spiritual and moral values of civilization.[50]

In fact, the congress of the Confédération Internationale d'Agriculture, which had always tried to hold a perilous balance between internationalist values and

---

[45] Guido Miglioli, 'Résolution de la commission paysanne au congrès français du Rassemblement Universel pour la Paix', ILO Archives Geneva, AG 1000/78, 2. On fascist agrarian propaganda, see Willson, *Peasant Women*; Perry Willson, 'Le virtù della terra. Due periodici per le contadine negli anni del fascismo', in Silvia Franchini and Simonetta Soldani, eds, *Donne e giornalismo: Percorsi e presenze di una storia di genere* (Milan: Franco Angeli, 2004), 259.

[46] *The New York Times* (12 December 1937).

[47] 'Relations with the International Bureau for Social Problems in Agriculture (Ufficio Internazionale per i Problemi Sociali in Agricoltura), Prof. Franco Angelini, Rome', ILO Archives Geneva, AG 0/10/01/13/2.

[48] Confédération Internationale d'Agriculture, 1937–1946, FAO Archives Rome, 1 IIA 73. On the organization, see also Chapter 1.

[49] Seventeenth International Congress of the Commission Internationale d'Agriculture, La Haye, ILO Archives Geneva, AG 1000/13/7. Report von Bülow, 14 September 1937, ILO Archives Geneva, AG 1000/13/7.

[50] 'Manifeste en faveur de la paix, adopté par le XVIIe Congrès International d'Agriculture, La Haye, à L'Assemblée plénière d'ouverture du 17 juin 1937', ILO Archives Geneva, AG 1000/13/7.

nationalist interests, brought out into the open some of the tensions and hostility that existed between liberal, socialist, and fascist representations.[51] As illustrated by various incidents during the conference, agricultural cooperation was increasingly becoming a pretext for ideological battles. A struggle broke out, for example, about who would host the new International Radio Service for Agriculture, that Italian and German delegations wanted to locate in Rome under the management of fascist associations.[52] As one participant of the conference recalled, the move was not successful, thanks to the forceful intervention of the small number of socialist representatives who countered the proposal. The group in question was composed of younger agrarian economists from France and Belgium, mobilized and prepared by Miglioli and the Belgian economist and socialist Léon Delsinne to intervene in the debate and to counteract Italian and other fascist influences.[53] During the closing meeting, a sympathizer of the Franco government, not officially registered as an attendant, was able to take the stage, causing an 'atmosphere of uneasiness' among liberal attendees.[54] In response, the Dutch delegate raised the question that was probably on the mind of many liberal internationalists, namely whether in the face of 'the unmistakable presence of German and Italian propaganda', it would not be better to transfer the organization of international conferences and preferably the entire International Agricultural Institute from Rome to 'an independent place such as Geneva or Paris.'[55] Clearly there was a feeling that if no action was taken, fascism would completely dominate agricultural debates and agrarian internationalism. Although there was no direct reference to fascism, the Dutch comment can also be read as a critique of fascist ruralization policies, which, as economists remarked, were not helping the agricultural working class.[56]

Peasants for Peace

In response to the growing fascist presence, left-wing agrarian circles sought to reinforce their mobilization and to step up their efforts to create a social and political movement. In October 1937, preparations started for the follow-up to

---

[51] See previous chapters. On the contradictions within agrarian internationalism, see also Fritz Georg von Graevenitz, *Argument Europa. Internationalismus in der globalen Agrarkrise der Zwischenkriegszeit (1927–1937)* (Frankfurt am Main: Campus Verlag, 2017).

[52] Report Hettvolk (Holland) on the Seventeenth International Congress of the Commission Internationale d'Agriculture, La Haye, 16–23 June 1937, ILO Archives Geneva, AG 1000/13/7.

[53] Report Hettvolk (Holland) on the Seventeenth International Congress of the Commission Internationale d'Agriculture, La Haye, 16–23 June 1937, ILO Archives Geneva, AG 1000/13/7.

[54] Report von Bülow, 14 September 1937, ILO Archives Geneva, AG 1000/13/7.

[55] Report Hettvolk (Holland) on the Seventeenth International Congress of the Commission Internationale d'Agriculture, La Haye, 16–23 June 1937, ILO Archives Geneva, AG 1000/13/7.

[56] Asher Hobson, 'Review of Carl T. Schmidt, *The Plough and the Sword: Labour, Land, and Property in Fascist Italy* (New York: Columbia University Press, 1938)', *The American Historical Review* 44, no. 2 (January 1939), 389–90.

Miglioli's Conférence Agraire Internationale of 1936, now under the new name of Peasant Peace Conference, a name that suggested the promotion of harmony and the opposition to militarization.[57] This time, the meeting was scheduled to be held in Geneva at the Palais des Nations in February 1938, indicating the movement's entry into official and prestigious international spheres. Once again, at least formally, this second conference was placed under the umbrella of Cecil's International Peace Campaign. But in fact, the moving spirit behind the event was that of communist sympathizer Louis Dolivet (né Ludovic Brecher), an Austro-Hungarian (and later French) émigré writer along with a group of radical trade unionists. Miglioli was no longer part of the organization committee.[58]

In preparation for the meeting, the conference organizers circulated yet another questionnaire asking participants to share 'their experience and their understanding of the problems of the countryside'.[59] There were specific questions about the form and availability of rural education services such as schools and study circles, and general means of information like the radio and the press in different countries, and about whether these could be used to propagate and publicize pacifist ideas and ideals. Conference organizers also wanted to know more generally how the divide between rural and urban populations could be overcome, and how the 'machinery of the League and the International Labour Organization' could address demands of greater representation and organization of agrarian populations. Quite obviously, this collection of information was modelled on previous ILO enquiries and thus invested with a certain amount of scientific legitimacy. Unfortunately, there are no traces of the answers, and it remains unclear whether the enquiry amounted to anything.

The meeting ran under the general banner of 'peasant action in favour of peace'. The constant reference to 'peasants' as the primary representatives of farming communities did not go unnoticed and it led to confusion among Western European observers. The term was not yet commonly used in English-speaking internationalist agrarian circles in Geneva, which preferred terms such as 'agricultural workers', 'farmers' or 'agriculturists'. The term 'peasant' would gain importance and become the new buzzword of international and regional developmentalist programmes from the late 1930s onwards and during and after the Second World War.[60] Although Miglioli's reference to 'peasants' was

[57] The name varies across sources: it is sometimes also referred to as World Peasant Peace Conference or just Preparatory Peasant Conference or Peasant Peace Conference. In the following I will use the name Peasant Peace Conference (in French Conférence Paysanne Préparatoire pour la Paix).
[58] Letter, E. A. Allen to Louis Dolivet, 29 October 1937, Peasant Peace Conference, IISH Archives Amsterdam, RUP, 181–5.
[59] Letter, Rassemblement Universel pour la Paix, about Peasant Peace Conference, 22 January 1938, ILO Archives Geneva, AG 1000/78/1.
[60] Peasants would increasingly appear in the scholarly literature of the late 1930s and early 40s. See, for example, Doreen Warriner, *The Economics of Peasant Farming* (London: Oxford University Press, 1939); Royal Institute of International Affairs, *Agrarian Problems from the Baltic to the Aegan: Discussion of A Peasant Programme* (London, New York: Royal Institute of International Affairs,

meant to encompass all people employed in agriculture, independently of farm size and land tenure system, it was understood by some as denoting small subsistence farmers, not usually associated with Western Europe.[61] Thus, upon receiving the invitation to the conference, British peace activist Adelaide Livingstone remarked that it would be 'impossible to arouse the interest of agricultural organizations in [Britain]', where agriculture had been commercialized and large estates were the norm, by an approach based on peasant interests and problems'.[62]

Whereas the imagery of the 'global peasant' was yet another manifestation of the overly abstract approach of international agrarian movements and organizations to agricultural life and work, the change of language was meaningful. It indicated a shift in the conceptualization of agricultural labour and the inclusion of small-scale, traditional agriculture in non-European countries. This also became apparent in the emergence of extra-European voices in the debate. Whereas the first meeting of Miglioli's Conférence Agraire Internationale in 1936 had been dominated by European campaigners, the 1938 event aimed for a much more global outreach.[63] Thus, the established group of European participants was joined by Shelley Wang, a Chinese delegate, political exile, and former chief of the ministry of agriculture of the Kuomintang. It also included Manuel Mesa, a member of the governing board of the Mexican national agricultural credit bank. Indian anti-colonial nationalist and later United Nations star diplomat V. K. Krishna Menon represented the interests of Indian peasants.[64] Whereas during the previous meeting of 1936 the conditions of agricultural populations outside Europe had been discussed by colonial critics and social reformers, now the representatives of these countries were sitting at the conference table. This also reflected a similar shift in the ILO's expert commissions, as we will see towards the end of this chapter.

The Peasant Peace Conference had announced that it 'would avoid all discussions of internal politics and religious conceptions' and that it would limit itself to the question of how to ensure international collaboration among peasants with regard to peace.[65] Indeed, most presenters underlined the sacrifices made by

---

1944). Irwin T. Sanders, 'The Characteristics of a Peasant Society', in E. de S. Brunner, I. T. Sanders, and D. Ensminger, eds, *Farmers of the World* (New York, 1945). G. Medici, 'Diagnosis and Pathology of Peasant Farming', Proceedings of the Seventh International Conference of Agricultural Economists, held 21–27 August 1949 in Stresa, Italy (Oxford University Press, 1950).

[61] Reply von Bülow, 19 January 1938, ILO Archives Geneva, AG 1000/78. On the ILO's attitude to peasants, see also Chapter 6.

[62] Letter, Adelaide Livingstone (British National Committee of the International Peace Campaign), 12 January 1938, ILO Archives Geneva, AG 1000/78.

[63] Amalia Ribi Forclaz, 'Guardians of the Countryside: The Associated Countrywomen of the World (ACWW) and International Rural Governance in the Interwar Years', in Ribi Forclaz and van de Grift, *Governing the Rural*.

[64] Letter, Louis Dolivet to P. J. Noel Baker, 31 January 1938, ILO Archives Geneva, AG 1000/78/1; International Secretariat of the International Peace Campaign, *A New Force for Peace: Proceedings of the Preparatory Peasant Peace Conference, 5–6 February 1938/Une force nouvelle: Débats de la conférence paysanne préparatoire pour la paix, 5–6 février 1938* (Geneva: Palais Wilson, 1938).

[65] Circular letter, International Peace Campaign/Rassemblement Universel pour la Paix, 29 October 1937, IISH Archives Amsterdam, RUP 181.

peasants and farmers during the First World War, and the disastrous impact that another conflict would have on these populations. French delegate Paul Vimeux, for example, vividly reminded the audience of the toll that war generally inflicted on agriculture and described how French farmers 'feared the return of a new catastrophe'.[66] But in such a charged political and social context, more controversial issues were brought up, and condemnations of imperialism could not be completely avoided. Wang thus outlined how Chinese peasants had been impacted by the 'Japanese aggression' in Manchuria, and spoke of the Chinese support of the International Peace Campaign. Menon too mentioned how millions of Hindu peasants supported the cause of peace and condemned the politics of aggression.[67]

Others talked more specifically about social justice for peasants and land workers as a condition for peace, focusing in particular on existing gaps in the international governance of social agrarian questions. Many acknowledged the role of the ILO but also pointed to the inadequacy of existing expert groups and of the overlaps between different institutions. The representative of the Swedish National Union of Peasants, Aake Guillander, spoke for many of the participants by calling for a coordinating body to organize the effective collaboration between peasant groups.[68] The conference went even further by openly criticizing the International Institute of Agriculture in Rome for its narrow focus on statistics, and demanding that the League of Nations and the ILO be more responsive to the plight of agrarian populations.[69] Peasants, farmers, and rural populations in general, all speakers agreed, should receive greater visibility and representation in international bodies. 'The peasants want, and must have the possibility of solving their vital problems through international collaboration, in the same way that the problems of other layers of the population are solved. It is a weakness of the League of Nations and the International Labour Organization that they have not been the instrument of this collaboration and this weakness must be remedied as soon as possible.'[70]

Thus, the main demand was not an improvement of social conditions but a greater representation of agricultural populations, which, as many stressed,

---

[66] Paul Vimeux, 'Le paysan francais et le travail pour la paix', in International Secretariat of the International Peace Campaign, *Une force nouvelle pour la paix*, 11-12, IISH Archives Amsterdam, RUP, 181-5.

[67] 'Les paysans hindous veulent contribuer à sauver la paix du monde', in International Secretariat of the International Peace Campaign, *Une force nouvelle pour la paix*, 25, IISH Archives Amsterdam, RUP, 181-5. On Menon see Brant Moscovitch, '"Against the Biggest Buccaneering Enterprise in Living History": Krishna Menon and the Colonial Response to International Crisis', *South Asian Review* 41, nos. 3-4 (2020), 243-54.

[68] Agence télégraphique RUP, 'The Peasant Peace Conference Opens', ILO Archives Geneva, AG 1000/78/1.

[69] 'Les organisations représentées se sont déclarées presque unanimement hostiles à la politique et l'action de l'institut international d'agriculture de Rome', anonymous and undated report, Peasant Peace Conference, February 1938, ILO Archives Geneva, AG 1000/78/1, 4.

[70] 'La justice sociale est une condition de la paix', in International Secretariat of the International Peace Campaign, *Une force nouvelle pour la paix*, 25, IISH Archives Amsterdam, RUP, 181-5.

represented 'more than half of humanity'. In its resolutions, the conference stressed the importance of galvanizing the support of agrarian populations for pacifist internationalism and for the League of Nations—not least as a way also to prevent them from becoming radicalized by fascist organizations. This was to be done through publicity and information campaigns, whose form was a subject of discussion. The general opinion was that farmers and peasants lacked the necessary education and time to read and therefore one needed to resort to 'rather lapidary forms of propaganda' in the form of illustrated posters rather than brochures.[71] Such a programme of mobilization, delegates were convinced, also necessitated improving and expanding existing means of information, especially the rural press, schools, rural radio programmes, but also study circles and meetings. This was essential to overcome the allegedly characteristic 'isolation' of the agricultural classes of the population. Agrarian populations were also to feature much more prominently in international organizations, starting with the planned instauration in the International Peace Campaign of a permanent agricultural section in charge of representing and organizing regular meetings. However, plans to hold a follow-up conference were defeated by the outbreak of war and although the beginning of hostilities did not completely erase the International Peace Campaign, it clearly put a stop to the rise of left-wing agrarian internationalism.

The Peasant Peace Conference also faced more general obstacles as not everybody was supportive of the event: tellingly, some of the organizers of the International Peace Campaign, including Lord Robert Cecil and Pierre Cot, as well as leading agricultural experts Daniel Hall and Ernst Laur, all excused themselves citing impediments. International associations such as the Associated Country Women of the World and the Commission Internationale d'Agriculture were missing too. This highlighted an obvious unease among liberal and more conservative officials about being connected to what they viewed as a radical initiative. Yet, the event was significative in that it succeeded in rallying a diverse crowd of agrarian interests under the banner (and in the name) of 'the peasant'— something which would have been unimaginable a few years earlier. In an echo of the early post-war years, a hitherto neglected and sometimes despised social group was brought to the attention of the largely white middle-class diplomacy of the League of Nations, with an emphasis on its political (and pacifist) potential. There was a marked shift from the ILO's previous discourse that described agrarian workers as 'the most despised and least protected' labourers in European economy.[72] Now, thanks to their capacity to mobilize beyond governmental spaces, they were put forward as 'a new force for peace'.[73]

---

[71] 'A New Force for the League of Nations, the Peasant Peace Movement', Preparatory Peasant Peace Conference, February 1938, IISH Archives Amsterdam, RUP 181–5.
[72] See Chapter 1.
[73] 'A New Force for the League of Nations, the Peasant Peace Movement', Preparatory Peasant Peace Conference, February 1938, IISH Archives Amsterdam, RUP 181–5.

The pacifist agrarian movement also anticipated broader changes in the representation of global issues. Not only did social mobilization happen outside of the boundaries of the ILO, but the meeting also stood out for its inclusion of increasingly stronger and more assertive voices from extra-European and colonial territories, mirroring the growth in similar networks in other domains.[74] This shift was apparent in concrete demands to be represented in agricultural committees according to numerical importance. When, in one of its final resolutions, the Peasant Peace Conference of February 1938 agreed to set up an organizing committee initially composed exclusively of European members, this choice was heavily criticized by Krishna Menon, who ironically remarked that the suggested composition of the committee represented 'about one-sixth of the world's population' and thus did not adequately represent the majority of the world's agrarian communities. 'On occasions like this [e.g. international committee elections]', he pursued more seriously, 'India, China and Africa must always remind [others] of their existence'.[75] Menon also suggested it would be a good idea to include some women, who had historically been underrepresented in ILO committees and whose experience and viewpoints would be crucial for a comprehensive discussion of the challenges of rural living. His words, at least with regard to geographical representation, predicted a change that would soon be felt in international commissions and committees, and that would transform international discussions on agrarian issues.

A New Expert Committee

The ILO had picked up on the wind of change regarding the increased demands for an efficient agricultural expert body and the calls for a more global and diverse outreach. The Regional Conference of 1936 had adopted resolutions that called for the statistical study of agricultural work in the Americas, for an enquiry into the conditions of agricultural workers in Latin American countries and for support for the establishment of rural schools and agricultural colleges.[76] This, together with the pressure emanating from the new social movements described earlier, infused the ILO's agricultural work with new energy. In February 1938,

---

[74] Andrew Arsan, Su Lin Lewis, and Anne-Isabelle Richard, 'Editorial: The Roots of Global Civil Society and the Interwar Moment', *Journal of Global History* 7, no. 2 (July 2012), 157–65.

[75] 'Membres de la commission permanente', in International Secretariat of the International Peace Campaign, *Une force nouvelle pour la paix*, 25, IISH Archives Amsterdam, RUP, 181–5, 40. This led to the inclusion of the Chinese delegate Wang into the organizing commission.

[76] International Labour Office, *Record of Proceedings of the Labour Conference of the American States Which Are Members of the International Labour Organisation*, Santiago (Chile), 2–14 January 1936, 169. Three years later, a second Regional Conference of American members held in Cuba would further highlight the central importance of agricultural workers in the economies of Latin American countries. See also Chapter 6.

exactly at the same time as the Peasant Peace Conference was putting forward its resolutions in a room of the Palais Wilson in Geneva, a new expert commission of the ILO gathered for its first meeting.[77] Founded in 1935 but then delayed until 1938, the Permanent Agricultural Committee was intended as an advisory body that would provide expertise on agricultural labour questions—not as a substitute but in addition to the already existing Mixed Advisory Agricultural Committee which had met every three years since 1923.

The new Permanent Agricultural Committee was a way for the ILO to signal its position as a global forum that stood above partisan questions and class warfare. The preparations for the first meeting, however, had been slightly chaotic, mirroring the deteriorating international situation. Two Italian experts who had been foreseen for the Committee stepped back, and no measures were taken to replace them.[78] The expert from India could not attend because of an 'impediment', whereas the Chinese expert had to be replaced at the last minute. Miglioli and Delsinne both asked to be officially invited, but were told—much to their dismay—that they could attend only as part of the general public.[79] In the end, forty agricultural experts convened at the ILO's headquarters in Geneva. Besides the usual employer and workers' delegates, the attendees included an extensive group of thirty seasoned agricultural experts.[80] Among the latter were well-known personalities from overseas, such as the above-mentioned Australian economist McDougall and Chinese agricultural expert Wang, the American Professor of rural sociology Lowry Nelson, the British-Indian entomologist and principal of a Punjabi agricultural college Muhammad Afzal Husain, as well as a group of Japanese, Mexican, Brazilian, and Argentinian economists.

The new committee considerably changed both the tone and geographical orientation of the debates about agriculture within the ILO: mirroring the changes observed at the Peasant Peace Conference, experts from India, Japan, Australia, and Mexico took part in the Permanent Agricultural Committee's first meeting alongside the usual group of French, British, and Italian experts who had dominated the debates for much of the 1920s and 30s.[81] The additional appointment

---

[77] Letter, International Labour Office to Zappi Recordati, ILO Archives Geneva, AG 1003/0/1. The event was intended to coincide with the meeting of the ILO's new agricultural expert commission, the Permanent Agricultural Committee, so as to facilitate an exchange of views and also outwardly demonstrate a united front against fascist organizations.

[78] Note von Bülow to Lafrance, 19 January 1938, ILO Archives Geneva, AG 1003/1. However, a report by Franco Angelini showcasing social in agriculture under fascism was still circulated. Report presented by Franco Angelini, president of the National Confederation of Fascist Trade Unions of Agricultural Workers, ILO Archives Geneva, AG 1003/1/101/34.

[79] Letter, Centre International Agraire, Brussels, to International Labour Office, 1 February 1938, ILO Archives Geneva, AG 1003/1/2.

[80] Permanent Agricultural Committee, first session, Geneva, 7 February 1938, ILO Archives Geneva, AG 1003/1/2.

[81] Note von Bülow to the Director, 30 October 1936, ILO Archives Geneva, AG 1003.

NEW VOICES OF THE COUNTRYSIDE   121

of Chinese expert Tsou Ping-Wen, Indian entrepreneur Walchand Hirachand, as well as the increasingly influential position of Frank McDougall, who had participated as an expert in previous agricultural meetings and now acted as the Committee's rapporteur, brought a new tone to the event.[82]

Initially, the meeting appeared much like previous agricultural meetings of the ILO. The agenda of the Permanent Agricultural Committee drew on the Organization's established repertoire and included questions that had been insufficiently discussed in 1921, such as the protection of child labour in agriculture, paid holidays, and working hours, and more generally the standards of living and economic conditions in agriculture. Workers' interests continued to be represented by the International Landworkers' Federation with its largely European membership. There were echoes of the ILO's very first discussions on agricultural labour, as Piet Hiemstra from the International Landworkers' Federation condemned the 'enormous and unjustified difference' between the treatment of agricultural workers and that of industrial ones, and predicted that such inequality would cause continued poverty and dissatisfaction for coming generations.[83] In an emotional appeal, Hiemstra urged the members of the Committee not to 'leave it to our grandchildren to solve the problems that we ought to solve'.[84]

Yet, there were also new voices that raised issues that had not been discussed before. Rather than sending out a questionnaire with the usual pre-conceived categories, the ILO had asked its member countries to supply short general outlines and 'surveys of agricultural labour problems', as well as trends in agricultural policies that could be used to discuss the global outlook. This raised some debates about terminology and the ILO's remit with regard to agricultural work. McDougall took this as an opportunity to draw attention to the terms of reference of the Committee, which still centred on waged agricultural workers and did not include, as McDougall thought it should, 'the general economic and social welfare of farmers and peasants'.[85] Throughout the meetings, McDougall continued to bring up the 'fundamental question of terminology', and challenged the Committee to define the meaning of 'agricultural labour' and to extend it 'to all those engaged in agriculture'.[86] This, McDougall thought, would finally shift the focus from a

[82] Letter, International Labour Office, China Branch, Shanghai, 29 January 1937, ILO Archives Geneva, AG 1003. Letter, von Bülow to Erulkar about India, 14 June 1937, ILO Archives Geneva, AG 1003.
[83] Stenographic record of the second sitting of the Permanent Agricultural Committee, Tuesday, 8 February 1938, ILO Archives Geneva, AG 1003/1/202/2.
[84] Stenographic record of the second sitting of the Permanent Agricultural Committee, Tuesday, 8 February 1938, ILO Archives Geneva, AG 1003/1/202/2.
[85] Stenographic record of the second sitting of the Permanent Agricultural Committee, Tuesday, 8 February 1938, 92, ILO Archives Geneva, AG 1003/1/202/2.
[86] Stenographic record of the second sitting of the Permanent Agricultural Committee, Tuesday, 8 February 1938, 92, ILO Archives Geneva, AG 1003/1/202/2.

narrow group of people in a small number of countries to a much larger global community of 'farmers, peasants, and small cultivators' worldwide.[87]

In a similar way, the Japanese delegate appealed to the Committee not to take the narrow road: 'After all, it would, as it seems to me, be rather a confession of failure if this committee were to disperse saying that they [...] were not interested in [the] problems [of Japan, India, and China] and could do nothing about them.'[88] He was seconded by his Indian colleague, who insisted that in countries such as India, where 89 per cent of the population was rural, the entire society rested on the class of agricultural labourers. To illustrate this point, the expert cited an Indian myth that underscored the economic importance and the fragility of agrarian populations: 'In Indian mythology a bullock is represented as carrying the earth on its horns, and when it gets tired it shifts the earth on to the other horn, causing earthquakes. Translated into modern economy, it comes to this: that the cultivator—the man behind the plough—carries the entire burden of human society. When he has reached the limit of his patience, he attempts to readjust the burden and we have social outbreaks aimed at a levelling up.'[89]

Reflecting on the meeting, the International Landworkers' Federation noted with satisfaction that the new sympathetic tone of the discussions was quite different from that of previous committee meetings. The discussions between experts demonstrated, so the trade unionist thought, a new understanding that workers in farming should be put centre stage and that the improvement of their standards of living should extend to the agricultural populations of the world.[90] The transformations of international expert debates was indeed impressive: the new balance between European, Latin American, and Asian participants had led to the emergence of a new type of language and vocabulary to talk about agriculture. This was particularly apparent in the Committee's report on *Social Problems in Agriculture*.[91] Whilst the report traced the ILO's work from the 1920s onwards, arguing that there was still much to do for agricultural workers in Europe, it also showed a new awareness about the economic and social inequalities of the global agricultural system. Mexican delegate Mesa, who had earlier participated in the Peasant Peace Conference, observed in the report that 'men who cultivate the soil ought everywhere to have a similar standard of living, whatever the geographical

---

[87] This mirrored similar discussions within the Mixed Advisory Agricultural Committee about running an enquiry on the living and working conditions of small independent farmers. Correspondence with International Institute of Agriculture regarding the enquiry into social and economic conditions of small farmers, 1938–39, ILO Archives Geneva, AG 100/110/01.

[88] Stenographic record of the third sitting of the Permanent Agricultural Committee, Wednesday, 9 February 1938, ILO Archives Geneva, AG 1003/1/202/3.

[89] Stenographic record of the third sitting of the Permanent Agricultural Committee, Wednesday, 9 February 1938, ILO Archives Geneva, AG 1003/1/202/3.

[90] W. Holmes, 'The Nations Discuss Farm Labour', *The Landworker* 19, no. 226 (March 1938), 5.

[91] International Labour Office, *Social Problems in Agriculture* (Record of the Permanent Agricultural Committee of the ILO, 7–15 February 1938), Studies and Reports, Series K (Agriculture), no. 14 (Geneva, 1938).

peculiarities of the region or the varying ways in which agricultural exploitation was organized'.⁹² To Mesa, this meant not only the standardization of working hours on farms everywhere, but also improving the 'social position of crofters, share croppers and tenants and small farmers, who in fact suffered from deplorable conditions, similar to those of wage-paid labour'.⁹³ According to the Mexican delegate, one of the major challenges that the ILO would have to face in the future was the existence of 'large numbers of people in the world who live on a bare minimum and [are] really under-nourished, while large numbers of people producing food [are] unable to get really satisfactory prices for it'.⁹⁴

Mesa's statement was pointing to the connections between poverty, malnutrition, and the economic hardship of food producers which would become central to postwar international development thinking. His was a global picture in which Indian peasants, Latin American farmworkers, and European agricultural workers toiled side by side at a time of social unrest, political tensions, and increasing anti-imperialist claims. It is notable that this newly global agricultural underclass (or an imaginary thereof) was present both in the ILO's official expert commissions and in the movements that formed around them. The creation of the ILO's Permanent Agricultural Committee in the late 1930s thus not only reasserted what has been described as the 'symbolic capital' of international Geneva and its social and political legitimacy as an international centre for agrarian affairs.⁹⁵ It also foreshadowed an international developmentalist discourse in which peasant farming, its cultural and folkloristic patterns, and its perceived manifold social and economic problems would move centre stage against a Cold War backdrop of developmentalist concerns and technocratic modernization.⁹⁶ However, the inclusion of certain regions and countries as deserving of attention also highlighted the continued exclusion of other colonial populations, especially in Africa.

Ultimately, the new energy and awareness that had gone into preparing this first meeting of the Permanent Agricultural Committee was cut short by the beginning of international hostilities. A second meeting, planned and prepared for April 1939 to discuss the extension of social insurance to rural populations, had to be postponed because of the outbreak of war.⁹⁷ It would be held as a partial

---

⁹² International Labour Office, 'Social Problem in Agriculture', 112.
⁹³ International Labour Office, 'Social Problem in Agriculture', 112.
⁹⁴ International Labour Office, 'Social Problem in Agriculture', 111.
⁹⁵ Carolyn Biltoft, *A Violent Peace: Media, Truth and Power at the League of Nations* (Chicago: University of Chicago Press, 2021), ch. 2.
⁹⁶ Nicole Sackley, 'Cosmopolitanism and the Uses of Tradition: Robert Redfield and Alternative Visions of Modernization during the Cold War', *Modern Intellectual History* 9, no. 3 (2012), 565–95.
⁹⁷ A detailed report on social insurance and medical services, sickness, old age, death, and invalidity, as well as accident insurance, was prepared for the session that did not take place. 'Extension of Social Insurance to Rural Population', second session of the Permanent Agricultural Committee, Geneva, April 1939, Extension of the social insurance scheme to rural population, ILO Archives Geneva, AG 1003/2/101.

meeting during the second Regional Conference of American members in Cuba in November 1939, further accelerating the ILO's shift away from Europe.[98] The original committee, however, was only able to resume its work in Geneva in 1947—by which time, as we will see, the ILO and the world had experienced a period of great change and transformation.

Cultivating Fields of Progress: Agriculture and the International Labour Organization, 1920s–1950s. Amalia Ribi Forclaz, Oxford University Press. © Amalia Ribi Forclaz 2025. DOI: 10.1093/9780191945014.003.0006

[98] See next chapter.

6
War, Disruption, and Transformation

> 'The tempest which threatened has since broken on the world with a fury beyond anything that the gloomiest forebodings could then contemplate. It has struck with unparalleled rapidity north and west and south and east. It rages on three continents and two oceans; and perhaps it has not yet reached its climax. It has been responsible for material ruin and human misery on a scale without precedent in history.'
> International Labour Office, 'The ILO and Reconstruction', Report by the Acting Director of the International Labour Office to the International Labour Conference, New York, October 1941, 2

When in early 1940 Western European countries fell to the invaders and the threat of war came perilously close to Geneva, the ILO—through its International Labour Office—started making plans for its own survival. The ILO's Governing Body had decided that the latter should continue to function and dispositions for relocation were made. In August 1940, under the helm of American Director John Winant, who had taken over leadership of the Organization from Butler in 1939, a small number of ILO staff settled at McGill University in Montreal, while the Geneva office was kept for the Organization's future return. The story of the perilous journey of a minimal ILO staff to its new headquarters in Canada has been told many times, by those who witnessed it first-hand as well as by historians.[1] It does not need to be recounted here but it goes without saying that this move represented the beginning of a new chapter in the Organization's history that was accompanied by considerable changes in international order, the transformation of governance structures, and the emergence of new social policy challenges.

The war brought material destruction, food shortages, threats of epidemics, and streams of refugees—a humanitarian crisis which would last until 1950.[2] The

---

[1] Edward Phelan, 'The ILO Sets Up Its Wartime Centre in Canada', *Studies: An Irish Quarterly Review* 44, no. 174 (1955), 151–70; Edward Phelan, 'The ILO Turns the Corner', *Studies: An Irish Quarterly Review* 45, no. 178 (1956), 160–86; Sandrine Kott, 'Fighting the War or Preparing for Peace? The ILO during the Second World War', *Journal of Modern European History* 12, no. 3 (2014), 359–76; Daniel Maul, *The International Labour Organization. 100 Years of Global Social Policy* (Berlin: De Gruyter; Geneva: International Labour Office, 2019); Véronique Plata-Stenger, *Social Reform, Modernization and Technical Diplomacy: The ILO Contribution to Development 1930–46* (Oldenbourg: De Gruyter, 2020).

[2] Ben Shephard, *The Long Road Home: The Aftermath of the Second World War* (New York: Alfred A. Knopf, 2011); Ben Shephard, 'Becoming Planning Minded: The Theory and Practice of Relief 1940–1945', *Journal of Contemporary History* 43 (2008), 405–19. For the impact of the Second

complete investment of resources—both material and human—of many European countries into the war effort, added to the disruption of international cooperation and trade. This chapter looks at how the ILO's displacement and the emergence of new approaches and institutions during the war affected the ILO's agricultural work. It traces the ILO's struggle to reaffirm its role as both a defender of social rights for agricultural workers and a centre for the production of knowledge on agriculture.

Institutionally, the outbreak of war caused major disruption for the Organization, including for the Agricultural Service which would move back to Switzerland only in January 1948. The move led to a reorganization of staff and, with it, of agricultural expertise within the Organization. Von Bülow, who oversaw the work of the Service, was encouraged to take early retirement and was not part of the staff that moved to Canada.[3] Neither was Olindo Gorni, who died in Geneva in September 1943. Louise Howard (née Matthaei), an important staff member who had continued to maintain some relations with the ILO and interest in its work, had moved to Britain, where she was helping to bring German Jewish refugees to safety. The international agricultural labour legislation and research carried out before the war entailed by definition a long-winded process that necessitated the exchange of potentially delicate information between government delegations, experts on agricultural production, and national, regional, and local organizations and interest groups. This work stopped almost completely during the war. In exile, and having had to leave without the Organization's archives, the reduced Montreal staff was unable to pick up the threads of its pre-war agricultural work.[4] The war also disrupted other parts of the ILO network. One of its most important partners with regard to agricultural labour rights, the International Landworkers' Federation, saw its activities brought to a standstill by the conflict. With many members forced to go into exile, a temporary office of the Federation was established in Stockholm.[5] Joseph Duncan, who had been a strong advocate for agricultural workers since 1919, continued to serve as its President and would do so until 1950. In general, however, trade unionist campaigning and politics were very much put on hold.

There were other changes too that turned the ILO's exile into an unsettled period. In January 1941, the American director Winant left the Organization after

---

World War on agricultural production and trade, especially in European countries, see Paul Brassley, Yves Segers, and Leen Van Molle, eds, *War, Agriculture and Food: Rural Europe from the 1930s to the 1950s* (New York: Routledge, 2012); Frank Trentmann and Just Flemming, 'Introduction', in Trentmann and Flemming, eds, *Food and Conflict in Europe in the Age of the Two World Wars* (Basingtoke: Palgrave Macmillan, 2006).

[3] ILO Archives Geneva, P 1733.

[4] In Montreal, ILO staff started new files for each country for the period 1942–47, many of which remained empty.

[5] See Leon A. Dale's unpublished study titled 'The International Landworkers' Federation', prepared for the United States Department of Labor in 1957, 8.

only two years of leadership, to the surprise and dismay of most of its staff. Edward Phelan, an Irishman who had been part of the Organization since its inception, succeeded him as director and held the post until 1948.[6] Phelan was particularly concerned about what he called the 'danger of disintegration' that the ILO faced as a result of the war and about the fact that member governments would have other priorities than labour legislation.[7] The International Labour Conference, scheduled for 1940, had been postponed because of the war and he therefore thought it urgent to organize a meeting that would remind member governments of their international commitment and the 'collective function' of their membership within the Organization.[8] A partial meeting of the thirty-three government delegations was held in October 1941 at Columbia University in New York to reflect on the ILO's strategic contribution to post-war reconstruction.[9] With hindsight and in view of what was to happen to other international organizations such as the League of Nations and the International Institute of Agriculture, neither of which survived the Second World War, the threat of disintegration was real and there was an imperative need for the Organization to assert its relevance in a rapidly changing world order, in which economic development would become a primary objective of international relations.[10]

The well-known story of the survival of the ILO in exile tends to cover up another important change: the rather abrupt (albeit temporary) loss of relevance of Geneva as an internationalist and diplomatic hub and as a platform for interwar agricultural cooperation. The future of the League of Nations looked uncertain and, with it, the status of Geneva. In September, a fragment of the League's technical sections was transferred to Princeton, where, supported by the American government, former League officials sought to preserve some of the organization's economic and financial work and to develop plans for after the war.[11] No one, at this point, could foresee the amount of change and the number of new institutions that would emerge in a relatively short period of time. Even if in 1948

---

[6] Geert Van Goethem, 'Phelan's War: The International Labour Organization in Limbo (1941–1948)', in Magaly Rodriguez Garcia, Jasmien Van Daele, and Marcel Van der Linden, eds, *ILO Histories. Essays on the International Labour Organization and its Impact on the World during the Twentieth Century* (Bern: Peter Lang, 2010), 313–40.

[7] Carter Goodrich, 'The Effect of the War on the Position of Labor', *The American Economic Review* 32, no. 1 (1942), 416–25.

[8] International Labour Organization, *Edward Phelan and the ILO: The Life and Views of an International Social Actor* (Geneva: ILO, 2009), 248. For a detailed background to the dilemmas faced by the ILO, see Plata-Stenger, *Social Reform*, 275–6.

[9] International Labour Office, *Record of Proceedings of the Conference of the International Labour Organization*, New York, 27 October–6 November 1941 (Montreal, 1941), 1. Appendix 1: Resolutions Adopted by the Conference, 163.

[10] International Institute of Agriculture, *The Work of the International Institute of Agriculture During the War (1940–1945)* (Rome, 1945). On post-war development and economic order, see Eric Helleiner, *Forgotten Foundations of Bretton Woods: International Development and the Making of the Postwar Order* (Ithaca, NY: Cornell University Press, 2014).

[11] Patricia Clavin, *Securing the World Economy: The Reinvention of the League of Nations, 1920–1946* (Oxford: Oxford University Press, 2015), 267–71.

the ILO and its Agricultural Service would ultimately return to the shores of Lake Geneva, they would do so in a profoundly changed world and with newly formulated social policy objectives.

Shifting Priorities

The 'total' war brought far-reaching changes to how national economies organized labour and production. The impact was particularly felt in the agricultural sector.[12] The interruption of trading and financial relations was causing the disappearance of European continental markets for agricultural exports, with disastrous repercussions on prices and living standards in exporting countries.[13] Moreover, the war turned agriculture into a weapon of military strategy and security. Labour and equipment were used for defence purposes. Military campaigns affected agricultural production as well as transport and distribution. The urgent need to increase food supply and boost agricultural production was felt all over Europe and, from 1940 onwards, became in the words of ILO Director Phelan 'a preoccupation of the first importance' and remained so well into the post-war years.[14] The priority given to short-term food production led to the expansion of state control over labour recruitment, land allocation, and the type and quantity of crops to be grown. Programmes to increase yields with a view to achieving greater self-sufficiency were implemented all over Europe—including in neutral countries such as Switzerland.[15]

Another inevitable consequence of the war was that labour regulations in agriculture were relaxed in many countries to permit longer working days, which ran counter to some of the ILO's pre-war objectives.[16] To secure an agricultural labour supply in the absence of men, some countries such as Great Britain resorted to the training of 'inexperienced' persons, including women and children.[17] Other

---

[12] This was also reflected in the writings of ILO staff in the *International Labour Review*, which continued to survey the impact of war on labour, producing publications on labour problems during wartime. See for example E. F Penrose, 'Economic Organisation for Total War with special Reference to the Workers', *International Labour Review* 42 (1940), 175–213; P. Waelbroeck, 'Labour Redistribution for War Industry', *International Labour Review* 45, no. 4 (1942), 367–94.

[13] International Labour Office, 'The ILO and Reconstruction', Report by the Acting Director to the International Labour Conference, New York, October 1941, 6, 7.

[14] International Labour Office, 'The ILO and Reconstruction', Report by the Acting Director to the International Labour Conference, New York, October 1941, 2.

[15] D. P. E., 'Food for Postwar Europe: Shortages of World Supplies', *Bulletin of International News* 22, no. 11 (1945), 465–74.

[16] For a discussion on the issue of hours of work, see Chapters 2 and 4. International Labour Office, 'Wartime Measures Affecting Hours of Work and Rest Periods', *International Labour Review* 40, no. 5 (November 1939), 665–76. For the situation in the United States, Jacob J. Kaufman, 'Farm Labour During World War II', *Journal of Farm Economics* 31, no. 1 (February 1949), 131–42.

[17] Judith Barrett Litoff and David C. Smith, 'To the Rescue of the Crops: The Women's Land Army during World War II', *Prologue* 25 (Winter 1993), 34; Richard Moore-Colyer, 'The Call to the Land: British and European Adult Voluntary Farm Labour, 1939–49', *Rural History* 17, no. 1 (2006), 83–101;

measures involved the use of prisoners of war in the fields, as Britain did with Italian and German captives.[18] Wartime policies also facilitated the importation of farm labour from occupied countries or other foreign countries, and the imposition of compulsory farm labour to certain age or class groups.[19]

Beyond feeding the troops and maintaining food security, there were also long-term social aspects to factor in, including the improvement of nutrition and adequate diet which would become central to reconstruction efforts.[20] The war gave birth to a plethora of food aid operations, ranging from national charities to international associations and humanitarian relief agencies helping specific groups of civilians.[21] A point in case are the activities of the Associated Country Women of the World, whose office continued to function despite the bombings in London, reflecting the shift towards food production. The association engaged in seed transfer activities with the United States and resorted to distributing pressure cookers and hand sealers, so that its farming members could preserve fruit and vegetables that would otherwise have gone to waste.[22]

One particular organization stood out for the sheer scale and breadth of its operations, its concern with agricultural rehabilitation, and its influence on post-war planning: the United Nations Relief and Rehabilitation Administration (hereafter UNRRA).[23] According to some observers, its first session, held in November 1943 and hosted by the American government in Washington, signalled the beginning of a new era of international cooperation.[24] The UNRRA

---

and Richard Moore-Colyer, 'Kids in the Corn: School Harvest Camps and Farm Labour Supply in England, 1940-1950', *The Agricultural History Review* 52, no. 2 (2004), 183-206.

[18] Johann Custodis, 'Employing the Enemy: the Contribution of German and Italian Prisoners of War to British Agriculture during and after the Second World War', *Agricultural History Review* 60, no. 2 (2012), 243-65.

[19] 'The ILO and Reconstruction', Report by the Acting Director to the International Labour Conference, New York, October 1941, 61-2. International Labour Office, 'Wartime Measures'.

[20] John Boyd-Orr, 'The Role of Food in Post-War Reconstruction', *International Labour Review* 47, no. 3 (1943), 279-96.

[21] Michael Bartlett, *Empire of Humanity: A History of Humanitarianism* (Ithaca: Cornell University Press, 2011), 132-58; Silvia Salvatici, *A History of Humanitarianism, 1755-1989: In the Name of Others* (Manchester: Manchester University Press, 2019).

[22] Associated Country Women of the World, Report of the Executive Committee, 1939-47, Archives of the Associated Country Women of the World, London.

[23] David L. MacFarlane, 'The UNRRA Experience in Relation to Development in Food and Agriculture'. *Journal of Farm Economics* 30, no.1 (1948), 69-77; George Woodbridge, *The History of the United Nations Relief and Rehabilitation Administration*, vols 1-3 (New York: Columbia University Press, 1950), 26.

[24] UNRRA has in recent years emerged as a major actor in international and transnational histories of post-war reconstruction. Jessica Reinisch, 'Introduction: Relief Work in the Aftermath of War', *Journal of Contemporary History* 43, no. 3 (2008), 371-404; Jessica Reinisch, 'Internationalism in Relief: The Birth (and Death) of UNRRA', *Past and Present* 210, suppl. 6 (2011), 258-89; Silvia Salvatici, 'Help the People to Help Themselves': UNRRA Relief Workers and European Displaced Persons', *Journal of Refugee Studies* 25 (2012), 452-73; Andrew J. Williams, 'Reconstruction before the Marshall Plan', *Review of International Studies* 31 (2005), 541-58. Recent studies, which for reasons of space cannot be cited here, have provided insights into relief work in specific countries, including Poland, France, Greece, Germany, Italy, China, and the Soviet Union.

embodied a novel approach to food and agriculture that focused on operational activities and became a laboratory for the nascent international development machinery. Beside responding to emergencies and providing food, shelter, and clothing to civilians (especially children and displaced persons), the UNRRA also offered technical assistance, scientific expertise, and development aid. In this respect, the agricultural rehabilitation plan of the UNRRA went well beyond the provision of food and encompassed a detailed programme of agricultural reconstruction with a supply of agricultural goods such as tractors and seeds, but also of knowledge and technology.[25] This represented an important shift in the internationalist way of thinking about agriculture. The scale and ambitions of the UNRRA programme, for example the transfer of hybrid maize crops from the United States to Europe, was unprecedented; as were the dissemination and transfer of agricultural techniques in Eastern and Southern Europe and China. Albeit short-lived, UNRRA's agricultural relief operations opened a new age of international agricultural development and asserted American leadership in this field.[26]

The ILO's participation in these efforts and its integration into post-war reconstruction plans was marginal.[27] In December 1943, a delegation of the International Labour Office led by Phelan was invited, together with other inter-governmental agencies, to take part in the first session of the council of the UNRRA. The meeting approved certain permanent arrangements for cooperation between the UNRRA and ILO, including the latter's participation as an observer in the meetings of the council as well as its committees and subcommittees.[28] But in effect the ILO did not succeed in establishing a working relationship with the UNRRA and was thus left out from one of the most important and innovative wartime reconstruction programmes.

New Institutional Births and Slow Demises

Of course, the major wartime institutional change that affected the ILO's work on agriculture was not the creation of UNRRA but that of the Food and Agriculture

---

[25] While the work of UNRRA on food provisions is relatively well known, there has been little research about the goals, organization, and implementation of its agricultural programme. On the Agricultural Rehabilitation Division, see Amalia Ribi Forclaz, 'The Latest Developments in Agricultural Knowledge and Practice from the Outside World': UNRRA's Agricultural Rehabilitation Work in Italy in the Aftermaths of the Second World War', in Heinrich Hartmann and Julia Tischler, eds, *Planting Seeds of Knowledge: Agriculture and Education in Rural Societies in the Twentieth Century* (New York, Oxford: Berghahn Books, 2023), 71–86. Gerard A. Mahler, 'UNRRA's Agricultural Rehabilitation Activities: History and Economic Appraisal'. United Nations Archives New York, S-1021-0008-06.
[26] Emanuele Bernardi, *Il mais 'miracoloso': Storia di un'innovazione tra politica, economia e religione* (Roma: Carocci editore, 2014).
[27] Antony Alcock, *History of the International Labour Organization* (Basingstoke: Macmillan, 1971), 174–5. Also, Maul, *The International Labour Organization*, 126.
[28] International Labour Office, 'The United Nations Relief and Rehabilitation Administration', *International Labour Review* 49, no. 2 (February 1944), 145–59, 157–8.

Organization (hereafter FAO) in the spring of 1943. The birth of this new organization would—in time—also lead to the demise of the ILO's former cooperation partner, the International Institute of Agriculture.[29] If, after the First World War, the competence of the International Labour Office over agricultural issues had been questioned by a handful of governments, now the ILO faced the threat of new organizations that, in the run to dismiss 'failed' interwar institutions, would take over its mandate of creating better living and working conditions for people in agriculture.

Already in the late 1930s, Frank McDougall had anticipated that, should a new war break out, agriculture would need an organization of its own to secure lasting peace.[30] Proposals for the 'marriage of food and agriculture' under one institutional framework had been put forward as early as in 1935 by the Australian delegation at the League Assembly.[31] Work on rural nutrition and hygiene had also picked up in the second half of the 1930s, culminating in a range of international conferences.[32] Nutrition was important not just with regard to calorie intake but also to ensure the labour efficiency of man-power, an aspect that was of great relevance for the colonies during the war.[33] Dismissing the ILO's work on agriculture to date, McDougall argued that the League of Nations had no section dedicated to agricultural problems, a shortcoming that he attributed to the prior existence of the International Institute of Agriculture. In his eyes, the latter was not a satisfactory institution, unable as it was to address many important issues connected to agriculture, such as the technological aspects of new methods of production or the scientific discoveries about nutrition.[34] This was a gap that waited to be filled by a new organization.

A first step towards the creation of such an institution was made in the spring of 1943, when plans for an organization specialized in food and agriculture were

---

[29] On this, see Chapter 3.

[30] McDougall, Memo, 'The Food and Agriculture Organization of the United Nations', 11 June 1947, FAO Archives Rome, RG 3.1, Series D8. On McDougall, see also John B. O'Brien, 'F. L. McDougall and the Origins of the FAO', *Australian Journal of Politics and History* 46, no. 2 (2000), 164–74.

[31] Although the creation of the FAO has been ascribed to Roosevelt and American New Dealers, its roots are more diverse and intimately connected with pre-war experiences and institutions. Amy Staples, *The Birth of Development: How the World Bank, Food and Agriculture Organization, and World Health Organization Changed the World, 1945–1965* (Kent, OH: The Kent State University Press, 2006); Ruth Jachertz, '"To Keep Food out of Politics": The UN Food and Agriculture Organization, 1945–1965', in Marc Frey, Soenke Kunkel, and Corinna R. Unger, eds, *International Organizations and Development, 1945–1990* (Basingstoke: Palgrave Macmillan, 2014), 75–100; Ruth Jachertz and Alexander Nützenadel, 'Coping with Hunger? Visions of a Global Food System, 1930–1960', *Journal of Global History* 6 (2011), 99–119.

[32] Sunil Amrith, *Decolonizing International Health: India and Southeast Asia, 1930–1965* (Cambridge: Palgrave Macmillan, 2006); Iris Borowy, *Coming to Terms with World Health: The League of Nations Health Organization, 1921–1946* (Frankfurt am Main: Peter Lang, 2009).

[33] International Labour Office, 'The Nutrition of Indigenous Workers', *International Labour Review* 41, no. 3 (1940), 307–17.

[34] McDougall, Notes and Comments, 1938–1939, FAO Archives Rome, RG 3.1, Series D3; McDougall, 'Need for an Investigation on the Agricultural, Trade and Financial Aspects of the Application of the New Science of Nutrition', 5 August 1939, FAO Archives Rome, RG 3.1, Series D8.

agreed upon at the Hot Springs Conference—a prelude to the FAO's formal constitution, which would take place in 1945. The new organization was to work towards improving nutritional standards, promoting agricultural reconstruction, and increasing rural prosperity and welfare. It was to do this through the promotion of research, dissemination of knowledge, the exchange of services, and the issuing of international recommendations.[35] Indelicately, the ILO was not invited to attend the Hot Springs meeting but simply asked to submit a 'memorandum' summarizing its 'interests and activities' with regard to food and agriculture.[36] To the dismay of the International Labour Office, the conference issued a string of resolutions regarding short-term and long-term agricultural production but also farm labour, land tenure, cooperative movements, social security, without even mentioning the work done by the ILO in this field.[37] The Hot Springs conference threatened to further undermine the ILO's international role by providing a powerful and attractive new platform for agricultural interest groups that had formerly cooperated with the Organization. These included the Confédération Internationale d'Agriculture (formerly Commission Internationale d'Agriculture). The Confédération was presided by no other than the indefatigable Swiss agronomist Ernst Laur who in 1940 had taken over the leadership from the Marquis de Vogüé.[38] Ironically, after challenging the ILO's work on agriculture for two decades on the basis that it would weaken government sovereignty, Laur was now keen to reaffirm his own organization's role in the post-war international order, and clearly regarded the future FAO as a more promising cooperation partner than the ILO.[39]

Narratives about the beginning of the FAO, especially those written by FAO staff, often praise the conferences of 1943 and 1945 as stepping stones to a new structure of governance of agricultural issues, without paying much attention to the bureaucratic processes that accompanied the demise of the FAO's predecessor.[40] The transition between old and new agricultural organizations, which entailed the liquidation of the International Institute of Agriculture, was in fact a much messier and complex process than might appear from official declarations and constitutions. In effect, much of the Institute's activities continued until the

---

[35] US Department of State: United Nations Conference on Food and Agriculture, Hot Springs, Virginia, 18 May–3 June 1943. Final act and section reports (Washington, DC, 1943). See *International Labour Review* 48 (August 1943), 139–56.

[36] Alcock, *History of the International Labour Organization*, 175.

[37] 'The United Nations Conference on Food and Agriculture', *International Labour Review* 48, no. 2 (August 1943), 151–2, Footnote 140.

[38] Confédération internationale d'Agriculture, 1937–46, FAO Archives Rome, 1 IIA 73.

[39] Telegram Laur to Hot Springs Conference, undated, probably May 1943. FAO Archives Rome, 1 IIA 73. See also Chapter 1.

[40] Gove Hambidge, *The Story of FAO* (New York: D. Van Nostrand Company, 1955); Paul Lamartine Yates, *So Bold an Aim: Ten Years of International Cooperation toward Freedom from Want: Québec, 1945–Rome, 1955* (Rome: FAO, 1955). Historians have done a better job: see for example Staples, *The Birth of Development*.

end of 1946 and, as long as they did, the FAO remained in a dormant state.[41] As late as August 1946, 120 staff members of the Institute were still working in the same building that had been transferred to the FAO by the Italian government and was now operating as the FAO's Rome office.[42]

This explains why even well-informed observers such as Laur and the general secretary of the International Institute of Agriculture Ugo Papi were hopeful that the Institute would continue to exist within the FAO.[43] Work carried on without much interruption across different sections of the Institute, including the secretariat, the statistical section, the economic and social sections, the technical and legislative sections, and the library.[44] The remaining staff attributed great importance to ensuring the continuity of its publications such as its international agricultural review, its monthly bulletin of agricultural science and practice, its international bulletin of plant protection, and its statistical yearbooks.[45] Those in charge feared serious criticism if the agricultural research and information work of the Institute was stopped before FAO's headquarters were able to take over. They insisted that the world and especially Europe relied on the Institute's publication.[46] By September 1946, however, a few months after the official dissolution of the League of Nations in April 1946, a delegation of three American experts led by economist Howard R. Tolley visited the Institute to arrange its shutdown. They decided that its statistical yearbooks for 1945 and 1946 should be published, after which the section would be liquidated and the staff discharged, thus finalizing the closure of the Institute and putting an end to four decades of research work and expert meetings.[47]

In the meantime, the formal constitution of the FAO at a conference in Québec in October 1945 was welcomed by activists such as Charlotte Boudreau, who represented the Associated Country Women of the World as an observer. Boudreau, who was the wife of American League of Nations health expert Frank Boudreau, noted with undisguised excitement how the atmosphere at the meeting was one 'of intensive thought', with delegates that were 'experts in various scientific lines',

---

[41] Extract from: Sections and various duties of the temporary office in Rome, 12 March 1947, FAO Archives Rome, 0/1/0/D/16, 7. See also Amalia Ribi Forclaz and Corinne Pernet, 'Confronting a Hungry World: The United Nations Food and Agricultural Organization in a Historical Perspective', *International History Review* 41, no. 2 (2019), 345-350.

[42] Memo, dated 1946, unsigned, in 'Papers Concerning Continuation of IIA Activities by FAO 1946-1947', FAO Archives Rome, 0/1/0/D/16.

[43] Letter, Laur to the International Institute of Agriculture, 31 July 1945, Archives of the International Institute of Agriculture, FAO Archives Rome, IIA 73. Reply from Ugo Papi to Laur, 17 September 1945, FAO Archives Rome, IIA 73.

[44] Memo, dated 1946, unsigned, 'Papers Concerning Continuation of IIA Activities by FAO 1946-1947', FAO Archives Rome, 0/1/0/D/16.

[45] See Chapter 2.

[46] Memo, dated 1946, unsigned, in 'Papers Concerning Continuation of IIA Activities by FAO 1946-1947', FAO Archives Rome, 0/1/0/D/16.

[47] Unsigned report on the International Institute of Agriculture, 2 October 1946, FAO Archives Rome, 0/1/0/D/16.

including 'a sparkling of practical farmers' who 'should produce valuable work'.[48] Boudreau was not the only one to feel excited and hopeful about the FAO's future work. Other experts familiar with interwar cooperation, such as McDougall, described the constitution of the FAO as 'something new in the world'.[49] McDougall praised the international community for committing to promoting 'common welfare' by raising standards of nutrition and improving agricultural production, bettering the 'condition of rural populations' and overall contributing to world economic growth. He also noted that these functions were 'much wider' than those of the International Institute of Agriculture, which the FAO had, by agreement, taken over.[50]

The FAO was not only seen by many as a much-improved version of the Institute: its mandate was also deemed to be substantially 'bolder', its terms of reference 'more vigorous' and more in tune with the needs of the post-war world than the approach followed by previous organizations, the ILO included.[51] Writing in the *International Labour Review* in 1945, economist Horace Belshaw (head of the FAO's rural welfare section) indirectly criticized the ILO's approach to improving labour and living conditions of agricultural workers through labour legislation. Belshaw observed that the Organization's narrow line of attack overlooked bigger structural issues such as the lack of agricultural transformation and economic development that hindered progress in the rural countryside: 'There is always the danger that specialists will use the microscope on the segment in which they are especially interested', thus failing to appreciate the 'broader economic and social problems which must first be solved'.[52] Increasing efficiency and restructuring the agricultural sector through reforms that prioritized expanded holdings, farmed by a smaller numbers of commercial and mechanized farmers, were seen as a prerequisite for future improvements.[53] Rural welfare as a precondition to rural well-being was the new buzzword in internationalist circles, and it was mostly directed towards improving the conditions in so-called agrarian societies in Asia, Latin America, and Africa, where the majority of the rural population lived from subsistence agriculture.[54] Belshaw, however, also conceded that increased efficiency and higher per capita income for farmers would not

---

[48] Boudreau to Associated Country Women of the World, 22 October 1945, Associated Country Women of the World Archives, London.
[49] McDougall, Memo, 'The Food and Agriculture Organization of the United Nations', 11 June 1947, FAO Archives Rome, McDougall Notes, 1946–50.
[50] McDougall, Memo, 'The Food and Agriculture Organization of the United Nations', 11 June 1947, FAO Archives Rome, Mc Dougall Notes, 1946–50, 3.
[51] Yates, *So Bold an Aim*, 54.
[52] Horace Belshaw, 'Foundations of Rural Welfare', *International Labour Review* 52, no. 3 (March 1945), 279–301, 280.
[53] Belshaw, 'Foundations of Rural Welfare', 292.
[54] Food and Agriculture Organization, *Essentials of Rural Welfare: An Approach to the Improvement of Rural Well-Being* (Washington, DC: Food and Agriculture Organization, 1949). On this shift, see also Yates, *So Bold an Aim*, 25–52.

necessarily lead to improved conditions for rural workers. Hence, he did not completely discount the usefulness of public policies and international labour standards to secure better wages, limited hours, improved housing, and social insurance.

All in all, the internationalist vision of agriculture had significantly shifted: agriculture, as various international bilateral and multilateral relief plans show, was a much bigger part of the post-war reconstruction program and of broader economic and developmentalist aims than it had been after the First World War.[55] Food aid and economic recovery programmes such as the Marshall Plan would play a crucial role in Europe's recovery and its agricultural production.[56] What was also new was the FAO's rhetoric about the need to secure adequate levels of food and nutrition globally through the intensification and increase of agricultural production. The Organization's first World Food Survey of 1946 made predictions about population growth and nutritional targets, planning, and long-term projections that would become characteristic of development organizations in the following decades.[57] Driven by bleak forecasts about how an increase in population would strain limited resources, a fresh technological optimism infused the nascent international machinery that would soon see the rise of new expert circuits and the emergence of development economist.[58] The social and economic rupture caused by the war and the challenges of reconstruction were seen as decisive turning points that called for a new agricultural revolution. According to McDougall, this revolution would be boosted by 'modern agricultural implements', including the new technologies that had been tested and promoted during the war such as the use of fertilizers, insecticides and pesticides. In the eyes of international agricultural experts, these new 'tools of production' would undoubtedly contribute to 'an upward spiral' of prosperity.[59]

For the ILO, the FAO's very different outlook yet overlapping mandate on agriculture raised the question of how to cooperate with the new and acclaimed organization. Faced with the latter's confident assertions that it was opening a new era of agricultural cooperation, the ILO felt left out and threatened.[60] And it

---

[55] Amalia Ribi Forclaz, 'From Reconstruction to Development: The Food and Agriculture Organization (FAO) and the Conceptualization of Rural Welfare, 1945–1950', *International History Review* 41, no. 2 (2019), 351–71.

[56] Heinrich Hartmann, 'Building an Old Institution: the Agricultural Extension Service and Village Institutes in Post-Second World War Rural Turkey', in Heinrich Hartmann and Julia Tischler, eds, *Planting Seeds of Knowledge: Agriculture and Education in Rural Societies in the Twentieth Century* (New York, Oxford: Berghahn Books, 2023), 87–103.

[57] Food and Agriculture Organization of the United Nations, World Food Survey, Washington, 1946. See also Jenny Andersson, 'The Great Future Debate and the Struggle for the World', *The American History Review* 117, no. 5 (2012), 1411–30.

[58] Michelle Murphy, *The Economization of Life* (Durham, NC: Duke University Press, 2017).

[59] McDougall, 'Memorandum on Long-term International Problems in the Field of Food and agriculture', 12 July 1946, FAO Archives Rome, McDougall Notes, 1946–50.

[60] International Labour Office, *The ILO and the United Nations* (Montreal, 1946), 10.

many ways it was. Confidential notes by FAO experts reveal that there were efforts of cooperation with other United Nations organizations, especially UNESCO, which was showing an early interest in the topics of food and population. Ideas were evoked such as a plan to build an International Academy of Agricultural Science named after the founder of the International Institute of Agriculture, David Lubin, and to cooperate on forest research, meteorology, and climatology. These plans did not consider the ILO's participation and seemed unaware of the organization's pre-war work.[61] Even though these cooperation efforts between new organizations were mostly prompted by the wish to share costs at a time when budgets were still small, it was clear to many observers that the ILO was completely sidelined in what was referred to as the new 'UN machinery'—a term which implied that the world had been equipped with an unprecedented organization and structure of governance designed to resolve new global tasks.

The ILO's director Phelan, who was steering the Organization through the bumpy post-war years, was well aware of the situation, but also critical of those who enthusiastically embraced the new institutions: 'Machinery', Phelan reflected, 'is a convenient word to use when we discuss international institutions; but its use tends perhaps to make us sometimes forget that the essential character of institutions is not something mechanical, that they are not structures which can be bolted and rivetted to a geometrical design following the blueprints of carefully worded texts.' Highlighting the ILO's history and pre-war experience, Phelan mused that in order to be effective, international institutions 'must become endowed with life, pushing out their roots and branches—the creation of gardeners rather than engineers'. Before the war the ILO's 'roots ha[d] spread wide and deep; not even the cyclone of the war could uproot the tree, and though some of its branches may have been broken in that tempest, its vitality is such that even as the winds began to abate, the buds of new growth [...] [were] already in vigorous evidence.'[62]

Still, despite its deep roots and illustrious pedigree, it was the ILO that made the effort to liaise with the new institution, and not the other way round. In August 1947, the new chief of the ILO's Agricultural Service Mukdim Osmay reached out to FAO's first director Sir John Boyd-Orr to brief him on the pre-war agricultural work of the ILO.[63] Osmay was a former Turkish attaché at the Paris Peace Conference and a staff member of the ILO since 1934, who had resettled to Montreal and become the new chief of the Agricultural Service. Notwithstanding

---

[61] McDougall, Note on 'FAO–UNESCO Cooperation', 7 October 1948, FAO Archives Rome, McDougall notes, 1946–50.

[62] International Labour Office, *The ILO and the United Nations*, 10. In 1946, the ILO became the first specialized agency of the United Nations.

[63] Osmay to Phelan, 20 August 1947, ILO Archives Geneva, P 2874.

his rather different profile from his predecessors and his lack of experience in agricultural matters (his expertise lay in his diplomatic work for Greek–Turkish prisoner exchange), he was put in charge of agricultural 'liaison' work during the war years. The result of his meeting with Boyd-Orr was an agreement between the FAO and the ILO that set forth measures to avoid competition and enable cooperation between the two organizations. It assured mutual consultation, exchange of information, and reciprocal representations in expert commissions on questions of common interests.[64] In reality, however, the overlaps would provide manifold frictions in the following decades, as both organizations embarked on a global quest for the improvement of the economic and social conditions of farmers and agricultural workers worldwide.

Extending Social Policy to 'Dependent Territories'

What also came to impact the future course of the ILO's work on agriculture during those wartime and early post-war years between 1943 and 1947 were the changes in the international world order, the crisis of empires, the beginning of decolonization, and the emergence of a more unified developmentalist notion. In many ways, when viewed through the prism of the ILO, the process of decentring Geneva as an international hub both institutionally and geographically had already started in the second half of the 1930s, through an increasing number of regional conferences which transferred agency away from the headquarters and particularly to Latin American and later Southeast Asian countries. The adherence of the United States to the ILO in 1934 and the Second World War accelerated this shift, bringing with it a re-interpretation of colonial responsibilities and—at least publicly—a new language of equality.

The International Labour Conference held in May 1944 in Philadelphia—the first regular session since 1939—stands out as a watershed: this is where the ILO announced its post-war policy, rephrased its charter, and committed to addressing labour problems in colonial territories.[65] The Philadelphia conference, which happened a few months before other post-war planning discussions such as the Bretton Woods Conference, reaffirmed the organization's commitment to social justice and to tripartism, but also outlined its expanded geographical horizons. As historians have noted, there was a perceptible change in rhetoric, which now reflected a combination of 'human rights' and developmentalist language such as

---

[64] 'Agreement of 1947 on Reciprocal Representation', ILO Archives Geneva, FAO 3.
[65] International Labour Office, *Record of Proceedings*, twenty-sixth session of the International Labour Conference, Philadelphia (Montreal: 1944); Edward Joseph Phelan, 'The Contribution of the ILO to Peace', *International Labour Review* 59, no. 6 (1949), 611.

the statement that 'all human beings, irrespective of race, creed or sex', should be able to freely pursue development and economic security.⁶⁶ This mirrored the developmentalist turn in the colonies exemplified by the British Colonial Development and Welfare Act of 1940 and similar reform policies in French and Belgian dependencies. It happened in a context of crisis, labour unrest, and increasing social demands from workers.⁶⁷ As has been stressed by various historians, development was a malleable notion, especially when it was invoked by European colonial governments. At the government level, development was used as a 'strategy' to improve the economic standing of colonies, to 'modernize colonialism', and to keep up the colonial relationship.⁶⁸

In preparation for the conference, the International Labour Office had compiled a report on 'Minimum Standards of Social Policy in Dependent Territories', which led to the adoption of a homonymous recommendation that extended to the colonies the social security measures hitherto reserved for European workers.⁶⁹ This meant that issues such as unemployment, unionization, and social insurance in colonial territories were now part of the agenda.⁷⁰ There was talk of 'a strengthening of a sense of international responsibility for improved standards of living throughout the world' and particularly in the colonies. Not only was there a new 'world interest in security and welfare'. Also, thanks to technical innovations such as the evolution of commercial flying, 'the remoteness of tropical regions'

---

⁶⁶ International Labour Office, *Record of Proceedings*, twenty-sixth session of the International Labour Conference, Philadelphia (Montreal, 1944). Appendix 13: Declaration adopted by the Conference, 621–3, 621. See Maul, *The International Labour Organization*, 127; Luis Rodríguez-Piñero, *Indigenous Peoples, Postcolonialism, and International Law: The ILO Regime (1919–1989)* (Oxford University Press, 2005), 36–8. Alain Supiot, *L'Esprit de Philadelphie. La justice sociale face au marché total* (Paris: Seuil, 2010). Véronique Plata-Stenger, *Social Reform, Modernization and Technical Diplomacy: The ILO Contribution to Development (1930–1946)* (Oldenbourg: De Gruyter, 2020), 281. On the Bretton Woods agreements that emerged around the same time, see Helleiner, *Forgotten Foundations of Bretton Woods*.

⁶⁷ On this shift, see Frederick Cooper, 'Modernising Colonialism and the Limits of Empire', in Craig Calhoun, Frederick Cooper, and Kevin W. Moore, eds, *Lessons of Empire: Imperials Histories and American Power* (New York: New Press, 2006), 66–8; Joanna Lewis, 'Tropical East Ends and the Second World War: Some Contradictions in Colonial Office Welfare Initiatives', *The Journal of Imperial and Commonwealth History* 28, no. 20 (2000), 51; Helen Tilley, *Africa as a Living Laboratory: Empire, Development, and the Problem of Scientific Knowledge, 1870–1950* (Chicago: University of Chicago Press, 2011), 71–3, 100–13.

⁶⁸ Corinna R. Unger, *International Development: A Postwar History* (London, Bloomsbury, 2018), 34–43.

⁶⁹ International Labour Office, twenty-sixth session of the International Labour Conference, Report V: 'Minimum Standards of Social Policy in Dependent Territories' (Montreal, 1944); International Labour Organization, Recommendation no. 70: 'Social Policy in Dependent Territories', 1944.

⁷⁰ Jeremy Seekings, 'The ILO and Social Protection in the Global South, 1919–2005', Centre for Social Research CSSR Working Paper, no. 238, December 2008. Frederick Cooper, *Decolonization and African Society* (Cambridge: Cambridge University Press, 1996), 216–17. On the ILO's interwar approach to the colonies, see Susan Zimmermann, '"Special Circumstances in Geneva": The ILO and the World of Non-Metropolitan Labour in the Interwar Period', in Rodriguez Garcia, Van Daele, Van der Linden, *ILO Histories*, 221–50.

was largely disappearing, but not the ambivalent discourse that measured the tropics against the geographical spaces of the temperate zones.[71]

The growing commitment and awareness of the international community towards colonial development and the needs of colonial populations did not mean that colonialism was questioned or that self-government (an aim of the interwar mandates system) was within close reach.[72] Rather, population in these colonies was often qualified as 'lethargic' (due to malnutrition, lack of services, and poverty) and depicted as 'psychologically unwilling or unable' to produce more food.[73] And although the war had exacerbated the use of forced labour in French and British colonies, it was only towards the end of the conflict that the ILO began to revisit its attitude towards colonial territories and their labourers, and to demonstrate a new commitment to improving social and economic conditions for the latter.

The international codification of colonial labour reform that took place in those years also served to strengthen the perceived distinction between 'industrialized' versus 'less industrialized' countries.[74] The distinction appeared at a time when techniques of economic measurement where increasingly used to quantify (or rather estimate) the gap between rich and poor countries. The latter countries were increasingly defined by economists according to their economic performance as 'underdeveloped countries' characterized by limited industrialization, difficult climates, and archaic agricultural practices.[75] With regard to agriculture, the inclusion of 'less industrialized countries' in the ILO's deliberations was a potentially significant change because it called for greater awareness of large agrarian economies, the challenges of modernizing peasant agriculture, as well as issues of land distribution and technological development. At the conference in Philadelphia, numerous delegates from Latin American and Eastern European countries drew attention to the need for agricultural industrialization and mechanization but also for the 'social advancement of the rural population' as

---

[71] International Labour Office, Twenty-Sixth session of the International Labour Conference, Report V: 'Minimum Standards of Social Policy in Dependent Territories' (Montreal, 1944), 4. Daniel Clayton and Gavin Bowd, 'Geography, Tropicality and Postcolonialism: Anglophone and Francophone Readings of the work of Pierre Gourou', *L'Espace Géographique* 3 (2006), 208–21.

[72] Jessica Lynne Pearson, 'Defending Empire at the United Nations: The Politics of International Colonial Oversight in the Era of Decolonisation', *The Journal of Imperial and Commonwealth History* 45, no. 3 (2017), 525–49; Mark Mazower, *No Enchanted Palace: The End of Empire and the Ideological Origins of the United Nations* (Princeton, NJ: Princeton University Press, 2009), 15; Glenda Sluga, *Internationalism in the Age of Nationalism* (Philadelphia: University of Pennsylvania Press, 2013), 92.

[73] International Labour Office, 'The Nutrition of Indigenous Workers', 307–17, 308.

[74] For a discussion of the ILO's early distinction between more and less advanced economies, see Thomas Gidney, 'The Development Dichotomy: Colonial India's Accession to the ILO's Governing Body (1919–1922)', *Journal of Global History* 18, no. 2 (2023), 259–80.

[75] Daniel Speich, 'The Roots of the Millennium Development Goals: A Framework for Studying the History of Global Statistics', *Historical Social Research* 41, no. 2 (2016), 218–37. Malgorzata Mazurek, 'Measuring Development: An Intellectual and Political History of Ludwik Landau's Scale of World Inequality', *Contemporary European History* 28 (2019), 156–71. Murphy, *Economization of Life*. Helleiner, *Forgotten Foundations of Bretton Woods*, 20.

problems which would require 'enormous change'.[76] They pointed out that in many colonial territories over three-quarters of the population was dependent on agriculture for its livelihood—a situation that was unlikely to change in the foreseeable future. It was necessary to give rural labour more attention within the very structure of the ILO, and delegates called for special sessions on agriculture. These statements were also echoed in a report drafted by Wilfrid Benson of the ILO's Native Labour Section on the basis of the deliberations in Philadelphia. The report was explicit about the role of agriculture, food, and nutrition in the improvement of living standards of workers in the colonies. It also differentiated between European versus 'native' production, mining versus agriculture, and plantations versus 'peasant crops', outlining several potential social and economic conflicts.[77]

The discussions started in Philadelphia continued at the next International Labour Conference held in Paris in autumn 1945, where supplementary and more concrete issues pertaining to agriculture were addressed.[78] One of these was the problem of land policies and ownership, which were recognized as essential elements in the pursuit of economic and social progress in the colonies. Workers' representatives viewed the expansion of land tenancy and the availability and accessibility of land for farming, as well as the regulation of share-cropping to ensure a fair system for those working the land, as fundamental conditions to secure 'minimum standards of living' for agricultural populations.[79] Whereas some governments, such as Belgium, were concerned about the loss of 'flexibility' in the colonization of 'vacant' land and did not appreciate the fact that the ILO was making statements about land policies, others rejoiced. Thus, the Mexican government wished for the ILO to go further in recognizing the importance of peasant land ownership in dependent territories: 'In view of the stimulus provided by the ownership of land to work and progress, the peoples should not only be entitled to own land but should be encouraged and assisted to do so.'[80]

This new regard to land ownership and the 'peasant' did not signify—at least at the time—a shift in the ILO's traditional agenda that focused on hired landless workers. To be sure, the organization echoed the statements of other UN

---

[76] Statement of Polish government delegate Jan Stanczyk, in International Labour Office, *Record of Proceedings*, twenty-sixth session of the International Labour Conference, Philadelphia (Montreal, 1944), 151.

[77] International Labour Office, *Social Policy in Dependent Territories*, Studies and Reports, Series B, no. 38 (Montreal, 1944), 14.

[78] International Labour Office, *Record of Proceedings*, twenty-seventh session of the International Labour Conference, Paris, 1945.

[79] For a discussion of the supplementary provisions, see International Labour Office, twenty-seventh session of the International Labour Conference, Questionnaire 1, Minimum Standards for Social Policy in Dependent Territories (Supplementary Provisions) (Montreal, 1945).

[80] International Labour Office, twenty-seventh session of the International Labour Conference, Questionnaire 1, Minimum Standards for Social Policy in Dependent Territories (Supplementary Provisions). (Montreal, 1945), 8–9.

organizations that increasing the 'welfare of the peasant cultivator' was a fundamental problem in colonial and postcolonial territories. But it also freely admitted that it was not equipped to deal with such problems, not only because it did not have the necessary expertise, but also because 'peasants' did not neatly fall into the ILO's conceptualization of labour relations.[81] In contrast to agricultural workers and farmhands, peasants were seen as independent small farmers who were not subject to employer–employee relationships or contracts. In other words, peasant welfare posed challenges that the ILO would not be able to solve through labour legislation.[82] Thus, the ILO preferred to stick, at least temporarily, to its traditional agenda of elaborating progressive labour legislation and social standards based on the industrial model. It would jump on the bandwagon of rural development and technical assistance in the early 1950s, when it joined other UN organizations to build the so-called Andean Indian programme (1952–72), aimed at providing technical assistance and development to indigenous communities in the Andean highlands.[83]

Change and Continuity

Much of the ILO's work on the expansion of its programme and the rethinking of social policy for colonial territories had taken place while the organization was still in exile. This changed in 1947, when Geneva reclaimed its standing as an international city. In the spring of 1947, the former centre of operation of the League of Nations at the Palais des Nations was formally announced as the new headquarters of the European Office of the United Nations. According to one observer, this step returned the Swiss city 'to some extent to its glory of the thirties', a time when it was a significant hub for international diplomacy, cooperation, and organization.[84] A year earlier, the closing Assembly of the League had drawn the curtain on the interwar organization and transferred its functions to the United Nations.[85] As a commentator professed, the clash between old and

---

[81] International Labour Office, Twenty-Sixth session of the International Labour Conference, Report V: 'Minimum Standards of Social Policy in Dependent Territories' (Montreal, 1944), 6.
[82] International Labour Office, Twenty-Sixth session of the International Labour Conference, Report V: 'Minimum Standards of Social Policy in Dependent Territories' (Montreal, 1944), 6.
[83] Jason Pribilsky, 'Development and the "Indian Problem" in the Cold War Andes: Indigenismo, Science, and Modernization in the Making of the Cornell-Peru Project at Vicos', *Diplomatic History* 33, no. 3 (2009), 405–26; Sebastian Gil-Riaño, 'Risky Migrations: Race, Latin Eugenics, and Cold War Development in the International Labor Organization's Puno–Tambopata Project in Peru, 1930–60', *History of Science* 60, no. 1 (2022), 41–68; David Webster, 'Development Advisers in a Time of Cold War: The United Nations Technical Assistance Administration 1950–1959', *Journal of Global History* 6 (2011), 249–72.
[84] B. M, 'Geneva in 1947: A Centre for International Activities', *The World Today* 3, no. 2 (June 1947), 261–8.
[85] Clavin, *Securing the World Economy*, 357.

new was inevitable: between a younger versus older generation of staff; between interwar diplomats and new technicians; and between seasoned officials called back from their wartime jobs, who looked back with nostalgia at their League years, and the new recruits who were adamant that the UN system should cut all ties with its interwar predecessor.[86]

As an organization so closely linked to the League, the ILO's experience in this period of transition was somewhat unique and the disruption less felt. Under Phelan's continued leadership (he would be replaced by David Morse in 1948), the Organization made its way back to Geneva, leaving part of its staff in Montreal. In June 1947, the ILO held its first International Labour Conference in the Swiss city since the war—a symbolic return to normalcy. On the surface, there were no major debates or reflections about how it should continue or re-invent its agricultural work. The fact that the League had 'failed' also did not have much bearing on the working of the Organization, which had always seen itself as a separate body. There were no attempts to deny or reject the ILO's interwar agricultural work but there was a sense that the study of international agricultural problems had grown in importance and would further 'intensify'.[87]

International agricultural trade unions, however, were slow to regroup. The International Landworkers' Federation, still the main representative of agricultural workers globally, had tentatively taken up its work at a post-war congress held in 1946 in London. The meeting was almost entirely devoted to the 'renewal of personal relations' among trade unionist leaders after the disruption of the war.[88] For now, the International Landworkers' Federation's focus continued to be on agricultural workers in Europe and it was slow to extend its interest to agriculture in so-called non-industrialized countries. The change would come, as we will see, not from the trade unions but from the ILO.

In fact, the ILO's most important agricultural expert body, the Permanent Agricultural Committee, was keen to pick up the threads of its pre-war work. In August 1947, the Permanent Agricultural Committee met in Geneva for its second official session (an exceptional wartime meeting held during the Regional Conference of American members in Cuba in November 1939 was not counted).[89] Familiar problems of labour standards, such as the question of wages and holidays with pay, were placed on the agenda and now deemed ripe for international regulation. This reflected processes that were taking place in countries across the globe and that saw the regulation of agricultural wages and the fixing of

---

[86] B. M, 'Geneva in 1947', 261–8.
[87] Osmay to Jenks, 28 May 1947, ILO Archives Geneva, ILO FAO 10–13.
[88] International Landworkers' Federation, Bulletin 1946–1950, IISH Archives Amsterdam, ZK 66057.
[89] Second session of the Permanent Agricultural Committee, Geneva, 1947, ILO Archives Geneva, AG 1001/1. See also Chapter 5.

minimum wages in a bid to stabilize the agricultural labour force and render agricultural work more attractive.[90]

Even though the way in which ILO categorized agricultural labour had not changed, its geographical focus had. For the first time, ILO experts in the Permanent Agricultural Committee made an explicit differentiation between two groups of countries—developed and underdeveloped —'with widely dissimilar conditions'. The main difference between these groups was that in the first a relatively small part of the population was engaged in commercial agriculture, whereas in the second as much as 80 per cent of the population lived off small agricultural subsistence activities.[91] Such explicit references that linked agriculture to notions of economic development were a clear change from interwar discussions, which had not explicitly dwelled on economic differences between countries but tended to look at communalities in how the workforce was treated. Whereas in the interwar years expectations about progress and modernization where more loosely defined, the new language also came with much more explicit assumptions about the higher economic productivity of industrial versus agricultural economies.[92]

A future meeting of the Permanent Agricultural Committee was scheduled for 1949 to discuss the general extension of social security measures to agricultural population in developing countries. This too was a logical step forward from the ILO's interwar work when these populations had been largely neglected.[93] The ILO staff was well aware that the Committee no longer adequately represented the international world order and that action was needed to reorganize the Committee and give it a more widely representative character.[94] Exactly how this would be achieved, however, was unclear. Osmay somewhat desperately wrote to American rural sociologist and ad hoc expert Lowry Nelson that 'any ideas or suggestions you may have in this respect which you would care to convey to me personally, would be extremely welcome.'[95] In reality, not much changed, and controversial European interwar experts such as Laur and Angelini continued to represent the interests of agricultural producers, whereas European trade

---

[90] Report of the Director to the thirtieth session of the International Labour Conference, Geneva, 1947, 81–2.
[91] Report of the Director to the thirty-first session of the International Labour Conference, Geneva, 1948, 110.
[92] Corinna Unger, 'Development', in Mlada Bukovansky, Edward Keene, Christian Reus-Smit, and Maja Spanu (eds), *The Oxford Handbook of History and International Relations* (Oxford: Oxford University Press, 2023), 349.
[93] Third session of the Permanent Agricultural Committee, Geneva, 1949, ILO Archives Geneva, AG 1003/100.
[94] Letter, Osmay to Booth, 14 March 1949, Third session of the Permanent Agricultural Committee, Geneva, 1949, ILO Archives Geneva, AG 1003/100.
[95] Letter, Osmay to Nelson, 15 March 1949, Third session of the Permanent Agricultural Committee, Geneva, 1949, ILO Archives Geneva, AG 1003/100.

unionists spoke for the workers.⁹⁶ The Permanent Agricultural Committee would continue to hold its sessions until its last one in 1965, before morphing into the Advisory Committee on Rural Development—reconceptualized as 'an organ of liaison with the rural world'.⁹⁷

With such continuity in existing expert commissions, change had to come from new bodies. By 1947, the work on agriculture in Geneva was buzzing and would increase even further over the following decade.⁹⁸ Expert commissions were proliferating all across Geneva. The FAO Committee on Rural Welfare established in 1949 or the WHO-ILO Committee on Occupational Health, which sought to address issues of labour safety in agriculture, were leading to more or less successful joint discussions.⁹⁹ Agricultural trade unions such as the International Landworkers' Federation also resumed their activities, and a new organization representing big farmers' interests, the International Federation of Agricultural Producers, was created.

If after the First World War the geographical focus of the International Labour Office had been on Eastern and Central Europe, now attention was paid to agricultural development and transformation in Southeast Asia, the Near and Middle East, Central and South America, and Africa. The ILO carried out advisory missions in all these regions in the early months of 1947. It is in this context that a new focus emerged and the conditions of work on tropical plantations finally garnered attention. Plantations as a capitalist agro-industrial enterprise were a dominant feature of tropical agricultural economies. They had long posed specific challenges of labour supply, social control, and the management of resistance for colonial states and private owners who often resorted to forms of coercion and exploitation to guarantee their profitability. These problems had never been openly discussed in international expert committees until 1947, when the ILO's Preparatory Asian Regional Conference decided to take a closer look at the working and living conditions of plantation workers.

Cultivating Fields of Progress: Agriculture and the International Labour Organization, 1920s–1950s. Amalia Ribi Forclaz, Oxford University Press. © Amalia Ribi Forclaz 2025. DOI: 10.1093/9780191945014.003.0007

---

⁹⁶ See correspondence with Ernst Laur, Walter Kwasnik, and Franco Angelini about participation. Third session of the Permanent Agricultural Committee, Geneva, 1949, ILO Archives Geneva, AG 1003/100.

⁹⁷ Circular, 167th session of the Governing Body, Geneva, 18–21 November 1969. Nineteenth Item on the Agenda: Reconstitution of the Permanent Agricultural Committee, ILO Archives Geneva, AG 1007/401.

⁹⁸ On the 'intensification of ILO work on agricultural questions', see letter Osmay to Francis Bouchard, 24 March 1949, ILO Archives Geneva, AG 1003/100.

⁹⁹ Meeting of FAO's Standing Advisory Committee on Rural Welfare, October 1948 and March 1950, ILO Archives Geneva, FAO, 1009/41/1/2.

7
The Tropics in Sight

> 'Millions of workers all over the world are participating in the process of agrarian production, and practically everywhere these hard-working labourers belong to that category which is most badly off as regards their wages and working conditions [...]. We don't forget our brothers in those tropical countries, where the sun shines hot and strong, and labour is heavy and life is often a plague. We are able now to do something for them in those countries; although they have to fight for themselves, we are willing to support them.' International Landworkers' Federation, *A Better Future for Plantation Workers* (Utrecht: 1953), 53

In the years after the Second World War, the focus of social policy debates and of knowledge production on agriculture changed within the ILO, in line with global political, economic, and social transformations. Wartime conferences had brought a sense of increased responsibility towards the non-European world and there was a marked shift in how the ILO viewed the geographical locus of its agricultural social policy. For many countries across Europe, including those of the Communist bloc, the post-war years would bring a period of intense agricultural growth with greater state intervention, technological innovation, but also structural changes including a substantial rural exodus.[1] But in contrast to the early 1920s, agricultural labour relations in these countries were no longer the ILO's primary concern. Instead, in the context of an emerging developmentalist agenda, the ILO, in line with an academic redefinition of tropical geography, manifested a growing interest in so-called tropical agriculture in Southeast Asia and Latin America.[2] As will be shown in the following pages, in the early postwar

---

[1] Miguel Martin-Retortillo and Vicente Pinilla, 'Patterns and Causes of the Growth of European Agricultural Production, 1950 to 2005', *The Agricultural History Review* 63, no. 1 (2015), 132–59; Carin Martiin, Juan Pan-Montojo, and Paul Brassley, eds, *Agriculture in Capitalist Europe, 1945–1970: From Food Shortages to Food Surpluses* (Abingdon: Routledge, 2016); N. F. R. Crafts, 'The Great Boom: 1950–73', in M. Schulze, ed., *Western Europe, Economic, and Social Change since 1945* (London: Routledge, 1999), 42–62; Giovanni Federico, *Feeding the World: An Economic History of Agriculture, 1800–2000* (Princeton: Princeton University Press, 2005); David Grigg, *The Transformation of Agriculture in the West* (Oxford, UK; Cambridge, US: Blackwell, 1992); Arnd Bauerkämper, 'The Industrialization of Agriculture and Its Consequences for the Natural Environment: An Inter-German Comparative Perspective', *Historical Social Research* 29 (2004), 124–49.

[2] Pierre Gourou, *Les Pays tropicaux: principes d'une géographie humaine et économique* (Paris: Presses Universitaires de France, 1947). David Arnold, 'Illusory Riches': Representations of the tropical world, 1840–1950', *Singapore Journal of Tropical Geography* 21, no. 1 (2000), 6–18. Daniel Clayton

years, the ILO's approach to agricultural labour underwent a significant shift. Fuelled by the beginning of decolonization, plantation agriculture as a particularly labour-intensive form of production finally came into full view of international labour experts. Plantation workers, especially in the major plantation regions for colonial crops such rubber, palm oil, tea and coffee in Malaya, Indonesia, the Philippines, India and Ceylon, suffered from poor living and working conditions: they were often exposed to long working hours, heat stress, malnourishment, and high death rates. The management of labour on the estates was characterized by control, penalties, coercion, and exploitation, and women were often the victims of sexual abuse.[3] The luxurious lifestyles of white expatriate European planters struck a strong contrast with the living conditions of their indentured workers, housed in inadequate and overcrowded lodgings on undrained ground with no access to running water, thus exposing the inhabitants to diseases such as malaria, typhoid, and dysentery. This chapter discusses the establishment of the ILO's Plantation Committee in 1948 and traces the Committee's early deliberations and meetings that resulted in the adoption of a Convention on plantation labour in 1958. The chapter explores the postcolonial dynamics of these discussions and the diverging perspectives of workers' representatives that brought to the fore that plantations were agricultural systems based on an extractive logic that often led to exploitative labour condition, whereas newly independent and former colonial governments considered them as necessary gateways to development. The following pages indicate a notable transformation both of the type of labour discussed and also a considerable shift in the organization's regional outlook away from Europe to Southeast Asia—a shift that also affected trade unionist organization and lobbying.

As discussed in previous chapters, for most of the interwar years the ILO's agricultural work focused on agricultural workers in European countries, with the exceptional integration of non–European perspectives but always avoiding colonial territories.[4] In fact, although colonial powers were technically meant, when possible, to apply ILO conventions to territories under their jurisdiction, the discussion and debates very rarely showed any concern for colonial workers.

---

and Gavin Bowd, 'Geography, Tropicality and Postcolonialism: Anglophone and Francophone Readings of the work of Pierre Gourou', *L'Espace Géographique* 3 (2006), 208–21.

[3] On the coercive nature of plantation labour in the first half of the twentieth century, see Ann Laura Stoler, *Capitalism and Confrontation in Sumatra's Plantation Belt, 1870–1979* (New Haven: Yale University Press 1985); Sidney W. Mintz, *Sweetness and Power. The Place of Sugar in Modern History* (New York: Viking, 1985); John Tully, *The Devil's Milk: A Social History of Rubber* (New York: Monthly Review Press, 2011); M. Dove, *The Banana Tree at the Gate: A History of Marginal Peoples and Global Markets in Borneo* (New Haven: Yale University Press, 2011); Jayeeta Sharma, *Empire's Garden: Assam and the Making of India* (Durham: Duke University Press, 2011); Rana Behal, *One Hundred Years of Servitude: Political Economy of Tea Plantations in Colonial Assam* (New Delhi: Tulika Books, 2014); Ulbe Bosma, *The Sugar Plantation in India and Indonesia: Industrial Production, 1770–2010* (Cambridge: Cambridge University Press, 2013); Alessandro Stanziani, *Labor on the Fringes of Empire: Voice, Exit and the Law* (New York: Palgrave Macmillan, 2018).

[4] See Introduction.

This contrasted with other reformist circles in which the problems of labour abuse in the colonial plantation sector were well known, especially in the case of rubber plantations in the Dutch East Indies, which had become the subject of highly popular planter narratives in the second half of the 1930s.[5] The ILO also knew about these problems through its relations with the Permanent Mandates Commission of the League of Nations and the work of the Native Labour Section. Even though colonial labour abuses often concerned agricultural enterprises, those seldom featured in international labour debates and, if they did (as in the context of the discussion on forced labour), they were portrayed as necessary or educational.[6] Agricultural economist and historian Charles Orwin brought this oversight to public attention when critically remarking in 1946 that 'for long years the natives were at best sources of cheap labour for the enterprises initiated by the colonists' and that 'it would be no exaggeration to say that any consideration for them, any recognition of their organizations and social institutions, or any feeling of responsibility for the improvement of their economic conditions, are things of very recent growth'.[7]

Indeed, until the end of the Second World War, the ILO's attitude towards labour in colonial territories was highly ambivalent. Thomas had shown an early interest in the regulation of forced labour and issues of involuntary labour recruitment, but he also believed that 'the problems of [colonial]territories were not the general problems of the twentieth century'.[8] In other words, colonial territories would not be ready for social policy reforms until they overcame such hurdles as the suppression of slavery and other forms of 'servile organization' and evolved from a 'slave mentality' to wage-earning labour or independent production.[9] The conditions of people working in agriculture in colonial settings were thus measured differently than those of European workers. They also appeared separately in the work of the Native Labour Section. One of the latter's main achievements, the Forced Labour Convention adopted in 1930, put a spotlight on colonial labour relations. However, its wording remained very general and made no reference to specific regions, sectors, sites, or types of work in which forced labour was used.[10] Instead, reflecting the influence of colonial powers

---

[5] See for example Madelon Székely-Lulofs, *Rubber* (Amsterdam: Elsevier, 1931); Madelon Székely-Lulofs, *Koelie* (Amsterdam: Elsevier, 1932); Eng. trans: Madelon H. Lulofs, *Coolie*, trans. G. J. Renier and Irene Clephane (Singapore: Oxford University Press, 1932); Leopold Ainsworth, *The Confessions of a Planter in Malaya: A Chronicle of Life and Adventure in the Jungle* (London: H. F. and F. G. Witherby, 1933).

[6] See Chapter 4.

[7] C. S. Orwin, 'Colonial Agricultural Production', *Nature* 159 (1947), 350–1.

[8] Report of the Director to the Tenth International Labour Conference, Geneva, 1927, 201.

[9] Report of the Director to the Tenth International Labour Conference, Geneva, 1927, 201.

[10] Suzanne Miers, *Slavery in the Twentieth Century: The Evolution of a Global Problem* (Walnut Creek, Calif.: Altamira Press/Lanham, Md.: Rowman and Littlefield Publishers, 2003); Daniel Maul, 'The International Labour Organization and the Struggle against Forced Labour from 1919 to the Present', *Labor History* 48, no. 4 (2007), 477–500.

within the ILO, the convention indirectly approved the use of forced labour for governmental purposes and certainly did not question colonialism as such.[11] What is more, it allowed recourse to forced labour to ensure food supply and even, as stated in article 21 of the Forced Labour Convention, as a measure of agricultural education, thus opening loopholes for all sorts of abuses.[12] The Belgian governmental delegate Edmond Leplae, president of the International Association for Tropical Agriculture (Association Internationale d'Agriculture Tropicale), insisted at the time that compulsory cultivation was not only indispensable for colonial prosperity, but also in the interest of the local populations. Rather cynically, the example that was given was the compulsory planting of Cinchona trees in Belgian colonies: the bark of these trees was used by the local population as an anti-malaria remedy and compulsory planting was thus presented as a life-saving measure.[13]

More specific instruments for the protection of colonial workers, who were still referred to at the time as indigenous labour, were adopted in the wake of the Great Depression, when there was a general tendency to revisit the value of 'native labour' and colonial agricultural production for national economies in Europe. From the mid-1930s onwards, the decentralization of international labour debates through the organization of regional conferences in Latin America, together with the opening of a number of new branch offices and the expansion of correspondent networks, had brought about a 'shift' in the balance of power and greater attention to the development of social policies in developing countries.[14] During those years, the ILO passed three conventions that dealt with colonial labourers: in 1936, it adopted a convention regulating the forced recruitment of workers in the colonies. The aim of this instrument was to limit abusive methods of obtaining the labour of persons 'who do not spontaneously offer their services' by persuading or deceiving them to enter into contracts.[15] In 1939 two additional conventions further regulated the contracts of employment and banned the use of penal sanctions for so-called indigenous workers.[16]

---

[11] J. P. Daughton, 'ILO Expertise and Colonial Violence in the Interwar Years', in Sandrine Kott and Joelle Droux, eds, *Globalizing Social Rights: The International Labour Organization and Beyond* (Basingstoke: Palgrave, 2013), 85–97.

[12] Article 21 of the Forced Labour Convention. This point was criticized by workers representatives.

[13] International Labour Office, *Record of Proceedings*, Twelfth International Labour Conference, Geneva, 30 May to 29 June 1929, 537–8.

[14] Véronique Plata-Stenger, *Social Reform, Modernization and Technical Diplomacy: The ILO Contribution to Development (1930–1946)* (Oldenbourg: De Gruytier, 2020); on early regional cooperation in Latin America, 61–83.

[15] International Labour Organization, Convention no. 50, Recruiting of Indigenous Workers (1936).

[16] International Labour Organization, Convention no. 64, Contracts of Employment of Indigenous Workers (1939); Convention no. 65, Penal Sanctions for Indigenous Workers (1939). On this see also Henrich Fechner, 'Standard-Setting in Colonial Labour Regulation and the Great Depression', in F. Nullmeier, Delia Gonzáles de Reufels, and Herbert Obinger, eds, *International Impacts on Social Policy: Short Histories in Global Perspective* (Palgrave Macmillan, 2022), 341.

In all these cases, the protective measures framed the issue as a problem of colonial labour management rather than general labour rights, thus reinforcing a divide and creating a system of inequality between colonial and non-colonial workers. Even though, by the early 1940s, the awareness of a new moral responsibility towards native welfare had increased and the ILO showed a new interest in the nutrition and health of workers in the colonies, many colonial labour enterprises remained outside of the ILO's remit.[17] There was an inherent notion, in the ILO's work, that the development of a waged labour force was only achievable through colonial rule and colonial discipline.[18] On the one hand, reformers condemned the colonial use of forced labour for war efforts; on the other, they also insisted that workers in the colonies lacked the capital and experience to develop their agricultural and mineral resources and their industrial potential. Therefore, 'capital and skilled direction' needed to come from the outside.[19]

In the colonial context of the interwar years, plantations were conceptualized as a gateway to economic development. As economist Ida C. Greaves observed in her PhD study in 1935, plantations were a means of bringing supposedly 'backward people' into the sphere of modern production and introducing 'modern improvements' in the tropics.[20] It is striking that until the late 1940s there was little reflection within the ILO on labour relations on large agricultural estates.[21] Whereas anti-slavery campaigning leaflets about labour conditions in rubber, cocoa, and other plantations had since the early twentieth century pointed sometimes dramatically to labour abuses, scientific works analysing the management of labour by colonial governments and private companies in these settings were few and far between.[22] The invisibilization of plantation labour was also apparent in the scientific literature of the time. A notable exception was Edgar Thompson's historical study of the Southern plantation which acknowledged the latter's role in the global economy, its reliance on slavery and its role in racializing labour and establishing hierarchical relations between white and non-white labourers.[23]

---

[17] International Labour Office, 'The Nutrition of Indigenous Workers', *International Labour Review* 41, no. 3 (1940), 307–17. See also Amalia Ribi Forclaz, *Humanitarian Imperialism: The Politics of Anti-Slavery Activism, 1880–1940* (Oxford: Oxford University Press, 2015).

[18] On this, see Luis Rodríguez-Piñero, *Indigenous Peoples, Postcolonialism, and International Law: The ILO Regime (1919–1989)* (Oxford University Press, 2005), 32–6.

[19] International Labour Office, *Social Policy in Dependent Territories*, Studies and Reports', Series B, no. 38 (Montreal, 1944), 123.

[20] Ida C. Greaves, *Modern Production among Backward Peoples* (London: Allen and Unwin, 1935), 170.

[21] Miguel Jéronimo Bandeira and José Pedro Monteiro, 'Colonialism on Trial: International and Transnational Organizations and the Global South Challenge to the Portuguese Empire (1949–1962)', *Humanity: An International Journal of Human Rights, Humanitarianism and Development* 13, no. 1 (2022), 104–26.

[22] Members of the British Anti-Slavery and Aborigines Protection Society wrote about various issues, including labour abuses on rubber plantations and child labour on Ceylonese tea plantations.

[23] Edgar T. Thompson, *The Plantation*, dissertation (University of Chicago, 1932). Reprinted as Edgar T. Thompson, *The Plantation*, edited with an introduction by Sidney W. Mintz and George Baca (Columbia: University of South Carolina Press, 2010).

But most existing works centred on development, efficiency, and commercial interests, with little consideration for social welfare.

This changed in the wake of the Second World War, when a new concern with social policy in dependent (and formerly dependent) territories crystallized within international organizations.[24] This concern was at least partly galvanized by the new role played by freshly decolonized states in international fora, where groups of anti-colonial nationalists and regional coalitions were rethinking the post-war international order.[25] Policy-makers from Latin American and Asia actively shaped the international system and the United Nations Organization became a crucial platform for an Arab–Asian coalition, for example, which contested existing frameworks, raised colonial questions, and introduced new ideas, including the reconceptualization of agricultural labour.[26] The change of direction, however, did not just come from above, and it was no coincidence that this more systematic concern for labour conditions on plantations emerged precisely at that time. The 1940s were a period of growing social unrest and with the admission of former colonial countries into the international governance structure, concerns about what the ILO euphemistically described as 'labour troubles' and their impact on post-colonial agricultural production and the global economy moved centre stage. Protests, strikes, and sometimes violent altercations on plantations had existed since the 1930s and as has been shown for colonial and postcolonial Sumatra, the maintenance of order and economic efficiency had become more difficult for the planters in the years leading up to the Second World War. Workers' mobilization grew increasingly vigorous after the war, and the violent and repressive 'politics of labour control' were no longer effective in upholding power relations on plantations.[27] Changes in ownership of plantations brought about by political decolonization did not affect this mobilization. Thus, the newly decolonized countries that were increasingly joining the membership of the ILO pushed for a new agenda.

India, which had been one of the founding members of the ILO in 1919 despite being a colony and had long enjoyed a special status within the organization,

---

[24] Chapter 5.

[25] On the agency of Southern actors in the negotiations of the post-war financial order, see Eric Helleiner, *Forgotten Foundations of Bretton Woods: International Development and the Making of the Postwar Order* (Ithaca, NY: Cornell University Press, 2014). Adom Getachew, *Worldmaking After Empire: The Rise and Fall of Self-Determination* (Princeton, NJ: Princeton University Press, 2019). Cindy Ewing, ' "With a Minimum of Bitterness": Decolonization, the Right to Self-determination, and the Arab-Asian Group', *Journal of Global History* 17, no. 2 (2022), 254–71.

[26] A. M. O'Malley and V. Thakur, 'Introduction: Shaping a Global Horizon: New Histories of the Global South and the UN', *Humanity: An International Journal of Human Rights, Humanitarianism, and Development* 13, no. 1 (2022), 55–65; Eva-Maria Muschik, *Building States: The United Nations, Development and Decolonization, 1945–1965* (Columbia University Press, 2022); Guy F. Sinclair, *To Reform the World: International Organizations and the Making of Modern States* (Oxford: Oxford University Press, 2017); Thomas G. Weiss and Pallavi Roy, 'The UN and the Global South, 1945 and 2015: Past as Prelude?', *Third World Quarterly* 37, no. 7 (2016), 1147–55.

[27] Stoler, *Capitalism and Confrontation*, 129.

took the lead in this process. In the decades leading up to the Second World War, Indian representatives had regularly intervened on behalf of Indian workers' interests and criticized the ILO's poor track record in bringing about labour improvements in the colonies.[28] In autumn 1947, a newly independent India hosted the Preparatory Asian Regional Conference of the ILO in New Delhi.[29] In his opening speech, Indian prime minister Pandit Nehru declared that the time had come to abandon the largely European perspective in favour of a 'world perspective' in which the social and economic conditions of agricultural work and food production would take centre stage.[30] Similarly to the situation faced by the ILO after the First World War, when it chose to address the living and working conditions of farmworkers in Europe against a backdrop of communist upheaval, the improvement of working conditions was perceived as necessary to maintain social peace and economic productivity, and there was a perceived urgency to act before labour relations would become uncontrollable.[31] The Indian workers' delegate, acknowledging the important place of plantation crops such as rubber, cinchona, tea, coffee, and sugarcane in the economy of a number of Asian countries, noted the unsatisfactory conditions of the labourers, and called the attention of governments to the 'immediate necessity' to put in place the appropriate legislation for improving their conditions. He successfully demanded that the ILO undertake a special enquiry of all the aspects of work organization, remuneration, and legislation.[32]

One of the most important outcomes of the 1947 Conference was the creation of a Plantation Committee. This expert commission was to look at commercial agri-capitalist enterprises in areas dedicated to the production of rubber, tea, coffee, cinchona, sisal, palm oil, and similar tropical crops.[33] Significantly, the new body did not fall under the umbrella of already existing agricultural units and

---

[28] Plata-Stenger, *Social Reform*, 98–9. On the role of Indian worker's delegate Joshi in the 1920s and 30s, see Gerry Rodgers, Sabyasachi Bhattacharya, and J. Krishnamurty, 'India and the ILO in Historical Perspective', *Economic and Political Weekly* 46, no. 10 (2011), 47. Also, Prabhu P. Mohapatra, *India and the ILO: Chronicle of a Shared Journey 1919–2019* (New Delhi: International Labor Organization, 2019).

[29] International Labour Office, *Record of Proceedings, Preparatory Asian Regional Conference, New Delhi, October–November 1947* (Geneva, International Labour Office: 1948); ILO Archives Geneva, IC IC 9/0/1 (1).

[30] International Labour Office, *Record of Proceedings, Preparatory Asian Regional Conference, New Delhi, October–November 1947* (Geneva, International Labour Office: 1948); ILO Archives Geneva, IC IC 9/0/1 (1).

[31] See Chapter 1. International Labour Office, *Record of Proceedings, Preparatory Asian Regional Conference, New Delhi, October–November 1947* (Geneva, International Labour Office: 1948), 5; ILO Archives Geneva, IC 9/0/1 (1). Erich H. Jacoby, *Agrarian Unrest in South-East Asia* (New York: Columbia University Press, 1949).

[32] International Labour Office, *Record of Proceedings, Preparatory Asian Regional Conference, New Delhi, October–November 1947* (Geneva, International Labour Office: 1948), 230–1; ILO Archives Geneva, IC 9/0/1 (1).

[33] Revised note on the proposed industrial committee on plantation (no date), ILO Archives Geneva, IC 9/0/1 (1).

expert commissions that had proliferated since the organization's early beginning. Rather, the International Labour Office decided to establish the Plantation Committee as a so-called 'industrial committee'. This was a new mechanism set up in 1945 to consider certain industrial sectors deemed important for post-war 'reconstruction' and development.[34] The application of the term 'industrial' to an agricultural issue echoes the ILO's earlier battle for its agricultural mandate and the theoretically inclusive interpretations of the term 'industrial' as applying to all productive labour. In fact, the meaning of this new categorization was ambiguous as it seemed to suggest a novel divide between industrial and non-industrial forms of agriculture. It also blurred the criteria that had been formerly used to distinguish between countries of chief industrial importance versus those that boasted a large agrarian economy.[35]

In contrast with the ILO's pre-war work, the plantation was framed as an economic and industrial institution in which the main activity was the production of crops for metropolitan markets, a feature which differentiated it from family farms and other middle- and large-sized landholdings. This signalled a shift in acknowledging the economic significance of some forms of agricultural labour, but it did not substantially alter the ways in which the ILO approached labour issues. Rather, the conditions of workers on these plantations were perceived as a natural extension of interwar discussions on waged agricultural workers and, therefore, as 'familiar ground'.[36]

Expanding Unionist Horizons

Another reason can explain why the shift to plantation labour was so readily undertaken: the beginning of a numerical decline of hired agricultural workers in Western Europe.[37] Whereas agriculture would remain a dominant economic sector in many regions until the 1960s, the rapid adoption of machinery, chemical fertilizers, pesticides, and herbicides, as well as increased specialization and the selection of animals and plants, were changing the face of Western European farms and the types of labour they employed.[38] From the reports of national

---

[34] John Price, 'The Industrial Committees of the International Labour Organization', *International Labour Review* 52, nos. 2-3 (1945), 139-53. The first industrial committees to be set up were the coal mines committee and the inland transport committee, followed by the iron and steel committee, the textile committee, and the building, civil engineering, and public works committee, as well as the petroleum committee.

[35] See Chapters 1-3.

[36] International Labour Office, twenty-seventh session of the International Labour Conference, Questionnaire 1, Minimum Standards for Social Policy in Dependent Territories (Supplementary Provisions) (Montreal: 1945), 6.

[37] David Grigg, 'The World's Agricultural Labour Force 1800-1970', *Geography* 60, no. 3 (July 1975), 194-202.

[38] Michel Mazoyer and Laurence Roudart, *A History of World Agriculture from the Neotlihic Age to the Current Crisis* (New York: Monthly Review Press, 2006), 375-440.

agricultural trade unions affiliated with the International Landworkers' Federation, it seemed that numbers of hired workers were falling as a result of post-war mechanization and rationalization of agriculture.[39] According to the Federation's statistical estimations, in most Western European countries the number of hired farmworkers now oscillated between 12 and 20 per cent of the total number of people engaged in agricultural production. There were of course important variations from one country to the next. In Denmark and the Netherlands, for example, a third of the people in agriculture were hired workers, whereas in Belgium and West Germany they made up only around 10 per cent of the agricultural population.[40] Not only were European workers less likely to stay on the farms, but their conditions also improved in the post-war years: in Denmark, for example, working hours were shortened. Generally, workers' wages increased in the sector and, in countries such as Germany and Switzerland, new laws about agricultural training and vocational education were changing the face of the profession.

By 1950, in response to these changes, the International Landworkers' Federation was envisioning a process of reorientation. Joseph Duncan retired after thirty years of service, as did Piet Hiemstra who would pass away a few years later in January 1953.[41] The new leadership was composed of Edwin G. Gooch, a long-standing member of the British National Union of Agricultural Workers, who presided the Federation between 1950 and 1959. Another important figure was Adrian de Ruijter of the Netherlands' Agricultural Workers Union, who became its new secretary.[42] For the Federation, the ILO remained the most important partner organization, and the agricultural trade unionists watched the Organization's statements about agriculture closely. In an echo of its interwar relationship with the International Institute of Agriculture, the Federation considered the FAO as less important for social policy questions. Trade unionists viewed the organization in Rome as a 'very idealistic, fresh, and fully alive organization' but not as a champion of social justice or labour improvements.[43]

The Federation was also undergoing a shift with regard to its geographical focus. In line with the changing orientation of the ILO, a turning point in the history of the International Landworkers' Federation came in August 1952, when agricultural trade unionists met for the Federation's twelfth congress in Salzburg. At the meeting it was decided to extend the field of its activities to plantation

---

[39] For a review of the various national affiliated unions, see International Landworkers' Federation, Report of the thirteenth Congress, Oslo, 17–19 August 1954 (Utrecht: 1954).

[40] See also International Landworkers' Federation, The Social Position of Agricultural Workers in Various Western European Countries, IISH Archives Amsterdam, Arch00632.

[41] International Landworkers' Federation, Report of the thirteenth Congress, Oslo, 17–19 August 1954 (Utrecht: 1954).

[42] Gooch was the president of the National Union of Agricultural Workers in Britain since 1930 and a significant figure in the British Labour Party.

[43] International Landworkers' Federation, Report on the fifteenth session of the Council of FAO, Rome, 9–4 June 1952, IISH Archives Amsterdam, Arch00632.

labourers.⁴⁴ From then on, the Federation devoted a large portion of its time and resources towards the creation of new affiliates, especially agricultural trade unions in Asia. British trade unionist Tom Bavin was tasked with establishing a special office in Singapore, from where he undertook study trips to secure and maintain relations with plantation unions in Asia.⁴⁵ Europe was still on the radar but there was a growing sense among activists that the discussions about agricultural integration was mainly catering to farm owners' interests.⁴⁶ To publicize its new focus, in February 1953 the International Landworkers' Federation published a booklet titled *A Better Future for Plantation Workers* which traced the evolution of its social policy agenda. The narrative that it put forward described how, in the first half of the twentieth century, European agricultural workers had achieved better conditions thanks to progress in social policy legislation and how it was now the time to organize plantation workers in Asia, Africa, and Latin America.⁴⁷ In May 1953 the first Union of Plantation Workers, an organization in British Cameroon, affiliated with the International Landworkers' Federation. Even though the latter continued to keep an eye on agriculture in Western Europe, and particularly on the European integration process, its focus was now firmly on the non-European world. Calls for defending the interests of the 'brothers in those tropical countries where the sun shines hot and strong, and labour is heavy and life is often a plague' were motivated by a sense of solidarity as well as the pragmatic view that those regions in which trade unions were not yet developed offered a promising field of action.⁴⁸

Framing Plantation Labour Globally

For the ILO, bringing attention to plantations meant opening up a new area of research that went far beyond its previous work on agriculture in Europe, and on which it had only scarce information. The International Labour Office wanted to offer a conceptual framework that underlined the global structural communalities among plantations despite their variability in size, ecological and social environment, and economic, commercial, and political context.⁴⁹ It also aimed to investigate the specific labour conditions that existed on plantations at that

---

⁴⁴ International Landworkers' Federation, Report on the twelfth Congress, Salzburg, 28–29 May 1952, IISH Archives Amsterdam, Arch00632, 28.

⁴⁵ International Landworkers' Federation, Report of the thirteenth Congress, Oslo, 17–19 August 1954 (Utrecht: 1954).

⁴⁶ International Landworkers' Federation, 'Integration of Agriculture in Western Europe', May 1952, IISH Archives Amsterdam, Arch00632.

⁴⁷ International Landworkers' Federation, *A Better Future for Plantation Workers* (Utrecht: 1953).

⁴⁸ International Landworkers' Federation, *A Better Future for Plantation Workers* (Utrecht: 1953), 53.

⁴⁹ On variability and on the broad use of the term 'plantation', see Corey Ross, 'The Plantation Paradigm: Colonial Agronomy, African Farmers and the Global Cocoa Boom, 1870–1940s, *Journal of Global History* 9, no. 1 (2014), 54.

precise moment in time. What was novel since the late 1940s was a strongly emerging interest among American rural sociologists and social anthropologists in the social, cultural, and economic fabrics of plantations. Eric Wolf and Sidney Mintz, in particular, embarked on a decade-long fieldwork research on Puerto Rican sugar plantations to investigate their 'industrial organization' and the resulting class structure and community.[50] They conceptualized post-war plantation labourers as a 'rural proletarian community' in which people earned wages, bought food in stores, were corporately employed, and therefore shared traits with the industrial working class.[51] But, in line with their agrarian origins, workers also maintained a liminal status as peasant-proletarians, often producing food for subsistence on small garden plots in parallel to their plantation work, an aspect which Wolf referred to as leading 'double lives'.[52]

Although there is no direct evidence that the ILO's work on plantations was inspired by American scholarship, there are parallels in how the Organization chose to conceptualize plantations as a research object in the late 1940s. In line with scholarly interpretations, the International Labour Office approached plantations as a global and comparative institution that followed similar patterns of labour control and labour management across diverse geographical regions.[53] The Office also defined plantations as 'commercialized' forms of agricultural production in which a 'large labour force' was used mostly 'for routine operations' and subjected to 'a centralized managerial machinery'.[54] Other features which distinguished the discussion from previous debates on agricultural labour was its focus on specific crops rather than countries, and an interest in the process of production of these crops and their role in the global food economy.

To prepare documentation on plantations for the first meeting of the Plantation Committee, which was to be held in 1950 in a yet undecided location, the Office

---

[50] In the 1950s, plantations featured at academic conferences and in collective publications. See Vera Rubin et al., eds, *Plantation Systems of the New World: Papers and Discussion Summaries of the Seminar Held in San Juan, Puerto Rico* (Washington, DC: Research Institute for the Study of Man and Pan-American Union, 1959).

[51] Sidney Mintz, 'The Folk-Urban Continuum and the Rural Proletarian Community', *American Journal of Sociology* 59, no. 2 (September 1953), 39; Eric R. Wolf, 'Specific Aspects of Plantation Systems in the New World: Community Sub-Cultures and Social Classes', in Vera Rubin et al., *Plantation Systems of the New World* (1959). Republished in Eric Wolf, *Pathways of Power: Building an Anthropology of the Modern World* (Berkeley, Los Angeles, London: University of California Press, 2001), 215–29.

[52] Eric Wolf, 'Specific Aspects of Plantation Systems in the New World', 143. For a discussion of the debate on this issue, see Ann Laura Stoler, 'Plantation Politics and Protest on Sumatra's East Coast', *Journal of Peasant Studies* 13, no. 2 (1986), 124–43.

[53] This view that large cash-crop agricultural systems shared certain characteristics across regions was also corroborated by later academic research: Edgar T. Thompson, *Plantation Societies, Race Relations and the South: The Regimentation of Populations* (Durham, NC: Duke University Press, 1975).

[54] Draft note (by Blelloch?) on the proposed industrial committee on plantation (no date), ILO Archives Geneva, IC 9/0/1 (1). Other aspects of the definition would cause considerable debate and were only discussed in detail in 1953.

put together a long questionnaire asking for detailed information on labour provisions, including legal and customary arrangements. Among the problems that needed to be addressed before starting the enquiry were its geographical outreach, whether it should embrace a regional or universal focus, and who should occupy a seat in the Committee.[55] As the International Labour Office argued, countries and territories in which the plantation system represented a significant sector of the economy could be found in all 'tropical regions', including Hawaii, Puerto Rico, the Belgian Congo, Brazil, Burma, India, Siam, Ceylon, Cuba, the Philippines, Liberia, as well as a large number of European dependencies in Africa, the Caribbean, Fiji Islands, Indochina, Indonesia, Mauritius, and Malaya. It was therefore important that the respective countries be represented—together, of course, with the European colonial powers.

Given the delicate political times of decolonization, the question of accountability was also raised. As plantations were usually based on foreign capital investments, one of the questions that arose was whether the responsibility about housing and the provision of medical and other services lay with the employer or the state.[56] International labour officials also wondered whether a distinction should be made between conditions in the colonies (now referred to as 'non-metropolitan' territories, a new term used from 1947 onwards to denote what formerly had been called colonies and other dependent territories) and the conditions in newly independent countries. There was concern, especially among British delegates and members of the colonial office, that the Committee would create the perception that the conditions on colonial plantations were 'particularly bad and need[ed] special attention'. Not wanting the Committee to create unnecessary political divisions, Ragunath Rao, assistant director-general since 1948, urged the Committee to 'avoid [...] any political implications as to the differences between colonial and independent territories' and to focus on crops rather than on countries.[57]

In March 1949 the questionnaire was sent out to ministries of labour, public health, and foreign affairs, requesting answers to an extensive and detailed list of queries. It began with a few introductory questions about types of crops, plantation size, and volume of production. Then a large section was devoted to questions about workers, their numbers, origins, and types of contracts. The employment of women and children also featured prominently, as well as the general conditions of work. There were numerous questions about working

[55] Revised note (by Blelloch?) on the proposed industrial committee on plantation (no date), ILO Archives Geneva, IC 9/0/1 (1).
[56] Revised note (by Blelloch?) on the proposed industrial committee on plantation (no date), ILO Archives Geneva, IC 9/0/1 (1).
[57] Rao to Blelloch, 11 June 1948. Reporting on a conversation with Mr Grossmith of the United Kingdom Delegation (Grossmith is from the Colonial Office) see note Rao to Rens, 30 June 1948, ILO Archives Geneva, IC 9–01 (1). On Rao, see also J. Krishnamurty, 'India and the International Labour Organisation', *Economic and Political Weekly* 46, no. 10 (2011).

hours, rest periods, wages, as well as discipline, labour control, and the role of overseers.[58] Another section focused on the workers' use of agricultural plots on the plantation, the existence of medical and social services (including schools) for their children, and the housing facilities. The tone of the questionnaire was largely sympathetic to plantation workers and showed a concern for their rights and the challenges they faced. It asked about the workers' degree of freedom to quit work, and that of employers to move workers at will. It also enquired about workers' rights to organize and unionize, and to what extent such unions were subject to control and oppression.[59]

All in all, the questionnaire took for granted the existence of a marginalized (and displaced) labour force and the potential for abuse of power. This was a marked shift from the previous lack of regard for the conditions of workers in tropical countries. But this does not mean that the ILO's framing of the problem was devoid of colonial and racial undertones. In particular, one last section sought information on racial and religious discrimination and tensions among workers on the estates.[60] It also asked for information about whether 'the people of a certain race [have] shown more ability in or adaptability to the work'—a question that echoed century-old racist stereotypes and superficial theories that professed that specific racial attributes made certain groups of workers less vulnerable and more suitable and adaptable to strenuous work in hot climates.[61] In contrast, there were no direct questions about plantation owners, their ethnicity, training, presence, involvement in managerial tasks, and attitude towards workers. Also, the fact that plantation systems were historically tied to coerced labour and the extent to which this continued to shape labour relations was not mentioned.

As had been the case with previous enquiries, governments were slow in replying, blaming the International Labour Office's unrealistic time frame to put together the reports.[62] The Office received answers to the questionnaire from sixteen countries and it deplored that among the governments replying late or not at all, such as the

---

[58] Questionnaire attached to letter from the International Labour Office to Fennema, Werkgevers Federatie voor internationale Arbeidazaken, 11 February 1949, ILO Archives Geneva, IC IC 9/0/1 (2).

[59] International Labour Office, 'Enquiry into Work in Plantations', March 1949, ILO Archives Geneva, IC 9/0/1 (2), 13.

[60] International Labour Office, 'Enquiry into Work in Plantations', March 1949, ILO Archives Geneva, IC 9/0/1 (2). 15.

[61] On stereotypes and racist theories, see Alan Derickson, '"A Widespread Superstition": The Purported Invulnerability of Workers of Color to Occupational Heat Stress', *American Journal of Public Health* 109, no. 10 (2019), 1329–35; Syed Hussein Alatas, *The Myth of the Lazy Native: A Study of the Image of the Malays, Filipinos, and Javanese from the Sixteenth to the Twentieth Century and its Function in the Ideology of Colonial Capitalism* (London: Frank Cass, 1977).

[62] A. Jawad from Agricultural Section to Official Relations Section, 22. 8. 1949, ILO Archives Geneva, IC 9/0/1 (2) asking to send a reminder regarding the enquiry on conditions of work in plantations. The questionnaire had been sent to Venezuela, Costa Rica, the Dominican Republic, Belgium, Brazil, Ceylon, France, Liberia, the Netherlands, Portugal, Thailand, United Kingdom, United States, Philippines, South Africa, Cuba, Mexico, Colombia, Guatemala, Salvador, Ecuador, Haiti, Panama, and Peru.

United States, the Philippines, and South Africa, were a number of countries for whom plantations constituted a pillar of their national economy.⁶³ Some of those who did reply often provided simple 'yes-or-no' answers that rendered the feedback meaningless. Reports also focused strictly on territories rather than on the geographical distribution of expatriate planters: for instance, the British government replied on behalf of its colonies but had nothing to say about British planters who owned and managed plantations outside the confines of the empire, such as in Indonesia.⁶⁴

In line with pre-war procedure, the documentation submitted by governments was used together with additional information to produce a report which identified 'basic problems' in the life and work of plantation workers and thus offered supposedly universal observations.⁶⁵ Although the Governing Body of the ILO had decided that the Plantation Committee should take an inclusive approach and cover 'plantations of all kinds, large and small, producing any crop', for practical reasons this first survey focused mainly on rubber, tea, coffee, and sugar estates (excluding other crops such as cotton, tobacco, and bananas). Among the aspects investigated were labour supply and especially the system of forced 'recruitment', which was known to result in displacement, indenture, and other forms of coerced labour. The system was also criticized for failing to repatriate the workers after the expiry of their contracts.⁶⁶ Moreover, the report outlined how the extent of legislation regarding working hours and weekly and daily rest periods varied widely from estate to estate and from country to country, as did provisions for food, housing, sanitation, and medical care. This strongly echoed the ILO's inter-war reform efforts for agricultural workers in Europe, and especially the attempts undertaken in the mid-1930s to standardize labour and rest periods in agriculture.⁶⁷ The repertoire of tropes was also quite familiar. As was the case with interwar European farms, the 'backward conditions' on plantations were largely attributed to the isolation of estates, the residency requirement which rendered workers more dependent, and the fact that much of the responsibility for the working and living conditions was up to employers and not to public authorities. Although the report did not make any recommendations, it implicitly hinted at the fact that these aspects needed attention. The similarities of issues that emerged, despite the ILO's different conceptualization of plantation work as industrial work,

---

⁶³ International Labour Office, *Basic Problems of Plantation Labour* (Geneva, International Labour Office: 1950), 3.

⁶⁴ Letter, UK Government to International Labour Office, 22 August 1949, enclosing replies for Barbados, British Guiana, Kenya, Northern Rhodesia, Southern Rhodesia, Dominica, and St Lucia, ILO Archives Geneva, IC 9/0/1 (2).

⁶⁵ ILO, *Basic Problems*.

⁶⁶ 'Recruitment and Engagement of Labour' in International Labour Office, *Basic Problems of Plantation Labour* (Geneva, International Labour Office: 1950), 33–43. On this see also Recruiting of Indigenous Workers Convention adopted in 1936.

⁶⁷ See Chapter 4.

ultimately also raises the question of why plantation workers were singled out as a specific category—rather than in line with the work already done on agriculture.

Postcolonial Dynamics and Disputed Realities

From January 1950 onwards, following the ILO's preparatory work, correspondence among ILO officials indicated the possibility that the first meeting of the Plantation Committee might be held in Indonesia, which had applied for membership and would become a member by summer 1950.[68] The decision to hold the meeting in Bandung, a city that would emerge as a crucial site for 'Asian internationalism' in the mid-1950s, was far from random.[69] Indonesia, had gained independence in a violent colonial war just a few months earlier after the Netherlands had been pressured to end colonial administration and transfer sovereignty to the new republic. During this process, the new state was receiving considerable support from Asian and Arab states in the UN.[70] Indonesia also continued to experience social and political unrest and although, geopolitically, the country was praised by contemporaries for its refusal to be drawn into the Cold War, observers were concerned about the rise of Communism which was gaining ground in Southeast Asia.[71] Like in other parts of Southeast Asia, where plantation economies predominated, low wages and human exploitation provided a fertile ground for communist agitation and there was widespread anxiety over the workers' mobilization and demands of redistribution.[72] By the time of the meeting, Indonesian plantations that continued to be under European ownership even after its independence in 1945, were undergoing waves of unrest and upheaval. In Sumatra, for example, strikes, plantation raids and estate seizures were leading planters to leave.[73]

By setting the first Plantation Committee in Indonesia, the International Labour Office, similarly to the situation after the First World War, hoped to create a symbolic buffer against what it saw as the dangerous activities of communist

---

[68] Letter, Osmay to Rao, 23 January 1950, ILO Archives Geneva, IC 9/0/1.
[69] Sunil Amrith, 'Asian Internationalism: Bandung's Echo in a Colonial Metropolis', *Inter-Asia Cultural Studies* 6, no. 4 (2005), 557.
[70] Cindy Ewing, 'With a Minimum of Bitterness': Decolonization, the Right to Self-determination, and the Arab-Asian Group', *Journal of Global History* 17, no. 2 (2022), 258.
[71] Press cutting, article by Justus van de Kroef, 'Indonesia: Independent in the Cold War, 1952', undated, ILO Archives Geneva, IC 9/1/115; Ragna Boden, 'Cold War Economics: Soviet Aid to Indonesia', *Journal of Cold War Studies*, 10 (2008), 110–29.
[72] Press cutting, Lawrence S. Finkelstein, Far Eastern Survey, Institute of Pacific Relations, 24 January 1951, ILO Archives Geneva, IC 9/1/303.
[73] Lisa Tilley, '"A Strange Industrial Order": Indonesia's Racialized Plantation Ecologies and Anticolonial Estate Worker Rebellions', *History of the Present* 10, no. 1 (April 2020), 67–83; Ben White, 'Remembering the Indonesian Peasants' Front and Plantation Workers' Union (1945–1966), *The Journal of Peasant Studies* 43, no.1 (2016), 1–16.

agitators who manipulated ignorant labourers.[74] Holding an international conference would not only demonstrate the political and economic presence and anti-communist support of the United Nations at a crucial time when the latter was embarking on a global technical assistance program to modernize 'less developed countries'.[75] It would also help both the ILO and the new government take control of the discourse on social improvements for plantation labourers without losing sight of productivist aims. Thus, some observers praised the economic as well as political importance of the ILO's Plantation Committee, claiming the meetings of the latter in Bandung would also be 'as a means for ensuring the maximum development of the vast resources of [these areas]'.[76]

In December 1950, delegations from a mix of colonial governments and newly independent territories convened for the first session of the Committee in Bandung, a city surrounded by plantations that was praised for its mild tropical climate and its comfortable grand hotels. Present at the meeting were fourteen delegations of Southeast Asian and Caribbean countries whose economies largely relied on plantations such as Burma, Ceylon, Cuba, India, Pakistan, the Philippines, Indonesia, Liberia, and Brazil. There were also a few European governments, all of which were colonial powers, including France, the Netherlands, Belgium, Portugal, and the United Kingdom. The meeting was dedicated to the 'basic problems common to workers on plantations' and to ways for the ILO to approach these issues within its framework. The word 'basic', more fittingly translated as *'fondamentaux'* (fundamental) in French, covered a wide-ranging agenda that included the discussion of the legal, economic, and social conditions of plantation labourers—from labour contracts to wages, housing, and food.[77]

The meeting was presided by none other than V. K. Krishna Menon who had participated in the meetings of the Peasant Peace Conference in the mid-1930s in Geneva and was now secretary of the Indian ministry of labour, further signalling the international rise of newly decolonized states and the role of regionalism in the political thinking of the leaders of these countries. As detailed in a previous chapter, in the 1930s Menon had criticized the narrow focus of agricultural labour discussions and the fact that no voice was given to countries in Asia, Latin America, and Africa.[78] Whereas governmental representation had notably improved on this front, the inclusion of workers from these regions continued to be an issue. In preparation for the Bandung meeting, the ILO had asked governments to

---

[74] Lisa Tilley notes that the portrayal of union members as 'ignorant natives, manipulated by propaganda from outside forces, fed into wider British narratives which dismissed plantation rebellions as the product of external communist agitation in a Cold War context'. Tilley, 'A Strange Industrial Order', 17.
[75] David Webster, 'Development Advisers in a Time of Cold War: The United Nations Technical Assistance Administration 1950–1959', *Journal of Global History* 6 (2011), 249–72.
[76] Press cutting, Eric Ford, 'Charter for Plantation Workers', *Eastern World* (December 1951), ILO Archives Geneva, IC 9/1/303.
[77] Minute Somay, 27 September 1950, ILO Archives Geneva, IC 9/1/100.
[78] See Chapter 5.

prepare tripartite delegations. As on previous occasions, the question of whether to invite trade unions and what status to bestow on them caused considerable discussion among ILO officials. The chief of the ILO's Agricultural Service emphasized the importance of transparency and communication with local trade unions and he was adamant 'that the organizations in question have the right to know from the beginning that the Committee exists, where and when it is to meet and what will be its business'.[79] He also pointed out that any reticence on the part of the Office to invite trade unions might expose it to criticism, and some countries might take issue with the inadequate representation of the workers' point of view. A circular letter was sent out to plantations workers' organizations in India, Latin America, Cuba, and Peru, informing them of the 'expanding programme of action' of the ILO. However, the letter also made clear that the message was purely informational and 'should in no way be considered as an invitation to attend the session'.[80] Invitations were also sent to the International Landworkers' Federation and the newly created International Federation of Agricultural Producers as 'observers'. Local trade unions, however, were less welcome or did not wish to attend. As the press relayed, the most powerful Indonesian trade union, the communist Sobsi, refused to participate in the meeting of the Plantation Committee and denounced the ILO as 'a capitalist-imperialist tool'.[81] From the perspective of communist workers' organizations that embraced a nationalization of plantations, what the ILO's Plantation Committee was doing was in fact to normalize the foreign-owned plantation system and help maintain its extractive nature in the face of workers' protests. As had been the case forty years earlier, when Thomas had been openly attacked and dismissed by Eastern European communists, the ILO's action was again perceived as an attempt at containing communist movements and was criticized by the latter 'as an instrument of capitalism'.[82]

The ILO also faced protests from other corners. Representatives of colonial powers as well as employer's delegates, for example, showed concern about the Committee's spotlight on the conditions of plantation workers and were keen to create an image of recent reform and social progress, detailing the latest achievements in social policy in the colonies and stressing the existence of some labour legislation, for example in the Belgian Congo and in the Portuguese overseas territories. They emphasized that 'employers did not wish to go back to the times when workers were treated as slaves and mere tools', but now saw them as 'partners in production'.[83] Given the absence of the Soviet Union, which had left the ILO in 1940, voices speaking against this distorted representation of colonial

[79] ILO Archives Geneva, IC 9/1/200/1.
[80] Circular letter by Jan Schuil, 1 November 1950, ILO Archives Geneva, IC 9/1/103/2.
[81] Press cutting, Lawrence S. Finkelstein, Far Eastern Survey, Institute of Pacific Relations, ILO Archives Geneva, IC 9/1/303.
[82] See Chapter 1.
[83] International Labour Office, 'The First Session of the Committee on Work on Plantations', International Labour Review 63, no. 6 (June 1951).

paternalism were somewhat limited.[84] Workers' delegates across all regions were the ones to question these statements, and insisted on the fact that the conditions on plantations were problematic, particularly in Africa and Asia where exploitation was rife.[85]

One central point of discussion were the methods of recruiting plantation labourers (as opposed to their voluntary engagement). After the Second World War, the practice continued to be used in colonial territories to guarantee labour supply. As the ILO had already pointed out in a report written in 1935 on the recruitment of colonial workers, the concern was that this often led to forced labour conditions and other forms of bonded labour. More generally, it had long-term socio-economic consequences in terms of food insecurity, social disintegration, and depopulation.[86] Almost two decades after the initial discussion of 1935, at the 1950 meeting of the Plantation Committee workers' representatives demanded the abolition of professional recruiters, and especially of those who also performed supervisory functions on the plantations. Further discussion points concerned the formulation of contracts and general labour legislation, as well as the conditions of employment, including the vexed question of working hours and of housing, which had generated much debate with regard to European agricultural workers in the interwar years.

The first meeting of the Plantation Committee resulted in a resolution that criticized the conditions of life and work of plantation labourers as 'unsatisfactory' and lacking transparency and regulation.[87] The conference highlighted the need and urgency of 'appropriate legislation' to improve these conditions, without of course any power to enforce such a call with the concerned governments. Various recommendations outlined the necessity of improvements in housing, vocational education, and medical services. The most concrete step taken by the International Labour Office was to decide to devote further time and effort to studying the employment and living conditions of this class of workers, a step which was hailed as a sign of progress.[88] As journalist Eric Ford commented for *Eastern World*, the Committee had 'cleared the ground and set the pace' for what he maintained was 'a new approach' to labour in tropical countries.[89] Ford evidently had high hopes for the development of labour policies that respected the rights of plantation labourers whilst enabling the good functioning of the plantation industry. It remained to be seen what these initial efforts would achieve.

---

[84] Daniel Maul, *The International Labour Organization: 100 Years of Global Social Policy* (Berlin: De Gruyter, Geneva: International Labour Office, 2019), 140.

[85] International Labour Office, 'The First Session of the Committee', 663.

[86] ILO, 'The Recruiting of Labour in Colonies and in Other Territories with Analogous Labour Conditions', Report IV, nineteenth session, Geneva: International Labour Office, 1935, 15 onwards.

[87] Resolution of the first meeting of the Plantation Committee.

[88] Dispatch to governments of decisions adopted, ILO Archives Geneva, IC 9/1/200/1.

[89] Press cutting, Eric Ford, 'Charter for Plantation Workers', *Eastern World* (December 1951), ILO Archives Geneva, IC 9/1/303.

By 1952, preparations for a follow-up meeting of the Plantation Committee that would take place in Havana in 1953 were well underway. The agenda included the discussion of a more concise and precise definition of the term 'plantation', which many delegates had argued needed a clearer conceptualization. The Committee also wanted to gain an overview of recent events affecting plantation work, and decide on possible future studies and enquiries. The choice of the location was motivated by the fact that Cuba was not only a major sugar-producing country, but also one of the leading economies in Latin America. It was of financial, economic, and also strategic importance to the United States, which had recently helped General Fulgencio Batista impose a military dictatorship on the country. There were even rumours that Batista himself, who was aligned with Cuba's land-owning class, would preside over the opening session of the Plantation Committee.

This time, positions defending the employers versus the workers were even more entrenched than during the first meeting of the Committee, and the ILO came under fire as soon as it started preparing documentation.[90] Several British colonial officials took issue with the ILO's representation of plantation workers as a poor, exploited, and sometimes coerced labour force. Sir Frederick Seaford, member of the East African Royal Commission and chairman of the employers' group, commented that the 'extent of suffering' of plantation labourers was exaggerated, that their living standards were 'not as low as would be suggested', and that suggestions of coercion were entirely false for British colonies.[91] Others pointed out the absence of thorough studies on wages and general living conditions, and the potential complexity of carrying out such research, as conditions varied from country to country. These objections illustrated the continued influence of colonial powers on the debates.

Things did not get better at the meeting of the Committee, which opened in Havana in March 1953—in Batista's absence but chaired by Venezuelan Victor Montoya. The discussion centred around the necessity for medical care services and sanitation as well as on the regulation of wages to stabilize earnings and employment. The employers' side was generally unhappy with what they viewed as an unbalanced discussion in favour of the workers. The employer's delegate from Ceylon criticized the Committee's proceedings for putting a spotlight on 'national problems' that should find 'national solutions', and condemned a concerted attempt to utilize the Plantation Committee 'for the exhibition and disposal of soiled parochial linen'.[92] Others criticized the trade unions for causing unrest and deplored that there was no mention of the workers' reciprocal responsibility

---

[90] ILO Plantation Committee, General Report submitted to the second session of the Committee (Cuba: 1953).
[91] Seaford, 19 December 1952, ILO Archives Geneva, IC 9/2/170/2.
[92] Seventh sitting of the Plantation Committee, Verbatim Records 1953, ILO Archives Geneva, IC 9/2/202.

towards their employers. Workers' representatives, on the other hand, reminded the audience of the slave roots of plantations, arguing that their growth and expansion were chiefly a result of the colonial use of slave labour. The remnants of this system, especially when it came to the management of labour, were hard to die out, sharpening the need for a change and for new labour laws.[93]

It would be an understatement to say that the ILO's efforts to discuss the grievances of plantation workers and its work towards a more transparent set of labour regulations generated mixed feelings in colonial circles. Echoes of the discussions reached London, where C. R. Harrison, a member of the British employers' delegation who had attended the Havana meeting, gave a critical report to the Ross Institute at the London School of Hygiene and Tropical Medicine. Describing his experience in Havana to a group of colonial officials and hygiene specialists, Harrison outlined how he had tried to show that 'for humanitarian and economic reasons' employers were on the same page as the workers concerning improvements in health and housing. Harrison decried that the ILO was biased towards the workers and that it presented a distorted picture of their conditions. His audience was incensed, and people criticized the staff of the International Labour Office as 'misguided enthusiasts, entirely on the side of labour'. They rejected the Plantation Committee for misrepresenting the planter 'as a man who drives on his labour with a whip in his hand and a revolver on each hip!'.[94]

In reality, the Plantation Committee was trying to find a way to accommodate the interests of both sides. The Committee was sympathetic to the planters' wish to increase the volume of output (and with it of their profits) in order to be competitive on the world market, while also taking into account the workers' interests. Compared to the Bandung meeting, the conference in Havana thus focused more strongly on promoting the economic rationale for a greater investment in labour that would lead to more efficient production. Historically, the International Labour Office had always emphasized that labour improvements and economic growth in production needed to go hand in hand.[95] The chairman of the Havana meeting Montoya echoed this by unequivocally stating that the standard of living of workers could only be raised if a substantial increase in their productivity was achieved.[96] The productivist logic of the Plantation Committee was also reflected in the fact that labour was only a small part of the discussion, which centred mostly on the fluctuating value of crops and the management of production

---

[93] Plantation Committee Verbatim Records 1953, ILO Archives Geneva, IC 9/2/202.

[94] Letter, Pickford, Director of the London office to the International Labour office, 30 June 1953, sending a report on the meeting of the Ross Institute Industrial Advisory Committee, including a report by Mr C. R. Harrison on his journey to Havana as one of the British employers' delegates on the Committee on Work on Plantations.

[95] See the discussion of its 1920s enquiries in Chapter 3.

[96] Plantation Committee Verbatim Records 1953, ILO Archives Geneva, IC 9/2/202, 12.

costs. This was also apparent from the reports of the Plantation Committee, which usually began with a long section dedicated to plantation crops and their role in world economy and a much smaller section dedicated to 'some problems of plantation labour'.[97]

'The Gleam of Human Amelioration'?

In 1954, drawing on the debates within the Plantation Committee, the Governing Body of the ILO decided to put the conditions of plantation workers on the agenda of one of its upcoming International Labour Conferences, a step which would ensure a wider international audience and thus highlight the relevance of this issue.[98] The Plantation Committee, tasked with deciding what topics would be suitable for discussion, forwarded a comprehensive list which included the classic issues of work time, rest periods, and the employment of women and children already discussed for European agricultural workers in 1921. Other issues were more specific to developing economies, such as the recruitment of workers, the regulation of contracts, and the promotion of labour inspections and support for organization and trade unionism.

As usual, to prepare for the conference which would ultimately take place in 1957, the International Labour Office circulated a detailed report that described and contextualized the various points of the agenda, and asked members states whether they would approve of the formulation of international regulation.[99] The report also contained a draft convention with over seventy articles that extensively covered all aspects of plantation work, regulating anything from maternity leave to the way wages should be paid, the role of independent labour inspections, and the rights of workers to unionize.[100] As with earlier discussions on improving the working conditions of farm labourers, the proposition evidently represented an attempt at creating more equal conditions between plantations and industrial settings. However, as had already been the case in earlier conferences about the protection of agricultural workers in Europe, the discussions highlighted a clear contrast between the views of employers' and workers' groups. The legislation was especially criticized by colonial governments and those on the side of the entrepreneurs. The Indian employers' delegate Mr Varghese tried to raise the pity of the audience for the tormented plantation owners.

---

[97] Committee on Work on Plantations, third session, Report I (Geneva: International Labour Office, 1955).
[98] International Labour Office, fortieth session of the International Labour Conference, Report VIII: 'Conditions of Employment of Plantation Workers' (Geneva: International Labour Office, 1957).
[99] International Labour Office, fortieth session of the International Labour Conference, Report VIII: 'Conditions of Employment of Plantation Workers' (Geneva: International Labour Office, 1957).
[100] Draft Convention.

166   CULTIVATING FIELDS OF PROGRESS

He called plantation workers 'a privileged class' and presented the employers as the 'victims of labour unrest', arguing that they were 'rather helpless' and had to try and survive in a fluctuating and competitive global market. To Varghese, it was the job of the ILO to promote 'an atmosphere of abiding peace' between employers and workers that would support production growth.[101] The British government similarly claimed that plantation labourers did not need any specific legislation, as they were an ill-defined category that varied from country to country.[102] Various British advisers took issue with the fact that the proposed convention was too extensive. One, in particular, the British employers' adviser Mr Hyde-Clarke, ridiculed it as an assemblage of existing regulations, adapted to cover every aspect of the lives of plantation workers 'from the cradle to the grave'.[103] According to the critic the world was not ready for such a plantation charter. This solicited a critical response from the Soviet delegations, whose re-admission in 1954 was changing the dynamics of international debates. The Soviet workers' representative Ivan Shkuratov rejected the speaker's comments as in 'bad taste', and retorted that the time span between birth and death for a plantation worker was, as he put it, very short.[104] Shkuratov was shut down for digressing off topic. In the end, the voices that disapproved of the convention were in the minority.

In spite of these controversies, a year later, the delegations attending the International Labour Conference voted in favour of a convention regulating the employment of plantation workers, which was ultimately adopted with a full majority of 118 votes to 32, with 16 abstentions.[105] In ninety-nine articles, the convention regulated issues ranging from the recruitment of migrant workers, banning the use of illegal pressure or fraudulent hire, and stipulating access to medical examination, adequate transport, and an (undefined) period of acclimatization. The Convention also stipulated the fixing of minimum wages, their regular payments, and the workers' access to a full day of weekly rest and to paid annual holidays. Paid maternity leave and compensation for accidents arising on the plantations were also included. The Convention also stated that workers should have a right to unionize and that appropriate machinery should be put in place to 'avoid disputes' and facilitate conciliation and that regular labour inspections should make sure the provisions were enforced.[106]

---

[101] International Labour Office, *Record of Proceedings*, fortieth session of the International Labour Conference (Geneva: International Labour Office, 1957), 419.

[102] International Labour Office, *Record of Proceedings*, fortieth session of the International Labour Conference (Geneva: International Labour Office, 1957), 417–22.

[103] International Labour Office, *Record of Proceedings*, fortieth session of the International Labour Conference (Geneva: International Labour Office, 1957), 429.

[104] International Labour Office, *Record of Proceedings*, fortieth session of the International Labour Conference (Geneva: International Labour Office, 1957), 429.

[105] International Labour Office, *Record of Proceedings*, forty-second session of the International Labour Conference (Geneva: International Labour Office, 1958), 475.

[106] C110 Convention concerning Conditions of Employment of Plantation Workers (1958).

Many saw this as a major achievement and even praised the ILO for 'lighting up a star' and 'doing away with man's inhumanity to man'.[107] In a poignant speech, Jorge Bocobo, the government adviser from the Philippines, chose to recite Edwin Markham's 1921 poem 'The Man with the Hoe', which described the wariness, desperation, and lack of better perspective of an exhausted field worker. Bocobo used Markham's words to capture the human experience and the struggles of a worker who '[B]owed by the weight of centuries [was] lean[ing] upon his hoe and gaz[ing] on the ground, the emptiness of ages in his face and on his back the burden of the world'.[108] The choice of poem was in itself remarkable, given that it was written shortly after the First World War and that it portrayed the exhaustion of a British agricultural worker, thus creating a direct (but probably unconscious) connection with the ILO's earlier work. Praising the new convention, Bocobo rejoiced that the ILO had given the nations of the world 'a gleam of human amelioration', which, after centuries of exploitation, would lead to better living and working conditions for plantation workers.[109]

In many ways, the overly optimistic tone of this statement and the hope that the new Convention would bring tangible improvements was to prove unfounded, and the much-praised 'gleam of human amelioration' was more of a flicker. In fact, the number of ratifications of the 1958 plantations convention remained very low throughout the second half of the twentieth century, and out of the ten signatories who in the next two decades signalled their support, most were not among the big producers of plantation crops.[110] Calls for revision of the Convention started to appear almost immediately after it entered into force, especially from Asian countries that argued that its provisions were too broad and not in line with the realities of many member states. The Indian and Malayan governments, for example, argued that the Convention was impractical because it did not include any indication of minimum size and minimum number of hired workers and thus could be understood to apply to any small agricultural undertakings that hired labourers and produced crops for commercial markets whereas Indian legislation, for example, stipulated a minimum number of thirty workers to qualify as a plantation.[111]

---

[107] International Labour Office, *Record of Proceedings*, forty-second session of the International Labour Conference (Geneva: International Labour Office, 1958), 360.

[108] International Labour Office, *Record of Proceedings*, forty-second session of the International Labour Conference (Geneva: International Labour Office, 1958), 360. Also, on the more general role of the Philippine government as an anti-colonial force in the UN from the late 1940s onwards, see Ewing, 'With a Minimum of Bitterness'.

[109] International Labour Office, *Record of Proceedings*, forty-second session of the International Labour Conference (Geneva: International Labour Office, 1958), 360.

[110] The signatories were Cuba, Côte d'Ivoire, Ecuador, Guatemala, Mexico, Panama, Uruguay, and the Philippines. Liberia and Brazil signed early but then denounced the convention in the early 1970s. See also D. Lincoln, 'Plantation Workers by Definition: The Changing Relevance of the ILO's Plantations Convention', *The International Journal of Sociology of Agriculture and Food* 17, no. 1 (2010), 51–71, 57.

[111] International Labour Office, sixty-eight session of the International Labour Conference, Revision of the Plantations Convention (No. 110) and Recommendation (No. 110) (Geneva: International Labour Office, 1982), 108.

Over the next four decades, until the mid 1990s, the Plantation Committee continued to meet every four to five years, keeping an eye on the evolution of work conditions on plantations.[112] Generation after generation of experts and officials reviewed the often limited measures taken by member countries to respond to the 1958 convention. In terms of implementation of plantation legislation, there was little progress over this time period, and much of the discussion centred on commodity market trends and other economic aspects rather than on plantation work. And even though in many countries the ownership of plantations changed over the next decades, it did so with little improvements for the workers. Rather, what emerged in the following decades was the 'persistent poverty' of the plantation workforce.[113] Surveys published by the ILO in the 1960s, 1970s, and 1980s highlighted that the living conditions of plantation workers were below those of other industrial workers, and that poverty, substandard living, and working conditions remained unchanged.[114] Well into the twenty-first century, unionization remains low and discrimination and exploitation rife.[115] The continued marginalization of plantation workers thus echoes some of the earliest observations made at the ILO on agricultural work over a century ago to the effect that agricultural workers were the 'most despised and least protected' workers internationally.[116]

Cultivating Fields of Progress: Agriculture and the International Labour Organization, 1920s–1950s. Amalia Ribi Forclaz, Oxford University Press. © Amalia Ribi Forclaz 2025. DOI: 10.1093/9780191945014.003.0008

---

[112] The tenth and last session of the Plantation Committee took place in 1994.
[113] G. L. Beckford, *Persistent Poverty: Underdevelopment in Plantation Economies of the Third World* (London: Oxford University Press, 1972).
[114] International Labour Office, *Plantation Workers*, Studies and Reports, New Series, No. 69 (Geneva 1966). Jean-Paul Sajhau and Jürgen Muralt, *Plantations and Plantation Workers* (Geneva: International Labour Office, 1986).
[115] Janina Puder, 'Cheap Labour, (Un) Organized Workers: The Oppressive Exploitation of Labour Migrants in the Malaysian Palm Oil Industry, in van Nederveen Meerkerk, Elise and Bauer, Rolf, eds, *Global Agricultural Workers from the 17th to the 21st Century* (Leiden, Boston: Brill, 2023), 438–461. Oliver Pye, 'A Plantation Precariate: Fragmentation and Organizing Potential in the Palm Oil Global Production Network', *Development and Change* 48, no. 5 (2017), 942–64.
[116] See Chapter 1.

Conclusion

From Post-War Efforts to Present Challenges

The history of the ILO's efforts to understand and improve labour conditions in agriculture in the three decades following the First World War is a history of pioneering reformist endeavours, of the recognition of a complex problem with a multitude of socio-economic ramifications, and of the building and standardization of unprecedented international socio-economic knowledge on a particular professional group. It is also the history of the complex and contested interactions between often opposed interest groups in the formulation of labour standards, of the possibilities and limits of international institutions and their uneven processes of governance, and ultimately, of the transformation and evolution of agricultural work itself.

By the early 1950s, after decades of focusing on agricultural workers in Europe, the ILO's normative and epistemic efforts had moved on in substantial ways that reflected the social, economic, and political transformations brought on by the Second World War. The 1950 report of ILO's director David A. Morse featured the conditions of agricultural workers in Puerto Rico alongside those of Swiss farmworkers. Technical aspects of social policy such as, for example, the instauration of old-age pension funds in Cuba and Czechoslovakia were mentioned in the same paragraph without distinction between geographical zones.[1] This would have been unimaginable ten years earlier. The new spotlight on waged agricultural labourers outside Europe, particularly in tropical regions, and also, to some extent, in former colonies, reflected post-war changes in world order and a transformation of the ILO's geographical outlook.[2] The agricultural worker had finally become a global figure, a symbol of the fault lines of modernization and capitalist productivity.

For three decades, the ILO had tried to establish agriculture as a field of social policy and to address problematic labour arrangements that were often shielded from national and international legislation because of their arguably customary, informal, and local character. Throughout the interwar years, agriculture had

---

[1] Report of the Director-General to the thirty-third session of International Labour Conference (Geneva: International Labour Office, 1950).

[2] Daniel Maul, 'The Morse Years 1948–1970', in Magaly Rodriguez Garcia, Jasmien Van Daele, and Marcel Van der Linden, eds, *ILO Histories. Essays on the International Labour Organization and its Impact on the World during the Twentieth Century* (Bern: Peter Lang, 2010), 365–400.

been an important sector of European economies, but also a sector predicted to decline. When looking through the ILO lens, however, it becomes clear that the decrease in importance of agriculture globally after 1945 was relative. The picture that is sometimes painted in histories of the twentieth century of a steep process of de-agrarianization and depeasantization after the Second World War widely exaggerates the decline.[3] Change happened gradually and unevenly. In Europe, commercial, political, and technical changes led to greater state intervention in agriculture and to a transformation of farming practices towards larger production units, greater investments in mechanization and technology, resulting in higher yields per acre and intensification of labour output.[4] From the late 1950s onwards, traditional small-scale farming that relied heavily on manual labour decreased as the sector became smaller, more industrialized, and dominated by state and institutional interventions such as the regulatory framework of the Common European Agricultural Policy.[5] Capital investments and the use of increased motorization, chemical fertilizers, and pesticides, as well as the application of new methods of accounting, and data management, required new skills and less manual labour.[6] Across industrialized European countries, the expansion of mechanization and the growth of other sectors also resulted in an accelerated rural exodus and in the death of small farms.[7] Remaining farmers were remodelled into increasingly specialized food producers and farm managers.

The process of agricultural industrialization was not limited to capitalist societies. From the 1950s onwards, agricultural industrialization also became a key policy in socialist states such as the GDR and the USSR, where gigantic agricultural infrastructure projects showcased the state's capital investments into mechanization and its appetite for technology.[8] Throughout the interwar years, Soviet

[3] On the alleged disappearance of Europe's 'peasantry', see Eric Hobsbawm, *Age of Extremes: The Short Twentieth Century, 1914–1991* (London: Michael Joseph, 1994), 288–9, 415.

[4] Carin Martiin, Juan Pan-Montojo, and Paul Brassley, eds, *Agriculture in Capitalist Europe, 1945–1970: From Food Shortages to Food Surpluses* (Abingdon: Routledge, 2016); Pedro Lains and Vicente Pinilla, eds, *Agriculture and Economic Development in Europe* (London, New York: Routledge, 2009); Paul Brassley, Yves Segers, and Leen Van Molle, eds, *War, Agriculture and Food: Rural Europe from the 1930s to the 1950s* (New York: Routledge, 2012).

[5] Kiran Klaus Patel, ed., *Fertile Ground for Europe? The History of European Integration and the Common Agricultural Policy since 1945* (Normos: Baden-Baden, 2009); Peter Moser, 'Kultivierung und Zerstörung lebender Organismen. Der bäuerliche Umgang mit chemisch-synthetischen Hilfsstoffen in der Übergangszeit von der agrarisch-industriellen zur industriell-agrarischen Wissensgesellschaft (1945–1975)', *Zeitschrift für Agrargeschichte und Agrarsoziologie* 1 (2017), 19–34; Venus Bivar, *Organic Resistance: The Struggle over Industrial Farming in Postwar France* (Chapel Hill: University of North Carolina Press, 2019).

[6] Karen Sayer, 'The Changing Landscape of Labour: Work and Livestock in Post-Second World War British Agriculture', *History: The Journal of the Historical Association* 104, no. 363 (February 2020), 911–40.

[7] David Grigg, 'The World's Agricultural Labour Force 1800–1970', *Geography* 60, no. 3 (July 1975), 194–202.

[8] Arnd Bauerkämper, 'The Industrialization of Agriculture and Its Consequences for the Natural Environment: An Inter-German Comparative Perspective', *Historical Social Research* 29, no. 3 (2004), 124–49, 131.

agricultural collectivization had been the often-imagined but largely invisible foil against which the ILO formulated its social policy aims. A fear of socialist uprisings and communist takeover accompanied many of the International Labour Office's reflections on creating more equal conditions between agricultural workers and those working in the industry. As Stalin's successors continued to embrace the kolkhozes and to expand pre-war experiments with giant mechanized grain farming on more marginal land in the Eastern regions of the Soviet Union, the ILO remained vigilant.[9] Fears of communist uprisings continued to motivate many of those who advocated for improvements. At the 1950 International Labour Conference, Justiniano Espinosa, secretary of the mainly agrarian Colombian Workers' Federation, called for social justice and dignity for agricultural workers but also warned against those who might use the workers' economic hardship as a tool for ideological influence: 'Let us give back to the man who cultivates the land what is only just that he should have, so that he may live decently and in accordance with human dignity. Let us protect him from pernicious agitators who try to exploit his poverty to the advantage of the diabolical power which hides itself behind the Iron Curtain. Let us raise his standard of living as a just reward for his labours. Let us encourage his pacific spirit, his pure affection for the family, his integrity, his spirit of sacrifice.'[10]

Agricultural industrialization and modernization were not confined to Europe, but they played out differently in countries where agriculture remained the dominant economic sector.[11] The rise of what has been termed a 'neoliberal' notion of development from the 1950s onwards helped consolidate unilinear models of progress, often determined by economic growth.[12] This also reinforced divisions between agricultural workers in supposedly 'developed' and 'under-developed' countries. At a surface level, and in the eyes of trade unionists, agricultural workers were now a global type: across cultures and countries, people who cultivated but did not own land were seen as sharing similar experiences and challenges including poverty, low wages and political and social disregard. Yet, the ILO's discourse also increasingly emphasized distinctions in advancement—not just between industrialized and developing countries but also between more advanced and less advanced metropolitan territories.[13] Some characteristics that were highlighted for agricultural workers in the less advanced regions had been absent in the discourse on Europe. In the discourse of employers, the pre-war trope of the

[9] Lazar Violin, 'Soviet Agricultural Policy after Stalin: Results and Prospects', *Journal of Farm Economics* 38, no. 2 (1956), 274–86.
[10] International Labour Office, *Record of Proceedings*, thirty-third session of the International Labour Conference (Geneva: International Labour Office, 1950), 61.
[11] Doreen Warriner, 'Changes in European Peasant Farming', *International Labour Review* (1957), 446–9; Grigg, 'The World's Agricultural Labour Force'.
[12] Michelle Murphy, *The Economization of Life* (Durham, NC: Duke University Press, 2017).
[13] Report of the Director-General to the thirty-third session of the International Labour Conference (Geneva: International Labour Office, 1950), 73.

uneducated and unskilled agricultural worker was substituted with the image of the lazy, unproductive native, but with an additional racial component.[14] Racialization and racial ordering was, and still is, a defining feature of (foreign-owned) modern plantations and of the workers' vulnerability.[15] This added a further layer to the marginalization of plantation workers that did not exist, or at least not in the same measure, on interwar European farms, and thus presented a new challenge to ILO action.

Asian, Latin American, and—to a lesser extent—African 'peasants' became the targets of multilateral and bilateral development and aid programmes.[16] Agricultural development, now dominated by the Malthusian logic of feeding a growing population with limited resources, became strongly entangled with the rise of Cold War antagonism, its particular geopolitical context and agenda, but also the cultural and scientific visions of the period.[17] The short-term production growth and doubling of yields resulting from the various technological Green Revolutions in Latin America and Southeast Asia were hailed as economic successes. But the social implications of these revolutions were less certain. Along the lines of commodity frontiers, the need for cheap labourers persisted and even increased.[18] Across Southeast Asia, plantation labourers who were often undocumented migrants continued to labour in conditions that were not only far from decent but also retained some of the coercive features of colonial times. In Europe too, waged agricultural labour did not just disappear but was transformed by new consumer demand for out-of-season fruit and vegetable and by access to cheap migrant workers.[19] One wonders what the participants of the 1921 International Labour Conference, who discussed issues such as housing, vocational education, child labour, and women's labour, would make of the current living and working conditions of migrant labourers from India and North Africa in agricultural and food-processing enclaves in Southern Europe. These workers who often live in

---

[14] Syed Hussein Alatas, *The Myth of the Lazy Native: A Study of the Image of the Malays, Filipinos, and Javanese from the Sixteenth to the Twentieth Century and its Function in the Ideology of Colonial Capitalism* (London: Frank Cass, 1977).

[15] See discussion in Chapter 5. Sharit K. Bhowmik, 'Ethnicity and Isolation: Marginalization of Tea Plantation Workers', *Race/Ethnicity: Multidisciplinary Global Contexts* 4, no. 2 (2011), 235–53. Janina Puder, 'Cheap Labour, (Un)Organized Workers: The Oppressive Exploitation of Labour Migrants in the Malaysian Palm Oil Industry', in Elise van Nederveen Meerkerk and Rolf Bauer, eds, *Global Agricultural Workers from the 17th to the 21st Century* (Leiden, Boston: Brill, 2023), 438–461.

[16] David Engerman and Corinna Unger, eds, 'Special Forum: Modernization as a Global Project', *Diplomatic History* 33, no. 3 (2009), 375–506.

[17] Nicole Sackley, 'The Village as a Cold War Site: Experts, Development, and the History of Rural Reconstruction', *Journal of Global History* 6 (2011), 481–504; Nick Cullather, 'Miracles of Modernization: The Green Revolution and the Apotheosis of Technology', *Diplomatic History* 28, no. 2 (2004), 227–54.

[18] Sven Beckert, Ulbe Bosma, Mindi Schneider, and Eric Vanhaute, 'Commodity Frontiers and the Transformation of the Global Countryside: A Research Agenda, *Journal of Global History* 16, no. 3 (2021), 435–50.

[19] Nicola Verdon, *Working the Land: A History of the Farmworker in England from 1850 to the Present* (London: Palgrave Macmillan, 2017).

slums with no claims to social rights or citizenship and have now become what trade unionists in the 1920s used to call the 'most despised and least protected workers' in the global economy.[20]

The story told in this book highlights the many continuities in how agricultural labour has and has not received attention from international institutions since the First World War. If today we tend to associate rural development with peasants in the Global South, the ILO's interwar records show that not so long ago, agricultural societies in Europe and especially landless labourers were conceptualized as a major site of social and economic development. The ILO thus contributed to the construction of a seemingly coherent European countryside that shared similar characteristics across many national borders. As is now well known, in the interwar years, ruralization, land reclamation, colonization, education, and public health schemes existed in liberal democracies as well as fascist regimes ranging from the north to the south of the European continent.[21] The debates within the ILO reflect some of these national phenomena but also demonstrate an attempt by an international reformist institution to go beyond national frameworks and towards the establishment of an international understanding and a uniform approach to the shortcomings of agricultural labour protection. The formulation of international standards remained arguably of limited outreach, but the production of knowledge and of a reformist language was considerable.

Through the ILO's work, agricultural labour and rural living was constructed into a distinct empirical category, defined by poverty, specific customs, the dependency on natural conditions, and relative isolation and backwardness. Agricultural workers shared traits across regions: workers were often displaced from their places of origins, living on their place of work, lacking social protection, poor and with little pay, thus making them vulnerable.[22] They were also associated with backward social development, a degree of stubbornness, and the menace of potential unrest and political mobilization. Their relationship with farmers, plantation owners, and managers was tense, and, because they did not own the land they worked on, it was implied that they had little motivation to increase their productivity.[23] There was a striking continuity and lack of variation in these themes. In ILO parlance, agricultural workers housed on plantations in India in the 1950s faced the same 'unsatisfactory conditions' that agricultural workers had faced on European farms in the 1920s and 30s. Recurring themes

[20] Jörg Gertel and Sarah Ruth Sippel, eds, *Seasonal Workers in Mediterranean Agriculture: The Social Costs of Eating Fresh* (London and New York: Routledge, 2014).
[21] Liesbeth van De Grift and Amalia Ribi Forclaz, eds, *Governing the Rural in Interwar Europe* (London: Routledge, 2018).
[22] R. Roux, 'Economic Conditions Affecting Social Policy in Plantations', *International Labour Review* 67, no. 3 (1953), 236–61.
[23] See Chapters 1–3.

were the dismal living conditions and the lack of ventilation, running water, and adequate sleeping quarters.[24]

In the early 1950s, the emergence of the so-called 'Third World' on the international scene further increased the necessity of a concerted policy of social, economic, and technical improvements in agricultural societies in the minds of development practitioners and experts.[25] Although the term 'Third World' has now gone out of fashion, the association between rural communities, poverty, archaic labour conditions, insufficient health care, illiteracy, and malnutrition persists.[26] The growing membership of countries with a dominant agrarian sector and a large number of subsistence farmers gave new meaning to agricultural and rural development. In many ways, however, the ILO's post-war work did not depart from its interwar frame but persisted in its focus on waged labourers. There were many continuities in the ILO's work, not least concerning the items of discussion, of which there was a fixed repertoire, but also with regard to its methods of research and the role of its expert committee. In the late 1940s and early 1950s, the Plantation Committee of the ILO raised the same issues about working hours, housing, and rest periods that early ILO conferences had raised in 1921 for European farmworkers. As the figure of the impoverished rural worker moved from the provincialized European countryside of the interwar years to more exotic settings, many of the tropes and remedies remained the same. Thus, one of the main items of the International Labour Conference of 1955 was the issue of vocational training in agriculture, echoing not only one of the ILO's very first discussions in 1921 but also the focus of a major enquiry in the 1920s.[27] Also, the conference brought back on the table issues such as recreation and utilization of leisure in rural areas, as well as the classical items of hours of work, minimum wages, and holidays with pay for agricultural workers.[28]

Throughout the 1920s, the ILO had played a key role in the construction of an international library of socio-economic knowledge on agriculture, and established itself as an international rural observatory. In the following three decades, the organization strengthened its position despite wartime disruption, competition, and a lack of resources that was to remain a major problem well into the

---

[24] International Labour Office, 'Worker's Housing Programmes in Asian Countries', *International Labour Review* 63, no. 4 (1951), 390–401.

[25] Ernesto Escobar, *Encountering Development: The Making and Unmaking of the Third World* (Princeton, NJ: Princeton University Press, 1995); Nick Cullather, *The Hungry World: America's Cold War Battle Against Poverty in Asia* (Cambridge, Mass.: Harvard University Press, 2010).

[26] United Nations, *The Sustainable Development Goals Report* (New York: United Nations Publications, 2022).

[27] International Labour Office, thirty-ninth session of the International Labour Conference. Fourth Item on the Agenda: Vocational Training in Agriculture, Report IV (1) (Geneva: International Labour Office, 1955).

[28] For a review of the activities of the Agricultural Service for the year 1955, see Osmay's personal file, ILO Archives Geneva, ILO P 2873.

second half of the twentieth century.[29] Under Osmay, the Agricultural Service continued its research activities, and its international enquiries were again one major feature of the ILO's work on agriculture. The ILO did expand its knowledge and repertoire. Its work on plantations in tropical regions was one of the major post-war innovations in this respect.[30] It highlighted problems in the living and working conditions of plantations workers and thereby challenged the power of colonial governments to shield their territories from ILO investigations which had led to the pre-war invisibilization of these issues. Increasingly, the ILO came under pressure to widen its repertoire to include other categories of agricultural workers, especially sharecroppers and small tenants. Both the Asian Regional Conference in 1950 and the 1955 meeting of the Permanent Agricultural Committee flagged this issue. Including these categories of workers raised new questions about land tenancy and lease payments, credit and indebtedness, on top of the classical issues of wages and living conditions. In 1957, the International Labour Office issued a study on living conditions of life and work of tenant farmers in Asia.[31] The report was 'intended to examine the specific problems which arise when agriculture is carried out by individuals who do not own the land they cultivate'. This was the first time—after the failed attempts to research agrarian reform in the 1920s—that some of the social, economic, and legal issues of land rights and the latter's implications for the workers' living conditions was put at the centre of attention.

Overall, the process of building a repertoire on agricultural labour conditions, however, was at times uneven and chaotic. The proliferation of committees and expert groups on agricultural labour in the 1920s and 1930s illustrates the ILO's attempts at finding the right instrument to address these issues. It also highlights one of the organization's major flaws, namely the duplication of work between the so-called Mixed Advisory Agricultural Committee and the Permanent Agricultural Committee. One could add to this the excessive bureaucratization of the ILO's work on agriculture, especially the International Labour Office's rigid methodology in researching specific issues. Moreover, the schematic accounts and technical language used in its studies made the results hardly accessible to the general population. Agricultural trade unionists and farmers alike often criticized the fact that the social reformers and diplomats of international Geneva seemed out of touch. It is true that there were only few occasions when people with firsthand knowledge of agricultural labour were involved in the discussions.

---

[29] On the continuing problem of 'inadequate staffing', see note Abbas Amar, 5 October 1962, ILO Archives Geneva, ILO P 2874.
[30] See Chapter 7.
[31] International Labour Office, 'Conditions of Life and Work of Share-croppers, Tenant Farmers and Similar Categories of Semi-Independent and Dependent Workers in Agriculture', Third Item of the Agenda of the Asian Regional Conference in New Delhi in 1957 (Geneva, International Labour Office: 1957).

This problem of representation of agricultural workers in international discussions persisted well into the second half of the twentieth century. In the 1950s and 60s, despite the reorganization of international agricultural trade unions and a re-focusing on plantation labour, their voices were still very much absent from international debates. This was partly due to the relative weakness of agricultural trade unionist organizations compared to industrial ones and partly a result of the exclusion of more political groups by the ILO. As various delegates pointed out in 1950, the reports submitted to the conference were those of governments keen to protect their prestige, and rarely gave a true picture of the conditions of workers. In addition, workers' delegates, especially for agriculture, were often not familiar with the specificities of the sector and, as a result, 'the real sentiments' of agricultural workers were rarely voiced.[32] There were further limitations to the ILO's work, partly imposed by its own tripartite logic of only considering formal employment relationships, which left out major groups of the population such as women. Whereas women's labour's contribution to agriculture featured prominently in the early international debates of the 1920s, the issue had disappeared from the debates in the 1950s and was to remain invisible until the 1970s and 80s, thus reflecting the continued marginalization and subordination of women's work.

Overall, what did not diminish but became even more pronounced in the 1950s and the following decades was the ILO's contribution to the narrative of the 'rural–urban divide' and the contradictory discourse between rural idyll, the romanticization of rural life, and rural hell, the emphasis of its grim and harsh conditions. Overall, the conceptualization and portrayal of static agrarian ways of living as fixed, unchanging, or deteriorating, played a central role in the emphasis of differences between urban and rural lifestyles. It also contributed to a discursive polarization between backward rural hinterlands and cities with higher educational level and better economies. If, for some, the rural countryside remained characterized by 'ancestral virtue' and 'finest moral strength', for others it was a place with poor labour legislation and a space dominated by the laws of Nature.[33]

Environmental and climatic constraints and the limits they imposed on productivity were a particularly salient element in international debates before the Second World War. The question of productivity remained a central issue that related the discussions of the 1950s with the debates of the 1920s and 30s. Since the beginning there had been a duality to the ILO's approach to improving the conditions in agriculture: reform was seen, on the one hand, as a way to attain social equality (and stability) between the agricultural and industrial sectors; on the other, as a means to achieve an increase in production—which was also

---

[32] International Labour Office, *Record of Proceedings*, thirty-third session of International Labour Conference (Geneva: International Labour Office, 1950).

[33] Colombian government delegate Vazquez Carrizosa speaking at the International Labour Conference in 1950. International Labour Office, *Record of Proceedings*, thirty-third session of the International Labour Conference (Geneva: International Labour Office, 1950), 70.

CONCLUSION 177

presented as a social objective. As the ILO experts progressed in their work, the enquiries became more specifically about the particular conditions of agricultural labour and ways to improve output. This becomes evident in the research on worktime in agriculture, which sought to understand the degree of dependency of agricultural work on natural and atmospheric factors and the correlations between hours worked and efficiency.[34] According to the ILO, labourers that were overworked, ill, and inadequately housed would simply not be productive. Since efficient utilization of agricultural resources and social progress went hand in hand, the expansion of social policy to tropical agricultural enterprises was a given. The ideal was a highly qualified and forward-looking labour force that produced enough for the growing industrial sector. If the enquiry into working hours thus showed early (but indirect) signs of a developmentalist mindset, in which agrarian labour productivity was to play a major role, by 1950 agricultural productivity was a more generally discussed subject.[35] A case in point are the objectives attributed to vocational education, which by 1955 stated clearly that the aim was to impart men and women in farming with skills so that they could make 'more effective use of land, labour and capital in agriculture, increase production and yields [...] and improve their income and standards of living'. The promotion of mechanization and the achievement of a proper balance between agriculture and other occupation was also seen as essential.[36]

For much of the interwar years, the ILO was regarded as the main reference by existing agricultural organizations and agrarian movements who championed social justice and labour improvements. This changed with the arrival of new institutions that—on the surface at least—shared similar mandates with the ILO, especially the FAO. If in the 1920s and 30s, frictions with the International Institute in Rome had been a constant of inter-institutional collaborative efforts, the situation did not improve with the arrival of the United Nations and its specialized agencies. From the early 1950s onwards, the ILO often struggled in its relations with the FAO, which stood for the new global post-war emphasis on worldwide food security, hunger, and rural welfare.[37] The latter's attention, led by a rising class of international experts—many of whom were agricultural economists—soon turned to the problem of agricultural underproductivity in

---

[34] See Chapter 3.
[35] On the developmentalist character of the work of the ILO in the 1930s, see also Véronique Plata-Stenger, *Social Reform, Modernization and Technical Diplomacy: The ILO Contribution to Development 1930–46* (Oldenbourg: De Gruyter, 2020). For current views, see Andrew Dorward, 'Agricultural Labour Productivity, Food Prices and Sustainable Development Impacts and Indicators', *Food Policy* 39 (April 2013), 40–50.
[36] International Labour Office, thirty-ninth session of the International Labour Conference. Fourth Item on the Agenda: Vocational Training in Agriculture, Report IV (1) (Geneva: International Labour Office, 1955), 5–6.
[37] Amalia Ribi Forclaz, 'From Reconstruction to Development: The Early Years of the Food and Agriculture Organization and the Conceptualization of Rural Welfare', *International History Review* 41, no. 2 (2019), 351–71.

developing countries. As had been the case with the International Institute of Agriculture, technological and scientific developments and statistical enquiries were FAO's primary focus, while the ILO' s gaze remained on the people working and living on the land and on social issues that were neglected by many other organizations. The outlook of the two organizations therefore significantly diverged, for example on new topics such as the use of pesticides, which were viewed by the ILO as a risk for the professional group of agricultural workers and by the FAO as a promising technological tool for the achievement of food security.[38]

Today, there still is a striking consistency in the ILO's approach, which reflects the fact that despite technological advances and major changes in food production, agricultural work remains physically demanding and often involves a marginalized, cheap, and casual labour force. Issues such as hours of work, low pay, child labour, and lack of social protection remain unresolved and have continued to occupy much of the ILO's work on agriculture. Thus, what in the 1920s initially seemed to be an awkward decision to focus on the category of 'waged agricultural labourer', has proven in the twenty-first century to have a rather surprising longevity.[39] Even though this concept homogenizes different forms of labour relationships and obscures individual experiences, the focus on agricultural waged labourers as a socially and economically precarious group is legitimate and remains a major labour and governance issue. Many men, women, and children who presently work in agriculture do not own or rent the land they cultivate, be it on smallholding or large industrialized farms and plantations. Due to processes of 'casualization' and 'flexibilization' of the labour force, the conditions of these workers appear to have worsened in the course of the last forty years or so.[40] Presently agriculture is the sector that relies the most on child labour, and although its hazardous conditions are now internationally recognized, the reduction let alone elimination of the labour of children encounters many obstacles which range from rural poverty to the pressures of global consumption, economic competition, and deregulation on production and labour costs. As social scientists have put it, this places agricultural workers 'at the bottom of the global value chain'.[41]

Across the globe, agriculture continues to be one of the sectors of the economy most associated with labour exploitation, not only in the Global South but also at the heart of Europe, where the demand for fresh, out-of-season fruit and

[38] Amalia Ribi Forclaz and Corinna Unger, 'Progress versus Precaution: International Organizations and the Use of Pesticides, 1940s to 1970s', *Comparativ—Zeitschrift für Globalgeschichte und vergleichende Gesellschaftsforschung* 32, no. 6 (2022), 750–68.

[39] International Labour Organization, *Agricultural Workers and their Contribution to Sustainable Agriculture and Rural Development* (Geneva: International Labour Office, 2007).

[40] Beatrice Conradie, 'What Do We Mean When We Say Casualization of Farm Work Is Rising?: Evidence from Fruit Farms in the Western Cape', *Agrekon* 46, no. 2 (2007), 173–94.

[41] Catherine S. Dolan, 'On Farm and Packhouse: Employment at the Bottom of a Global Value Chain', *Rural Sociology* 69, no. 1 (2004), 99–126.

vegetable has led to the development of racialized 'agri-food enclaves'. Notorious examples in Southern Europe include countries such as Italy and Spain, where seasonal migrant workers from Eastern Europe, North and West Africa, and India are paid a pittance for excessive hours of work, are housed in degrading conditions in camps and slums, without social rights and legal protection.[42] The lack of standardization and implementation of existing international instruments continues to be a major issue in global governance, and one on which the ILO has been working continuously for the last century. Raising awareness about agricultural labour conditions in ways that go beyond the current policy discourses on sustainable development and technological responses to climate change and environmental degradation, and that also address the longstanding social and legislative inequalities that exist with regard to workers' rights in the sector, will continue to be a major challenge.

Cultivating Fields of Progress: Agriculture and the International Labour Organization, 1920s–1950s. Amalia Ribi Forclaz, Oxford University Press. © Amalia Ribi Forclaz 2025. DOI: 10.1093/9780191945014.003.0009

---

[42] International Labour Organization, *Policies to Prevent and Tackle Labour Exploitation and Forced Labour in Europe* (Geneva: 2021); Gertel and Sippel, eds, *Seasonal Workers*; Irene Peano, 'Turbulences in the Encampment Archipelago: Conflicting Mobilities between Migration, Labour and Logistics in Italian Agri-Food Enclaves', *Mobilities* 16 (2021), 212–23.

Archival Sources and Bibliography

Archival Sources

Archives of the International Labour Organization, Geneva

Series AG Agriculture
Series I
Series P Personal Files
Series IC Industrial Committees
Series PWR Postwar Reconstruction
Series FAO Food and Agriculture Organizations
Proceedings of International Labour Conferences, 1919–60
Minutes of the Governing Body
Director's Reports
Industrial and Labour Information
Studies and Reports Series
Conventions and Recommendations
International Labour Review
Official Bulletin

Archives of the League of Nations, Geneva

Registry (R) series
10 D Economic
50 General

Archives of the International Institute for Social History, Amsterdam

RUP (Rassemblement Universel pour la Paix) 76–80
RUP (Rassemblement Universel pour la Paix) 181–50
Bulletins of the International Landworkers' Federation

Archives of the International Institute of Agriculture (in Archives of the Food and Agriculture Organization, Rome)

Series G Liquidation of the International Institute of Agriculture
Series I Participation in the work of the League of Nations and connected institutions
Series N Congresses, conferences and meetings
Papers Concerning Continuation of IIA Activities by FAO

Archives of the Food and Agriculture Organization, Rome

Frank McDougall Notes and Correspondence, 1946–50
Agriculture Institutions and Services Division
Rural Welfare Branch

Archives of the Associated Countrywomen of the World, London

Uncatalogued and unsorted materials relating to organization of conferences (1929–45)
Correspondence with adhering societies
Correspondence with Charlotte Boudreau

Private Papers and Unpublished Manuscripts

Leon Estabrook, diary, National Agricultural Library Washington, Estabrook MSS, box 1–5

Asher Hobson Papers, University of Wisconsin Archives
Louise Howard (Matthaei), private family archives, Birmingham
Olivia Rossetti Agresti, manuscript, *Anecdotage of an Interpreter. The Reminiscences of Olivia Rossetti Agresti* (1958), Yale Beinecke Rare Book and Manuscript Library

University of Warwick, Modern Records Centre
The Landworker (1919–50)

Bibliography

Adams, Caitlin, 'Rural Education and Reform Between the Wars', in Brassley, Paul, Burchardt, Jeremy, and Thompson, Lynne, eds, *The English Countryside between the Wars: Regeneration or Decline?* (Woodbridge: Boydell & Brewer, 2006), 36–52.
Aeroboe, Friedrich, *Die ländliche Arbeiterfrage nach dem Kriege* (Berlin: Parey, 1922).
Aglan, Ayla, 'Albert Thomas, historien du temps présent', Les cahiers Irice 2, no. 2 (2008), 23–38.
Aglan, Ayla, Feiertag, Olivier, and Kévonian, Dzovinar, eds, *Humaniser le travail. Régimes économiques, régimes politiques et organisation internationale du travail (1929–1969)* (Brussels: Peter Lang, 2011).
Ainsworth, Leopold, *The Confessions of a Planter in Malaya: A Chronicle of Life and Adventure in the Jungle* (London: H. F. and F. G. Witherby, 1933).
Alary, Éric, *La Grande Guerre des civils* (Paris: Perrin, 2013).
Alary, Éric, *L'Histoire des paysans français* (Paris: Perrin, 2016).
Alatas, Syed Hussein, *The Myth of the Lazy Native: A Study of the Image of the Malays, Filipinos, and Javanese from the Sixteenth to the Twentieth Century and Its Function in the Ideology of Colonial Capitalism* (London: Frank Cass, 1977).
Alcock, Antony, *History of the International Labour Organisation* (Basingstoke: Macmillan, 1971), 3–17.
Aldcroft, Derek H., *Europe's Third World: The European Periphery in the Interwar Years* (Aldershot, UK: Ashgate, 2006).
Allen, Alice Maud, *Sophy Sanger. A Pioneer in Internationalism* (Glasgow: Robert Maclehose and Co., 1958).
Alquier, Jules, L'agriculture dans l'évolution de la crise Mondiale (Paris: Alcan, 1933).
Amrith, Sunil, 'Asian Internationalism: Bandung's Echo in a Colonial Metropolis', *Inter-Asia Cultural Studies* 6, no. 4 (2005), 557–69.
Amrith, Sunil, *Decolonizing International Health: India and Southeast Asia, 1930–1965* (Cambridge: Palgrave Macmillan, 2006).
Andersson, Jenny, 'The Great Future Debate and the Struggle for the World', *The American History Review* 117, no. 5 (2012), 1411–30.
Armiero, Marco, 'Introduction: Fascism and Nature', *Modern Italy* 19, no. 3 (2014), 241–5.
Arnold, David, *The Problem of Nature: Environment, Culture and European Expansion* (Oxford: Blackwell Publishers, 1996).
Arnold, David, 'Illusory Riches': Representations of the Tropical World, 1840–1950', *Singapore Journal of Tropical Geography* 21, no. 1 (2000), 6–18.
Arsan, Andrew, Lewis, Su Lin and Richard, Anne-Isabelle, 'Editorial: The Roots of Global Civil Society and the Interwar Moment', *Journal of Global History* 7, no. 2 (July 2012), 157–65.
Auderset, Juri, 'Manufacturing Agricultural Working Knowledge: The Scientific Study of Agricultural Work in Industrial Europe, 1920s–60s', *Rural History* 32, no. 2 (October 2021), 233–48.
Augé-Laribé, Michel, 'La crise agricole et ses effets sur la classe paysanne en France', *Revue internationale d'agriculture* (1931), 174–80.
Augé-Laribé, Michel, 'Labour Conditions in French Agriculture', *International Labour Review* 25, no. 1 (1932), 23–57.
Bairoch, Paul and Limbor, Jean-Marie 'Changes in Industrial Distribution of the World's Labour Force by Region, 1850–1960', *International Labour Review*, 98, no. 4 (October 1968), 311–36.

Balachandran, Gopalan, 'Subaltern Cosmopolitanism in the Imperial Metropole: Notes towards a Prehistory of Racism and Multiculturalism', *Working Papers in International History* 8 (September 2011).
Bänziger, Peter-Paul and Suter, Mischa, eds, *Histories of Productivity: Genealogical Perspectives on the Body and Modern Economy* (London: Routledge, 2016).
Baron, Ava and Boris, Eileen, 'The Body as a Useful Category for Working-Class History', *Labor* 4, no. 2 (2007), 23–43.
Barrett Litoff, Judith and Smith, David C., 'To the Rescue of the Crops: The Women's Land Army during World War II', *Prologue* 25 (Winter 1993), 34.
Bartlett, Michael, *Empire of Humanity: A History of Humanitarianism* (Ithaca: Cornell University Press, 2011).
Barton, Gregory, *The Global History of Organic Farming* (Oxford: Oxford University Press, 2018).
Bauer, Steven, 'The Road to the Eight-Hour Day', translated by Maylander, Alfred, *Monthly Labor Review* 9, no. 2 (August 1919), 41–65.
Bauerkämper, Arnd, 'The Industrialization of Agriculture and Its Consequences for the Natural Environment: An Inter-German Comparative Perspective', *Historical Social Research* 29, no. 3 (2004), 124–49.
Béaur, Gérard and Chiapparino, Francesco, eds, *Agriculture and the Great Depression: The Rural Crisis of the 1930s in Europe and the Americas* (London: Routledge, 2023).
Beckert, Sven, Bosma, Ulbe, Schneider, Mindi, and Vanhaute, Eric, 'Commodity Frontiers and the Transformation of the Global Countryside: A Research Agenda, *Journal of Global History* 16, no. 3 (2021), 435–50.
Beckford, George, *Persistent Poverty: Underdevelopment in Plantation Economies of the Third World* (London: Oxford University Press, 1972).
Behal, Rana, *One Hundred Years of Servitude: Political Economy of Tea Plantations in Colonial Assam* (New Delhi: Tulika Books, 2014).
Belshaw, Horace, 'Foundations of Rural Welfare', *International Labour Review*, no. 3 (March 1945), 279–301.
Bemmann, Martin, 'Cartels, Grossraumwirtschaft and Statistical Knowledge: International Organizations and Their Efforts to Govern Europe's Forest Resources in the 1930s and 1940s', in van De Grift, Liesbeth and Ribi Forclaz, Amalia, eds, *Governing the Rural in Interwar Europe* (London: Routledge, 2018), 233–58.
Bernardi, Emanuele, *Il mais 'miracoloso': Storia di un'innovazione tra politica, economia e religione* (Roma: Carocci editore, 2014).
Bhowmik, Sharit K., 'Ethnicity and Isolation: Marginalization of Tea Plantation Workers', *Race/Ethnicity: Multidisciplinary Global Contexts*. 4, no. 2 (2011), 235–53.
Bianciardi, Silvia, *Argentina Altobelli e la 'buona battaglia'* (Milan: Franco Angeli, 2013).
Biltoft, Carolyn, 'Sundry World Within the World: Decentred Histories and Institutional Archives', *Journal of World History* 31, no. 4 (December 2020), 729–60.
Biltoft, Carolyn, *A Violent Peace: Media, Truth and Power at the League of Nations* (Chicago: University of Chicago Press, 2021).
Bivar, Venus, *Organic Resistance: The Struggle over Industrial Farming in Postwar France* (Chapel Hill: University of North Carolina Press, 2019).
Bluma, Lars and Uhl, Karsten, eds, *Kontrollierte Arbeit—disziplinierte Körper? Zur Sozial- und Kulturgeschichte der Industriearbeit im 19. und 20. Jahrhundert* (Bielefeld: Transcript Verlag, 2012).
Boden, Ragna, 'Cold War Economics: Soviet Aid to Indonesia', *Journal of Cold War Studies* 10 (2008), 110–29.
Boilley, Paul, 'La Journée de huit heures et le travail intensif', *La revue socialiste* 11 (January–June 1890), 712–15.
Bonnet, Romain, *La Terre et le Plomb. Violence politique, question agraire et crise du parlementarisme libéral dans l'Italie du premier après-guerre (1918–1922) et dans l'Espagne républicaine (1931–1935)*, PhD thesis (European University Institute, 2016).

Booth, Anne, 'Varieties of Exploitation in Colonial Settings: Dutch and Belgian Policies in Indonesia and the Congo and their Legacies', in Frankema, Ewout and Buelens, Frans, eds, *Colonial Exploitation and Economic Development: The Belgian Congo and the Netherlands Indies Compared* (London: Routledge, 2016).

Boris, Eileen, Hoethker, Dorothea, and Zimmermann, Susan, eds, *Women's ILO: Transnational Networks, Global Labour Standards, and Gender Equity, 1919 to Present* (Leiden, Boston: Brill, 2018), 38.

Borowy, Iris, *Coming to Terms with World Health: The League of Nations Health Organization, 1921-1946* (Frankfurt am Main: Peter Lang, 2009).

Bosma, Ulbe, *The Sugar Plantation in India and Indonesia: Industrial Production, 1770-2010* (Cambridge: Cambridge University Press, 2013).

Boulet, Michel, ed., *Les enjeux de la formation des acteurs de l'agriculture, 1760-1945* (Dijon: Educagri, 2000).

Boyd-Orr, John, 'The Role of Food in Post-War Reconstruction', *International Labour Review* 47, no. 3 (1943), 279-96.

Brassley, Paul, 'British Farming between the Wars', in Brassley, Paul, Burchardt, Jeremy, and Thompson, Lynne, eds, *The English Countryside between the Wars: Regeneration or Decline?* (Woodbridge: Boydell & Brewer, 2006).

Brassley, Paul, 'Agricultural Education, Training and Advice in the UK, 1850-2000', in Vivier, Nadine ed., *The State and Rural Societies: Policy and Education in Europe, 1750-2000* (Brepols: Turnhout, 2008).

Brassley, Paul, Segers, Yves, and Van Molle, Leen, eds, *War, Agriculture and Food: Rural Europe from the 1930s to the 1950s* (New York: Routledge, 2012).

Bravo, Anna, 'Italian Peasant Women and the First World War', in Marwick, Arthur, Simpson, Wendy, and Emsley, Clive, eds, *Total War and Historical Change. Europe, 1914-1955* (Maidenhead: Open University Press, 1989), 45-73.

Bruisch, Katja, *Als das Dorf noch Zukunft war: Agrarismus und Expertise zwischen Zarenreich und Sowjetunion* (Cologne et al: Böhlau, 2014).

Bruisch, Katja, 'Knowledge and Power in the Making of the Soviet Village', in Ribi Forclaz and van de Grift, eds, *Governing the Rural in Interwar Europe* (London: Routledge, 2018).

Burchardt, Jeremy, 'The Rural Idyll: A Critique', in Elson, Verity and Shirley, Rosemary, eds, *Creating the Countryside: The Rural Idyll Past and Present* (London: Paul Holberton, 2017), 64-73.

Butler, Harold, 'The Washington Conference, 1919', in Solano, E. J., ed., *Labour as an International Problem* (London: Macmillan, 1920), 197-246.

Camic, Charles, Gross, Neil, and Lamont, Michele, eds, *Social Knowledge in the Making* (Chicago: University of Chicago Press, 2011).

Cathcart, Edward Provan, *The Human Factor in Industry* (London: Oxford University Press, 1928).

Cayet, Thomas, 'Travailler à la marge: le Bureau International du Travail et l'organisation scientifique du travail (1923-1933)', *Le Mouvement social* 3, no. 228 (2009), 39-56.

Cazzola, Franco, 'Les salariés agricoles de la plaine du Pô. Naissance et déclin d'une classe 'dangereuse', Hubscher, Ronald and Farcy, Jean-Claude, eds, *La Moisson des Autres: Les salariés agricoles aux XIXe et XXe siècles* (Paris: Créaphis, 1996), 153-76.

Cerutti, Mauro, 'Olindo Gorni', *Dictionnaire historique de la Suisse*, https://hls-dhs-dss.ch/fr/articles/027942/2004-10-27 (last accessed 28 January 2024).

Cipolla, Carlo M., *Before the Industrial Revolution: European Society and Economy, 1000-1700* (New York: Norton, 1976).

Clavien, Alain and Valsangiacomo, Nelly, *Les intellectuels antifascistes dans la Suisse de l'entre-deux- guerres* (Lausanne: Antipodes, 2006).

Clavin, Patricia, 'Explaining the Failure of the World Economic Conference', in James, Harold, ed., *The Interwar Depression in an International Context* (Munich: Oldenbourg Wissenschaftsverlag, 2002), 77-99.

Clavin, Patricia, *Securing the World Economy. The Reinvention of the League of Nations, 1920-1946* (Oxford: Oxford University Press, 2013).

Clavin, Patricia and Sluga, Glenda, eds, *Internationalisms: A Twentieth-Century History* (Cambridge: Cambridge University Press, 2017).
Clayton, Daniel and Bowd, Gavin, 'Geography, Tropicality and Postcolonialism: Anglophone and Francophone Readings of the work of Pierre Gourou', *L'Espace Géographique* 3 (2006), 208–21.
Clout, Hugh, *After the Ruins. Restoring the Countryside of Northern France after the Great War* (Exeter: University of Exeter Press, 1996).
Cobble, Dorothy Sue, 'The Other ILO Founders: 1919 and Its Legacies', in Boris, Eileen, Hoethker, Dorothea, and Zimmermann, Susan, eds, *Women's ILO: Transnational Networks, Global Labour Standards, and Gender Equity, 1919 to Present* (Leiden, Boston: Brill, 2018), 38.
Coghe, Samuel, 'Reordering Colonial Society: Model Villages and Social Planning in Rural Angola, 1920–45', *Journal of Contemporary History* 52 (2016), 16–44.
Conférence Agraire Internationale, *Le Monde Agraire et la Paix* (Paris: Editions Agraires Internationales, 1936).
Conford, Philip, *The Origins of the Organic Movement* (Edinburgh: Floris, 2001).
Conradie, Beatrice, 'What Do We Mean When We Say Casualization of Farm Work Is Rising?: Evidence from Fruit Farms in the Western Cape', *Agrekon* 46, no. 2 (2007), 173–94.
Cooper, Frederick, 'Modernising Colonialism and the Limits of Empire', in Calhoun, Craig, Cooper, Frederick, and Moore, Kevin W., eds, *Lessons of Empire: Imperials Histories and American Power* (New York: New Press, 2006), 63–72.
Cooper, Frederick, Holt, Thomas C., and Scott, Rebecca J., *Beyond Slavery: Explorations of Race, Labour, and Citizenship in Post-Emancipation Societies* (Chapel Hill: University of North Carolina Press, 2000).
Crafts, Nicholas, 'The Great Boom: 1950–73', in Schulze, M. ed., *Western Europe, Economic, and Social Change since 1945* (London: Routledge 1999), 42–62.
Cross, Gary, 'Les Trois Huits: Labor Movements, International Reform, and the Origins of the Eight-Hour Day, 1919–1924', *French Historical Studies* 14, no. 2 (Autumn 1985), 240–68.
Cullather, Nick, 'Miracles of Modernization: The Green Revolution and the Apotheosis of Technology', *Diplomatic History* 28, no. 2 (2004), 227–54.
Cullather, Nick, *The Hungry World: America's Cold War Battle against Poverty in Asia* (Cambridge Mss: Harvard University Press, 2010).
Custodis, Johann, 'Employing the Enemy: The Contribution of German and Italian Prisoners of War to British Agriculture during and after the Second World War', *Agricultural History Review* 60, no. 2 (2012), 243–65.
D. P. E., 'Food for Postwar Europe: Shortages of World Supplies', *Bulletin of International News* 22, no. 11 (1945), 465–474.
D'Onofrio, Federico, *Knowing to Transform: Three Ways for Agricultural Economists to Observe Italy, 1900–1940*, PhD thesis (University of Utrecht, 2013).
D'Onofrio, Federico and Mignemi, Niccolò, 'The International Institute of Agriculture and the Information Infrastructure of World Trade (1905–1946), *Histoire & Mesure* 48 (2023), 13–38.
Dahlén, Marianne, *The Negotiable Child: The ILO Child Labour Campaign, 1919–1973*, Doctor of Laws thesis (Uppsala University 2007).
Daughton, James P., 'ILO Expertise and Colonial Violence in the Interwar Years', in Kott, Sandrine and Droux, Joelle, eds, *Globalizing Social Rights: The International Labour Organization and Beyond* (Basingstoke: Palgrave, 2013), 85–97.
Derickson, Alan, '"A Widespread Superstition": The Purported Invulnerability of Workers of Color to Occupational Heat Stress', *American Journal of Public Health* 109, no. 10 (2019), 1329–35.
Derlitzki, Georg, 'Die Landarbeitsforschung, dargestellt an den Arbeiten der Versuchsanstalt für Landarbeitslehre Pommritz', in Derlitzki, Georg, ed., *Berichte über Landarbeit* (Stuttgart: 1927).
Devinat, Paul, *Scientific Management in Europe*, Studies and Reports, Series B (Economic Conditions), no. 17 (Geneva: International Labour Office, 1927).
Dhermy-Mairal, Marine, 'Du danger des enquêtes savantes. Faire oeuvre de science dans l'entre-deux-guerres au Bureau International du Travail', *Revue d'histoire moderne & contemporaine* 62, no. 4 (2015), 7–32.

Dhermy-Mairal, Marine and Piguet, Laure, 'Enquiring into Others: The International Labour Office's Attempts to Grasp the Early Soviet Labour System (1920)', *Cadernos Sociedade e Trabalho* (Lisbon: MTSSS/GEP, 2021), 149–62.

Dingsdale, Alan, *Mapping Modernities: Geographies of Central and Eastern Europe, 1920–2000* (London: Routledge, 2002).

Dolan, Catherine S., 'On Farm and Packhouse: Employment at the Bottom of a Global Value Chain', *Rural Sociology* 69, no. 1 (2004), 99–126.

Domènech Feliu, Jordi and Miley, Thomas, 'Structural Change, Collective Action, and Social Unrest in 1930s Spain', *IFCS Working Papers in Economic History* (Universidad Carlos III de Madrid, Instituto Figuerola: 2013).

Dop, Louis, *Le Présent et l'avenir de l'institut international d'agriculture* (Rome: Imprimerie de L'institut international d'agriculture 1912).

Dorward, Andrew, 'Agricultural Labour Productivity, Food Prices and Sustainable Development Impacts and Indicators', *Food Policy* 39 (April 2013), 40–50.

Dove, Michael R., *The Banana Tree at the Gate: A History of Marginal Peoples and Global Markets in Borneo* (New Haven: Yale University Press, 2011).

Duncan, Joseph, 'A New Policy for Agricultural Labour', *International Labour Review* 25, no. 2 (February 1932).

Dunlop, Walter, *An Investigation of Certain Processes and Conditions on Farms* (London: National Institute of Industrial Psychology, 1927).

Dunlop, Walter, 'Labour Efficiency Investigations in English Farming', *International Labour Review* 21, no. 5 (1930), 700–10.

Dunnage, Jonathan, *Twentieth-Century Italy. A Social History* (London: Routledge, 2002).

Eisenberg, Jaci, 'Butler, Harold Beresford', in Reinalda, Bob, Kille, Kent J., and Eisenberg, Jaci Leigh, eds, *IO Bio: Biographical Dictionary of Secretaries-General of International Organizations*, www.ru.nl/fm/iobio (last accessed 28 January 2024).

Engerman, David and Unger, Corinna, eds, 'Special Forum: Modernization as a Global Project', *Diplomatic History* 33, no. 3 (2009), 375–506.

Ermacora, Matteo, 'Rural Society', in Daniel, Ute, Gatrell, Peter, Janz, Oliver, Jones, Heather, Keene, Jennifer, Kramer, Alan, and Nasson, Bill, eds, *1914–1918: International Encyclopedia of the First World War* (Berlin: Freie Universität Berlin, 2015), https://encyclopedia.1914-1918-online.net/article/rural_society.

Escobar, Ernesto, *Encountering Development: The Making and Unmaking of the Third World* (Princeton, NJ: Princeton University Press, 1995).

Eurofound, *Bridging the Rural–Urban Divide: Addressing Inequalities and Empowering Communities* (Luxembourg: Publications Office of the European Union, 2023).

Ewing, Cindy, 'With a Minimum of Bitterness': Decolonization, the Right to Self-determination, and the Arab-Asian Group', *Journal of Global History* 17, no. 2 (2022), 254–71.

Farcy, Jean-Claude, 'Les grèves agricoles de 1936–1937 dans le bassin parisien', in Ronald Hubscher and Jean-Claude Farcy, eds, *La Moisson des Autres: Les salariés agricoles aux XIXe et XXe siècles* (Paris: Créaphis, 1996), 303.

Farrugia, Peter, 'Mésentente Cordiale: Anglo-French Collaboration in the Rassemblement Universel pour la paix', *Synergies. Royaume-Uni et Irlande* 4 (2011), 105–16.

Febvre, Lucien, 'Albert Thomas historien', *Annales d'histoire économique et sociale* 4 (July 1932), 381–4.

Fechner, Henrich, 'Standard-Setting in Colonial Labour Regulation and the Great Depression', in Nullmeier, F., Gonzáles de Reufels, Delia, and Obinger, Herbert, eds, *International Impacts on Social Policy: Short Histories in Global Perspective* (Palgrave Macmillan, 2022).

Federico, Giovanni, *Feeding the World: An Economic History of Agriculture, 1800–2000* (Princeton: Princeton University Press, 2005).

Feiertag, Olivier, 'Humaniser la crise économique (1929–1934): l'expertise du BIT dans la crise de mondialisation des années 1930', in Aglan, Ayla, Feiertag, Olivier, and Kévonian, Dzovinar, eds, *Humaniser le travail. Régimes économiques, régimes politiques et organisation internationale du travail (1929–1969)* (Brussels: Peter Lang, 2011), 19–38.

Fernandez-Prieto, Lourenzo, Pan-Montojo, Juan, and Cabo, Miguel, eds, *Agriculture in the Age of Fascism: Authoritarian Technocracy and Rural Modernization, 1922–1945*, series *Rural History in Europe* 13 (Turnhout: Brepols 2014).

Fiti Sinclair, Guy, *To Reform the World: International Organizations and the Making of Modern States* (Oxford: Oxford University Press, 2017).

Fitzgerald, Deborah, *Every Farm a Factory: The Industrial Ideal in American Agriculture* (New Haven, CT and London: Yale University Press, 2003).

Folsom, Josiah C., 'Review of *Labour in Agriculture: An International Survey* by Louise E. Howard', *Journal of Farm Economics* 18, no. 2 (May 1936), 439–44.

Food and Agriculture Organization, *Essentials of Rural Welfare: An Approach to the Improvement of Rural Well-Being* (Washington, DC: Food and Agriculture Organization, 1949).

Foot, John M., 'White Bolsheviks? The Catholic Left and the Socialists in Italy, 1919–1920, *The Historical Journal* 40, no. 2 (1997), 415–33.

Forney, Jérémie, 'Idéologie agrarienne et identité professionelle des agriculteurs: la complexité des images du paysan Suisse', *Yearbook of Socioeconomics in Agriculture* 4, no. 1 (June 2011), 13–33.

Galligani Casey, Janet, 'Farm Women, Letters to the Editor, and the Limits of Autobiography Theory', *Journal of Modern Literature* 28, no. 1 (2004), 89–106.

Galpin, Charles, *Rural Life* (New York: The Century Co., 1918).

Galpin, Charles, *Rural Social Problems* (New York: The Century Co., 1924).

Gamble, Harry, 'Peasants of the Empire. Rural Schools and the Colonial Imaginary in 1930s French West Africa', *Cahiers d'études africaines* 195 (2009), 775–804.

Garrier, Gilbert, 'L'apport des récits de vie et des romans paysans', in Hubscher, Ronald and Farcy, Jean-Claude, eds, *La Moisson des autres: Les salariés agricoles aux XIXe et XX siècles* (Paris: Créaphis, 1996).

Gentili Zappi, Elda, *If Eight Hours Seem Too Few: Mobilization of Women Workers in the Italian Rice Fields* (New York: State University of New York Press, 1991).

Gertel, Jörg, and Sippel, Sarah Ruth, eds, *Seasonal Workers in Mediterranean Agriculture: The Social Costs of Eating Fresh* (London and New York: Routledge, 2014).

Getachew, Adom, *Worldmaking after Empire: The Rise and Fall of Self-Determination* (Princeton, NJ: Princeton University Press, 2019).

Geyer, Martin H. and Paulmann, Johannes, eds, *The Mechanics of Internationalism: Culture, Society, and Politics from the 1840s to the First World War* (Oxford, Oxford University Press, 2001).

Gidney, Thomas, 'The Development Dichotomy: Colonial India's Accession to the ILO's Governing Body (1919–1922)', *Journal of Global History* 18, no. 2 (2023), 259–80.

Gil-Riaño, Sebastian, 'Risky Migrations: Race, Latin Eugenics, and Cold War Development in the International Labor Organization's Puno–Tambopata Project in Peru, 1930–60', *History of Science* 60, no. 1 (2022), 41–68.

Gillette, John Morris, *Rural Sociology* (New York: Macmillan, 1922).

Goddard, Nicholas, 'The Development and Influence of Agricultural Periodicals and Newspapers, 1780–1880', *The Agricultural History Review* 31, no. 2, British Agricultural History Society (1983), 116–31.

Gong, Gerrit W., *The Standard of 'Civilization' in International Society* (Oxford: Clarendon Press, 1984).

Goodrich, Carter, 'The Effect of the War on the Position of Labor', *The American Economic Review* 32, no. 1 (1942), 416–25.

Gorman, Daniel, *The Emergence of International Society in the 1920s* (New York: Cambridge University Press, 2012).

Gourou, Pierre, *Les Pays tropicaux: principes d'une géographie humaine et économique* (Paris: Presses Universitaires de France, 1947).

Gove Hambidge, *The Story of FAO* (New York: D. Van Nostrand Company, 1955).

Grant, Kevin, *A Civilized Savagery: Britain and the New Slaveries in Africa, 1884–1926* (New York, 2005).

Greaves, Ida C., *Modern Production among Backward Peoples* (London: Allen and Unwin, 1935).

Grieves, Keith, 'War Comes to the Fields. Sacrifice, Localism and Ploughing Up the English Countryside', in Beckett, Ian, ed., *1917. Beyond the Western Front* (Leiden, Boston: Brill, 2009), 159–168.

Grigg, David, 'The World's Agricultural Labour Force 1800–1970', *Geography* 60, no. 3 (July 1975), 194–202.

Grigg, David, *The Transformation of Agriculture in the West* (Oxford, UK; Cambridge, US: Blackwell, 1992).

Grovers, Ernest R., *The Rural Mind and Social Welfare* (Chicago: University of Chicago Press, 1922).

Groves, Reg, *Sharpen the Sickle! The History of the Farm Workers' Union* (London: Merlin Press Limited, 2011).

Handy, Jim, '"Almost Idiotic Wretchedness": A Long History of Blaming Peasants', *Journal of Peasant Studies* 36, no. 2 (2009), 325–44.

Hartmann, Heinrich 'Building an Old Institution: the Agricultural Extension Service and Village Institutes in Post-Second World War Rural Turkey', in Hartmann, Heinrich and Tischler, Julia, eds, *Planting Seeds of Knowledge: Agriculture and Education in Rural Societies in the Twentieth Century* (New York, Oxford: Berghahn Books, 2023), 87–103.

Hartmann, Heinrich, and Tischler, Julia, 'Introduction', in Hartmann, Heinrich, and Tischler, Julia, eds, *Planting Seeds of Knowledge: Agriculture and Education in Rural Societies in the Twentieth Century* (New York, Oxford: Berghahn Books, 2023), 9–23.

Harvey Smith, J., 'Agricultural Workers and the French Wine-Growers' Revolt of 1907', *Past & Present* 79, no. 1 (May 1978), 101–25.

Harwood, Jonathan, *Technology's Dilemma. Agricultural Colleges between Science and Practice in Germany, 1860–1934* (Frankfurt: P. Lang, 2005).

Heinzen, James W., *Inventing a Soviet Countryside: State Power and the Transformation of Rural Russia, 1917–1929* (Pittsburgh, PA: University of Pittsburgh Press, 2004).

Helleiner, Eric, *Forgotten Foundations of Bretton Woods: International Development and the Making of the Postwar Order* (Ithaca, NY: Cornell University Press, 2014).

Herren, Madeleine, *Internationale Organisationen seit 1865: Eine Globalgeschichte der Internationalen Ordnung* (Darmstadt: Buchgesellschaft, 2009).

Herren, Madeleine, 'Fascist Internationalism', in Clavin, Patricia and Sluga, Glenda, eds, *Internationalisms: A Twentieth-Century History* (Cambridge: Cambridge University Press, 2017), 191–212.

Hervieu, Bertrand and Purseigle, Francois, 'The Sociology of Agricultural Worlds: From a Sociology of Change to a Sociology of Coexistence', *Review of Agricultural and Environmental Studies* 96, no. 1 (2015), 59–90.

Hidalgo-Weber, Olga, *La Grande-Bretagne et l'Organisation internationale du travail (1919–1946). Une nouvelle forme d'internationalisme* (Louvain-la-Neuve: Academia—L'Harmattan, 2017).

Hobsbawm, Eric, *Age of Extremes: The Short Twentieth Century, 1914–1991* (London: Michael Joseph, 1994).

Hobson, Asher, 'The Landless Agricultural Laborer in Italy', *The Journal of Land & Public Utility Economics* 1, no. 4 (1925), 425–34.

Hobson, Asher, 'An International Organization of National Farm Associations', *Journal of Farm Economics* 10, no. 7 (April 1928).

Hobson, Asher, 'Review of Carl T. Schmidt, *The Plough and the Sword: Labour, Land, and Property in Fascist Italy* (New York: Columbia University Press, 1938)', *The American Historical Review* 44, no. 2 (January 1939), 389–90.

Hodge, Joseph Morgan, *Triumph of the Expert: Agrarian Doctrines of Development and the Legacies of British Colonialism* (Athens, OH: Ohio University Press, 2007).

Hoethker, Dorothea and Kott, Sandrine, eds, *À la rencontre de l'Europe au travail: récits de voyages d'Albert Thomas (1920–1932)* (Sorbonne/Bureau International du Travail, 2015).

Howard, Louise Ernestine, *Labour in Agriculture: An International Survey* (Oxford: Oxford University Press, 1935).
Howkins, Alun, *Poor Labouring Men. Rural Radicalism in Norfolk 1870–1923* (Boston: Routledge and Kegan Paul, 1985).
Howkins, Alun, 'Labor History and the Rural Poor, 1850–1980', *Rural History* 1, no. 1 (1990), 113–22.
Hubscher, Ronald, 'Révolution aux champs. La Fédération nationale des travailleurs de l'agriculture (1920–1981)', in Hubscher, Ronald and Farcy, Jean-Claude, eds, *La Moisson des Autres: Les salariés agricoles aux XIXe et XXe siècles* (Paris: Créaphis, 1996), 343–59.
Institut International d'Agriculture, *L'organisation scientifique du travail agricole en Europe* (Rome: Imprimerie de la Chambre des Députés Charles Colombo, 1931).
International Institute of Agriculture, *The Agricultural Situation in 1930–31* (Rome: 1932).
International Institute of Agriculture, *The Work of the International Institute of Agriculture During the War (1940–1945)* (Rome: 1945).
International Labour Office, *First International Congress of Landworkers' Unions affiliated to the International Federation of Trade Unions Amsterdam, 17–19 August 1920*, Studies and Reports, Series K, no. 1 (Geneva: International Labour Office, 1920).
International Labour Office, *Report on Special Measure for the Protection of Agricultural Workers* (Geneva: International Labour Office, 1921).
International Labour Office, *The International Labour Organization and Agriculture* (Geneva: 1924).
International Labour Office, *The Relation of Labour Cost to Total Costs of Production in Agriculture* (Geneva: 1926).
International Labour Office, 'The Science of Farm Labour: Scientific Management and German Agriculture', *International Labour Review* 15, no. 3 (1927), 379–413.
International Labour Office, *The Representation and Organisation of Agricultural Workers*, Studies and Reports, Series K (Agriculture), no. 8 (Geneva: 1928).
International Labour Office, 'The Nutrition of Indigenous Workers', *International Labour Review* 41, no. 3 (1940), 307–17.
International Labour Office, *Labour Problems in Agriculture: General Report for the Thirty-Third Session of the International Labour Conference* (Geneva: International Labour Office, 1950).
International Labour Office, *Plantation Workers*, Studies and Reports, New Series, No. 69 (Geneva 1966).
International Labour Office and International Institute of Agriculture, *Studies on Movements of Agricultural Population: I, The Rural Exodus in Germany* (Geneva: 1933).
International Labour Office and International Institute of Agriculture, *Studies on Movements of Agricultural Population: II, The Rural Exodus in Czechoslovakia* (Geneva: 1935).
International Labour Organization, *Edward Phelan and the ILO: The Life and Views of an International Social Actor* (Geneva: ILO, 2009).
International Labour Organization, *Policy Guidelines for the Promotion of Decent Work in the Agri-food Sector* (Geneva: May 2023).
International Secretariat of the International Peace Campaign, *A New Force for Peace: Proceedings of the Preparatory Peasant Peace Conference, 5–6 February 1938/Une force nouvelle: Débats de la conférence paysanne préparatoire pour la paix, 5–6 février 1938* (Geneva: Palais Wilson, 1938).
Isobe, Keizo, 'Aux marges de la description géographique et de l'enquête sociale: Notes sur Jacques Valdour', in Claval, P., ed., *Autour de Vidal de la Blache* (Paris: CNRS Éditions, 1993), 65–9.
Jachertz, Ruth, '"To Keep Food out of Politics": The UN Food and Agriculture Organization, 1945–1965', in Frey, Marc, Kunkel, Soenke, and Unger, Corinna R., eds, *International Organizations and Development, 1945–1990* (Basingstoke: Palgrave Macmillan, 2014), 75–100.
Jachertz, Ruth and Nützenadel, Alexander, 'Coping with Hunger? Visions of a Global Food System, 1930–1960', *Journal of Global History* 6 (2011), 99–119.

Jacoby, Erich H., *Agrarian Unrest in South-East Asia* (New York: Columbia University Press, 1949).
Jasanoff, Sheila, ed., *States of Knowledge: The Co-Production of Science and Social Order* (London: Routledge, 2004).
Javal, Adolphe, *La Confession d'un agriculteur* (Paris: Fayard, 1929).
Jensen, A. S., 'Rural Opinion of Educational Philosophy', *Journal of Rural Education* (November 1925).
Jensen, Jill, 'From Geneva to the Americas: The International Labor Organization and Inter-American Social Security Standards, 1936–1948', *International Labor and Working-Class History*, no. 80 (2011), 215–40.
Jéronimo Bandeira, Miguel and Monteiro, José Pedro, 'Colonialism on Trial: International and Transnational Organizations and the Global South Challenge to the Portuguese Empire (1949–1962), *Humanity: An International Journal of Human Rights, Humanitarianism and Development* 13, no. 1 (2022), 104–26.
Johnston, George Alexander, *The International Labour Organization. Its Work for Social and Economic Justice* (London: Europa Publications, 1970), 254.
Jones, Elizabeth B., 'Seeing Is Believing: Sites/Sights of Agricultural Improvement in Germany (1840–1914)', *Rural History* 30, no. 1 (2019), 37–51.
Jones, Peter, *Agricultural Enlightenment: Knowledge, Technology, and Nature, 1750–1840* (Oxford: Oxford University Press, 2016).
Kaufman, Jacob J., 'Farm Labour during World War II', *Journal of Farm Economics* 31, no.1 (February 1949), 131–42.
Kitchen, Fred *Brother to the Ox: The Autobiography of a Farm Labourer* (London, 1939; 1981 edn).
Kopecek, Michael, 'Czechoslovak Interwar Democracy and its Critical Introspections', *Journal of Modern European History* 17 (2019), 7–5.
Kott, Sandrine, 'Les organisations internationales, terrains d'étude de la globalisation. Jalons pour une approche socio-historique', *Critique internationale* 52 (2011), 11–16.
Kott, Sandrine, 'Fighting the War or Preparing for Peace? The ILO during the Second World War', *Journal of Modern European History* 12, no. 3 (2014), 359–76.
Kott, Sandrine, *A World more Equal: An Internationalist Perspective on the Cold War* (New York: Columbia University Press, 2024).
Kott, Sandrine and Droux, Joelle, eds, *Globalizing Social Rights: The International Labour Organization and Beyond* (Basingstoke: Palgrave, 2013).
Kozma, Liat, Rodriguez Garcia, Magaly, and Rodogno, Davide, eds, *The League of Nations' Work on Social Issues: Visions, Endeavours and Experiments* (Geneva: United Nations, 2016).
Krishnamurty, J., 'India and the International Labour Organisation', *Economic and Political Weekly* 46, no. 10 (2011).
Kurian, Rachel, 'Dynamics of the Plantationcene: Finance Capital and the Labour Regime on British Colonial Plantations in Nineteenth-Century South Asia', in van Nederveen Meerkerk, Elise and Bauer, Rolf, eds, *Global Agricultural Workers from the 17th to the 21st Century* (Leiden, Boston: Brill, 2023), 268–292.
Lains, Pedro and Pinilla, Vicente, eds, *Agriculture and Economic Development in Europe since 1870* (London, New York: Routledge, 2009).
Lamartine Yates, Paul, *So Bold an Aim: Ten Years of International Cooperation Toward Freedom from Want: Québec, 1945–Rome, 1955* (Rome: FAO, 1955).
Langthaler, Ernst, 'Landflucht, Agrarsystem und Moderne: Deutschland 1933–1939', in Oltmer, Jochen, ed., *Nationalsozialistisches Migrationsregime und 'Volksgemeinschaft'* (Paderborn: Schöningh, 2012), 111–36.
Laqua, Daniel, ed., *Internationalism Reconfigured: Transnational Ideas and Movements Between the World Wars* (London: Tauris Academic Studies, 2011).
Lebow, Katherine, Mazurek, Małgorzata, and Wawrzyniak, Joanna, 'Making Modern Social Science: The Global Imagination in East Central and Southeastern Europe after Versailles', *Contemporary European History* 28, no. 2 (May 2019), 137–42.

Lembré, Stéphane, 'The Experience of Itinerant Agricultural Education in the Nord Region (1900-1939)', *Histoire et Sociétés rurales* 34, no. 2 (2010), 149-80.
Leonori, Franco, *No guerra, ma terra! Guido Miglioli, una vita per i contadini* (Milan, Rome: CEI, 1969), 75-92.
Lespinet-Moret, Isabelle and Liebeskind-Sauthier, Ingrid, 'Albert Thomas, le BIT et le chômage: expertise, catégorisation et action politique internationale', *Les cahiers Irice* 2, no. 2 (2008), 157-79.
Lespinet-Moret, Isabelle and Viet, Vincent, eds, *L'organisation internationale du travail. Origine, développement, avenir* (Rennes, Presses universitaires de Rennes, 2011).
Lewis, Joanna, 'Tropical East Ends and the Second World War: Some Contradictions in Colonial Office Welfare Initiatives', *The Journal of Imperial and Commonwealth History* 28, no. 20 (2000), 42-66.
Lewis, Su Lin, 'Decolonising the History of Internationalism: Transnational Activism across the South', *Transactions of the Royal Historical Society* (2023), 1-25.
Liaison Committee on Rural Women's and Homemakers' Organisations, *What the Country Women of the World Are Doing* (London: Chapman and Hall, 1932).
Lih, Lars T., *Bread and Authority in Russia 1914-1921* (Berkeley: University of California Press, 1990).
Lincoln, David, 'Plantation Workers by Definition: The Changing Relevance of the ILO's Plantations Convention', *The International Journal of Sociology of Agriculture and Food* 17, no. 1 (2010), 51-71.
Lipmann, Otto, 'Hours of Work and Output', *International Labour Review* 9, no. 4 (April 1924).
Lutz, Raphael, 'Die Verwissenschaftlichung des sozialen als methodische und konzeptionelle Herausforderung für eine Sozialgeschichte des 20. Jahrhunderts', *Geschichte und Gesellschaft* 22 (1996), 165-93.
Lutz, Raphael, 'Knowledge, Skills, Craft? The Skilled Worker in West German Industry and the Resilience of Vocational Training, 1970-2000', *German History* 37, no. 3 (2019), 359-73.
Lynch Dungy, Madeleine, 'The Global Agricultural Crisis and British Diplomacy in the League of Nations in 1931', *The Agricultural History Review* 65, no. 2 (2017), 297-319.
Lynch, Edouard, 'Interwar France and the Rural Exodus: The National Myth in Peril', *Rural History* 21, no. 2 (2010), 165-76.
Maat, Harro, 'Agriculture and Food Production', in Corinna R. Unger, Iris Borowy, and Corinne A. Pernet, eds, *The Routledge Handbook on the History of Development* (Abington, New York: 2022), 190-203.
MacFarlane, David L., 'The UNRRA Experience in Relation to Development in Food and Agriculture'. *Journal of Farm Economics* 30, no. 1 (1948), 69-77.
MacMillan, Margaret, *Paris 1919: Six Months that Changed the World* (New York: Random House, 2002).
Madsen, Jakob B., 'Agricultural Crises and the International Transmission of the Great Depression', *The Journal of Economic History* 61, no. 2 (2001), 327-65.
Maier, Charles, 'Between Taylorism and Technocracy: European Ideologies and the Vision of Industrial Productivity in the 1920s', *Journal of Contemporary History* 5, no. 2 (1970), 27-61.
Maier, Charles S., *Recasting Bourgeois Europe: Stabilization in France, Germany, and Italy in the Decade after World War I* (Princeton: Princeton University Press, 1988).
Mamudi, Rod, *A Survey of the Great Depression as Recorded in the International Labour Review, 1931-1939* (Geneva: International Labour Office, 2009).
Manela, Erez, *The Wilsonian Moment: Self-Determination and the International Origins of Anti-Colonial Nationalism* (Oxford, New York: Oxford University Press, 2007).
Marchisio, Sergio, di Blase, Antonietta, *The Food and Agriculture Organization (FAO)* (Dordrecht: M. Nijhoff, 1991).
Marks, Sally, 'Mistakes and Myths: The Allies, Germany, and the Versailles Treaty, 1918-1921', *The Journal of Modern History* 85, no. 3 (2013), 632-59.
Martiin, Carin, Pan-Montojo, Juan, and Brassley, Paul, eds, *Agriculture in Capitalist Europe, 1945-1970: From Food Shortages to Food Surpluses* (Abingdon: Routledge, 2016).

Martin, John, *The Development of Modern Agriculture: British Farming since 1931* (London: Macmillan, 2000).
Martin-Retortillo, Miguel and Pinilla, Vicente 'Patterns and Causes of the Growth of European Agricultural Production, 1950 to 2005', *The Agricultural History Review* 63, no. 1 (2015), 132–59.
Martini, Manuela, 'Conflits sociaux et organisations paysannes dans les campagnes italiennes, du *Risorgimento* à l'arrivée du fascisme au pouvoir', *Ruralia* 16/17 (2005), http://journals.openedition.org/ruralia/1072 (last accessed 27 January 2024).
Marung, Steffi 'A 'Leninian Moment'? Soviet Africanists and the Interpretation of the October Revolution, 1950s–1970s, *Journal für Entwicklunspolitik* 33, no. 3 (2017), 21–48.
Maslow, Abraham, 'A Theory of Human Motivation', *Psychological Review* 50, no. 4 (1943), 370–96.
Matthaei, Louise E., 'More Mechanisation in Farming', *International Labour Review* 23, no. 3 (March 1931).
Matthaei, Louise E., 'Some Effects of the Agricultural Depression on Agricultural Labour', *International Labour Review* 23, no. 4 (April 1931).
Maul, Daniel, 'The International Labour Organization and the Struggle against Forced Labour from 1919 to the Present', *Labor History* 48, no. 4 (2007), 477–500.
Maul, Daniel, 'The Morse Years 1948–1970', in Rodriguez Garcia, Magaly, Van Daele, Jasmien, and Van der Linden, Marcel, eds, *ILO Histories. Essays on the International Labour Organization and Its Impact on the World during the Twentieth Century* (Bern: Peter Lang, 2010), 365–400.
Maul, Daniel, *The International Labour Organization: 100 Years of Global Social Policy* (Berlin: De Gruyter; Geneva: International Labour Office, 2019).
Mazower, Mark, *No Enchanted Palace: The End of Empire and the Ideological Origins of the United Nations* (Princeton, NJ: Princeton University Press, 2009).
Mazoyer, Michel and Roudart, Laurence, *A History of World Agriculture from the Neotlihic Age to the Current Crisis* (New York: Monthly Review Press, 2006).
Mazurek, Malgorzata, 'Measuring Development: An Intellectual and Political History of Ludwik Landau's Scale of World Inequality', *Contemporary European History* 28 (2019), 156–71.
Mazuy, Rachel, 'Le Rassemblement Universel pour la Paix: une organisation de masse?', *Matériaux pour l'Histoire de Notre Temps* 20, no. 1 (1993), 40–4.
Medici, Senatore G., 'Diagnosis and Pathology of Peasant Farming' *Proceedings of the Seventh International Conference of Agricultural Economists, held 21–17 August 1949 in Stresa, Italy* (Oxford University Press, 1950).
Miers, Suzanne, *Slavery in the Twentieth Century: The Evolution of a Global Problem* (Walnut Creek, Calif.: Altamira Press/Lanham, Md.: Rowman and Littlefield Publishers, 2003).
Miglioli, Guido, *Le village soviétique* (Paris: Librairie du Travail, 1927).
Mignemi, Niccolò, *Nel regno della fame. Il mondo contadino italiano fra gli anni Trenta e gli anni Cinquanta* (Rome: Aracne, 2010).
Mignemi, Niccolò, 'Agriculteurs du monde entier, associez-vous! Robert de Rocquigny: du Musée social à l'Institut International d'Agriculture', *Histoire et Sociétés Rurales* 1, no. 45 (2016), 43–67.
Mignemi, Niccolò, 'Rome, capitale mondiale de la documentation agricole: de la bibliothèque de l'Institut international d'Agriculture à la David Lubin Memorial Library de la FAO', *Mélanges de l'École française de Rome. Italie et Méditerranée modernes et contemporaines*, no. 132-1 (2020), 215–35.
Mintz, Sidney, 'The Folk-Urban Continuum and the Rural Proletarian Community', *American Journal of Sociology* 59, no. 2 (September 1953), 39.
Mintz, Sidney W., *Sweetness and Power. The Place of Sugar in Modern History* (New York: Viking, 1985).
Mohamedou, Mohammad-Mahmoud Ould, 'Arab Agency and the UN Project: the League of Arab States between Universality and Regionalism', *Third World Quarterly* 37, no. 7 (2016), 1219–33.

Mohapatra, Prabhu P., *India and the ILO: Chronicle of a Shared Journey* 1919-2019 (International Labor Organization: New Delhi, 2019).
Moore-Colyer, Richard, 'Kids in the Corn: School Harvest Camps and Farm Labour Supply in England, 1940-1950', *The Agricultural History Review* 52, no. 2 (2004), 183-206.
Moore-Colyer, Richard, 'The Call to the Land: British and European Adult Voluntary Farm Labour, 1939-49', *Rural History* 17, no. 1 (2006), 83-101.
Moscovitch, Brant, '"Against the Biggest Buccaneering Enterprise in Living History": Krishna Menon and the Colonial Response to International Crisis', *South Asian Review* 41, nos. 3-4 (2020), 243-54.
Moser, Peter, 'Kultivierung und Zerstörung lebender Organismen. Der bäuerliche Umgang mit chemisch-synthetischen Hilfsstoffen in der Übergangszeit von der agrarisch-industriellen zur industriell-agrarischen Wissensgesellschaft (1945-1975)', *Zeitschrift für Agrargeschichte und Agrarsoziologie* 1 (2017), 19-34.
Moser, Peter and Gosteli, Marthe, eds, *Une paysanne entre ferme, marché et associations: Textes d'Augusta Gillabert-Randin, 1918-1940* (Baden: hier+jetzt, 2005), 257.
Moser, Peter and Varley, Tony, eds, *Integration through Subordination: The Politics of Agricultural Modernization in Industrial Europe* (Brepols: Turnhout, 2013).
Mouton, Marie-Renée, 'Les huit heures en agriculture? Un conflit entre la France et l'OIT', *Relations internationales* 4 (1975), 53-79.
Müller, Dietmar, and Harre, Angela, eds, *Transforming Rural Societies. Agrarian Property and Agrarianism in East Central Europe in the Nineteenth and Twentieth Centuries* (Innsbruck: Studienverlag, 2011).
Munguía, Enrique, 'The Agrarian Problem in Mexico: I', *International Labour Review* 36, no. 1 (1937), 49-85.
Murphy, Michelle, *The Economization of Life* (Durham, NC: Duke University Press, 2017).
Muschik, Eva-Maria, *Building States: The United Nations, Development and Decolonization, 1945-1965* (Columbia University Press, 2022).
Muşat, Raluca 'Prototypes for Modern Living: Planning, Sociology and the Model Village in Interwar Romania', *Social History* 39 (2014), 157-184.
Muşat, Raluca 'Making the Countryside Global: The Bucharest School of Sociology and International Networks of Knowledge', *Contemporary European History* 28 (2019), 205-19.
Natchkova, Nora and Schoeni, Céline, 'The ILO, Feminists and Expert Networks: The Challenges of a Protective Policy (1919-1934)', in Kott, Sandrine and Droux, Joelle, eds, *Globalizing Social Rights: The International Labour Organization and Beyond* (Basingstoke: Palgrave, 2013), 49-64.
Newby, Howard, Bell, Colin, Rose, David, and Saunders, Peter, *Property, Paternalism and Power* (Madison: University of Wisconsin Press, 1987).
Noël, Gilbert, 'La solidarité agricole européenne: des congrès d'agriculture à la politique agricole commune', in Canal, Jordi, Pécout, Gilles, and Ridolfi, Maurizio, eds, *Sociétés rurales du XXe siècle. France, Italie et Espagne* (Rome: École française de Rome, 2004), 311-25.
O'Brien, John B., 'F. L. McDougall and the Origins of the FAO', *Australian Journal of Politics and History* 46, no. 2 (2000), 164-74.
Oldfield, Sybil, 'Howard, Louise Ernestine, Lady Howard (1880-1969)', *Oxford Dictionary of National Biography* (Oxford: Oxford University Press, 2004), http://www.oxforddnb.com/view/article/37576 (last accessed 28 January 2024)].
Olsson, Tore C., *Agrarian Crossings: Reformers and the Remaking of the US and Mexican Countryside* (Princeton: Princeton University Press, 2017).
O'Malley, Alanna and Thakur, Vineet, 'Introduction: Shaping a Global Horizon: New Histories of the Global South and the UN', *Humanity: An International Journal of Human Rights, Humanitarianism, and Development* 13, no. 1 (2022), 55-65.
Owens Patricia, Rietzler Katharina, Hutchings, Kimberly, Dunstan, Sara C., eds, *Women's International Thought: A New History* (Cambridge: Cambridge University Press, 2021).
Orwin, Charles Stewart, 'Colonial Agricultural Production', *Nature* 159 (1947), 350-1.

Packer, Ian, *Lloyd George, Liberalism and the Land: The Land Issue and Party Politics in England, 1906–1914* (New York: Boydell and Brewer, 2001).
Paisant, Marcel, *La Commission Internationale d'Agriculture et son rôle dans l'économie europenne* (Paris, 1936).
Pan-Montojo, Juan, and Mignemi, Niccolò, 'International Organizations and Agriculture, 1905 to 1945: Introduction', *Agricultural History Review* 62, no. 2 (2017), 237–53.
Patel, Kiran Klaus, ed., *Fertile Ground for Europe? The History of European Integration and the Common Agricultural Policy since 1945* (Normos: Baden-Baden, 2009).
Patel, Kiran Klaus, 'The Green Heart of Governance: Rural Europe during the Interwar Years', in Ribi Forclaz, Amalia, and van de Grift, Liesbeth, eds, *Governing the Rural in Interwar Europe* (London: Routledge, 2018).
Paxton, Robert O., *French Peasant Fascism: Henry Dorgères's Greenshirts and the Crises of French Agriculture, 1929–1939* (New York, Oxford: Oxford University Press, 1997).
Peano, Irene, 'Turbulences in the Encampment Archipelago: Conflicting Mobilities between Migration, Labour and Logistics in Italian Agri-Food Enclaves', *Mobilities* 16 (2021), 212–23.
Pearson, Jessica Lynne, 'Defending Empire at the United Nations: The Politics of International Colonial Oversight in the Era of Decolonisation', *The Journal of Imperial and Commonwealth History* 45, no. 3 (2017), 525–49.
Pedersen, Susan, 'Back to the League of Nations', *The American Historical Review* 112, no. 4 (2007), 1091–1117.
Pedersen, Susan, *The Guardians. The League of Nations and the Crisis of Empire* (Oxford: Oxford University Press, 2015).
Penrose, Ernest Francis, 'Economic Organisation for Total War with special Reference to the Workers', *International Labour Review* 42 (1940), 175–213.
Perren, Richard, 'Farmers and Consumers Under Strain. Allied Meat Supplies in the First World War', *Agricultural History Review* 53, no. 2 (2005).
Phelan, Edward, 'The Labour Proposals before the Peace Conference', in Shotwell, James T., ed., *Origins of the International Labor Organization*, 2 vols (New York: Columbia University Press, 1934), vol. 1, 199–220.
Phelan, Edward, 'The Contribution of the ILO to Peace', *International Labour Review* 59, no. 6 (1949), 607–32.
Phelan, Edward, 'The ILO Sets Up Its Wartime Centre in Canada', *Studies: An Irish Quarterly Review* 44, no. 174 (1955), 151–70.
Phelan, Edward, 'The ILO Turns the Corner', *Studies: An Irish Quarterly Review* 45, no. 178 (1956), 160–86.
Phelan, Joseph, 'The Contribution of the ILO to Peace', *International Labour Review* 59, no. 6 (1949), 607–32.
Plata-Stenger, Véronique, *Social Reform, Modernization and Technical Diplomacy. The ILO Contribution to Development 1930–46* (Oldenbourg: De Gruyter, 2020).
Pribilsky, Jason, 'Development and the "Indian Problem" in the Cold War Andes: Indigenismo, Science, and Modernization in the Making of the Cornell-Peru Project at Vicos', *Diplomatic History* 33, no. 3 (2009), 405–26.
Price, John, 'The Industrial Committees of the International Labour Organization', *International Labour Review* 52, nos. 2–3 (1945), 139–53.
Prochasson, Christophe, 'Entre science et action sociale: le réseau Albert Thomas et le socialisme normallien 1900–1914', in Topalov, Christian, ed., *Laboratoires du nouveau siècle. La nébuleuse réformatrice et ses réseaux en France 1880–1914* (Paris, 1999), 141–58.
Puder, Janina, 'Cheap Labour, (Un) Organized Workers: The Oppressive Exploitation of Labour Migrants in the Malaysian Palm Oil Industry', in van Nederveen Meerkerk, Elise and Bauer, Rolf, eds, *Global Agricultural Workers from the 17th to the 21st Century* (Leiden, Boston: Brill, 2023), 438–461.
Pye, Oliver 'A Plantation Precariate: Fragmentation and Organizing Potential in the Palm Oil Global Production Network', *Development and Change* 48, no. 5 (2017), 942–64.

Rabinbach, Anson, *The Human Motor: Energy, Fatigue and the Origins of Modernity* (New York: Basic Books, 1990).
Rabinbach, Anson, *The Eclipse of the Utopias of Labor* (New York: Fordham University Press, 2018).
Raeburn, John Ross and Jones, Owen J., *The History of the International Association of Agricultural Economists: Towards Rural Welfare World Wide* (Aldershot and Brookfield: Dartmouth Publishing Company Ltd, 1990).
Reinalda, Bob, *Routledge History of International Organizations: from 1815 to the Present Day* (Abingdon: Routledge, 2009).
Reinalda, Bob, Kille, Kent J., and Eisenberg, Jaci Leigh, eds, *IO Bio: Biographical Dictionary of Secretaries-General of International Organizations*, www.ru.nl/fm/iobio (last accessed 28 January 2024).
Reinisch, Jessica, 'Introduction: Relief Work in the Aftermath of War', *Journal of Contemporary History* 43, no. 3 (2008), 371–404.
Reinisch, Jessica, 'Internationalism in Relief: The Birth (and Death) of UNRRA', *Past and Present* 210, suppl. 6 (2011), 258–89.
Ribi Forclaz, Amalia, 'A New Target for International Social Reform: The International Labour Organisation and Working and Living Conditions in Agriculture in the Interwar Years', *Journal of Contemporary European History* 20, no. 3 (2011), 307–29.
Ribi Forclaz, Amalia, *Humanitarian Imperialism: The Politics of Anti-Slavery Activism, 1880–1940* (Oxford: Oxford University Press, 2015).
Ribi Forclaz, Amalia, 'Agriculture, American Expertise, and the Quest for Global Data: Leon Estabrook and the First World Agricultural Census of 1930', *Journal of Global History* 11, no. 1 (2016), 44–65.
Ribi Forclaz, Amalia, 'Shaping the Future of Farming: The International Labour Organization and Agricultural Education in the Interwar Years', *The Agricultural History Review*, 65, no. 2 (2017), 320–339.
Ribi Forclaz, Amalia, 'Guardians of the Countryside: The Associated Countrywomen of the World (ACWW) and International Rural Governance in the Interwar Years', in Ribi Forclaz and van de Grift, eds, *Governing the Rural in Interwar Europe* (London: Routledge, 2018).
Ribi Forclaz, Amalia, 'From Reconstruction to Development: The Food and Agriculture Organization (FAO) and the Conceptualization of Rural Welfare, 1945–1950', *International History Review* 41, no. 2 (2019), 351–71.
Ribi Forclaz, Amalia, 'A Bed, a Cover, and Possibly a Pillow: Improving the Living Conditions of Agricultural Workers in the Interwar Years', *Capitalism. A Journal of History and Economics* 3, no. 1 (2022), 136–59.
Ribi Forclaz, Amalia, 'The Latest Developments in Agricultural Knowledge and Practice from the Outside World': UNRRA's Agricultural Rehabiliation Work in Italy in the Aftermaths of the Second World War', in Hartmann, Heinrich and Tischler, Julia, eds, *Planting Seeds of Knowledge: Agriculture and Education in Rural Societies in the Twentieth Century* (New York, Oxford: Berghahn Books, 2023), 71–86.
Ribi Forclaz, Amalia and Pernet, Corinne, 'Confronting a Hungry World: The United Nations Food and Agricultural Organization in a Historical Perspective', *International History Review* 41, no. 2 (2019), 345–350.
Ribi Forclaz, Amalia and Taratko, Carolyn, 'Experimenting with Scientific Management: New Approaches to Agricultural Labour in the Twentieth Century', in van de Grift, Liesbeth, Müller, Dietmar, and Unger, Corinna, eds, *Living with the Land: Rural and Agricultural Actors in Twentieth-Century Europe: A Handbook* (Berlin: De Gruyter, 2022), 205–25.
Ribi Forclaz, Amalia and Unger, Corinna, 'Progress versus Precaution: International Organizations and the Use of Pesticides, 1940s to 1970s', *Comparativ—Zeitschrift für Globalgeschichte und vergleichende Gesellschaftsforschung* 32, no. 6 (2022), 750–68.
Ribi Forclaz, Amalia, and van De Grift, Liesbeth, eds, *Governing the Rural in Interwar Europe* (London: Routledge, 2018).

Richter, Klaus, 'Post-War Agrarian Economic Policies (East Central Europe)', in Daniel, Ute, Gatrell, Peter, Janz, Oliver, Jones, Heather, Keene, Jennifer, Kramer, Alan, and Nasson, Bill, eds, *1914–1918-online. International Encyclopedia of the First World War* (Berlin: Freie Universität Berlin, 2015), https://encyclopedia.1914-1918-online.net/article/post-war_agrarian_economic_policies_east_central_europe.

Riddell, Walter Alexander, 'The Influence of Machinery on Agricultural Conditions in North America', *International Labour Review* 13 (March 1926), 309–26.

Riegelman, Carol, 'War-Time Trade-Union and Socialist Proposals', in Shotwell, James T., ed., *Origins of the International Labor Organization*, 2 vols (New York: Columbia University Press, 1934).

Rinaudo, Yves, 'Ouvriers agricoles provençaux en grève, 1890–1939', in Hubscher, Ronald and Farcy, Jean-Claude, eds, *La Moisson des Autres: Les salariés agricoles aux XIXe et XXe siècles* (Paris: Créaphis, 1996), 281–301.

Rodgers, Daniel T., 'Bearing Tales: Networks and Narratives in Social Policy Transfer', *Journal of Global History* 9 (2014), 310–11.

Rodgers, Gerry, Bhattacharya, Sabyasachi, and Krishnamurty, J., 'India and the ILO in Historical Perspective', *Economic and Political Weekly* 46, no. 10 (2011).

Rodriguez Garcia, Magaly, Van Daele, Jasmien, and Van der Linden, Marcel, eds, *ILO Histories. Essays on the International Labour Organization and Its Impact on the World during the Twentieth Century* (Bern: Peter Lang, 2010).

Rodríguez-Piñero, Luis, *Indigenous Peoples, Postcolonialism, and International Law: The ILO Regime (1919–1989)* (Oxford University Press, 2005).

Rose, Adam, 'Agricultural Workers and Agrarian Reform in Central Europe', *International Labour Review* 18, no. 3 (September 1928), 307–338.

Ross, Corey, 'The Plantation Paradigm: Colonial Agronomy, African Farmers and the Global Cocoa Boom, 1870–1940s', *Journal of Global History* 9, no. 1 (2014), 54.

Rossetti Agresti, Olivia, *David Lubin: A Study in Practical Idealism* (Boston, 1922).

Roux, R., 'Economic Conditions Affecting Social Policy in Plantations', *International Labour Review* 67, no. 3 (1953), 236–61.

Royal Institute of International Affairs, *Agrarian Problems from the Baltic to the Aegan: Discussion of a Peasant Programme* (London, New York: Royal Institute of International Affairs, 1944).

Rubin, Vera et al., eds, *Plantation Systems of the New World* (Washington, DC: Research Institute for the Study of Man and Pan-American Union, 1959).

Sackley, Nicole, 'The Village as a Cold War Site: Experts, Development, and the History of Rural Reconstruction', *Journal of Global History* 6 (2011), 481–504.

Sackley, Nicole, 'Cosmopolitanism and the Uses of Tradition: Robert Redfield and Alternative Visions of Modernization during the Cold War', *Modern Intellectual History* 9, no. 3 (2012), 565–95.

Sajhau, Jean-Paul and Jürgen Muralt, *Plantations and Plantation Workers* (Geneva: International Labour Office, 1986).

Salvatici, Silvia, 'Help the People to Help Themselves': UNRRA Relief Workers and European Displaced Persons', *Journal of Refugee Studies* 25 (2012), 452–73.

Salvatici, Silvia, *A History of Humanitarianism, 1755–1989: In the Name of Others* (Manchester: Manchester University Press, 2019).

Sanders, Irwin T., 'The Characteristics of a Peasant Society', in Brunner, E. de S., Sanders, I. T. and Ensminger, D., eds, *Farmers of the World* (New York, 1945).

Saraiva, Tiago, 'Fascist Modernist Landscapes: Wheat, Dams, Forests, and the Making of the Portuguese New State', *Environmental History* 21, no. 1 (2016), 54–75.

Saraiva, Tiago, *Fascist Pigs: Technoscientific Organisms and the History of Fascism* (Cambridge, MA: MIT Press, 2016).

Sayer, Karen, 'The Changing Landscape of Labour: Work and Livestock in Post-Second World War British Agriculture', *History: The Journal of the Historical Association* 104, no. 363 (February 2020), 911–40.

Schmidt, Georg, *Lohnformen and Arbeitsverhältnisse in der Landwirtschaft: ein Beitrag zur Beurteilung der Lage der deutschen Landarbeiterschaft* (Berlin: Deutscher Landarbeiterverband, 1913).

Schultz, Helga and Harre, Angela, eds, *Bauerngesellschaften auf dem Weg in die Moderne. Agrarismus in Ostmitteleuropa, 1880 bis 1960* (Wiesbaden: Harrassowitz, 2010).

Seebohm Rowntree, Benjamin, and Kendall, May, *How the Labourer Lives: A Study of the Rural Labour Problem* (London: Thomas Nelson, 1913).

Seedorf, Wilhelm, *Die Vervollkommnung der Landarbeit und die bessere Ausbildung der Landarbeiter unter besonderer Berücksichtigung des Taylor-Systems* (Berlin: Deutsche Landbuchhandlung, 1919).

Seekings, Jeremy, 'The ILO and Social Protection in the Global South, 1919–2005', Centre For Social research CSSR Working Paper, no. 238, December 2008.

Segers Yves and Van Molle, Leen, eds, *Agricultural Knowledge Networks in Rural Europe, 1700–2000* (Woodbridge: The Boydell Press, 2022).

Sharma, Jayeeta, *Empire's Garden: Assam and the Making of India* (Durham: Duke University Press, 2011).

Sharp, Allan, *The Versailles Settlement: Peacemaking in Paris, 1919* (Basingstoke, New York: Palgrave Macmillan, 2008).

Shephard, Ben, 'Becoming Planning Minded: The Theory and Practice of Relief 1940–1945', *Journal of Contemporary History* 43 (2008), 405–19.

Shephard, Ben, *The Long Road Home: The Aftermath of the Second World War* (New York: Alfred A. Knopf, 2011).

Shotwell, James T., ed., *Origins of the International Labor Organization*, 2 vols (New York: Columbia University Press, 1934).

Sinclair, Guy F., *To Reform the World: International Organizations and the Making of Modern States* (Oxford: Oxford University Press, 2017).

Sircana, Giuseppe, 'Guido Miglioli', *Dizionario Biografico degli Italiani*, vol. 74 (Rome: Istituto dell'Enciclopedia Italiana, 2010).

Slobodian, Quinn, *Globalists: The End of Empire and the Birth of Neoliberalism* (Cambridge, MA: Harvard University Press, 2018).

Sluga, Glenda, 'Editorial: The Transnational History of International Institutions', *Journal of Global History* 6 (2011), 219–22.

Sluga, Glenda, *Internationalism in the Age of Nationalism* (Philadelphia: University of Pennsylvania Press, 2013).

Sluga, Glenda, 'From F. Melian Stawell to E. Greene Balch: International and Internationalist Thinking at the Gender Margins, 1919–1947', in Owens Patricia, Rietzler Katharina, Hutchings, Kimberly, Dunstan, Sara C., eds, *Women's International Thought: A New History* (Cambridge: Cambridge University Press, 2021), 223–243.

Sollai, Michele, 'How to Feed an Empire? Agrarian Science, Indigenous Farming and Wheat Autarky in Italian-Occupied Ethiopia, 1937–1941', *Agricultural History* 96, no. 2 (2002), 379–416.

Speich, Daniel, 'The Roots of the Millennium Development Goals: A Framework for Studying the History of Global Statistics', *Historical Social Research* 41, no. 2 (2016), 218–37.

Spillman, W. J., 'The Agricultural Ladder', *The American Economic Review* 9, no. 1 (1919), 170–9.

Stanziani, Alessandro, 'Beyond Colonialism: Servants, Wage Earners and Indentured Migrants in Rural France and on Reunion Island (ca 1750–1900)', *Labour History* 54, no. 1 (2013), 64–87.

Stanziani, Alessandro, *Labor on the Fringes of Empire: Voice, Exit and the Law* (New York: Palgrave Macmillan, 2018).

Staples, Amy L., *The Birth of Development. How the World Bank, Food and Agriculture Organization, and World Health Organization Changed the World, 1945–1965* (Kent, OH: Kent State University Press, 2006).

Steffek, Jens, 'Fascist Internationalism', *Millennium : Journal of International Studies* 44, no. 1 (2015), 3–22.

Stoler, Ann Laura, *Capitalism and Confrontation in Sumatra's Plantation Belt, 1870–1979* (New Haven: Yale University Press 1985).

Stoler, Ann Laura, 'Plantation Politics and Protest on Sumatra's East Coast', *Journal of Peasant Studies* 13, no. 2 (1986), 124–43.
Stone, Judith F., *The Search for Social Peace: Reform Legislation in France, 1890–1914* (Albany: State University of New York, 1985).
Storey, William K., 'Plants, Power and Development: Founding the Imperial Department of Agriculture for the West Indies, 1880–1940', in Jasanoff, Sheila, ed., *States of Knowledge: The Co-Production of Science and Social Order* (London: Routledge, 2004), 109–30.
Supiot, Alain, *L'Esprit de Philadelphie. La justice sociale face au marché total* (Paris: Seuil, 2010).
Székely-Lulofs, Madelon, *Rubber* (Amsterdam: Elsevier, 1931).
Székely-Lulofs, Madelon, *Koelie* (Amsterdam: Elsevier, 1932); Eng. trans: Madelon H. Lulofs, *Coolie*, trans. G.J. Renier and Irene Clephane (Singapore: Oxford University Press, 1932).
Tauger, Marc B., 'Stalin, Soviet Agriculture, and Collectivization', in Frank Trentmann and Just Flemming, eds, *Food and Conflict in Europe in the Age of the Two World Wars* (Basingtoke: Palgrave Macmillan, 2006), 109–42.
Taylor, Carl C., *Rural Sociology: A Study of Rural Problems* (New York and London: Harper, 1926).
Tennstedt, Florian, *Vom Proleten zum Industriearbeiter: Arbeiterbewegung und Sozialpoliitk in Deutschland 1800 bis 1914* (Cologne: Bund-Verlag, 1983).
Thompson, Edward Palmer, 'Time, Work-Discipline, and Industrial Capitalism', *Past and Present* 38 (December 1967), 56–97.
Thompson, Edgar T., *The Plantation*, dissertation (University of Chicago, 1932). Reprinted as Edgar T. Thompson, *The Plantation*, edited with an introduction by Mintz, Sidney W. and Baca, George (Columbia: University of South Carolina Press, 2010).
Thompson, Sarahelen, 'Agrarian Reform in Eastern Europe Following World War I: Motives and Outcomes', *American Journal of Agricultural Economics* 75, no. 3 (1993), 840–4.
Tilley, Helen, *Africa as a Living Laboratory: Empire, Development, and the Problem of Scientific Knowledge, 1870–1950* (Chicago: University of Chicago Press, 2011).
Tilley, Lisa, '"A Strange Industrial Order": Indonesia's Racialized Plantation Ecologies and Anticolonial Estate Worker Rebellions', *History of the Present* 10, no. 1 (April 2020), 67–83.
Tischler, Julia, 'Education and the Agrarian Question in South Africa, c. 1900–40', *The Journal of African History* 57, no. 2 (2016), 251–70.
Tooze, Adam, *The Deluge: The Great War and the Remaking of the Global Order* (London, New York: Allen Lane, 2014).
Topalov, Christian, ed., *Laboratoires du nouveau siècle. La nébuleuse réformatrice et ses réseaux en France 1880–1914* (Paris, 1999).
Tosi, Luciano, *Alle orgini della FAO. Le relazioni tra l'Istituto Internazionale di Agricoltura e la Società delle Nazioni* (Milan: Franco Angeli, 1989).
Tosstorff, Reiner, 'The International Trade-Union Movement and the Founding of the International Labour Organization', *International Review of Social History* 50 (2005), 399–433.
Tracy, Michael, *Government and Agriculture in Western Europe, 1880–1988* (New York: New York University Press, 1988).
Trentmann, Frank and Flemming, Just, 'Introduction', in Trentmann, Frank and Flemming, Just, eds, *Food and Conflict in Europe in the Age of the Two World Wars* (Basingtoke: Palgrave Macmillan, 2006).
Tully, John, *The Devil's Milk: A Social History of Rubber* (New York: Monthly Review Press, 2011).
Tyler, Hannah, 'In Numbers We Trust? A History of the US Department of Agriculture and its Agricultural Surveys during the 1920s', *Histoire & Mesure* 48 (2023), 39–46.
Uekötter, Frank, *Die Wahrheit ist auf dem Feld. Eine Wissensgeschichte der deutschen Landwirtschaft* (Göttingen: Vandenhoeck & Ruprecht, 2010).
Unger, Corinna R., 'Agrarwissenschaftliche Expertise und ländliche Modernisierungsstrategien in der internationalen Entwicklungspolitik, 1920er bis 1980er Jahre', *Geschichte und Gesellschaft* 41 (2015), 552–79.
Unger, Corinna, 'Development', in Mlada Bukovansky, Edward Keene, Christian Reus-Smit, and Maja Spanu, eds, *The Oxford Handbook of History and International Relations* (Oxford, Oxford University Press, 2023).

Unger, Corinna R., Iris Borowy, and Corinne A. Pernet, eds, *The Routledge Handbook on the History of Development* (Abington, New York: 2022), 190–203.

Valade, Bernard, 'Un marginal de la science sociale: Jacques Valdour', *Revue européenne des sciences sociales* 5, no. 1 (2013), online version http://journals.openedition.org/ress/2344; DOI: 10.4000/ress.2344 (last accessed 30 Avril 2019).

Valdour, Jacques, *L'ouvrier agricole: Observations vécues* (Paris: Arthur Rousseau, 1919).

van Beusekom, Monica M., *Negotiating Development: African Farmers and Colonial Experts at the Office du Niger, 1920–1960* (Oxford: James Currey, 2002).

Van Daele, Jasmien, 'Engineering Social Peace. Networks, Ideas, and the Founding of the International Labour Organization', *International Review of Social History* 50, no. 3 (2005), 435–66.

van De Grift, Liesbeth and Ribi Forclaz, Amalia, eds, *Governing the Rural in Interwar Europe* (London: Routledge, 2018).

van de Grift, Liesbeth, Müller, Dietmar, and Unger, Corinna, 'Introduction', in van de Grift, Liesbeth, Müller, Dietmar, and Unger, Corinna, eds, *Living with the Land: Rural and Agricultural Actors in Twentieth-Century Europe: A Handbook* (Berlin: De Gruyter, 2022), 1–13.

van de Grift, Liesbeth, Müller, Dietmar, and Unger, Corinna, eds, *Living with the Land: Rural and Agricultural Actors in Twentieth-Century Europe: A Handbook* (Berlin: De Gruyter, 2022), 1–13.

Van der Linden, Marcel, 'Labour History: The Old, The New and the Global', *African Studies* 66 (2007), 169–80.

van der Ploeg, Jan Douwe, *The New Peasantries: Struggles for Autonomy and Sustainability in an Era of Empire and Globalization* (London: Earthscan, 2008).

Van Goethem, Geert, 'Phelan's War: The International Labour Organization in Limbo (1941–1948)', in Rodriguez Garcia, Magaly, Van Daele, Jasmien and Van der Linden, Marcel, eds, *ILO Histories. Essays on the International Labour Organization and its Impact on the World during the Twentieth Century* (Bern: Peter Lang, 2010), 313–40.

van Nederveen Meerkerk, Elise and Bauer, Rolf, eds, *Global Agricultural Workers from the 17th to the 21st Century* (Leiden, Boston: Brill, 2023).

Vandervelde, Émile, *L'exode rural et le retour aux champs* (Paris: Felix Alcan, 1903).

Vanhaute, Eric, *Peasants in World History* (New York: Routledge, 2021).

Vaught, David, *Cultivating California. Growers, Specialty Crops, and Labor, 1875–1920* (Baltimore: John Hopkins University Press, 2002).

Verdon, Nicola, 'Agricultural Labour and the Contested Nature of Women's Work in Interwar England and Wales', *The Historical Journal* 52, no. 1 (2009), 109–30.

Verdon, Nicola, 'The Modern Countrywoman: Farm Women, Domesticity and Social Change in Interwar Britain', *History Workshop Journal* 70, no. 1 (Autumn 2010), 86–107.

Verdon, Nicola, *Working the Land: A History of the Farmworker in England from 1850 to the Present Day* (London: Palgrave Macmillan, 2017).

Verschuur, Christine, 'From the Centre to the Margins and Back Again: Women in Agriculture at the ILO', *International Development Policy*, no. 11, November 2019, 152–76.

Viola, Lynne, Danilov, V. P., Ivitskii, N.A., and Kozlov, Denis, eds, *The War against the Peasantry, 1927–1930: The Tragedy of the Soviet Countryside* (New Haven: Yale University Press, 2005).

Violin, Lazar, 'Soviet Agricultural Policy after Stalin: Results and Prospects', *Journal of Farm Economics* 38, no. 2 (1956), 274–86.

Vogt, Paul, *Introduction to Rural Sociology* (New York: Appleton & Co., 1917).

von Bülow, Fritz Wilhelm, 'Social Aspects of Agrarian Reform in Latvia', *International Labour Review* 13, no. 3 (September 1928).

von Graevenitz, Fritz Georg, *Argument Europa: Internationalismus in der globalen Agrarkrise der Zwischenkriegszeit (1927–1937)* (Frankfurt am Main: Campus Verlag, 2017).

Waelbroeck, Pierre, 'Labour Redistribution for War Industry', *International Labour Review* 45, no. 4 (1942), 367–94.

Walker, B., 'The World of Farmworkers', *The Landworker* (April 1921).

Warriner, Doreen, *The Economics of Peasant Farming* (London: Oxford University Press, 1939).
Warriner, Doreen, 'Changes in European Peasant Farming', *International Labour Review* 76, no. 5 (1957), 446–9.
Washington, Booker T., with the collaboration of Robert E. Park, *The Man Farthest Down: A Record of Observation and Study in Europe* (Garden City: Double Day, 2012).
Weber, Max, *Die Verhältnisse der Landarbeiter im ostelbischen Deutschland (Preussische Provinzen Ost- und Westpreussen, Pommern, Posen, Schlesien, Brandenburg, Grossherzogtümer Mecklenburg, Kreis Herzogtum Lauenburg)* (Leipzig: Duncker & Humblot, 1892).
Weber, Max, 'Zur Psychophysik der industriellen Arbeit', *Archiv für Sozialwissenschaft* 28 (1908).
Webster, David, 'Development Advisers in a Time of Cold War: The United Nations Technical Assistance Administration 1950–1959', *Journal of Global History* 6 (2011), 249–72.
Weiss, Thomas G. and Roy, Pallavi, 'The UN and the Global South, 1945 and 2015: Past as Prelude?', *Third World Quarterly* 37, no. 7 (2016), 1147–55.
White, Ben, 'Remembering the Indonesian Peasants' Front and Plantation Workers' Union (1945–1966), *The Journal of Peasant Studies* 43, no.1 (2016), 1–16.
Williams, Andrew J., 'Reconstruction before the Marshall Plan', *Review of International Studies* 31 (2005), 541–58.
Willson, Perry, *Peasant Women and Politics in Fascist Italy: The Massaie Rurali* (London: Routledge, 2002).
Willson, Perry, 'Le virtù della terra. Due periodici per le contadine negli anni del fascismo', in Silvia Franchini and Simonetta Soldani, eds, *Donne e giornalismo: Percorsi e presenze di una storia di genere* (Milan: Franco Angeli, 2004), 259.
Wolf, Eric, 'Specific Aspects of Plantation Systems in the New World: Community Sub-Cultures and Social Classes', in Vera Rubin et al., *Plantation Systems of the New World* (Washington, DC: Research Institute for the study of Man and Pan-American Union, 1959). Republished in Wolf, Eric, *Pathways of Power: Building an Anthropology of the Modern World* (Berkeley, Los Angeles, London: University of California Press, 2001), 215–29.
Woodbridge, George, *The History of the United Nations Relief and Rehabilitation Administration*, vols 1–3 (New York: Columbia University Press, 1950).
Yearwood, Peter J., *Guarantee of Peace: The League of Nations in British Policy 1914–1925* (Oxford: Oxford University Press, 2009).
Ziemann, Benjamin, 'Agrarian Society', in Winter, Jay, ed., *The Cambridge History of the First World War*, vol. 3 (Cambridge: Cambridge University Press, 2014), 382–407.
Zimmermann, Susan, '"Special Circumstances in Geneva": The ILO and the World of Non-Metropolitan Labour in the Interwar Period', in Rodriguez Garcia, Magaly, Van Daele, Jasmien, and Van der Linden, Marcel, eds, *ILO Histories. Essays on the International Labour Organization and Its Impact on the World during the Twentieth Century* (Bern: Peter Lang, 2010), 221–50.
Zimmermann, Susan, 'A Struggle over Gender, Class and the Vote: Unequal International Interactions and the Formation of the 'Female International' of Socialist Women', in Janz, O., and Schönpflug, D., eds, *Gender History in a Transnational Perspective* (New York: Berghahn, 2014), 101–26.
Zimmermann, Susan, 'The Agrarian Working Class Put Somewhat Centre Stage: An Often Neglected Group of Workers in the Historiography of Labour in State-Socialist Hungary', *European Review of History* 25, no. 1 (2018), 79–100.

Index

Since the index has been created to work across multiple formats, indexed terms for which a page range is given (e.g., 52–53, 66–70, etc.) may occasionally appear only on some, but not all of the pages within the range.

Advisory Committee on Rural Development: *see* Permanent Agricultural Committee
agrarian education: *see* education
agrarian reforms 13–14, 16–17, 24–5, 42–4, 58–61, 74–9, 108, 158–9, 174–7
   See also: Czechoslovakia; enquiries; International Institute of Agriculture; Mixed Advisory Agricultural Committee; Romania
agricultural census (1924–1929) 60, 63–4, 95–6
   See also: International Institute of Agriculture
Agricultural Section: *see* Agricultural Service
Agricultural Service 174–5
   history and mission 57–63
   collaboration with League of Nations 83–4
   on scientific management of agricultural labour 87
   enquiry on hours of work 67–8, 95–8. *See also*: enquiries; worktime
   enquiry on rural education 69–72. *See also*: enquiries; education
   enquiry on rural exodus 81–3. *See also*: rural exodus
   expansion of repertoire 174–5
   See also: enquiries; Gorni, Olindo; Matthaei, Louise; Osmay, Mukdim; Riddell, Walter Alexander; rural sociology; Second World War; von Bülow, Wilhelm
'agricultural worker/labour', use of term and perception 1–4, 9, 19–20, 26–31, 49–50, 115–16, 121–2
   See also: 'farmer', use of term; 'industrial', use of term; 'landworker', use of term; 'peasant', use of term; Weber, Max
Altobelli, Argentina 38, 53–4, 65–6
   leader of Federterra 33
   in International Landworkers' Federation 33
   participation in third session of International Labour Conference (1921) 38, 53–4
   considered for Mixed Advisory Agricultural Committee 65–6

   See also: experts; Federterra; International Labour Conference; International Landworkers' Federation; socialism
Angelini, Franco 112–13, 120 n.77, 143–4
   See also: fascism
antifascism: *see* Conférence Agraire Internationale; Gorni, Olindo; Miglioli, Guido; Peasant Peace Conference
Argentina
   not included in International Landworkers' Federation 33–4
   enquiry on hours of work 98, 100–2
   meeting of Confédération Internationale d'Agriculture (1937) 113
   See also: Coni, Emilio A.; enquiries; eurocentrism; hours of work; worktime
Asian Regional Conference (New Delhi, 1947) 144, 150–2, 174–5
   creation of Plantation Committee 151–2
   See also: Asia; India; Plantation Committee; plantations
Associated Country Women of the World 11
   creation and mission 84–5
   absent from Peasant Peace Conference 118
   during Second World War 129
   participates in first FAO conference (1945) 133–4
   See also: Boudreau, Charlotte; women's labour
Australia
   discussed by McDougall at Mixed Advisory Agricultural Committee 87
   enquiry on hours of work 98
   participation in first meeting of Permanent Agricultural Committee 120–1
   See also: eurocentrism; McDougall, Frank
Austria
   International Landworkers' Federation membership 32–3
   child labour 51
   regulation of hours of work after Second World War 102–3

Belgium
  statistics on hired labourers 3–4, 152–3
  International Landworkers' Federation membership 32–3
  regulation of hours of work after Second World War 102–3
  Belgian colonies 137–8, 147–8, 155–6
Bolshevik revolution: *see* October revolution
Brecher, Ludovic: *see* Dolivet, Louis
Boudreau, Charlotte
  represents Associated Country Women of the World at first FAO conference (1945) 133–4
  See also: Associated Country Women of the World
Boyd-Orr, Sir John 136–7
  FAO's first director 136–7
  See also: Food and Agriculture Organization
bracciante: *see* 'landworker', use of term
Brazil
  not included in International Landworkers' Federation 33–4
  enquiry on hours of work 98, 101–2
  and ILO convention on plantation labour 167 n.109
  See also: plantation labour; slavery; worktime
Britain: *see* Great Britain
Bulgaria 3–4, 56 n.5, 102–3, 108
  statistics on hired labourers 3–4
Butler, Harold
  ILO director 89–91, 98–9, 125
  On hours of work 94

Canada 29–30, 50, 71 n.89, 113
  ILO's move to 125–6
Cecil, Lord Robert
  organizer of International Peace Campaign 106, 118
  See also: International Peace Campaign; pacifism
child labour 13, 19–22, 25–7, 34, 37–8, 48–53, 61, 69–71, 83–4, 107–8, 121, 128–9, 149 n.22, 156–7, 165, 172–3, 178
Chile 39–40, 71 n.89, 107–8, 113
  first Regional Conference in Santiago de Chile (1936) 105–8
  See also: Regional Conference of American states
China
  excluded from International Landworkers' Federation 33–4
  participation in first meeting of Permanent Agricultural Committee 120–1
  Japanese aggression 111, 116–17
  See also: Asia; eurocentrism; Japan

Cold War 14, 123, 159, 172–3
  involvement of United States and USSR in ILO: *see* United States
  See also: communism; Soviet Union; United States
Colonial Development and Welfare Act (1940) 137–8
  See also: Britain; colonies
colonies
  exclusion from discourse 6–14, 30–1, 50, 98, 123, 137–41, 145–68
  colonial stereotypes 30–1, 93
  and education 69
  Native Labour Section 92–3, 139–40, 146–8
  Conférence Agraire Internationale 109–10
  discussions at Peasant Peace Conference 116, 119
  International Labour Conference (Philadelphia, 1944) 137–9
  International Labour Conference (Paris, 1945) 140
  land ownership 140
  See also: decolonisation; enquiries; eurocentrism; land ownership; Native Labour Section; plantations; slavery; 'tropical', use of term
Commission on International Labour Legislation 18–20. *See also*: Expert Commissions
Commission Internationale d'Agriculture: *see* Confédération Internationale d'Agriculture
Committee of Agricultural Work
  creation 95
  relationship with Mixed Advisory Agricultural Committee 95
  relationship with International Institute of Agriculture 95, 98
  1934 enquiry on hours of work 95–8
  See also: enquiries; International Institute of Agriculture; Mixed Advisory Agricultural Committee
communism
  fear of spread 16–20, 23–5, 76–7, 150–1, 159–61, 170–1
  sympathizers 106, 108, 115
  diffidence vs. international organizations 160–1
  See also: Cold War; October revolution; Soviet Union
Confédération Internationale d'Agriculture 20
  meeting in La Haye (1937) 113–14
  absent from Peasant Peace Conference 118
  changes name from Commission Internationale d'Agriculture 113, 131–2

Hot Springs Conference (1943) 131–2
See also: de Vogüé, Marquis Louis de; Laur, Ernst, Méline, Jules
Conférence agraire internationale (1936) 106–11, 114–16
 relation with International Peace Campaign 106, 111
 participants 108
 eurocentrism 108
 participation of International Landworkers' Federation 108
 pacifist message 108–9
 relationship with League of Nations 109–11
 preparatory enquiry 109
 colonial issues 109–10
 ILO does not accept invitation 110–11
 focus away from governments 111
 See also: International Peace Campaign; League of Nations; Miglioli, Guido; pacifism; socialism; Wanner, Léo
Conférence Paysanne Préparatoire pour la Paix: *see* Peasant Peace Conference
Coni, Emilio A. 100–1
 See also: Argentina; worktime
Cuba 53–4, 155–6, 157 n.62, 160–1, 167 n.109, 169
 second Regional Conference in Havana (1939) 119 n.74, 123–4, 142–3
 second meeting of the Plantation Committee (1953) 163–5
Czechoslovakia
 Pardos' enquiry on working hours (1920–1921) 42–4, 75
 child labour 51
 land redistribution 76–7
 enquiry on agrarian reform (1924) 78
 Gorni and von Bülow's enquiry on rural exodus (1930–1932) 81–3
 living conditions 87

de Vogüé, Marquis Louis 8–9
 president of Commission Internationale d'Agriculture 65–6
 Mixed Advisory Agricultural Committee 86
 on Great Depression 87
 See also: Commission Internationale d'Agriculture; experts; Mixed Advisory Agricultural Committee
Decolonisation 14, 137, 146–7, 150, 156, 160–1
 See also: colonies, plantations
dependencies: *see* colonies
De Michelis, Giuseppe
 director of International Institute of Agriculture 77–8, 91, 94–5
 See also: International Institute of Agriculture

de Zayas Bazan, Laura
 on womens' work 53
Delsinne, Léon
 counteracts fascist influence at Confédération Internationale d'Agriculture 113–14
 not invited to Permanent Agricultural Committee 120
 See also: socialism
Denmark
 statistics on hired labourers 3–4, 152–3
 International Landworkers' Federation membership 32–3
 housing 46–7
 women's labour 50
 child labour 51
 International Landworkers' Federation's statistics on hired workers 152–3
depression: *see* Great Depression
Dolivet, Louis
 organizer of Peasant Peace Conference 115
 See also: Peasant Peace Conference
Dragoni, Carlo
 in Mixed Advisory Agricultural Committee 65–6
 General secretary of International Institute of Agriculture 65–6
 See also: experts; International Institute of Agriculture; Mixed Advisory Agricultural Committee
Duffy, Michael 90–1
 Farmworkers' representative 90–1
Duncan, Joseph 8–9
 editorial in *Scottish Farm Servant* 15–17
 International Landworkers' Federation 33
 Mixed Advisory Agricultural Committee 65–6, 86
 on Great Depression 80
 president of International Landworkers' Federation 88, 126
 on working hours 97–8, 101
 retires 153
 See also: International Landworkers' Federation; Mixed Advisory Agricultural Committee
(Nederlandsche Bond van Arbeiders in het Landbouw- Tuinbouw- en Zuivelbedrijf)" 32–3, 153

Economic Committee (League of Nations)
 draft report 83–4
economic crisis: *see* Great Depression
education 2, 5–6, 13, 25–9, 37, 40, 51–2, 57–8, 66–72, 75–6, 79, 85–6, 109–13, 115, 117–18, 128–9, 147–8, 152–3, 162, 172–4, 176–7

employers' organizations
 ILO structure 4–5, 25–6, 31–2, 38, 64–5,
 mobilization 35–6, 43–4, 52–3, 60–1, 65–7, 82–3, 92–5, 98–9, 161–6
 criticism by Hiemstra 35–6
enquiries
 methods and objectives 3–4, 61–2, 79, 121–2, 174–8
 1919 Jacques Valdour's enquiry on agricultural working life in France 46
 1920 on labour conditions in Soviet Russia 24–5
 1920 on women's labour 49–51, 62
 1920 survey on child labour 51–2
 1920–1921 on worktime reduction in Czechoslovakia 42–4, 75
 1921 on housing 46–8
 1923–1924 on rural education 69–72
 1926 on scientific management of agricultural labour 72–6
 1925 on agrarian reforms 77–9
 Late 1920s on indigenous labour 92–4
 1930–1931 on rural exodus 81–3
 1930–31 impact of economic downturn 85–8
 1934 on hours of work 13, 95–103
 pre-1936 on impact of military rearmament 109
 1949 on plantations 155–9
 pre-1938 on propagation of pacifist ideals 115
 See also: Agricultural Service; Committee of Agricultural Work; International Institute of Agriculture; Mixed Advisory Agricultural Committee; Thomas, Albert
environmental constraints: see natural constraints
eurocentrism 6, 13–14, 29–30, 32–4, 50, 58–9, 66, 89–90, 98, 103, 108, 121
 expanding the focus 32 n.100, 66, 102, 105–6, 116, 119–24, 137–41, 143–69, 171–2
experts
 expert commissions 4, 8–9, 13, 18–21, 30–1, 58–9, 64–6, 71–2, 102–3, 105–6, 112–13, 116–17, 119–20, 123, 136–7, 144, 151–2
 expertise 20–1, 23, 30–1, 58–9, 66, 81, 84–5, 95, 119–20, 129–30, 136–7, 140–1, 155
 expertise vs. first-hand experience 11–12, 38, 44, 46, 55, 72, 109, 175

'farmer', use of term 110
 See also: 'agricultural worker/labour', use of term and perception; 'industrial', use of term; 'landworker' 'peasant', use of term; Weber, Max

fascism
 polarization between socialist and fascist agrarian reformers 13–14, 113–14
 pressure on International Institute of Agriculture 20, 77–8
 impact on trade unions 99
 use of international platforms for Nationalistic goals 111–12
 emergence of Italian-led international agrarian organizations 112–13
 tensions at Confédération Internationale d'Agriculture 113–14
 See also: Angelini, Franco; Italy; Mussolini, Benito
Fédération Internationale des Travailleurs Agricoles Chrétiens: see International Federation of Christian Landworkers' Unions
Federazione Internazionale dei Lavoratori della Terra: see Federterra
Federterra 33–5, 38, 65–6
 See also: Altobelli, Argentina; Italy
Finland 3–4, 56 n.5
 statistics on hired labourers 3–4, 152–3
 women's labour 50
First World War
 aftermath of 1–15, 32–3, 40, 51–2, 66, 83–4, 88, 169, 173
 agricultural legislation before First World War 29
 visibility of women 49–50
 emergence of rural sociology 59–61
 impact on economic crisis 83–4, 87
 See also: Versailles Peace Conference and Treaty; League of Nation
Fjelstad, Anders
 on Agricultural Service 63
 represents the International Institute of Agriculture 64 n.50
 See also: International Institute of Agriculture
Food and Agriculture Organization
 creation 14, 130–7
 supplants International Institute of Agriculture 14, 132–4
 use of statistics 133, 177–8
 Committee on Rural Welfare 144
 relationship with International Landworkers' Federation 153
 relationship with ILO 177–8
France
 statistics on hired labourers 3–4
 agricultural strikes 17, 28
 participation in third session of International Labour Conference (1921) 38–9

living conditions 28
reforms 29
International Landworkers' Federation membership 32–3
hours of work 35, 40, 100–3
participation in third session of International Labour Conference (1921) 39–40, 43–4
1919 Jacques Valdour's enquiry on agricultural working life in France 46
housing 46–7
scientific management of agricultural labour
Thomas on living conditions 87
migrant labour 102
forced labour in colonies 139–40

Gautier, Jules
in Mixed Advisory Agricultural Committee 65–6, 86
about enquiry on agrarian reform 77–8, 86, 98–101
about enquiry on working hours 122–3
on industrial vs. agricultural work 100–1
Germany 32–3
Versailles Peace Conference and Treaty 17–18
inequality between industrial and agricultural workers 29
International Landworkers' Federation membership 32–3
German Landworkers' Union 33
housing 46–7
scientific management of agricultural labour 73–4
enquiry on rural exodus 81–3
Nazification of trade unions 99
regulation of hours of work after Second World War 102–3
tensions at Confédération Internationale d'Agriculture 113–14
statistics on hired workers 152–3
new laws about vocational education 152–3
Gillabert-Randin, Augusta 12, 38, 38 n.3, 44, 55
participation in International Labour Conference (1921) 38, 55
on hours of work 44
Global South 14, 102–3, 173, 178–9
Governing Body (ILO) 6, 23–6, 29–30, 38–9, 69, 81–2, 89–90, 93–5, 125, 158–9, 165
Gooch, Edwin G.
president of International Landworkers' Federation 153
career 153 n.42
Gorni, Olindo 58–9, 81–2, 110–11, 126
enquiry on rural exodus in France, Germany, and Czechoslovakia 81–3
See also: Agricultural Service; socialism

Great Britain 128–9, 156–8, 157 n.62, 160, 163
exploitative relationship between farm owners and labourers 27
inequality between industrial and agricultural workers 29
statistics on hired labourers 3–4
trade unions 31–4
International Landworkers' Federation membership 32–3
strikes 40
housing 45–6
scientific management of agricultural labour 73–4
at Conférence Agraire Internationale 108
impact of Second World War 128–9, 139–40
British colonial Development and Welfare Act of 1940 137–8
forced labour in colonies 139–40
on plantations 156–8, 163, 165–6
Great Depression 13, 20–1, 58–9, 75, 80–103, 148

Hall, Daniel
attends Conférence Agraire Internationale 108
organizer of International Peace Campaign 118
See also: pacifism
Havana: see Cuba
Health and medical care 15–16, 18, 40, 46–7, 50–2, 60, 71, 83–4, 89–90, 92, 100–1, 109–10, 123 n.96, 149, 156–9, 162–4, 166, 173–4
Hiemstra, Piet
leader of International Landworkers' Federation 32–3
criticises employers' organisations and Swiss Farmers' Association 35–6
participation in Conférence Agraire Internationale 108
participation in Permanent Agricultural Committee 121
retires from International Landworkers' Federation 153
Holland: see Netherlands
Hours of Work: see Worktime
Housing 1–4, 10–11, 13, 22–8, 34, 37–8, 45–8, 54, 57–8, 60–1, 67–8, 71, 74, 79, 82–4, 89–90, 100–1, 134–5, 156–60, 162, 164, 172–4
See also: enquiries
Howard, Louise Ernestine: see Matthaei, Louise
Hungary
statistics on hired labourers 3–4
labour insurrections 28
rise of fascism 99
working hours 102–3

206 INDEX

India
    early inclusion in ILO 29–30, 150–1
    Conférence agraire internationale 109–10
    Peasant Peace Conference 116, 119–21
    Permanent Agricultural Committee 120–2
    hosts Asian Regional Conference 150–1
    participation in International Labour
        Conference (1954) 165–7
    Indian employers' delegate defends employers'
        perspective 165–6. *See also*: Varghese
    Plantation workers in 1950s 173–4
'indigenous', use of term 92–3
    See also: enquiries
indigenous labour: *see* native labour
Indonesia 102–3, 155–8
    regulation of hours of work after Second
        World War 102–3
    meeting of Plantation Committee
        (1950) 159–62
    non-involvement in Cold War 159
'industrial', use of term 19–20, 19 n.26
    See also: 'agricultural worker/labour', use of
        term and perception; 'farmer', use of term;
        industrial vs. agricultural labour;
        'landworker', use of term; 'peasant',
        use of term
industrial vs. agricultural labour
    differences 4, 6–7, 15, 19, 22, 29, 40–2, 49–53,
        67, 96, 100–1
    expertise gap 38, 62
    industrialization of agriculture 72–6, 169–72
    in plantations 151–2, 154–5, 158–9, 165–6,
        168, 176–7
    regulation and social standards 1–2, 5–6, 15,
        22, 29, 31–2, 34–6, 53–7, 87–8, 93–4,
        121, 140–1
industrialization
    industrialized vs. non industrialized
        countries 10–11, 14, 24–5, 29–30, 45, 48,
        139–40, 142, 169–72
    agricultural industrialization 9–10, 24–5,
        60–1, 139–40, 169–72, 178
    capitalist industrialization 24–5
    See also: industrial vs. agricultural labour
International Association of Agricultural
    Economists 97–8
    See also: International Conference of
        Agricultural Economists
International Conference of Agricultural
    Economists 84–5, 87
    See also: International Association of
        Agricultural Economists
International Federation of Agricultural
    Producers 144, 160–1

International Institute of Agriculture
    creation 20
    forms Mixed Advisory Agricultural
        Committee with ILO 13, 64–6, 64 n.48
    correspondence with Matthaei 60
    relationship with ILO 62–7, 77–8
    relationship with League of Nations 62–3
    participation in third ILO session (1921) 69–71
    on scientific management of agricultural
        labour 72–3
    on rural exodus 81–3
    methods 83–4
    on agrarian reforms 77–9
    relationship with new Committee of
        Agricultural Work 95, 98
    Mussolini's attempt to control 111–12
    criticized at Peasant Peace Conference 117
    use of statistics 77, 83–4, 95–6, 177–8
    end of Institute 14, 126–7, 130–4
    supplanted by FAO 132–4
    comparison with FAO 153, 177–8
International Labour Conference 6,
    18–19, 35, 165
    1919 session 22, 41–2
    1921 session 13, 15 *q*., 37–40, 37 *q*., 45, 62–3,
        69–70, 172–3
    1930 session 93
    1933 session 91, 94–5
    1941 session 125 *q*., 127–8
    1944 session 137–8
    1945 session 140
    1947 session 142
    1950 session 170–1
    1955 session 174
    1957 session 165–6
    1958 session 166
International Landworkers' Federation
    creation and membership 32–4
    first meeting (1920)
    participation of agricultural trade unions 33
    resistance of employers' organizations 35
    on child labour 48–9
    on International Institute of Agriculture 63–4
    on land redistribution 76–7
    impact of rise of fascism 99
    participation in Conférence Agraire
        Internationale 108
    participation in Permanent Agricultural
        Committee 121–3
    impact of Second World War 126
    use of statistics 153
    after Second World War 142, 144, 153
    relationship with FAO 153
    statistics on hired workers 152–3

new focus on plantation labourers 153–4
invited to Plantation Committee as 'observer' 160–1
International Office for Social Problems in Agriculture 112–13, 113 n.45
International Peace Campaign (Rassemblement Universel pour la Paix) 114–18
organisation of Conférence Agraire Internationale 106–11
organisation of Peasant Peace Conference 114–19
plan for inclusion of agricultural section 117–18
Peace Pavilion at *Exposition Internationale* (Paris 1937) 111
boycott of Japan 111. *See also*: Japan
'international peasant's day for Peace' 111
See also: Conférence Agraire Internationale; pacifism; Peasant Peace Conference
Italian Federation of Agricultural Workers: *see* Federterra
International Federation of Christian Landworkers' Unions (Fédération Internationale des syndicats chrétiens de travailleurs de la terre) 32–3, 32 n.100, 108
Italy
  statistics on hired labourers 3–4
  agricultural strikes 17, 28
  food rationing after First World War 16–17
  labour insurrections 28, 53–4
  inequality between industrial and agricultural workers 29
  reforms 29
  trade unions 31–2
  International Landworkers' Federation membership 32–3
  housing 46–7
  child labour 51
  Italian migrant workers to France 66–7
  invasion of Ethiopia 110
  use of international platforms for nationalistic goals 111–12
  tensions at Confédération Internationale d'Agriculture 113–14
  migrant workers to Italy 178–9
  See also: fascism; Federterra

Japan 29–30, 33–4, 39–40, 56 n.5, 71 n.89, 78, 81–2, 120–2
  not included in International Landworkers' Federation 33–4
  enquiry on agrarian reform (1924) 78
  participation in first meeting of Permanent Agricultural Committee 120–1
  aggression of China 110–11, 116–17

Javal, Adolphe
  on scientific management of agricultural labour in France 74
Joint Advisory Committee on Agriculture: *see* Mixed Advisory Agricultural Committee

Kautsky, Karl 76–7
Kendall, May
  survey on living conditions 46
  See also: Rowntree, Seebohm
Keynes, John Maynard 90–1
Kjelsberg, Betzy
  on womens' work 53–4
Klindera, Ferdinand 8–9
  Mixed Advisory Agricultural Committee 66, 86,
  on Great Depression 87

Latin America
  overlooked 1, 160–1
  delegates participate in International Labour Conference (1921) 39–40
  demand to put agricultural workers centre stage 107–8
  separation of European and Latin American movements 108
  ILO's new interest in tropical geography 145–6, 160–1
  Regional conferences in Latin America in mid-1930s 148
  Green revolutions 172–3
Landarbeiter: *see* 'landworker', use of term
land ownership 75–7, 140–1
  See also: colonies
'landworker', use of term 26–8
  See also: 'agricultural worker/labour', use of term and perception; 'farmer', use of term; 'industrial', use of term; 'peasant', use of term; Weber, Max
Laur, Ernst 133, 143–4
  Leader of Swiss Farmers' Association 35
  against regulation of agriculture 35–6
  participation in Mixed Advisory Agricultural Committee 86
  organizer of International Peace Campaign 118
  president of Confédération Internationale d'Agriculture 131–2
League of Nations
  creation and history 7–8, 17–18, 81
  relationship with ILO 20–1, 30–1, 83–4, 90–1, 142
  slavery 20–1, 30–1
  Permanent Mandates Commission 30–1, 147–8

League of Nations (*cont.*)
  Slavery Commission 30–1
  correspondence with Matthaei 60
  relationship with International Institute of Agriculture 62–3
  Great Depression 81, 83–4
  Health Organization 83–4
  disconnect from agricultural masses 104, 109, 118
  And Conférence Agraire Internationale 109–11
  Italy leaves 113
  Peasant Peace Conference 115, 117–18
  end of League 126–8, 133
  United Nations 141–2
Lipmann, Otto
  on hours of work 94
Living conditions 2–4, 8–10, 20–6, 28–31, 34, 45–8, 50, 54, 60, 63, 75–6, 80–1, 85–7, 97, 102–5, 107–10, 121–3, 128, 130–1, 134–5, 138–40, 144–6, 150–1, 155, 158–9, 162–5, 167–8, 170–8
Livingstone, Adelaide
  'peasant', use of term 115–16
Lubin, David
  founder of International Institute of Agriculture 20, 135–6

Mesa, Manuel
  Mexican delegate 116, 122–3
McDougall, Frank
  participation in conferences 83–4
  and League of Nations 86
  and Mixed Advisory Agricultural Committee 86–7
  and Permanent Agricultural Committee 120–2
  and Food and Agriculture Organization 131, 133–5
  See also: Australia
Martin, Louis: *see* Valdour, Jacques
Matthaei, Louise Ernestine
  as Louise Howard 89, 126
  enquiry on economic downturn 85–6.
  See also: enquiries
  life and career at 8–9, 57–60, 77–8, 85–6, 108–9
  pacifist activism 58–9
  corresponds with International Institute of Agriculture and League of Nations 60
  retirement from ILO 89, 95–6
  See also: Agricultural Service; International Institute of Agriculture; League of Nations

Méline, Jules
  president of Commission Internationale d'Agriculture 20
Menon, Krishna V. K.
  at Peasant Peace Conference 116–17, 119
  at Plantation Committee 160–1
  Indian ministry of labour 160–1
Mertens, Corneille
  on women's work 54
Miglioli, Guido
  leads Conférence Agraire Internationale 106, 114–16
  pacifist 106
  ILO does not accept his invitation to Conference 110–11
  concerned about rise of fascist agrarian organizations 112–14
  not invited to Permanent Agricultural Committee 120
migrant workers 26–8, 33–4, 66–7, 102
Mintz, Sidney
  study on Puerto Rican Plantations 155
  Wolf, Eric
Mixed Advisory Agricultural Committee
  creation 13, 64–6, 64 n.48
  relationship between ILO and International Institute of Agriculture 64–7
  on rural education (1924) 69–72
  on scientific management of agricultural labour 74–6
  on agrarian reforms 77–9
  on rural exodus 81–3
  impact of economic downturn 85–8
  relationship with new Committee of Agricultural Work 95
  relationship with Permanent Agricultural Committee 119–20, 119 n.75, 175
Montoya, Victor
  chairing of Plantation Committee 163–4
Morse, David A.
  ILO director 142
  1950 report 169
Mussolini, Benito 34–5, 112–13. *See also*: fascism

National Union of Agricultural Workers 31 n.95, 33, 99, 153
native labour 6–7, 30–1, 92–3, 98, 148
  See also: colonies; Native Labour Section
Native Labour Section (ILO) 92–3, 139–40, 146–8
  See also: colonies; native labour
natural constraints 3, 6, 37, 41–2, 44, 52–3, 72–5, 96–103, 173–4, 176–7

INDEX 209

Nazism 99
   See also: Germany; Austria
Nelson, Lowry 120, 143–4
   See also: rural sociology
Netherlands
   statistics on hired workers 5 152–3
   International Landworkers' Federation membership 32–3
   Dutch Federation of Agricultural, Horticultural, and Dairy Workers 32–3
   International Landworkers' Federation's statistics on hired workers 152–3
Netherlands' Agricultural Workers Union: *see* Dutch Federation of Agricultural, Horticultural, and Dairy Workers

October revolution (1917) 16–19, 78
   See also: Cold War; communism; Soviet Union
Osmay, Mukdim 136–7, 143–4, 174–5
   See also: Agricultural Service
ouvrier agricole: *see* 'landworker', use of term
overseas territories: *see* colonies

Pacifism
   Conférence agraire internationale (1936): *see* Conférence agraire internationale
   International Peace Campaign: *see* International Peace Campaign
   Enquiry on propagation of pacifist ideals: *see* enquiries
Pardo, Guido
   enquiry on working hours in Czechoslovakia 42–3
Paris Peace Conference: *see* Versailles Peace Conference and Treaty (1919)
Parsons, S.R.
   participation in International Labour Conference (1921) 37, 52–3
   on natural constraints 37, 52–3
'peasant', use of term 115–16, 141
   See also: 'agricultural worker/labour', use of term and perception; 'farmer', use of term; 'industrial', use of term; 'landworker', use of term
Peasant Peace Conference (Geneva, 1938) 104, 111, 114–23, 160–1
   name variations 114 n.55
   sponsored by International Peace Campaign 114–15
   colonial issues 116, 119
   criticizes International Institute of Agriculture 117

Permanent Agricultural Committee 119–24
   participants 120
   participation of International Landworkers' Federation 121–3
   expansion of Eurocentric focus 120–1
   working hours 102–3, 121–3
Phelan, Edward Joseph
   ILO director 126–7, 142
   on food supply during Second World War 128
   ILO's involvement in UNRRA programmes 130
   on FAO 136
'plantation' and 'plantation work', use of term 154 n.49, 163
   in relation to industrial work: 152, 154–5
Plantation Committee 31, 145–6, 155–6, 158–65, 168, 174
   creation 14, 151–2
   Havana meeting (1953) 163–5
   Indonesia meeting (1950) 159–62
   invites International Landworkers' Federation as 'observer' 160–1
   preparatory enquiry on plantations: 155–9
   See also: Asian Regional Conference; enquiries; Cuba; Indonesia; plantations
plantations 6–7, 14, 31–2, 42, 47–8, 102–5, 139–40, 144–68, 171–6, 178
   congress of International Landworkers' Federation (1952) 153–4
   use of term in relation to industrial and agricultural work: *see* 'plantation', use of term
   enquiries: *see* enquiries
Poland
   agricultural strikes 16–17
   Polish migrant workers to France 66–7
   land redistribution 76–7
   Albert Thomas' trip to 24 n.49
Preparatory Peasant Conference: *see* Peasant Peace Conference
Productivism 3, 159–60, 164–5

questionnaires: *see* enquiries

Rassemblement Universel pour la Paix: *see* International Peace Campaign
Regional conferences of American member states
   Santiago di Chile (1936) 105–8
   Cuba (1939) 119 n.74, 123–4, 142–3
   use of statistics 119–20

Restrepo, Antonio José
  advocates for agricultural work as Colombian delegate at International Labour Conference of 1921 15, 39–40
  on industrial vs. agricultural work 15
Riddell, Walter Alexander 57–8
  See also: Agricultural Service
Romania
  land redistribution 76–7
  enquiry on agrarian reform (1924) 78
  regulation of hours of work after Second World War 102–3
romanticization of rural life 4–5, 23, 25, 51–2, 93, 100–1
  See also: industrial vs. agricultural work; rural idyll
Rowntree, Seebohm Benjamin
  survey on living conditions 46
  See also: Kendall, May
rural education: see education
rural exodus 2, 22–4, 29, 42–3, 59–60, 66–7, 73–5, 79, 81–3, 145–6, 169–70
  and unemployment 66
  and wages 66–7
  Gorni and von Bülow's enquiry on rural exodus (1930–1932) 81–3
'rural idyll' 25, 50–1, 176
  See also: romanticization of rural life
rural sociology 59–61, 66–7, 120
rural-urban migration: see rural exodus

Schmidt, Georg 33, 63–6, 86, 99
  in International Landworkers' Federation 33
  in Mixed Advisory Agricultural Committee 65–6, 86
  resigns from International Landworkers' Federation 99
science of work: see scientific management of agricultural labour
scientific management of agricultural labour 13, 40, 60–1, 67–8, 72–6, 85, 97, 109–10
  See also: education; enquiries; International Institute of Agriculture; Mixed Advisory Agricultural Committee; Taylorism
Scottish Farm Servant's Union 15–16, 33
Second World War 4–5, 14, 58–9, 102–3, 115–16, 125–48, 150–1, 162, 169–70, 176–7
servitude: see slavery
slavery
  and League of Nations 20–1, 30–1
  ILO report 47–8
  in colonies and plantations 101, 147–50, 164
  See also: colonies; plantations; League of Nations; Thompson, Edgar

socialism 11, 16–17, 29, 32–3, 104–5, 113–14, 170–1
  polarization between socialist and fascist agrarian reformers 13–14
  limitation of hours of work in France 40
  at Conférence Agraire Internationale
  See also: Altobelli, Argentina; Delsinne, Léo; Gorni, Olindo; International Landworkers' Federation; Miglioli, Guido; Schmidt, Georg; Thomas, Albert; Wanner, Léo
Soderini, Count Edoardo
  represents the International Institute of Agriculture 64 n.50, 69–70
  on education 69–70
South Africa
  reliance on plantations 157–8
  women's labour 50
Soviet Union 24–5, 71, 102, 106, 129 n.24, 161–2, 170–1
  1920 enquiry on labour conditions in Soviet Russia
  Initial absence from ILO 30–1, 38, 71, 102
  Join ILO 1934 30–1 (US,R)
  Leaves ILO 161–2
  Agricultural industrialization 170–1
  See also: Cold War; communism; enquiries; October Revolution
Spain
  agricultural strikes 16–17
  regulation of hours of work 42–3, 94–5
  Spanish migrant workers to France 66–7
  rise of fascism 99
  Spanish civil war 117
  migrant workers to Spain 178–9
statistics 28, 59–61, 63–4, 81, 97–8
  statistical misrepresentation of women workers 62
  and International Institute of Agriculture 77, 83–4, 95–6, 177–8
  and Regional Conference 119–20
  statistics on hired labourers 3–4, 152–3
  and FAO 133, 177–8
surveys: see enquiries
Sweden
  International Landworkers' Federation membership 32–3
  Public health act (1919) 46–7
  strikes 16–17
Swiss Farmers' Association (Schweizerischer Bauernverband) 35–6
  See also: employers' organizations; Laur, Ernst; Hiemstra, Piet
Swiss Farmers Unions: see Swiss Farmers' Association

Switzerland
  hours of work 35
  against international regulations 35–6
  participation in third session of International Labour Conference (1921) 39–40, 43–4
  strikes 40
  romanticization of agriculture 51–2
  on living conditions 54
  Agricultural Service moves back to Switzerland (1948) 126
  impact of Second World War 128
  ILO's move back to Switzerland (1947) 141–2
  new laws about vocational education 152–3
  International Labour Conference (1947)
  See also: Gillabert-Randin, Augusta; Laur, Ernst; Second World War; Swiss Farmers' Association

Taylorism 72–4
  See also: scientific management of agricultural labour
Thomas, Albert
  advocates for agricultural work as ILO director 23–5, 56–9
  on working hours 42
  ILO research methods 61
  on rural exodus 66–7, 82
  on education 69
  on agrarian reforms 76–7
  Relationship with International Institute of Agriculture 77–8
  on living conditions in France 87
  on Great Depression 85–7
  death 88–9, 94
  on colonies and slavery 147–8
  See also: enquiries; France; International Institute of Agriculture
Thompson, Edgar
  study on slavery in plantations 149–50
trade unions 6, 8–13, 15–18, 23, 25–7, 31–6, 38–40, 43–5, 48–9, 51, 55, 60–1, 63, 65–6, 74–5, 83–5, 88, 92, 98–9, 102–4, 108, 112–15, 122–3, 126, 142–6, 152–4, 160–1, 163–5, 171–3, 175–6
  See also: Federterra: International Landworkers' Federation
'tropical', use of term 30–1
tropical regions 98, 138–9, 144–69, 174–7
  See also: colonies

unemployment 22, 37, 138–9
  insurance for unemployment 25–6
  regulation of hours of work as countermeasure 40, 91, 94–5, 102
  and rural exodus 66
  and Great Depression 75, 89–90, 93–4
  Unemployment Committee (ILO) 89–90, 93–4
Unemployment Committee (ILO) 89–90, 93–4
UNESCO 135–6
United Kingdom: see Great Britain
United Nations 14, 129–30, 135–6, 141–2, 150, 159–60, 177–8
  See also: League of Nations; UNESCO; United Nations Relief and Rehabilitation Administration
United Nations Relief and Rehabilitation Administration 129–30, 129 n.24, 25
United States
  initial absence from (by analogy with Soviet Union) ILO 30–1, 38, 71, 102
  participates as 'observer' to International Labour Conference of 1933 92–3
  reliance on plantations 157–8
  adherence to ILO (1934) 105–6, 137
  strategic importance of Cuba as venue for Second Regional Conference 163
  See also: Cold War
UNRRA: see United Nations Relief and Rehabilitation Administration

Valdour, Jacques 27, 46, 66–7
  See also: enquiries; France; rural sociology
Varghese
  defends employers' perspective as Indian employers' delegate 165–6
  See also: India
vocational training: see education
Vimeux, Paul
  French delegate at International Peace Campaign 115–16
Vogt, Paul 56, 66–7
  See also: rural sociology
von Bülow, Wilhelm
  Agricultural Service 58–9, 95–6
  enquiry on agrarian education 69–70
  enquiry on rural exodus in France, Germany, and Czechoslovakia 81–3
  retirement 126

wages
  payment in kind 27–8, 47–8, 87
  working without wages on family farms 49–50
  and rural exodus 66–7
  minimum wages 107–8, 142–3, 145, 166, 174
Wanner, Léo
  at Conférence Agraire Internationale 109–10
Weber, Max
  definition of 'landworker' 26

Winant, John
   ILO director 125–7
Wolf, Eric
   study on Puerto Rican Plantations 155
   See also: Mintz, Sidney
women's labour 13, 16, 21–2, 25–6, 28, 31–2, 34, 37–8, 44, 48–54, 61–2, 69–70, 84–5, 109–10, 128–9, 145–6, 156–7, 165, 172–3, 176
   during First World War 49–50
   statistical misrepresentation of women workers 62
working hours: *see* worktime

worktime 3, 5–7, 10–11, 13, 18–20, 22–4, 28, 34–5, 37, 39–44, 47–51, 52 n.78, 65–7, 74–5, 79, 81, 83–4, 88, 91–104, 121–3, 145–6, 152–3, 156–9, 162, 174, 176–9
World Peasant Peace Conference: *see* Peasant Peace Conference

Zulueta y Gomis, José
   expert in Mixed Advisory Agricultural Committee 65–6
   on education 69–70